# THE WORKING CLASSES

# IN THE VICTORIAN AGE

# VICTORIAN SOCIAL CONSCIENCE

A series of facsimile reprints of selected articles from
*The Edinburgh Review*, *The Westminster Review*, *The Quarterly Review*, *Blackwood's Magazine* and *Fraser's Magazine*
1802–1870

THE SERIES INCLUDES:

Poverty 4 vols.
Urban Problems 2 vols.
The Working Classes 4 vols.
Prostitution
Emigration
Population Problems 2 vols.
Trade Unions 4 vols.
Working Conditions
Public Health 2 vols.

# THE WORKING CLASSES IN THE VICTORIAN AGE

Debates on the issue

from 19th century critical journals

With an introduction

by

C. J. Wrigley

Volume I

## POLITICAL ECONOMY AND WHIG REFORMS

1815–1837

1973

GREGG INTERNATIONAL PUBLISHERS LIMITED

© Editorial matter Gregg International
Publishers Limited, 1973

Complete set ISBN 0 576 53256 8
This volume ISBN 0 576 53257 6

Published in 1973 by Gregg International Publishers Limited
Westmead, Farnborough, Hants., England

Printed in Germany

# CONTENTS

# INTRODUCTION

Ever since Engels wrote *The Condition of the Working Class in England* (1845) there has been considerable controversy over the state of the British working class in the first half of the nineteenth century. In recent years many learned articles and books have been written on the subject, especially on living standards in the early decades of industrialisation.

The major documents which historians have used have been reprinted in recent years, and so are easily available to students of the period. The major source for the period is the hundreds of volumes of Parliamentary Papers, some of which are referred to in the articles reproduced here; many of these Papers have recently been reprinted by the Irish University Press. *Hansard*, *The Times* and some of the working class periodicals are now available in microfilm or reprints. Also the more important contemporary monographs, including Engels' major study and the works of various of the major classical economists, have in recent years been republished with learned introductions.

One important source which hitherto has not been readily available is the multitude of articles on social conditions in the nineteenth century periodicals. Even the main Reviews, such as the *Edinburgh* and the *Quarterly*, are rarely found except in major libraries; and even these often have incomplete collections.

Informed contemporary discussions on Government and private enquiries and the various proposed remedies for bad social conditions appeared in these journals. As such the articles provide not only a guide to the conditions of the time, but indicate more what the politically influential felt the conditions to be, and reveal the nature of the debate as to what aims and limits there should be in public policy towards the conditions of the working class.

The contemporary debate on these matters was much wider than one would be led to think by reading published work on the period. Important elements of the debate were never given a trial. Such arguments, though important at the time, have been too frequently put aside by many historians, who have tended to make the development of the past to the present a clear-cut route, devoid of inconsistencies and dead-ends.

Some of the authors of the articles are still well-known, such as George Eliot; many of the other people were influential men of letters or political economists, some of whom wrote anonymously; and even today it is not always possible to identify them.

Britain emerged from the Napoleonic wars victorious. Her efforts in the war, subsidising her Allies and financing her own forces, displayed the wealth of the country (Article 1). But the Wars also partly concealed the great changes taking place socially through the coming of industrialisation, and at the end of the war the propertied classes were faced with a slump and considerable social disorder.

In this period economists, for the first time, took a leading part in the discussion of social policy. The writings of men such as Adam Smith and David Ricardo had a profound influence on contemporary thought and social policy. This body of thought, later termed "classical economics" by Karl Marx, favoured as little State intervention in the economy as possible, believing that the economy would prosper most (and hence the working class) if a free play of market forces was allowed. Nevertheless, they recognised the need for an institutional framework of law and order within which their economic freedom could work and, as with all groups, there were significant differences between each of the leading economists on certain policy issues. Adam Smith, like several of the later classical economists, was as much a social philosopher as an economist—and individual economic freedom was part of a larger liberal outlook. These views, often popularised into a blind dogma of *laissez-faire*, naturally found favour amongst the aspiring commercial and industrial middle class of early nineteenth century Britain; and were a marked contrast to the stultifying aristocratic and authoritarian outlooks dominant in Prussia, Austria and Russia, Britain's Allies in the Napoleonic Wars.

In the Reviews, the classical economists' views were regularly and forcefully expressed in the *Edinburgh*, founded in 1802, from the beginning Whig in sympathies, and which subsequently became increasingly a spokesman for the Whig Party, and the *Westminster*, founded by Jeremy Bentham and James Mill in 1824. Robert Torrens in his critique of Robert Owen's proposals to better the lot of the working class, makes a typical claim for political economy: that "whether with respect to the conduct of private life, or to the administration of public affairs cases, are perpetually occurring, in which, without a competent knowledge of its principles, it is impossible either to judge correctly or to act with wisdom" (Article 2).

A blunt statement of the classical economists' position is given in one article in this collection (Article 6) which rejects Sadlers' Factory Bill:

> "It is a principle in political philosophy ... that he legislates best, legislates least .... Restrictive laws, interfering with the internal regulations of commerce, may prevent the recurrence of some specific evils which they are intended to remove, but they effect this by ultimately occasioning extensive embarrassment to trade, and consequently inflicting serious ills on the working classes. Hence, nothing but the strongest necessity can justify legislative interference with commercial concerns ...."

The leading classical economists generally opposed legislative reduction of adults' hours of work, though they recognised children required special protection. They argued that shorter hours would reduce production and diminish wages, or masters might resort to speeding up their machinery; overall profits would be reduced to levels dangerous for the nation's well-being, and foreign rivals would gain in British markets (Article 6).

Many of these writers, imbued with Malthusian gloom, felt that intervention on behalf of the poor could only make matters worse. Torrens severely commented, "Benevolence and Charity, when not under the guidance of economical science, frequently degenerate into ministers of mischief, aggravating the misery they endeavour to relieve ...." (Article 2). As well as demoralising the working class, Poor Law payments were deemed to have encouraged "the most wretched of the working class" marrying at an early age (Article 6).

The Wage Fund theory, which argued that the level of wages was exactly determined by the means available for payment divided by the number of employees, reinforced the classical economists' rejections of certain proposed reforms. It was argued that charitable payments could only come out of the money for wages or out of profits, and that these would, therefore, lower wage rates or restrict capital investment, which in turn would reduce the number of jobs. Dr. Kay deplored the Poor Laws thus: "A rate levied on property for the support of indigence is, in a great degree, a tax on the capital from whose employment are derived the incentives of industry and the rewards of the frugal, ingenious and virtuous poor" (Article 6).

Many of the political economists followed Nassau Senior in opposing trade unionism. The activities of the unions were seen as futile, if not actually harmful, in their disregard of the iron law of the Wage Fund. One writer comments on them being "engaged in impolitic, vexatious contests with their employers" (Article 6). Another, commenting on their aims "of permanently raising the standard of wages", asserts "It is clear that trades unions must fail to do this in the mode they propose, because the rate of wages depends on the supply of labour which is brought into the market, and not upon the arbitrary regulations of either master or men" (Article 9). In contrast many warmly approved of co-operation, which they felt had no such bad effects on the working of market forces. In free market conditions some took the line that Spencer and to a lesser extent Malthus took of equating poverty with stupidity and wealth with brains: "Poverty is only another name for Ignorance; while Intelligence may be regarded as the synonyme of Comfort" (Article 9).

The classical economists' remedies to the condition of the working class were to remove various checks to the free working of the economy. The main evil was the Corn Laws, which protected Britain's grain farmers from an influx of cheap foreign corn. Though many of the classical economists were indifferent to the Anti-Corn Law League's campaign for immediate repeal, most of them held the Corn Laws to be an intolerable check to the economy and a cause of depressed real wages for the working class (Article 6). Another major remedy they proposed was to remove heavy taxation. This was opposed as it restricted capital formation and caused capital to flow out of the country, both of which would harm employment. Thus Torrens, in rejecting Owen's socialist plans to relieve distress, urges "Give Freedom to Commerce, and lighten the pressure of Taxation, and we shall have no complaining in our streets" (Article 2).

In contrast to the classical economists' views, there were the remedies put forward in the Tory journals. Many of these articles are the fruit of a paternalistic Toryism, which was frequently at odds with the Tory Party's leaders.

In the two decades after Waterloo the major Tory journals were the *Quarterly Review*, founded in 1809 to combat the success of the Whig

*Edinburgh Review*, *Blackwood's Magazine*, founded in 1817, and *Fraser's Magazine*, founded in 1830, which in 1847 was taken over by the leaders of the Broad Church Movement and became Liberal. The most lively of these was usually *Blackwood's*, affectionally known as the "Maga". One observer later in the century commented, "With a rare consistency it has contrived to appear for over three score years and ten as a spirited and defiant advocate of all those who are at least five years behind their time. Sometimes *Blackwood's* is fifty years in the rear, but that is a detail of circumstance. Five or fifty it does not matter so long as it is well in the rear".

Many of these writers argued that the ruling class had a duty to maintain the working class even if this cut profits and economic expansion. These Tories were horrified at how industrialisation had undermined the old relationship between rich and poor, where each had known their place and their duties (Article 3). They feared the lower orders of society, the hordes of unskilled casual labourers and riff-raff collected together in the urban centres. As one writer put it "Anarchy, spoliation and plunder, are topics which occupy their idle thoughts by day and their dreams by night", and should they break loose "remembrance of the horrors of the French revolution would be lost in scenes of much greater atrocity" (Article 7). To the paternalistic Tories the Whigs were injuring the poor by their callous laws and were liable to drive the masses to revolution (Article 9).

The paternalistic Tories vigorously attacked the ideas of the political economists. The cult of "cheapness" was denounced, and the new social relationship of the "cash nexus" between labourer and employer, where the labourer was left to starve if his labour was not required, was vigorously deplored. Some pointed out that the break up of the old relationship forced the working class to organise to protect themselves (Article 3). The Malthusian doctrines were rejected by many such writers (Articles 3, 4). Above all, writers such as Alfred Mallalieu made classic indictments of the factory system and the rigours of the New Poor Law. The Whigs were accused of crucifying the poor for popularity among the middle class—"Why? Because the poor have no votes, and rate payers have" (Articles 10, 11). In short, the Whigs were accused of dividing society, of creating Two Nations.

In essence, the old Tories distrusted industrialisation and the new position of the urban class. Southey, after emphasising the great growth of wealth stemming from manufacturing, still stated, "The real intrinsic value, power, and independence of a nation must ultimately be found in its soil" (Article 1). Many responded to the slumps of industry by urging a policy of Back to the Land, where "the victims of our manufacturing system" could be "settled in peaceful, virtuous and happy competence" (Articles 2, 3). They loathed the factory system for its cruelties, but also, surely, because it was alien to the traditional society for which they stood.

They were willing to raise taxes for the unemployed. Many of them recognised that society owed maintenance to the poor who were unemployed through no fault of their own. Southey commented that circumstances beyond a man's control could pauperise a man—

"... such as a sudden rise in the necessaries of life, or a supply of labourers beyond the demand for work; and sickness or other calamity may throw out of employment, for a time, many workmen with the best disposition to be industrious. It would be cruel and unjust to withhold relief from persons so circumstanced. They have, indeed, the strongest claims on all those classes of society whose incomes are derived from their labour, when from any calamity or misfortune, more especially from those which no prudence nor foresight could prevent, they are unable to continue that labour".

He urged that this would be very expensive, "but be the amount what it may, we cannot deny their claims to a maintenance from the public" (Article 1). Although few were as enlightened as Southey, the Tory paternalists were undoubtedly much more willing to raise taxes to support the poor (Articles 3, 5).

Nevertheless, the Tory responses to the condition of the working class were conservative. There was the harking back to the land. There was the paternalism of the old Poor Law. There was the call for protection—above all for agriculture. There was the call for better education—but this was to be a force for social discipline, which would lift them out of improvidence and sedition (Article 7). One writer at least, felt that " we do not believe that any education which it is possible to give them will ever render the working classes capable of thoroughly understanding and consequently, of being trusted with the regulation of their own interests, so as to relieve their superiors from the duty of guiding and protecting them " (Article 5). Some even called for the development of the colonies to take surplus labour and capital as an alternative to repealing the

Corn Laws, a proposal which many of the classical economists supported (Article 5). The Tories remained cautious of reform. As one writer proclaimed "... a wise and considerate Statesman will oppose all innovation until it has been so generally and so unequivocally demanded by public opinion, that to resist any longer would be inexpedient, if not unsafe; his conduct under such circumstances should put it into his power to say to the injured individual, or class, with an honest conscience, "I have protected your particular interest as long as I could; but I can no longer contend against the united voice of the community: I, therefore, give you warning, to make the best preparation you can against the moment when the change thus called for must be carried into effect" (Article 4).

As well as containing this major debate over policy, these articles contain a mass of material on living conditions and the way of life of the working class. As well as comments on work conditions and housing there are descriptions of such matters as the prevalence of food adulteration and the effects of bad bankruptcy and debtor laws (Article 8). This selection of articles contains a great diversity of opinion on remedies for alleviating the distress of the working class and a rich stock of descriptive material. No commentary can be a wholly satisfactory alternative to the student of any period reading first hand the views and impressions of the people of the time.

C. J. Wrigley

Art. V.—*A Treatise on the Wealth, Power, and Resources of the British Empire, in every Quarter of the World, including the East Indies; the Rise and Progress of the Funding System explained; with Observations on the National Resources for the beneficial Employment of a redundant Population; and for rewarding the Military and Naval Officers, Soldiers, and Seamen, for their Services to their Country during the late War: illustrated by copious Statistical Tables, &c.*— By P. Colquhoun, LL.D. London, 1814.

MR. COLQUHOUN contrives to arrest the attention of his readers, rather by the magnitude and distribution of his subjects, than by their novelty. The objects exhibited in his ' Police of the Metropolis' were familiar to every reader. No inhabitant of this great town could be ignorant that its vast population was mixed up with swindlers and pickpockets, thieves, vagrants, beggars, and prostitutes ; but Mr. Colquhoun enabled us to trace them to their lurking-places :—he gave to each class a ' local habitation ;' —he brought them to our view in groups amounting to thousands, and their pilfering and plunder to millions. Familiar as such objects must have been to him, from his official situation, the systematic villainy which he disclosed was so monstrous, and at the same time

so

so methodically planned, the scale of operations was so extensive,
that the truth of his statements was called in question; we believe,
however, it has been pretty well ascertained, that there was more
foundation for them than the superficial observer had ever imagined.

Mr. Colquhoun has now taken a bolder flight, and entered upon
a research of a much wider range. With uncommon labour, and
some ingenuity, he has attempted to collect into one great mass,
the sum total of the ' wealth, power, and resources, of the British
empire, in every quarter of the world.' This splendid view is
exhibited in four Tables, elucidated by explanatory notes ; and
the principles on which they are constructed are explained in four
corresponding chapters. These tables and chapters occupy about
one-fourth part of the volume ; the remainder being employed on
historical accounts of the public revenue and expenditure, and the
public debt; on the settlements and colonies of Great Britain ;
and the territories under the management of the East India Company.

The first chapter is dedicated to the interesting and important
subject of population. The increase in that of Great Britain, according to the census taken in 1801 and 1811, appears to be as
under :—

|  | England and Wales. | Scotland. | Total in Great Britain. |
|---|---|---|---|
| In 1801 - - - - | 8,872,980 | 1,599,068 | 10,472,048 |
| In 1811 - - - | 10,150,615 | 1,805,688 | 11,956,303 |
| Increase in 10 years - | 1,277,635 | 206,620 | 1,484,255 |

The extraordinary addition of nearly a million and a half to the
population of Great Britain in the period of ten years, and in the
midst of a widely extended war, created some doubt as to the accuracy of the returns made in 1801. It was objected, that the
novelty of the measure necessarily produced imperfect returns; and
some affected to say, that the apprehension of an intention on the
part of government to lay on a poll-tax influenced those returns,
and that many concealed the real number of their families. There
are, however, several facts, which, coupled with collateral circumstances, amount almost to proof, that the increase is not more than
might be expected. It is true, that in great towns, false returns
might easily be made without fear of detection—a man might sink
a part of his family, though he would not find it quite so feasi-
ble to bury his house out of sight. Now, it appears from the
same returns, that the houses in Great Britain had increased from
1,937,489 in 1801 to 2,163,946, in 1811, being 226,457 in the
same

same period of ten years : which gives pretty nearly the same increase of population, as stated in the returns. *

A variety of causes have co-operated to this progressive increase. No one will deny that the wealth of the country has very much increased ; it is equally certain that this must have occasioned an increased demand for labour; this demand would as certainly raise the price of labour, as well as require additional hands to supply it. The change too in the manners and habits of the people has been favourable to an increasing population. The upper and middling classes of society are more abstemious, especially in the article of wine ; and the tradesmen, mechanics, and lower orders, generally, in the use of spirituous liquors. The almost universal use which the article of tea has obtained, is, perhaps, one of the greatest blessings, both to the rich and poor, that was ever conferred on the nation, not even the potatoe root excepted : the habitual use of this beverage has contributed in no small degree to the health and comfort of every class of society ; yet we have heard, that a supposed increase of the number of insane persons has been absurdly ascribed to the frequent use of tea. The visionaries, who entertain such fancies, would do well, before they propagate them, to inquire whether madness is a prevailing disease among the Chinese, who may be said, ' to eat their tea, drink their tea, and sleep on their tea.' The potatoe was, for a long time, held to be an unwholesome and poisonous root.†

A habit of cleanliness, which for some years has gained considerable ground in all ranks of society, and the almost universal use of vegetable clothing, either linen or cotton, next to the skin, to the exclusion of animal substances, as silks and woollens, have produced the most beneficial effects, in preserving health, and add-

---

* For Ireland, the returns have not yet been received ; but in 1812 a census was ordered to be taken of its population, which, there is reason to think, has increased in a more extraordinary degree than in Great Britain. In 1695, as appears from the rolls for collecting a poll-tax, its population amounted to 1,034,000 ; but, allowing for the usual evasions, it was, unquestionably, much higher. Mr. Rickman, who collected and arranged the census taken in Great Britain, at the commencement of the last century, at 1,500,000, and that, in 111 years, it has reached 4,000,000; but Mr. Newenham extends it to a still greater number. Mr. Colquhoun, in his tables, takes the middle path, and sets it down at 4,500,000.

† The labouring people of Scotland live chiefly on potatoes and oatmeal ; in the northern counties of England, these furnish the principal part of every meal ; and it is well known, that nine-tenths of the population of Ireland subsist almost entirely upon them. The enormously increasing population of Ireland is an unequivocal proof of the wholesome and nutritive quality of this root. ' When I see,' says Arthur Young, ' the people of a country with well-formed vigorous bodies, and their cottages swarming with children—when I see their men athletic, and their women beautiful, I know not how to believe them subsisting on unwholesome food.'

ing

ing to length of days. *  The improvements that have taken place
in the treatment of diseases, and the perfection to which the sur-
gical art has been brought, have considerably abridged the usual
mortality; and the invaluable discovery of vaccination has annually saved thousands from an early grave, and would, no doubt,
soon exterminate one of the most destructive diseases that afflict
mankind, if prejudice and envy, or interested and other unworthy
motives, did not shed their malignant influence, and keep alive the
variolous infection.

Of the favourable operation of those changes in our habits which
have contributed to the improvement of health, we have a proof in
the report on the population returns compiled by Mr. Rickman,
in which it is stated, ' that the annual number of burials, as collected in pursuance of the population acts of 1801 and 1811, au-
thorizes a satisfactory diminishing mortality in England since the
year 1780.'  The result was as follows :—

> In 1780, one person in 40 died annually.
> 1790, one  do.  in 45      do.
> 1800, one  do.  in 47      do.
> 1810, one  do.  in 49 or 50 do.

The same good effects, by a regular system of management,
and by timely precautions in preventing or destroying contagion by
white-washing, fumigation, dry air, and cleanliness, have been
experienced in those great national institutions where disease and
mortality once most prevailed; namely, in prisons, in hospitals,
and in the army and navy.

If the jail fever, as it is usually called, once so common and
so fatal, should by chance now show itself, it is subdued immediately.  The prison-ships and establishments on shore for prisoners of war, who are, of all others, most difficult to manage, were,
nevertheless, kept in such clean, dry, and excellent order, that,
though more than 70,000 prisoners were at one time in confinement, no contagious fever was known in any of them.  A petition
from certain prisoners at Dartmoor was sent to Mr. Whitbread,
complaining, among other grievances, of the sick being neglected.
A commission, composed of Lieutenant-General Stephens, Rear
Admiral Martin, and Mr. Hawker, a justice of the peace of Ply-
mouth, was in consequence deputed to inquire into the truth of the
alleged grievances; the petition was disowned instantly by the body
of the prisoners, amounting then to 8000; and the three who had

---

* Nothing but the most rigid cleanliness will prevent animal matter from creating
cutaneous disorders, and, we believe, even worse complaints.  The upper classes of
Chinese, whose silken vests contiguous to the skin are seldom changed till worn out,
are, almost to a man, either infected with the itch or the leprosy, or swarming with
vermin ; which, we believe too, flannel is equally efficacious in promoting.

sent

sent it were ashamed and repentant, and denied that they had any cause of complaint. ' We observed,' says the report, ' in passing through the three first prisons, that the men had a very striking appearance of good health; and, with the exception of the fourth, which contains the prisoners who call themselves *Romans*,* their health is universally good.' Previously to this complaint, a person, who has since fled from justice, attempted to raise a clamour against the prison, by representing it as a scene of wretchedness and mortality. In consequence of this, it was visited by a member of the Transport Board in 1811. The number of prisoners then in confinement amounted to 6572, of whom 36 only were in the hospital, and *one* had died in the course of the week; an example of health not to be found, perhaps, in an equal population, either in this or any other country.

It is well known, that in Greenwich and Chelsea Hospitals, into which are admitted only worn-out, disabled, and helpless seamen and soldiers, there are to be found more instances of longevity than in any other bodies of men whatever.

That part of the army which has been serving abroad has suffered much from battle and disease; but, in the navy, the mortality has been incredibly small; and, as very erroneous ideas are entertained on this subject, our readers will be gratified to see the result of the official returns, which is as curious as it is satisfactory.

| | Seamen and Marines. | | Seamen and Marines. |
|---|---|---|---|
| There were on board the ships of war in all parts of the world, | On 1st Jan. 1811—138,581<br>1st Jan. 1812—136,778<br>1st Jan. 1813—138,324 | Died of disease, drowned, and killed in battle. | In 1810—5,185<br>1811—4,265<br>1812—4,211 |

Thus it appears that the average number of the crews of His Majesty's ships, taken for three years, amounted to 137,894: and that the average deaths in the year by disease, accident, and battle, amounted to 4,554, being one in $30\frac{637}{2277}$, or little more than one

---

* These persons, to the amount of some hundreds, exhibited a striking and detestable scene of depravity. These wretches, who were headed by a person calling himself ' General of the Romans,' are thus described :—' Regardless of every principle of religion, they absolutely forfeit all claim to be considered as human beings, by the practice of the most detestable and abominable vices; they go nearly naked, some of them quite so, from gambling away their clothes. Some have been starved to death by gambling away their provisions, a practice which has been discovered to extend even to their provisions *for months to come;* and the countenances of many whom we saw denoted a degree of wretchedness that exceeds all description.' It appears, that the experiment of placing armed soldiers over them, to compel them to eat their food, was resorted to, but this was soon found to be unsafe, with a people as ferocious as they were infamous.

man

man in 30¼.* The returns do not distinguish those who died from accident and from disease, but there are good grounds for stating the latter at not more than one in 60.

Compare these, and many other benefits which the present generation enjoys, with the havoc formerly made by ' plague, pestilence, and famine,' by infectious fevers, the nature of which was but ill understood, by leprosy, scurvy, and small-pox, and we shall no longer be surprised at the rapidly progressive increase of the population of the Britsh islands. The rate at which this increase took place, prior to 1801, cannot be ascertained with any degree of accuracy; but from all the data that could be collected from the number of births, marriages, and burials, it has been calculated, that from 1700 to 1811, being a period of 111 years, the population of Great Britain has nearly doubled itself; and that, in the same period, the population of Ireland has increased more than 160 per cent.

On the accuracy of the population of the different dependencies in Europe, and the foreign colonies, (amounting, by Mr. Colquhoun's account, to fifty-three in number,) exclusive of the territorial possessions under the management of the East-India Company, it will be obvious that no reliance can be placed. There are no official returns, and the documents afforded by those who have incidentally written on the colonies cannot be considered as authentic. The following, however, is a summary view of the details, exhibited in the copious table annexed to this chapter :—

|  | Europeans. | Free Persons of colour. | Negro Labourers. | Total. |
|---|---|---|---|---|
| Population (in 1811) of Great Britain and Ireland, exclusive of the army and navy - | 16,456,303 | ——— | ——— | 16,456,303 |
| British subjects in the different dependencies in Europe - - | 180,300 | ——— | ——— | 180,300 |
| Ditto, in the British possessions in North America - | 486,146 | ——— | ——— | 486,146 |

---

* These returns are worthy the attention of Mr. Morgan, the intelligent actuary of the ' Equitable Assurance Office for Lives.' He will perceive from them, that it is not *equitable* to make the officers of the Navy, who may be desirous of providing for their families, pay premiums so disproportionate to the actual risk; the less so, as the additional per centage for *military* and *sea* risk is raised on the *premium*, whether it be 2 per cent. or 6 per cent., though these extra risks of a man of 60 and a man of 20 must be precisely the same.

British

|  | Europeans. | Free Persons of colour. | Negro Labourers. | Total. |
|---|---|---|---|---|
| British subjects in the West India Colonies - - | 64,994 | 33,081 | 634,096 | 732,171 |
| Ditto, in the conquered countries, ditto - - | 35,829 | 26,253 | 372,800 | 434,882 |
| Ditto, in the British settlements in Africa - - | 20,678 | 108,299 | ———— | 128,977 |
| Ditto, in colonies, dependencies in Asia - - | 61,059 | 1,807,496 | 140,450 | 2,009,005 |
| East-India Company's territorial possessions - - | 25,246 | 40,033,162 | ———— | 40,058,408 |
| British navy, army, marines, and naval seamen in registered vessels, including foreign corps in the British service - | 671,241 | ———— | ———— | 671,244 |
| Total amount of the population of the British empire | 18,001,796 | 42,008,291 | 1,147,346 | 61,157,433 |

Although population is the source from which all wealth and power must be derived, it does not therefore necessarily follow that all populous countries should be wealthy or powerful : this consequence must depend much on local circumstances, and still more on the nature of the government and the genius and habits of the people. France is a populous and a powerful nation, but not wealthy. Holland and Hamburgh, Venice, Genoa, and some of the smaller states, were once populous and wealthy, without being powerful ; and India and China swarm with population, without being either rich or powerful. Great Britain, throughout the long and arduous struggle in which she has been engaged, has exhibited to the world the singular example of uniting within herself the three attributes of wealth, power, and population, acting reciprocally on one another, and mutually tending to aggrandizement. It is here that the desire of acquiring property receives an additional impulse from a conviction of the perfect security which the laws afford to it when acquired—it is here that capital is thrown into active circulation by a perfect confidence in the faith

of

of the government, which has never yet been broken with the subject.

To discover what the materials are that compose the public and private property of the British dominions; that accumulation of wealth, which, aided by credit and character, has raised this favoured nation to the highest pitch of grandeur, and set her on an eminence far above all other empires, forms the subject of the second chapter of Mr. Colquhoun's volume, and its corresponding table. He sets out with observing, that the same rules and principles, to which individuals resort, on all emergencies, will apply to the affairs of nations ; that the object of both is to have recourse to an accurate view of the resources in possession, and to the means of rendering those resources as productive as possible ; that the resources of nations are derived from the productive labour of the people ; and that this labour is augmented or diminished according to forms of government, and the intelligence, ability, and zeal, or the want of them, in those who direct the affairs of states and empires ; implying, however, we take for granted, a corresponding capital and expenditure for the maintenance of that labour. Our author also thinks, and in this we are disposed to concur with him, that, considering the limited territory and population of the British islands, when compared with those of many other states and kingdoms in the world, we may legitimately conclude, that the rapid strides it has made towards wealth and power, may fairly be attributed to the form of its government, and the wisdom of its councils ;—we would add, however, to the solid good sense of the people at large, who have co-operated in giving effect to those councils which they judged to be conducive to the public good.

The simple fact of our rapid progress to a state of wealth, power, and prosperity, unparalleled in the history of nations ; the noble stand which, with our seventeen millions of people we have been able to make against a population of more than one hundred millions ;—the conquests we have made of every foreign possession and dependency of our most deadly and inveterate foe, who had the persons and property of all these millions at his disposal ;—the annihilation of his navy and his commerce,—are invincible proofs of the unexampled power and prosperity of the British nation.

To ascertain what the vast resources are which have enabled this nation to accomplish such great and extraordinary events ; to trace the elements of which they consist, and to estimate their value upon the same principle as commercial men estimate their stock in trade, is, indeed, an ' arduous task;' and though, as Mr. Colquhoun observes, accuracy, to a point, in so extensive and complicated a range, is impracticable, yet, on a subject of such importance, an approximation to the truth, if attainable, we agree with him, must be very valuable.

' In

'In forming the estimates,' says Mr. Colquhoun, 'which are exhibited in the Tables annexed, the ablest writers in this branch of political economy have been consulted, and copious notes have been introduced, calculated to elucidate, as far as elucidation has been practicable, the grounds upon which the author has proceeded. From the scarcity of materials, much has been left to the exertion of the mind, and to laborious and intricate calculations, when information could not be derived from books or public documents.'—(p. 51.)

The Table No. 2, which is annexed to this chapter, contains the estimate of the public and private property in Great Britain and Ireland, with its dependencies, and is divided into eight general sections, as under :—

1. Exhibiting the value of landed and other public and private property, in Great Britain and Ireland, amounting to - - - - £2736,640,000
2. —— in 9 dependencies in Europe - - 22,161,330
3. —— in 7 colonies and settlements in North America - - - - 46,575,360
4. —— in 14 colonies and settlements in the West Indies - - - - 100,014,864
5. —— in 14 conquered colonies in the West Indies 75,220,000
6. —— in 4 settlements in Africa - - 4,770,500
7. —— in 5 settlements and colonies in Asia - 38,721,090

Total   53 colonies and dependencies   - - £3024,103,144
8. Territory of India under the control and management of the East India Company - - 1072,427,751

Total estimated value of the landed and public and private property of the British empire in all parts of the world - - - - £4096,530,895

It would be too long for us to enter into a detail of the particulars on which Mr. Colquhoun has constructed the table of which this is an abstract ; we must therefore content ourselves with briefly stating the component parts of the first and most important article in that abstract. They are classed, in the first place, under the three general heads, of 1. *Productive private property*; 2. *Unproductive private property*; 3. *Public property.* These classes are again subdivided into a variety of branches, and the value of each branch is set down in four columns, one for England and Wales, the second for Scotland, the third for Ireland, and the fourth for Great Britain and Ireland. At the end of the line, enumerating the subdivisions of property, is a reference to 'explanatory notes,' shewing the authority from which the several sums have been taken or the principle upon which the computations have been made. Our readers may wish to see, and it is all we can afford
ford

ford to extract, that column which exhibits the total value in Great Britain and Ireland of each distinct branch of property.

## 1. *Productive Private Property.*

| | |
|---|---:|
| * Lands cultivated in grain of all sorts, grass, hops, nurseries, gardens, &c. - - - | 1,200,640,000 |
| Tythes belonging to the laity exclusive of those in possession of the clergy - - - | 80,000,000 |
| Mines and minerals - - - | 75,000,000 |
| Canals, tolls, and timber - - - | 50,000,000 |
| Dwelling-houses, including warehouses and manufactories - - - - | 400,000,000 |
| Manufactured goods in progress to maturity and in a finished state, deposited in manufactories, warehouses, and shops for sale - - | 140,000,000 |
| Foreign merchandize, deposited in warehouses, shops, &c. either paid for, or virtually paid for, by debts owing to this country by foreigners - | 40,000,000 |
| British shipping of every description, employed in trade, including vessels on the stocks - | 27,000,000 |
| Agricultural property, consisting of grain, hay, straw, cheese, butter, and other productions of farms, including implements of husbandry - - | 45,000,000 |
| Animals, namely, horses, horned cattle, sheep, hogs, goats, asses, deer, wild animals, and poultry - | 183,000,000 |
| Fisheries round the coast of Great Britain and Ireland, including inland fisheries - - | 10,000,000 |
| Total of Productive Private Property - - | £2250,640,000 |

---

* As a specimen of Mr. Colquhoun's 'Explanatory Notes,' we extract the following :
'It appears, from the returns to the Tax Office for the year ending 5th April, 1804, that the *rental* of *real property* in England and Wales, including mines, canals, &c. calculated on 37,334,400 statute acres, amounted to 38,000,000 : it is, however, known to have much increased since that period. The cultivated lands may be distributed as follows—

| | | Acres. | L. | L. |
|---|---|---:|---:|---:|
| Gardens and nurseries, - - | about | 20,000 | at 70 | 1,400,000 |
| Lands highly cultivated in the vicinity of large towns - - - } | | 500,000 | 50 | 25,000,000 |
| Hop grounds - - - | | 100,000 | 40 | 4,000,000 |
| Lands cultivated of a superior quality - - | | 12,000,000 | 30 | 360,000,000 |
| Lands cultivated of an inferior quality - | | 18,000,000 | 20 | 360,000,000 |
| Total of cultivated lands in England and Wales | | 30,620,000 acres, estimated at - | | 750,400,000 |
| Lands cultivated in Scotland, estimated at one-fifth of England and Wales - - - - - } | | | | 150,080,000 |
| Lands cultivated in Ireland, estimated at two fifths - | | | - | 300,160,030 |
| Making a total for Great Britain and Ireland, of | | - | - | 1200,640,000 |

2. *Unpro-*

## 2. *Unproductive Private Property.*

|  |  |
|---|---:|
| Waste lands, .at present unproductive, after including all such as are incapable of any improvement adequate to the expense, including ways and waters | 132,000,000 |
| Household furniture in dwelling houses　　- | 185,000,000 |
| Wearing apparel in dwelling houses　-　　- | 20,800,000 |
| Plate, jewels, and other ornamental articles in dwelling-houses　-　　　-　　　-　　　- | 44,200,000 |
| Specie in circulation and hoarded, namely, gold, silver, and copper coin, including Bank dollars and tokens | 15,000,000 |
| Total of Unproductive Private Property　　- | £397,000,000 |

## 3. *Public Property.*

|  |  |
|---|---:|
| Public buildings, as palaces, churches, hospitals, prisons, bridges, &c.　　-　　　-　　　- | 27,000,000 |
| Public arsenals, castles, forts, and all other places of defence, with the artillery, stores, &c. thereunto belonging　-　　　-　　　-　　　- | 17,000,000 |
| Dock-yards and all materials for ship-building and repairs　-　　:　　　-　　　- | 10,000,000 |
| Ships of war, in number about 1000, of which 261 are of the line, in employment, including those in ordinary and building　-　　　-　　　- | 25,000,000 |
| Military and naval ordnance, and other public stores | 10,000,000 |
| Total of public property　　- | £89,000,000 |

Aggregate value of every species of property, public and private, in Great Britain and Ireland, as mentioned in the first of the eight general heads into which the Table, No. 2, is divided　-　　　- £2736,640,000

Of the immense property of 4081,530,895*l.*, Mr Colquhoun estimates the colonies and dependencies taken from the enemy during the late war, exclusive of ships and other floating property captured since 1792, to amount to 106,917,190*l*; and the captures by sea and land, he thinks, may amount to fifty or sixty millions more : but of these we surrendered at the peace of Europe, colonies to the value of 87,707,130*l.* This will reduce the amount of the national property to 3993,823,765*l.*, which, he says, will be found on the strictest examination to fall considerably short of its real value. ' It exhibits,' says Mr. Colquhoun, ' in glowing colours, the proud height to which this great empire has arrived in the scale of nations. It proves incontestably the immense resources of the state, and the rapid growth of the wealth of the people; and what is of more importance, the facility

lity and power of rendering this wealth productive to a greater extent than prevails in any other nation of the world.' To what extent this productive capital is carried, it is the object of the third chapter and its accompanying table to explain.

This chapter professes to be ' an attempt to estimate the new property annually created in the British empire, by the labour of the people employed in agriculture, manufactures, trade, commerce, navigation, fisheries, and other branches of productive industry.' The attempt is certainly a bold one ; but the author ' entertains a confident hope, that the estimates will be found, in all the different branches of productive labour, to fall short of the actual value of the new property created.' He tells us fairly upon what principle the different calculations have proceeded ; and he endeavours to elucidate them by copious explanatory notes ; so that every one may judge for himself how far the author is borne out in his conclusions. In the pursuit of a species of statistical knowledge interesting to all nations, and particularly to the British nation, he laments that the official materials are so scanty ; but he assures us, that no labour, on his part, has been wanting to supply this deficiency, by obtaining the best information that could be had on each particular branch of the subject, and that the aid of official documents has been called in wherever they could be rendered available.

This curious inquiry commences, as indeed it ought to do, with *agriculture*, that being the most important branch of national industry ; which, in Great Britain and Ireland, is presumed to give employment and afford support to 5,500,000 of the population or nearly one-third of the united empire. The population of Great Britain and Ireland, including the army and navy, was estimated, in 1811, at . . . . . . . . . . . . . . . 17,096,803
Estimated increase in three years, since that time . . 903,197

Probable population in 1814 . 18,000,000
depending principally on the soil of the British islands for subsistence.*

It is calculated that the grain, potatoes, hops, fruit
and vegetables, butter and cheese, grain, hay, turnips, &c., for cattle, poultry, &c. will amount to . £ 127,690,541
For the food of horses, horned cattle, sheep, hogs,
goats, &c., and labour in feeding and attending　　75,117,376

---

* We wish the British islands were made to produce this subsistence, of which they are surely capable—yet in the year 1802, the value of corn, flour, and other grain imported, amounted to the enormous sum of ten millions sterling, which, after all, was little more than one month's consumption. In 1810, the value of corn, &c. imported, amounted to nearly five millions sterling.

Brought up . . . . . . .        202,807,917

Wool, hemp, flax, timber, for manufactures; nurse-
ries and miscellaneous . . . . . . . . .        14,009,707

Making the amount of new property, created by the
cultivation of the land . . . . . . . . . £216,817,624*

The next branch is the yearly revenue derived from *mines* and *minerals*, which, moderately enough we think, is estimated at nine millions sterling : we should have thought on a rough guess that the important articles of iron, salt, and coals, would have amounted nearly to that sum, exclusive of the valuable products of the copper, lead, and tin mines. It must be observed, however, that this is the value only of the raw material.

Next follows the important head of *manufactures*, whose rapid progress, within the last thirty years, almost exceeds credibility. The astonishing improvement of the steam-engine, and the various machinery to which it is now applied, for facilitating some of the most important branches of our manufactures, has, by the number of workmen displaced, fully counterbalanced the excess of the price of manual labour in this country above that of the continent. Some idea may be formed of the value of machinery from the simple fact, that cotton twist spun in England may be carried to India and there sold, at a profit, under the price of the twist manufactured by hand in that country, where the wages are not more than twopence or threepence a day. Hitherto it is very certain that no foreign nation possesses either the skill or capital which the British manufacturers have acquired, though we must not disguise the truth, that the French are, in some particular branches, as in the cotton manufactures for instance, treading closely on our heels, though generally they are far behind us in skill, and at an infinite distance in point of capital. We have heard of apprehensions that they will be able to cut us off from the foreign markets, from the low prices of labour which they pay to the manufacturers; but in truth, there is little to be feared on this score. The application of machinery is become so extensive in Great Britain, that the high price of labour is now but a secondary consideration. If the French had iron as plentiful and as cheap, and could work it as well as ourselves; if they had coals in equal abundance to allow them to substitute steam-engines for horses and men, then indeed

---

* We can only refer to the Table No. 3 for the several items which make up this amount. The quantity of wheat, barley, oats, rye, beans and peas, consumed by man, is estimated at 18,750,000 quarters ; by animals, at 11,829,000 ; in beer and spirits, 4,250,000 ; in various manufactures, 171,000 ; making a total of 35,000,000 quarters, estimated (wheat at 70s. per quarter, and oats at 29s. per quarter,) at 73,734,291*l.*—Horses in Great Britain and Ireland, 1,800,000 ; horned cattle, 10,000,000 ; sheep and lambs, 42,000,000, consume in *hay, grass, straw, vetches, turnips, &c.* 103,400,000*l.*, &c. &c.

there

there might be some grounds for apprehension ; but the possession even of these would still require something else to enable them to rival us in the foreign markets—there must be capital to set them in motion; and we may be perfectly well assured that whenever the French shall possess that capital and can afford a proportionate expenditure to ours, the wages of labour will be just as high in France as in England.

The different kinds of manufactures are stated by Mr. Colquhoun to give employment to more than 3,000,000 of the population of the united kingdom, including their families ; of which fabrics the cotton, woollen, leather, linen, fabricated metals, glass, and porcelain are the most extensive.

The various manufactures are estimated to produce, from labour alone, after deducting the raw materials, 114,230,000*l.* yearly : of this sum the British and Irish produce and manufactures exported on an average for the last three years, according to the public accounts, amounted to 54,571,054*l.* ; but as this sum includes the produce of the mines (9,000,000*l.*) the remainder, 68,658,946*l.*, may be considered as consumed at home, and by the army and navy in different parts of the world.*

The next branch into which Mr. Colquhoun has divided his subject is that of *inland trade,* from which the property of the individual is increased, though it does not appear to add to the general public stock of the nation : by enriching the individual, however, the resources and the revenues of the state are augmented. The sum annually created under this head he estimates at 31,500,000*l.*, which being raised principally by productive labour, from comparatively small capital, is supposed to employ 4,500,000 individuals, including their families. These consist principally of warehousemen and shopkeepers of all descriptions, employed in collecting and vending British manufactures of all kinds, to the consumer or the merchant ; and under this head are included the labour and profits of innkeepers and publicans ; the profits of proprietors of barges

---

* Forty-four different branches of manufacture are enumerated in the table, of which the highest annual produce is that of *cotton,* being 23,000,000*l.*, the lowest, that of the labour employed on floor-cloths, oil-cloths, &c. being estimated at 30,000*l.* ; *woollens* amount to 18,000,000*l.*, and *straw hats, bonnets, toys, &c.* to 500,000*l.*—We transcribe the ' Explanatory note' on ' Woollens.'

' A respectable and intelligent manufacturer, who was examined before a committee of the House of Commons, in 1800, estimated the produce of the woollen manufacture at 19,000,000*l.* a year, and Mr. M'Arthur, in 1803, valued the whole, including the fine fabrics from foreign wool, at 25,560,000*l.* We see by Lord Sheffield's printed report at the meeting at Lewes wool fair on the 27th July, 1812, that on a medium of the six years, from 1806 to 1811, both inclusive, there were imported 7,329,795 pounds of Spanish wool ; the average price of which, on the 16th July, was 7*s.* 9*d.* a pound. The manufactures from British wool may be estimated at 20,000,000*l.*, and those from Spanish wool at perhaps 6,000,000*l.* Total, 26,000,000*l.*—Allowing 8,000,000*l.* for the raw materials, the net value will be 18,000,000*l.*'

D D 2                                                    and

and other small craft, employed in rivers and canals; the labour performed on rivers and canals; the profits of the proprietors of coaches and waggons; &c.

*Foreign Commerce and Shipping* are stated to have produced new property to the enormous amount of £ 46,373,748 in the year 1812, and to have given employment to 406,350 individuals, including their families; consisting of ship-owners, merchants, agents, consignees, brokers, clerks, and labourers. The magnitude of this commerce is apparent from the official returns of the value of imports and exports for the year above-mentioned, which, in the aggregate, stood thus:

| | |
|---|---:|
| Exported to all countries        -       -       - | £ 73,725,602 |
| Imported from all countries        -       -       - | 60,424,876 |

Total    £ 134,150,478

The ships and vessels engaged in this immense commerce are stated in the table at 28,061, carrying 3,160,293 tons, and employing 184,352 men.

Next follows the *Coasting Trade*, which is stated to employ at least 3000 vessels of every description, which are classed as under:

| | Vessels. | Annual Voyages. |
|---|---:|---:|
| From the outports to London        -       - | 700 making | 6,920 |
| From Newcastle and Sunderland, with coals to London        -       -       - | 450 | 3,750 |
| From ditto to other ports        -       - | 470 | 4,000 |
| From Whitehaven, in the coal trade        - | 250 | 2,700 |
| Coasting vessels conveying produce and merchandize | 1,200 | 10,000 |
| Total | 3,070 | 27,370 |

' Estimating these vessels to average 100 tons each, which is somewhat less than an official return made in 1798, of the coasting trade to the port of London, the number of tons conveyed from one port to another of produce, including coals and merchandize of all kinds, would amount to 2,737,000 tons, outwards; and, supposing only half a cargo homewards, on an average, the total would be 4,105,500 tons, which, taken at ten shillings a ton, would give a profit, arising from labour and capital, amounting to the sum of two millions, estimated to be the new property created annually from this trade.'

We consider this estimate as far too low. The voyages performed may perhaps be fewer, but the number of vessels employed, we are quite certain, is underrated.

We now come to the *Fisheries,* and we confess our regret that an object of such vast national importance should make so poor and insignificant an appearance in the list of ' resources,' from
which

which the national wealth is derived.   It is really disgraceful to
this great maritime nation that, surrounded as the British islands
are with fish of the most nutritive and wholesome description,
swarming on banks of many leagues in extent, each acre of which
is far more productive of food than the richest acre of land,
the article of fish should nevertheless be a luxury, in all the great
cities and towns of the empire, confined to the upper ranks of
society.   It has been proved, by direct and positive facts, that,
with a due portion of encouragement, the finest mackerel and herring may be sold in London, and millions of them actually have
been so sold with a reasonable profit, at one penny a-piece; instead
of which, the usual price is from 8 d. to 18 d.   Such indeed is
the productive nature of the fisheries, and so easy would it be to
render them a source of nutritious food for general consumption,
not only in the maritime towns, but in all the inland districts of
Great Britain and Ireland, that an adequate supply might be and
has been furnished at 2 d. a pound, or about £17 a ton, when the
price of butchers' meat was £70 a ton.   This difference in the
price is much more than sufficient to purchase the accompaniments
of potatoes and butter, which would reconcile the mass of the
people to the use of fish, and afford them a better and more relish-
ing meal than a scanty portion of butchers' meat with bread.   On
this subject we have lifted up our voice already, but we fear in
vain.   We hear no more of the 'Fish Association,' nor of the
worthy baronet at the head of it, who is not apt, on slight grounds,
to give up the pursuit of any object of which he may undertake the
management; and we therefore are reluctantly compelled to suppose, that the case is hopeless:—we know, indeed, that the imposition in London, far from being checked, is more flagrant than
before; and that the most infamous arts are put in practice to
enhance the price.   How can it be otherwise? the trading in fish
is a complete monopoly; there is but one market, and the salesmen
and the owners of the fishing-smacks being joint proprietors, that
market is just fed to keep it alive; but good care is taken that it shall
not die of a surfeit.   The distance too of that market, and its approaches, which are not the most convenient, are against its ever
being troubled by three-fourths of London; but these difficulties
may be the very reason why the Lord Mayor and Aldermen are so
tenacious of the privilege of confining the sale of fish to that precious spot called Billingsgate.

We understand that a suggestion was made in the proper quarter, of the expediency of bringing in a bill for establishing another
market towards the west end of the town, which, by creating a
competition, might break up the present scandalous monopoly,

and

and that the answer was, What will the city of London say? We should be glad to know what the city of London has done to entitle it to this or any other exclusive privilege, at the expense of the rest of the community in this great metropolis? There is an act, indeed, which empowers the establishment of a new fish-market in some part of Westminister; and which, as we apprehend, requires only the appointment of new commissioners to carry it into effect. The finest situation imaginable for such a market is that on the Surry side of the new Strand bridge, the more convenient from its contiguity to Covent Garden market; and as profit is the great stimulus to exertion, and several of the directors and proprietors of that magnificent undertaking, which does honour to the spirit and enterprize of individuals, are members of the House of Commons, we do not despair of seeing this desirable object accomplished. The increase of the foot-tolls alone, in consequence of such a market, would amount at least to £ 5000 a year.

Well may Mr. Colquhoun say, ' it is lamentable to reflect, that while £ 45,000,000 sterling is estimated as the value of butchers' meat, and other animal food consumed annually, the property created by the labour employed in the coast and river fisheries can only be estimated at £ 1,500,000, including the herrings and pilchards exported.' The value of the labour of the people employed in the northern and southern whale and seal fisheries, is estimated at £ 600,000 a year, which makes the total of the new property annually created by the fisheries, £ 2,100,000. The Dutch, when they first emerged out of their mud banks, far exceeded, in their fisheries, the greatest efforts that this country has yet made in the height of its prosperity; and even now, after years of unparalleled oppression, ' one hundred and ten herring-busses,' says their secretary of state, ' have sailed this season to the Great fishery, that source of Dutch prosperity.'

Want of example, of encouragement, of capital and skill, have hitherto retarded the progress of the fisheries; yet we should think that a small portion of each would be sufficient to ensure the success of an object which, in every point of view, is of such national importance. While it increased the public wealth, it would add most abundantly to the stock of subsistence; and train up a body of hardy seamen. It would at once give employment, on their own element, to the seventy-five thousand seamen and marines who have been, and half as many more who are about to be, discharged from the navy,* many of whom must either seek employment in foreign countries, or become a burthen to their own.

---

\* The number of seamen and marines voted for the navy in 1813 was  145,000
In 1814  70,000

Discharged  75,000

The

The next subject which engages the attention of Mr. Colquhoun in his endeavours to trace the wealth of the nation through all its ramifications, is the business of the Banker, through the intervention of whom a certain quantity of circulating medium is made to perform the functions of ten, fifty, or a hundred times its value; and the use of the precious metals, and what is of far more importance in mercantile transactions, time, are greatly economized. Millions of money may be paid and received with a degree of facility and security which specie could never perform. Mr. Colquhoun states, that the money paid and received daily, in the metropolis, amounts, on an average, to five millions sterling, or one thousand five hundred and fifty millions in a year, through the medium of bankers only. To count five millions of guineas, at the rate of a guinea every second, and to work twelve hours a day, would employ one person nearly four months, or 120 persons a whole day, or occupy two clerks in every banking house in London. But all the specie in the world would not suffice in the present state of the commerce of the country, to carry it on without a large circulation of bank notes, aided by the drafts or checks of private bankers. By discounting bills of exchange, which otherwise would not be convertible to mercantile purposes for weeks or months, they accommodate the trader, and accelerate business. And such is the facility with which the immense circulation of the checks or drafts given by the bankers, and the notes that pass through their hands, is settled among themselves, that by a clerk from each banking-house meeting at a particular spot, which they call the ' Clearing House,' at a fixed hour every day, millions are paid and received in the course of an hour by an exchange of checks, and the balances are finally settled by a general assemblage of the collecting clerks of the respective bankers. It appeared in the report of the Bullion Committee, that of the 71 private bankers of the metropolis, 46 were in the habit of settling their accounts in this manner; that the daily payments made to them amount, on an average, to £4,700,000, or yearly to one thousand four hundred and fifty-seven millions; yet the whole of these payments are adjusted daily, by means of £220,000, this sum being about the average differences, which are paid by bank notes. If we extend our inquiries a little farther, and take into consideration the payments made by the remaining bankers, by individuals to each other, by the Bank of England, besides the notes issued for the loans, the dividends and Exchequer bills, we shall probably find, that the annual payments in paper, in the metropolis alone, do not fall far short of three thousand millions sterling; while the whole amount of bank notes in circulation does not exceed twenty-seven millions and a-half.

　　　　　　　　　　　　　　　　Mr.

Mr. Colquhoun therefore is justified in saying, that ' in no country in the world is this velocity of circulation carried to such a degree of perfection as in the British metropolis.' It is the result, as he observes, of *public credit* supported by *punctuality*, in the transactions between man and man, which generates unbounded confidence, and gives energy to commercial enterprize—a character almost peculiar to Great Britain, which distinguishes her from all the nations of the earth.

|  | Capitals. |
|---|---|
| There are 5 chartered banks, one in England, three in Scotland, and one in Ireland, whose united capitals are estimated at | £ 30,500,000 |
| 72 private bankers in London - - | 4,000,000 |
| 659 country bankers in England - - | 4,000,000 |
| 72 banking establishments in Scotland - | 800,000 |
| 63 banking houses in Ireland - - | 1,400,000 |
| 871 banking establishments, with a capital of | £ 40,700,000 |

Upon which capital he reckons the profits to amount annually to £ 3,500,000.

The last branch of property annually created which engages the attention of our author is the *Amount of remittances* made to this country, from the *colonies* annexed to the British crown. The amount of property, arising from land and labour in those colonies, is valued, exclusive of the territories under the direction of the East India Company, at £ 50,740,470 sterling a year; and that part of the surplus profits of this land and labour remitted to England annually, is estimated at £ 5,000,000, though Mr. Colquhoun thinks there are strong grounds to believe, that it considerably exceeds this sum.

The account then of *property created in Great Britain and Ireland in the year* 1812-13, will, according to Mr. Colquhoun, stand thus :

| | |
|---|---|
| Agriculture and all its branches - - | £ 216,817,624 |
| Mines and minerals, coals, &c. - - | 9,000,000 |
| Manufactures in every branch - - | 114,230,000 |
| Inland trade in all its branches - - | 31,500,000 |
| Foreign commerce and shipping - - | 46,373,748 |
| Coasting trade - - - | 2,000,000 |
| Fisheries, exclusive of the colonial fisheries of New-foundland - - - | 2,100,000 |
| Chartered and private bankers - - | 3,500,000 |
| Foreign income remitted - - - | 5,000,000 |
| Total in Great Britain and Ireland | £ 430,521,372 |

In

|  | Brought over | - | £430,521,372 |
|---|---|---|---|

In fifty-three colonies and dependencies,
annual produce of labour　　-　　£50,740,470
Possessions in India　　　-　　-　　211,966,494

　　　　　　　　　　　　　　　　　　　262,706,964

　　　　　　　　　　　　Total　　£693,228,336

'The magnitude and splendour,' says Mr. Colquhoun, ' of the resources which have been thus developed, cannot fail to fill the mind of every British subject with exultation, and gratitude to the Supreme Being for the numerous blessings conferred on this highly favoured nation.'

The next chapter is, we believe, quite original. Having, as we see, taken a general view of the population—the capital or wealth—and the new property annually acquired from land and labour—Mr. Colquhoun now attempts ' to discover, as far as discovery is practicable, by approximating details, in what manner, and in what proportions, this property is divided among the various classes of society in Great Britain and Ireland.' And with this view a Table (No. 4.) is annexed to the chapter, being, as he calls it, ' a map of civil society, exhibiting in one view the proportions of created wealth which is allotted annually to every class of the community, from the sovereign, in regular gradation, down to the pauper.' The inquiry is certainly curious, and not wanting in interest; and though it cannot be otherwise than inaccurate, Mr. Colquhoun's ingenious divisions and subdivisions, with their several allotments, serve to shew, at one glance, what classes of the community, by their labour, tend to increase the national capital, and what other classes consume it. If Mr. Colquhoun be at all near the truth, in stating the new property created annually from the different manufactures of this country, at 114 millions, and that this addition to our wealth is created by the labour of three millions of the population, it will require no extraordinary skill in political arithmetic to discover that the profit of manufacturing labour is, in proportion to the numbers employed, nearly as great as that derived from the produce of the soil, which, according to Mr. Colquhoun, amounts to an aggregate of 216 millions created by the labour of five millions and a half of the population. We would not, however, be understood to insinuate, that if the manufactures of the country contributed to the national capital and the national revenue in an equal degree with agriculture, and with half the number of hands, they ought to be held in equal estimation. The real intrinsic value, power, and independence of a nation must ultimately be found in its soil.

In exhibiting a view of the population of the United Kingdom
of

of Great Britain and Ireland, as separated into eight distinct classes, Mr. Colquhoun mixes up into one class the labourers of every description; after which, however, we are presented with a summary view of a classification into productive and unproductive labourers.    His first division is as follows:

| Class. | Heads of families. | Total persons composing their families. |
|---|---|---|
| ' 1st. The royal family, the lords spiritual and temporal, the great officers of state, and all above the degree of a baronet, with their families    -    -    - | 576 | 2,880 |
| 2d. Baronets, knights, country gentlemen, and others, having large incomes, with their families    -    - | 46,861 | 234,305 |
| 3d. Dignified clergy, persons holding considerable employments in the state, elevated situations in the law, eminent practitioners in physic, considerable merchants, manufacturers upon a large scale, and bankers of the first order, with their families    -    -    - | 12,200 | 61,000 |
| 4th. Persons holding inferior situations in church and state, respectable clergymen of different persuasions, practitioners in law and physic, teachers of youth of the superior order, respectable freeholders, ship owners, merchants and manufacturers of the second class, warehousemen and respectable shopkeepers, artists, respectable builders, mechanics, and persons living on moderate incomes, with their families    -    - | 233,650 | 1,168,250 |
| 5th. Lesser freeholders, shopkeepers of the second order, innkeepers, publicans, and persons engaged in miscellaneous occupations, or living on moderate incomes, with their families    -    - | 564,799 | 2,798,475 |
| 6th. Working mechanics, artisans, handicrafts, agricultural labourers, and others who subsist by labour in various employments, with their families    - | 2,126,095 | 8,792,800 |
| Menial servants    -    - | | 1,279,923 |
| 7th. Paupers and their families, vagrants, gipsies, rogues, vagabonds, and idle and disorderly persons supported by criminal delinquency    -    - | 387,100 | 1,828,170 |
| | 3,371,281 | 16,165,803 |

Separate

                    Brought over  -   3,371,281    16,165,803
*Separate Class.*

Officers of the army, navy, and marines, including officers on half-pay and superan-
nuated, with their families      -         10,500         69,000
Non-commissioned officers in the army,
navy and marines, soldiers, seamen and
marines, including pensioners of the army,
navy, &c. and their families     -        120,000        862,000
                                          ————————      ————————
                    Grand total       3,501,781    17,096,803'

The other statistical distribution made by Mr. Colquhoun is
that of the productive and unproductive labourers; and this he
deems to be correct ' as far as approximating facts could be
obtained.' It is as follows:

' *Productive labourers,* by whose exertions a new property is created
every year.

|  | Families. | Persons. | Income. |
|---|---|---|---|
| Agriculture, mines, &c. | 1,302,151 | 6,129,142 | £ 107,246,795 |
| Foreign commerce, ship-<br>ping, trade, manufac-<br>tures, fisheries, &c. | 1,506,774 | 7,071,989 | 183,908,352 |
| Fine arts      - | 5,000 | 25,000 | 1,400,000 |
| Total | 2,813,925 | 13,226,131 | £ 292,555,147 |

' *Unproductive labourers,* whose exertions do not create any new
property.

|  | Families. | Persons. | Income. |
|---|---|---|---|
| Royalty, nobility and gentry | 47,434 | 416,835 | £ 58,923,590 |
| State and revenue, army and<br>navy, half-pay and pensi-<br>oners      -      - | 152,000 | 1,056,000 | 34,036,280 |
| Clergy, law, physic      - | 56,000 | 281,500 | 17,580,000 |
| Universities, schools, and mis-<br>cellaneous      - | 45,319 | 567,937 | 17,555,355 |
| Paupers      - | 387,100 | 1,548,400 | 9,871,000 |
| Total | 687,856 | 3,870,672 | £ 137,966,225' |

If this statement be correct, or if it approaches to the truth, the
conclusion is, that about ¾ of the population are productive labourers,
and divide somewhat more than ½ of their gains among themselves;
that the other fourth part of the community are unproductive
labourers, and that this class consumes nearly the other half of the
annual produce.

Political economists are not quite agreed as to the precise line
                                                                    to

to be drawn between productive and unproductive labourers, some classing the liberal and military professions with the former, and others considering them to belong to the latter class. The truth perhaps lies in this, as in most disputed points, in the middle. They form of themselves an intermediate class, that may with great propriety be denominated useful labourers; men who, though they do not immediately add to the actual stock of national wealth, contribute at least to the security and protection of property from fraud and violence, and to the improvement of the health and morals of society. Men of talent and ingenuity, though not themselves efficient labourers, add to the stock of wealth in giving the proper direction, by their superior skill and intelligence, to productive labour; for without intelligence to direct, the mere labourer might exhaust his strength to very little purpose.

For a more detailed account of Mr. Colquhoun's partition of society, and its various subdivisions, we must refer the reader to the table itself, wherein are specified the different pursuits and occupations of the whole community, their numbers, and their means of subsistence. Such a table, if constructed from official returns, might, it is true, as Mr. Colquhoun observes, ' suggest many useful hints to the statesman and politician;' but that these ' hints' would ' lead to arrangements highly beneficial to the nation,' we may be permitted to entertain very strong doubts. No measure that is injurious to individual interests can be beneficial to the nation; and it is very certain, that the limited degree of inquisitorial power, which is given to the commissioners for inspecting the returns under the property-tax act, might be rendered not only obnoxious, but ruinous to individuals. Such meddling with and prying into the private concerns of families, would be inconsistent with the spirit of the British constitution, incompatible with the national character, and the greatest inroad that has yet been made upon the independence of the subject—and for these reasons we cannot join in the ' confident hope' of Mr. Colquhoun, ' that the period is not far distant, when such a measure will be adopted by the legislature.' Our hope on the contrary is, that such a period may never arrive, though we have no objection to ingenious men, like our author, speculating on such subjects, and constructing tables for their own amusement, and for general information.

It would be too much to expect, that the splendid and magnificent picture which Mr. Colquhoun has exhibited of the wealth, power, and resources of the British empire, should be free from blemishes. Of this description may be reckoned the maintenance of the poor—the paper currency—the public debt and taxes— faults, it is true, which every one conceives himself to be at liberty

to

to censure—with the exception of our author who, on the contrary, is gifted with the happy disposition of finding ' good in every thing.'

The system of the poor laws founded on the 43d of Elizabeth, is, we think, right in principle, however it may be condemned in practice.  By this act the justices are empowered to levy whatever assessments they may think necessary for the relief of the poor, and to judge who are fit objects of public charity.  The meaning is obvious, though there may be too much latitude in the expression;—the justices may abuse the trust by making the assessments unequal and oppressive in extending relief to persons who are unfit, and by an improper distribution of that relief ; perhaps there may be some too, who, like Gil Blas's friend in Madrid, ' become rich by taking care of the poor'—these are evils that affect not the general principle of the laws.  The act is sufficiently clear in the intention of limiting the relief to the indigent and helpless; for in the same act the justices are directed to do what, indeed, might be difficult and even impossible for them to do—to set poor children to work, and to find employment for those who are capable of it.  The distinction, however, between the capable, the idle, and the indigent, perhaps could not be always attended to.  Circumstances have occurred to prevent it, such as a sudden rise in the necessaries of life, or a supply of labourers beyond the demand for work ; and sickness or other calamity may throw out of employ, for a time, many workmen with the best disposition to be industrious.  It would be cruel and unjust to withhold relief from persons so circumstanced.  They have, indeed, the strongest claims on all those classes of society whose incomes are derived from their labour, when from any calamity or misfortune, more especially from those which no prudence nor foresight could prevent, they are unable to continue that labour.

Of the various plans which, at different times, have been brought forward for the amendment of the poor laws, for improving the condition of the poor, and reducing the number of those who receive parochial relief, none have yet.produced the desired effect.  Some have been too indulgent, and liable to abuse—others, too inhuman for civilized society to tolerate—and others too speculative to be carried into practice.  They have each figured their day and departed, and we shall not rake up their ashes; but we cannot let the subject pass without a few cursory remarks.

It is a very general and we think a very erroneous opinion, that the increase of pauperism is mostly to be attributed to the high prices of the necessaries of life.  It would perhaps be more correct to say, that it is the necessary consequence of an increased population and active capital ; but after all is it greater than ought

to

to be expected?—we think not. When the number of poor per‑
sons receiving parochial relief in England and Wales amounted to
500,000; when the funds levied for their maintenance were one
million; and when the price of day labour was six-pence, the bur‑
den of maintaining the poor was just as oppressive to the nation,
and as loudly complained of, as when the number receiving parish
relief had increased, as in 1803, to one million persons, and the
funds raised for their support, to ten millions sterling: but be the
amount what it may, we cannot deny their claim to a maintenance
from the public. We give a considerable share of the national
income to those whose duty it is to direct the morals, and to pro‑
tect the public and private property of the nation—where then
would be the justice of excluding the unfortunate and helpless of
that part of the community from whose labour that income is
derived?

The general introduction of machinery into our manufactures,
by abridging the demand for labour, and the great and rapid im‑
provements that have taken place in husbandry, requiring fewer
hands, might occasion a temporary increase of the number of pau‑
pers; but the fluctuation in the prices of the necessaries of life has
been, in our estimation, a far more fertile source. This is a question
so nearly allied to a measure of vital importance to the future pro‑
sperity of the nation, now under the consideration of the legislature,
that it would be unpardonable to pass it over:—we allude to the
framing of a law for keeping steady the price of corn, which, in
fact, will have the effect of keeping steady the price of labour, and
thereby conduce more to the comfort of the poor, than the too
prevailing delusion of having bread *cheap*—a vague and indefinite
term, which has no meaning, unless when used in comparison with
the wages of labour.

Wheat may be *cheap* at 90s. the quarter, and dear at 30s.; and
the labouring poor may be wretched with the quartern loaf at six-
pence, and comfortable when it is at sixteen-pence; the active capital
and the expenditure of a nation will determine the demand for
labour, and this demand will regulate the wages of that labour, so
as to bear a just proportion to the price of the necessaries of life.
For it will be found that where the supply of labourers is nearly
balanced with the demand, there will the wages of labour be re‑
gulated by the price of provisions, and especially by the price of
corn. A sudden rise or fall of the prices of articles of the first ne‑
cessity must very severely affect the condition of the labouring
poor, but those prices and the wages of labour will gradually tend
to a level.

We have lately heard a great deal of the cheapness of living on
the continent. In France, we are told that beef and mutton may
be

be had from 3½*d*. to 4*d*. a pound, and that the quartern loaf is not above seven-pence; but then those who wish to extol the cheapness of living in France do *not* tell us that the wages of a common labourer are a *franc* or *ten-pence*, and that a weaver or other mechanic may earn, by close application, from thirteen to eighteen-pence a day: the common labourer in England, who earns from two shillings to half-a-crown a day, and who gets his pound of good meat for eight-pence, and his quartern loaf for a shilling, has nothing     envy the labourer of France; much less has the manufacturer and mechanic of England, whose daily wages amount to five shillings and from that sum to half-a-guinea. If the delusion of the word *cheapness* is to seduce any one from his native country, we should recommend him to take up his abode in Russia, where he may purchase as much beef as he can devour for about three halfpence, drink as much *quass* as he can swallow for a penny, and get plenty of garlic for nothing; and he may probably earn by hard labour about three-pence a day: or if he extends his journey to China, he may purchase as much rice as he can eat for a penny, an inch of fat pork to season it for a halfpenny, and a cup of *seau-chew* to to wash it down for another halfpenny, and by working like a Chinese, he may perhaps earn two-pence halfpenny a day.

The wages of labour, in point of fact, are higher in England at this time, when compared with the price of corn, than they are in any other country, and at least equal to what they were at any former period in this. When wheat was sold in the market at 52*s*. the quarter, the quartern loaf was six-pence halfpenny; and when this was the price of wheat corn, the price of labour was from six-pence to nine-pence a day. Take the present price of corn at 66*s*. the quarter, the quartern loaf ought to be 8½*d*. (why it is 11*d*. we leave the Lord Mayor and the Corporation of the City of London to explain,*) and the wages of a common daylabourer are from two shillings and upwards : that is, the labourer in the former period earned little more than his quartern loaf by a day's work, whereas he now earns more than two quartern loaves; and yet we are for ever reminded of the happy condition of the poor in former days.

The condition of the labouring poor, as connected with the price of grain, and the policy of affording an equal degree of protection to the agricultural and the manufacturing interests of

---

* The prices of provisions in London are shamefully kept up by monopolies, arising out of overgrown capitals. When that ridiculous remnant of corporation-meddling, known by the name of ' Assize,' shall be abolished ; when the baker becomes independent of the mealman, the publican of the brewer, the coal dealer of the coal carrier or ship-owner, the fishmonger of the Billingsgate salesman, and not till then, we shall have bread, porter, coals and fish at reasonable prices.

Great

Great Britain, are well argued in a speech, now before us, of the Honourable Mr. Baron Hepburn,* of Smeaton, on the subject of the corn laws, delivered at a numerous and respectable meeting of the county of East Lothian, ' to consider of a petition to the House of Commons,' on this important question.

In examining the history of the Saxon kings, he finds that corn was a regular article of commercial export; that however under the Norman race of kings a contrary policy was adopted, and the export of every denomination of food, even down to *cured h rings,* prohibited; and what was the consequence? ' the quarter of wheat, the year after this prohibition, (a very favourable and productive season,) was at *three shillings,* and a large surplus beyond the consumption remained an useless incumbrance upon the hands of the husbandman;' but ' in the course of two or three years thereafter,' adds the baron, ' you will find the quarter of wheat as high, one writer says, as *nineteen pounds,* and another *twenty-two pounds* sterling of our money; and historians tell us, that several thousands of people died in London of absolute want, and many went into the country and gathered and eat the ears of green corn, merely to preserve themselves in existence.'

This woeful change, then considered as ' a severe visitation of God for the sins of the people,' was the natural consequence of the farmer ceasing to grow wheat for which there was no market; and ploughing only as much land as would produce grain for his own consumption; turning the rest into pasture for the support of that stock which would not spoil by keeping a few years longer.

The same mistaken policy produced similar results in France. When its affairs were directed by that able and upright statesman, Sully, who used to say, that ' agriculture and pasture were the two great breasts of nature,' every facility was afforded to the transport and export of corn; and the consequence was, that France became so flourishing and productive, as to enable her, after paying freight and all other charges, to undersel the English farmer in his own market. But mark the difference when Richelieu became minister! Weakly aspiring to eclispe the glory of Sully, by doing something greater for France than Sully had done, he began his operations by establishing the manufacture of silk in the city of Lyons. To encourage this manufacture, under the absurd idea of lowering the price of corn, and with it that of labour, he not only prohibited the export of corn from France, but forbade the transport of it, under severe penalties, from one province to another: the unavoidable consequence was, as Baron Hepburn observes,

---

* Baron Hepburn is an excellent practical farmer in a district of Great Britain which confessedly yields to none in the perfection to which the agricultural art has been carried.

' that,

' that, in populous provinces, such as those round Paris, the price
of bread rose to an enormous rate; and, across an ideal line, corn
was a cumbrous, useless load, for the want of a market; and
agriculture, thus trammelled and shackled, soon languished, and
died.'

Under these regulations of Richelieu, France remained for more
than a century, until the report of M. Turgot on the depressed state
of her agriculture brought that nation to its senses; and, as we
know to our cost, she has again become an exporter of corn.

The French economists considered agriculture as the only productive employment If they had known to what pitch of improvement manufactures could be carried by the aid of machinery, they
must have confessed the absurdity of their theory. In England we
have felt the importance of manufactures, and afforded them a degree of protection and encouragement which, if popular clamour
were attended to, would now be withheld from agriculture; yet,
as the author whom we have just been quoting observes, ' it is
the clearest of all clear propositions, that they are most intimately
connected together; for the manufacturers eat what the agriculturists grow; and the latter wear what the former weave, and if one
thrive, the other must thrive.' This is the true way of viewing the
subject, and this necessarily leads to the conclusion, that the same
protection ought to be given to the manufacture of corn, that is
given to the anufacture of woollens and cottons: the prices of all
the necessaries of life, which are regulated by the price of corn,
would then become steady, and ' *steady prices* (as the baron observes) are always *cheap*, because they fix and keep equally *steady*,
the price of labour,'—and we may safely add, they tend to diminish
the number of paupers.

This, we are aware, is not the popular doctrine—the man who
professes it must not expect to be gratified by seeing his name emblazoned in chalk on every blank wall. If such be his ambition he
will better succeed by preaching up ' no corn laws'—' lower your
rents,' &c. It is not rent, we apprehend, that occasions the high
price of corn. Those who are most conversant on the subject declare that, even at the present prices, full one-third part of the land
now under cultivation, consisting of the high, the light, and the
poor soils, would do little more, even if rent free, than repay the
expenses; they require all the labour that the richer lands do,
greater expense of manure, pay all parochial and parliamentary
taxes, and after all yield but a scanty crop.* The delay of some

---

* It is stated in more than one of the petitions to parliament, that the average of rents
does not exceed *one-sixth* part of the annual expenses laid out on the lands; and that ten
or twelve pounds an acre are frequently bestowed on one crop on land the rent of which
does not exceed twenty shillings an acre.

legis-

legislative provision—the doubts that exist, lest a suitable protection may not be afforded to agriculture, have already put a stop to the inclosing of wastes and the improvement of poor lands; but if by bringing those into a high state of cultivation, Great Britain can be made, as is generally admitted, capable of yielding a sufficient supply for its own consumption, it would appear to be little short of madness to continue to send yearly from three to ten millions sterling *in specie* to buy corn in foreign countries, instead of expending it in the improvement of agriculture at home.

Whatever importance may be attached to our manufactures, and none will deny their importance, they are, nevertheless, not without their concomitant evils. By the general introduction of working by the task or job, the best workmen earn in four days more than is sufficient for the week; and the consequence too frequently is, that the other three days are spent in idleness and dissipation: while the sudden stoppage of any particular branch of manufacture, whether through the caprice of fashion, or the decrees of an enemy, usually send multitudes to the poorhouse, whose subsistence had been derived solely from that branch. Among the crowds, too, that large manufacturing towns and districts draw together there must be a number of idle and depraved characters, whose pernicious example infects but too generally the younger part of the community.

And yet, extraordinary as it may appear, the proportion of persons who have received parish relief, in some of the first manufacturing counties, is much less than in some of the richest agricultural counties. Thus it appears from the return to parliament, in 1803, of the number of paupers in England, that in the great manufacturing county of Lancashire, the number of paupers was about 7 in the 100, or about one-fourteenth part of the population; while in Oxford they amounted to 20 and in Berkshire to 21 in the 100, or one-fifth of the inhabitants of those highly cultivated counties.

This singular fact can only be explained by the practice which has recently prevailed in all the great towns, and more especially in manufacturing towns, of the labouring poor and the artisans forming themselves into benefit societies, whose funds are applied to the support of those whom sickness or a temporary want of work may have deprived of their usual earnings.

Mr. Colquhoun observes that

‘ Wherever oatmeal, barleymeal, potatoes and milk form the chief part of the food of the labouring people, as in the several counties of England north of the Trent, and in the whole of Wales, Scotland and Ireland, a greater abundance prevails; and that wherever the country exhibits the greatest and most general attributes of fertility; wherever the surface is covered with the most abundant crops, and the
                                                                        fines-

finest verdure, there generally is to be found the greatest portion of indigence'—

and he instances the returns abovementioned, wherein it appears, that in Sussex and Wiltshire the number of paupers average 23 per cent. or nearly one-fourth part of the population, whereas in Cumberland they do not exceed 5 per cent. or one-twentieth part of the population.

We have no doubt, indeed, that if potatoes were made the principal article of food, in the southern and middle, as they are in the northern counties and in Scotland, the number of paupers would be diminished, and the expense of their maintenance greatly reduced. For while we admit the indigent and helpless to have a right to a maintenance at the expense of the rest of the community, we cannot consent to the propriety of dealing out to them the best meat or the best bread, or to proportion the quantum of relief to the existing price of corn. A regulation of this kind, which, however, has been adopted, is a sort of premium for raising paupers; it is equally unjust to the public by increasing the burden beyond what is necessary, and to the industrious labourer, who sees the idle and dissolute better fed than himself. The indigent consist of a variety of classes, which are separated by Mr. Colquhoun into various divisions, and we do not see why they should not be as variously treated, in the quality as well as the quantity of food assigned to them ; this would tend more than any thing else to get rid of a great portion of those who have been admitted as objects of parochial relief, not from unavoidable but some of the ' culpable causes of indigence,' enumerated by Mr. Colquhoun.

It is but too true we fear, that, within the last thirty years, a considerable degradation of moral character has been observable among the lower ranks of society ; we wish we could say that it mounted no higher. The ostentatious display of charitable donations, posted in the front of the public newspapers, would seem to have subdued that pride and independence of feeling, which would once have shrunk from being held up as the objects of such charity; but now an address to the ' charitable and humane,' from ' a reduced officer, an unfortunate tradesman, or a gentleman who has seen better days,' is an easy and elegant way of acquainting the purchasers of charitable fame, at what banking houses their names and subscriptions will be registered.

We do not agree with Mr. Colquhoun and many very worthy people that this moral debasement had its origin in the French revolution. It is the natural consequence, we fear, of the general diffusion of wealth, of the increased population of manufacturing towns and villages, and above all of the want of education to check and restrain the propensity to vice.

E E 2                                                            Great

Considerable improvements have taken place within the last thirty years, in the condition of the great body of the people. Whoever is in the habit of travelling must be sensible how much the comforts of the lower classes have been extended; he sees them better fed, better clothed, and better housed than they were at any former period—more cleanly in their persons and dwellings, themselves and their children more healthy and vigorous. He will observe the avenues to every town enlivened with comfortable small villas and neat cottages; and in the manufacturing districts whole towns erected, where not a dwelling-house stood before. Instead of 'miserable mud hovels by the sides of the public roads, choked up as they still are in Ireland and in France, with a dunghill in front and a puddle behind—instead of a few listless beings covered with dirt and rags, whose squalid looks bespeak not merely a state of poverty, but of extreme indigence and misery, once too common a sight in this country—he will now observe the humblest cottage clean and comfortable, its little garden laid out in beds of herbs and flowers; and the woodbine and the jessamine overspreading the doors and windows: these are indications of comfort and plenty; for when men plant roses they are not in want of the necessaries of life.

The next blot, or what many will consider as false colouring, in Mr. Colquhoun's picture, is the paper-currency of Great Britain. The late bullion question, which occupied the attention, and employed the pens, of many able men, shewed how much opinions were at variance. The merchants entertained one idea respecting the paper currency, the bankers another, and the money-dealers a third; and the resolutions of a committee of the House of Commons, who had taken great pains to ascertain the truth, were set aside by resolutions of a contrary tendency passed by the whole house.

The general opinion, however, was, that the paper currency was depreciated, and consequently that the circulation of it, while unjust to individuals, was injurious to the national credit. This depreciation was supposed to arise from an excessive issue, which made paper, like every other article in the market whose supply exceeds the demand, to fall in value; and the evil thereby occasioned was a rise in the price of every necessary of life; an effect, however, which would have been precisely the same and to the same extent, from an excess of any circulating medium, no matter whether it were gold, or silver, or paper. In foreign countries the evil arising from an excessive issue of paper would be the loss of credit by the loss of confidence in the paper itself.

In consequence of the passing of the Bank restriction bill in
1797,

1797, a great increase in the Bank issues certainly took place. In 1797 the amount of its notes in circulation was about  8½ millions.

| | |
|---|---|
| In 1799 - - - - - - - - - - - - - 14 | ditto |
| 1801 - - - - - - - - - - - - - 16 | ditto |
| 1809 - - - - - - - - - - - - - 19 | ditto. |
| 1810 - - - - - - - - - - - - - 23 | ditto |
| 1812 - - - - - - - - - - - - - 25 | ditto |
| 1814 - - - - - - - - - - - - - 27½ | ditto |

It cannot be doubted that the six millions of paper thrown into circulation in the two years following the passing of the act, must have been employed chiefly to replace the guineas hoarded or withdrawn for other purposes. From the commencement of the parliamentary inquiry in 1810, these wholly disappeared ; and it is worthy of remark that in the *eight years* preceding that inquiry, the increase in the issue of paper was no more than *three* millions, whereas in that year alone it was *four* millions. There are no means of ascertaining what the amount was of gold coin in circulation, when the Bank suspended its cash payments; it has been conjectured at about 15 millions ; and if so, the difference between 23½ millions of mixed currency in 1797, and 27½ millions in 1814, would not be equivalent to the difference of the national capital and expenditure at the two periods, were not those four millions of Bank notes capable of performing more business, and in less time, than in gold.

The depreciation of paper was inferred from another circumstance. The market price of bullion rose so high above the mint price, that the guinea, after its disappearance from circulation, was sold for 26s. paper currency, instead of its standard value of 21s. At this period various causes contributed to raise the price of bullion. That which operated most powerfully was our immense foreign expenditure. The wants of government were so urgent to supply Lord Wellington's army with specie, that there was a constant competition in the market between the government and the private dealer, each striving who should bid most for an acticle of which the one had an interest in raising the price, and the other an imperious necessity of purchasing. Some idea may be formed as to the amount of bullion and specie sent to Spain for the use of our army in the course of five years, from the declaration of the Chancellor of the Exchequer, that within six months, the sum of four millions sterling in specie had been sent from England to enable that army to move. This state of things could not fail to produce a very unfavourable rate of exchange ; aggravated probably by the balance of trade being against us : the continental system had, in fact, put an end to all trade, except that of a limited importation by licences in exchange for bullion; it was not merely the *balance* of trade, therefore, but the whole amount of trade that was against England.

That the high price of bullion and the great depreciation of the foreign exchanges were in a great degree occasioned by the magnitude of our expenditure on the continent, is obvious from the following facts. Soon after the peace with France was concluded, the price of bullion fell from £5 : 10s. to £4 : 10s. the ounce, or 22 per cent. and the exchange with Hamburgh became more favourable and gradually rose 22 per cent. or approached as near to par as the market price of bullion had subsided to the mint price of gold.

The experiment of suspending all cash payments, it must be confessed, was a bold one; and, as Lord Liverpool pronounced it, in his reply to Lord Grenville's crimination of a measure which he himself had been a humble instrument in promoting,

' one of the most memorable among the whole number of the eminent services of that great man whom we all deplore—one that was characteristic of his genius—one that bore the strongest impression of that magnanimous spirit which, knowing the evil interpretation and the obloquy that would be thrown upon the measure, was yet fully prepared to encounter prejudice for the public welfare. He knew the alarm which it must create in its commencement—the strong prejudices that must be excited—the dark forebodings to which so new and formidable a step must give rise ; and,' continues his lordship, ' while I cannot sufficiently admire and applaud the spirit which, anticipating all those consequences, boldly resolved at once upon the measure, I cannot but regard it as the source of our most successful efforts in the general cause—as, in no slight degree, the very means of national salvation.'

We verily believe, indeed, on looking back to that portentous time, that had not Mr. Pitt's comprehensive mind anticipated, what afterwards happened, with regard to the disappearance of specie, but delayed the measure till the evil day came, no expedients, no exertions, no sacrifices on the part of individuals could by any possibility have enabled us to struggle through a war unexampled in its duration and expenditure. Every new alarm would have occasioned a run upon the bank ; every guinea drawn from thence would have been hoarded, melted, or exported ; public credit would have been shaken—all trade and commerce at a stand, and a peace been submitted to on any terms.

On the national debt, loans, and taxes, our observations must be very brief; but we wish to notice the erroneous opinions which many entertain of them. When Mr. Hume predicted the bankruptcy of Great Britain whenever her public debt should amount to one hundred millions, we have no doubt a majority of his readers acquiesced in the truth of the prophecy. If any one had then ventured
tured

tured to maintain that ten times that sum would one day have been raised by individuals for the exigencies of the state, he would have incurred the suspicion of being a visionary or a madman. A thousand and a thousand times have we been told that this debt could be carried no higher; that it loads, and clogs, and presses down the energies of the nation, and yet in spite of all those ponderous epithets, its weight has increased from year to year, and still the nation is buoyant! It has been represented as the greatest of national evils, and yet none can deny that the nation has continued to flourish. That it has a limit is most certain; but it is as certain that none will pretend to fix the point where that limit is to be placed.*

The

---

| | Principal. | Interest. |
|---|---|---|
| * Its progress is thus stated by Mr. Colquhoun : | | |
| The national debt at the revolution - - | 664,263 | 39,855 |
| *Increase* in the reign of King William - - | 15,730,439 | 1,271,087 |
| Debt at the accession of Queen Anne - - | 16,394,702 | 1,310,942 |
| *Increase* during the reign of Queen Anne | 37,750,661 | 2,040,416 |
| Debt at the accession of George I. - - | 54,145,363 | 3,351,338 |
| *Decrease* during the reign of George I. - - | 2,053,128 | 1,133,807 |
| Debt at the accession of George II. - - | 52,092,235 | 2,217,551 |
| *Decrease* during the peace - - - | 5,137,618 | 253,526 |
| Debt at the commencement of the Spanish war 1739, | 46,954,623 | 1,964,025 |
| *Increase* during the war - - - | 31,338,689 | 1,096,979 |
| Debt at the end of the Spanish war - - | 78,293,312 | 3,061,004 |
| *Decrease* during the peace - - | 3,721,472 | 664,287 |
| Debt at the commencement of the war 1755 - | 74,571,840 | 2,396,717 |
| *Increase* during the war - - - | 72,111,004 | 2,444,104 |
| Debt at the conclusion of the peace 1762 - | 146,682,844 | 4,840,821 |
| *Decrease* during the peace - - - | 10,739,793 | 364,000 |
| Debt at the commencement of the American war 1776 | 135,943,051 | 4,476,821 |
| *Increase* during the war - - - | 102,541,819 | 3,843,084 |
| Debt at the conclusion of the American war 1783 | 238,484,870 | 8,319,905 |
| *Decrease* during the peace - - - | 4,751,261 | 143,569 |
| Debt at the commencement of the Revolutionary war 1793, | 233,733,609 | 8,176,336 |
| *Increase* during the war - - - | 327,469,665 | 12,252,152 |
| Debt at the conclusion of the Revolutionary war 1801 | 561,203,274 | 20,428,488 |
| *Increase* during the peace - - - | 40,207,806 | 307,478 |
| Debt at the commencement of the French war in 1803 | 601,411,080 | 20,735,966 |
| *Increase* during the war - - - | 341,784,871 | 9,693,468 |

Total

The establishment of the sinking fund for the redemption of this debt was another proof of that consummate wisdom which will immortalize the memory of Mr. Pitt. Such was the effect of this measure that the 3 per cent. stock, which, at the close of the last war in 1784, was at 54, rose in the course of 1786 to 76 per cent., and in 1792 reached 96 per cent. This sinking fund was first fixed at a million a-year; it was afterwards raised to £1,200,000; and in 1793 was still farther increased by the addition of one per cent. on all loans raised subsequent to that period : And as a sinking fund of one per cent. will redeem the principal in 37, 41, or 47 years, according as the rate of interest shall be 5, 4, or 3, per cent., the amount borrowed will always be redeemed in a determined number of years. This circumstance alone should disarm the national debt of its terrors; its practical effects have indeed been satisfactorily proved by a solemn declaration of the legislature; ' that the total capital of the funded debt of Great Britain, amounting on the 5th of January, 1786, to £238,231,248 : 5s. 2¾d. had, on or before the 1st of March, 1813, been wholly satisfied and discharged, the commissioners for the reduction of the national debt having actually purchased £238,350,143 : 18s. 1d., exceeding the aforementioned sum by £118,895 : 12s. 10¾d.' The objection to loans, that they divert capital from a more beneficial employment in agriculture, trade, and manufactures, is, in some degree, founded. But when we have witnessed the progressive growth of all these branches of our national wealth and power, under the pressure of the very heavy loans which the late contest has compelled us to raise, we find in this circumstance the strongest and most gratifying evidence of the extent of our resources ; and that the annual drain on capital already accumulated, great as it has been, has been more than replaced in each succeeding year of war, by the still greater influx of capital created by the productive and renovating powers of this mighty empire.

But the evil may be said to consist in the taxes required to pay the interest of the national debt arising from these accumulated loans ; and that taxes are evils, very few, we believe, will be disposed to deny—every one feels their effect—many are grievously

| | | |
|---|---|---|
| Total funded and unfunded debt 1st of Feb. 1813 | 943,195,951 | 30,429,434 |
| Debt redeemed    -    -    -    - | 236,801,742 | 7,748,562 |
| Debt 1st of Feb. 1813    - | L.706,394,209 | 22,680,872 |

If to this be added the vast sums that were raised in 1813, amounting to more than 64 millions, together with that raised in the course of the present year, and the whole reduced to sterling money or 5 per cent. stock on each L.100, the total of the national debt unredeemed may be taken at L.600,000,000, bearing an interest of nearly L.25,000,000 sterling.

oppressed

oppressed by them, and the pressure must grow with the growing amount to be raised. But even the amount of taxation gives a spur to the national industry, and calls forth national energies. It is true that taxes increase the price of labour, and may on that account, in a certain degree, check the export of manufactures; they affect also the annuitants, or those who have a fixed income; but these are partial evils, from which, even ' universal good' cannot be exempt.

Though something odious attaches itself to the very name of a tax, yet a nation without taxes can have reached only a very low degree of civilization, or power. Thomas Jefferson, in his ' philosophical Messages to Congress,' boastingly demanded who had ever seen a tax-gatherer in America? Professing ourselves among the number of those who experience no very particular degree of affection for our transatlantic ' brethren,' we are not disposed to rejoice that this wretched impostor has lived long enough to answer the question himself: we could rather have wished (as far as we are concerned) that our loving kindred had been still permitted to feed on Johnny cake, and hominy, without molestation from the tax-gatherer.

The ' Message' of Jefferson was merely foolish; but the speech of an English Chancellor of the Exchequer, in which it was declared that taxation had nearly reached its limits, was both unwise and hurtful—unwise because it was known not to be true—and hurtful because, whether true or false, it tended to lower the public credit and the public confidence, by which this country has been enabled to struggle through the contest, and without which all the wealth of the nation would not have availed it at the trying moment when the bank withheld its cash payments. It was not by planting the seeds of despondency that Mr. Pitt taught the people of England to weather the storm. The pilot at the helm should be the last man to hint at danger.

Art. XI.  1. *A New View of Society; or, Essays on the Forma-*
*tion of Human Character, preparatory to the Development of*
*a Plan for ameliorating the Condition of Mankind.*
2. *Observations on the Effects of the Manufacturing System.*
3. *Two Memorials on Behalf of the Working Classes, presented to*
*the Governments of America and Europe.*
4. *Three Tracts; and an Account of Public Proceedings relative*
*to the Employment of the Poor.*  By ROBERT OWEN, of New
Lanark.

POLITICAL economy, when considered in all its bearings, is
one of the most important and useful branches of science.
It has a connexion more or less intimate with almost every
question of politics and morals; and, whether with respect to
the conduct of private life, or to the administration of public
affairs, cases are perpetually occurring, in which, without a
competent knowledge of its principles, it is impossible either to

4

judge correctly, or to act with wisdom. Benevolence and charity, when not under the guidance of economical science, frequently degenerate into ministers of mischief, aggravating the misery they endeavour to relieve, and resembling, in their effects, those splendid but baneful meteors, which throw a deceitful lustre over the disorder they create.

These remarks have been suggested to us by the degree of public attention and countenance, which, on some recent occasions, have been given to Mr Owen's plans for relieving the national distress. We are quite willing to grant that this gentleman is a most estimable person. Indeed, it is impossible to contemplate his disinterested labours and perfect benevolence, without feeling personally attached to the amiable enthusiast; and, whether his plans are practicable or not, the motives which induce him to pursue them are sufficient to command our approbation and respect. While, therefore, an anxious desire to contribute what we can to the formation of correct opinions respecting the causes of public distress, and the means which should be employed for removing or mitigating it, constrains us to enter into a free and rigid examination, both of the practicability of his particular plans, and of the soundness of his general principles, we can assure Mr Owen, that no particle of angry feeling mingles itself with our opposition, and that we cordially esteem the man whose projects we venture unequivocally to condemn.

In politics, as in medicine, the regular practitioner, before he prescribes his remedies for any existing disorder, will endeavour to ascertain its nature and its cause. When we examine into the condition of the labouring classes in this country, we immediately perceive that their distress arises from *Want of Employment;* and, on pushing the inquiry a step further, we find, that want of employment is occasioned by the depressed state of agriculture, manufactures, and trade. In tracing the causes of the existing distress, therefore, the ultimate question for our consideration is, why are these great branches of our national industry in a state of depression? Our soil and climate are not changed; our varied and admirable machinery for abridging and perfecting labour has undergone no deterioration; and our working population has, as yet, lost nothing in point of energy or skill. But if all these original sources of wealth and instruments of production continue unimpaired, whence is it that prosperity is suspended, that the capitalist obtains no adequate return, and that the labourer remains without employment?

These interesting and momentous questions cannot be answered in a manner completely satisfactory, unless we refer to first principles, and trace those general laws which at one period raise the rate of profit so high, that capital accumulates with rapidity, and is eagerly demanded for reinvestment; and at another period, depress the rate of profit so low, that capital either ceases to accumulate, or passes off to foreign countries, to seek that beneficial occupation which cannot be obtained at home. This preliminary inquiry we will endeavour to render as clear and as brief as possible : though, before entering upon it, we must be allowed to say one word in answer to an objection which persons conversant only with the particular details of business not unfrequently urge against general disquisition and theory, on the ground of their being at variance with experience and inapplicable to facts. In all the sciences, except those which relate to number and quantity, a principle is nothing more than a general rule, ascertained by the process of induction, from an examination of particular cases. To lay down a principle, therefore, is merely to assert that some one attribute, or circumstance, is common to a whole class of phenomena; and if, upon actual observation, or experiment, this attribute, is found not to be common to the class, the assumed principle must necessarily be erroneous. A general law or principle embraces particulars; and that which does not embrace particulars, ceases to be a general law. The objection, therefore, that general principles, or theory, may be at variance with experience, and contrary to facts, is applicable to those erroneous theories only, which have no foundation beyond hypothesis, and cannot be justly urged against a correct theory deduced analytically from observation or experiment, and which affords a satisfactory solution of the facts it is applied synthetically to explain. With this very simple explanation of the nature of general reasoning, we shall now proceed to trace, with as much brevity as possible, the laws which regulate the rate of profit, and thereby accelerate or retard the prosperity of nations.

Profit is that net surplus which remains with the capitalist after the complete replacement of all his advances :—And the first circumstance which influences its rate is, the quality of the Soil under cultivation. If the farmer occupy land so fertile that the expenditure of a capital of 100 quarters of corn in tillage yields him a reproduction of 150 quarters, it is self-evident that the net surplus will be 50 quarters; and that, supposing no rent to be paid, the rate of agricultural profit will be fifty per cent. But, should the farmer cultivate a soil so inferior that the expenditure of 100 yields a reproduction of no more than 105, it is equally self-evident, that the rate of profit will sink from

fifty to five per cent.; while, if, from the next quality of land to
be taken in, the expenditure of 100 quarters creates a reproduction of no more than 100 quarters, the further employment of
agricultural capital could be attended with no surplus or profit
whatever.  In the first case, capital, and the demand for labour, might double every two years; in the second, they could
not double in less than twenty years; and, in the third, no additional capital could be created, and therefore no additional
labour could be employed,—and the country would have arrived
at that stationary and melancholy state, in which every birth
beyond what is necessary to keep up the existing population,
must be followed by a death brought on by want.

The second circumstance which influences the rate of profit,
is the degree of Skill and economy with which labour is employed, whether in agriculture, or in manufactures.  If a farmer expend 100 quarters of corn, or the value of 100 quarters, in cultivation, and obtain a reproduction of 200 quarters, it makes
not the smallest difference with respect to the rate of profit,
whether this return be raised from a very fertile soil unskilfully
managed, or from one of inferior quality judiciously managed.
In either case there are 100 quarters expended, and 200 produced; and though the cause of the increased proportion in
which the return exceeds the advance is different, the effect
is the same, and the rate of profit in either case is cent. per
cent.

Improvements in manufactures have the same influence on
the rate of profit as improvements in agriculture.  If a farmer
were to employ 50 labourers in cultivating fields which yielded
150 quarters of corn, and were to expend 60 quarters on the
food and seed, and 60 on the clothing and implements they consumed while at work, his total surplus or profit would be 25
per cent.; but if an improvement in manufacturing industry
were to take place, which so reduced the productive cost, and
consequently the exchangeable value of wrought necessaries,
that the farmer could purchase the clothing and implements
consumed by his 50 labourers for 40, instead of 60 quarters of
corn, his profit would rise from 25 to 50 per cent.; for, in this
case, the reproduction of 150 quarters would be obtained by
an advance of 60 quarters for food and seed, and 40 for clothing and implements.

Now, the two causes which we have mentioned, namely, the
quality of the land under cultivation, and the degree of skill with
which labour is applied, have precisely the same effect in regulating the rate of manufacturing that they have in regulating
the rate of agricultural profit.  When a master-manufacturer,
by advancing to 100 labourers their clothing and tools, with

food and material equal to these in value, can fabricate clothing and tools for 300, his surplus of product above expenditure will be 50 per cent. But if, in consequence of cultivating inferior soils, or of pursuing a less skilful mode of husbandry, the productive cost, and consequently the exchangeable value of agricultural produce should be so increased, that for the food and raw material furnished to his 100 labourers he is obliged give clothing and tools for 150 instead of for 100, his profit would sink to 20 per cent.; because, in producing clothing and tools for 300, he would have expended the clothing and tools of 250.

The third circumstance which influences the rate of return upon capital, is the real amount of Wages, or the quantity of the products of labour advanced to the labourer while performing his work. When a farmer, in cultivating a field which yields him 300 quarters of corn, employs 150 labourers, and expends 100 quarters in supplying them with seed and implements, then, if he gives them 50 quarters more as their wages, his profit will be cent. per cent.; while, if he is obliged to advance 100 quarters as their wages, his profits will sink to 50 per cent. In like manner, when a master-manufacturer employs a set of labourers in fabricating 300 suits of clothing, and expends the value of 100 suits in supplying them with material and tools, he will obtain a profit of cent. per cent., if he pay them 50 suits as their wages; and a profit of only 50 per cent., if he pay them 100 suits. While real wages remain stationary, profit will rise or fall as the effective powers of industry are increased or diminished; and while the effective powers of industry remain stationary, the capitalist will receive a larger portion of its products as the labourer receives less; or, in other words, profits will rise as wages fall. Improvements in the effective powers of industry, however, may raise the rate of profit and the amount of wages at one and the same time. If a farmer and a master-manufacturer, by employing 100 labourers each throughout the year, obtain the one 300 quarters of corn, and the other 300 suits of clothing,—then, supposing the yearly wages of a labourer to be 1 quarter and 1 suit, the rate of profit will be 50 per cent. But were an improvement to take place in the effective powers of industry, enabling the master-manufacturer and farmer to obtain, the one 500 quarters and the other 500 suits from the work of the same men —then, though the annual wages of the labourer should be increased to $1\frac{1}{2}$ quarters and $1\frac{1}{2}$ suits, the rate of profit would rise to 66 per cent. For, a quarter of corn and a suit of clothing being equal in productive cost, would be also equal in exchangeable value; and, consequently, the farmer's advance to his 100 labourers of 150 quarters and 150 suits, would be equivalent to 300 quarters, while his return would be 500 quarters. In like manner, the master-manufacturer's advance to his 100 labourers would be equivalent to 300 suits, while his return would be 500. The total expenditure of the farmer and master-manufacturer being 300 quarters and 300 suits, and their total reproduction 500 quarters and 500 suits, it is evident that the aggregate profit of our little society would be 66 per cent. But the aggregate profit of the society is composed of the particular profits of individuals. Were the farmer to obtain more or less than 66 per cent., the manufacturer would obtain less or more. Yet, though such an irregularity might occasionally occur, the law of competition would prevent its continuance, and, on the average, would render the products of equal capitals equivalent, and the rate of profit equal.

There are three causes then,—the quality of the soil under cultivation,—the degree of skill with which labour is applied,—and the proportion of the produce absorbed as wages, which determine the rate of return upon productive capital, and which may at any time accelerate, retard, or even suspend the prosperity of a country. The two first, however, exert a much more powerful influence than the third. When a larger quantity of the products of labour fall to the share of labourers, their numbers are always found to increase; and hence, as the supply of labour augments with the demand, wages scarcely ever retain an elevation sufficient to depress the rate of profit in any material degree. Neither can the return upon capital be permanently raised by the reduction of wages below their natural level; because when the labouring classes do not obtain that quantity of the necessaries of life which climate and custom have rendered essential to their healthful existence, distress diminishes their numbers, until the failing supply of labour restores its value in the market. Very different is the case with respect to the quality of the soil under cultivation, and the degree of skill with which labour is applied. These causes exert a powerful and permanent influence on the rate of return upon productive capital; and it is only by a due consideration of the manner in which they operate in any given circumstances, that we can obtain a satisfactory solution of the difficult but most important problem, Why a country at one period should advance rapidly in prosperity, and at another should, without any external disaster, approach the limits of her prosperity, or verge sensibly to decay.

In new, or in thinly peopled countries, no lands except those of the first quality, and most eligible situation, will be resorted to for the supply of food and materials; and consequently the effective powers of Agricultural industry will be extremely high. But as the division of employment is limited by the extent of the market, and can be perfectly established only amongst a dense population, it follows, that in new or thinly inhabited countries, the effective powers of Manufacturing industry must be extremely low. Hence, in the progress of society, the two main causes which determine the rate of return upon productive capital, are as antagonist muscles, modifying and balancing the action of each other. As increasing population compels us, on the one hand, to resort to inferior soils, and thus raises the natural price of raw produce, so it leads, on the other, to more accurate divisions of employment, and to that extension of machinery which is at once their cause and their effect, and thus lowers the natural price of all wrought goods. Thus, as population and improvement advance, manufactured articles are constantly falling in value, as compared with agricultural produce. But, on the principles already unfolded, increased facility in producing wrought necessaries, has the same effect in raising the rate of profit, which diminished facility in producing food and material has in lowering it. And hence it will frequently happen, that a greater degree of economy and skill in the application of labour may completely counteract the effects of resorting to inferior soils; and that the return upon productive capital may rise, on the whole, though the difficulty of obtaining food and material should increase. Such a process, however, could not continue long. Under any given degree of skill and economy in the application of labour, the return upon capital will be determined by the quality of the land in cultivation ; and as inferior soils are resorted to, the rate of profit will constantly diminish, until that stationary state is attained, in which no additional capital can be employed, and all tendency to increased population must be checked by famine.

In considering the causes which accelerate or retard prosperity, it is important to remark, that any country which has started before her neighbours in wealth and population, will arrive at the stationary state long before the next quality of land to be taken in becomes so inferior that it will not replace the expenses of cultivation, with the lowest rate of profit for the sake of which the capitalist will engage in production. That constant desire on the part of individuals to turn their capital to the best account, which equalizes the rate of profit throughout the different districts of a country, tends also to equalize it throughout the different countries of the world. If in France the customary rate of profit were 20 per cent., while in England it was only 10 per cent.; then, allowing property to be equally secure in the two countries, British capital would inevitably flow to France. *. If the inequality in the rate of profit arose from the higher degree of skill possessed by France in the application of her labour, it would be corrected as soon as England adopted the more accurate divisions of employment, or copied the superior machinery of her neighbour. But if the inequality arose from England's having resorted to soils inferior to those under cultivation in France, it could not be corrected; and consequently the efflux of British capital could not be checked, until the progress of wealth and population in France compelled her to obtain additional supplies of agricultural produce from soils incapable of returning a larger surplus than those under cultivation in England. No superiority of skill in the application of labour could enable England to retain in tillage soils very much inferior to those under the plough in France. The divisions of employment, and the use of machinery, on which superiority in the application of labour depends, would be speedily copied by an intelligent people living under a free government; and, when copied, they would immediately raise the rate of profit in France, in the same proportion in which they had raised it in England; and the equilibrium which had been established, when different degrees of skill in the application of labour counterbalanced different degrees of fertility in the land, would be again disturbed, when skill became equal and the inequality in the soil resorted to for the supply of food and material, was left, uncounteracted, to produce its natural effect. Should this inequality be considerable, the rate of profit would be much higher in France than in England; and the desire of improving their condition becoming too powerful for those associations which bind men to their native land, capitalists would emigrate with their productive stock from the former to the latter country. When the next quality of land to be taken in cannot yield a produce sufficient to replace expenditure, it is *physically* impossible that wealth and population should continue to increase; and when the next quality of soil to which any particular nation is compelled to resort, in order to obtain an additional supply of food, is very much inferior to the soils under cultivation in neighbouring countries, it becomes *morally* impossible that they should continue to increase. In either case, a country will have reached, for the present, the limits of its resources; and will have attained that stationary and languid state, in which the pressure of distress causes a premature death to follow upon every birth

---

* See an admirable article on the Corn Laws and Trade, in the Supplement to the Encyclopædia Britannica.

beyond what is necessary to keep up the actual numbers of the labouring population.

That stationary and melancholy state, to which, from the o-peration of natural and necessary causes, every country is gradually approaching, may however be prodigiously accelerated by artificial and accidental circumstances; and forced prematurely upon us by *unwise Commercial Regulations*, or by *the pressure of Taxation*. To enter into a scientific exposition of the effects of these upon the production, distribution, and consumption of wealth, would far exceed the limits we have prescribed to ourselves in the present article. But lest, in assigning the causes of the distress which has recently overspread this country, we should appear to reason from principles the truth of which we are not prepared to demonstrate, it may be necessary to resort to one or two very brief illustrations, in order to show how Restrictive systems and heavy Taxes influence the rate of return upon productive capital.

In old and advanced countries, the great obstacle to the further increase of wealth and population, is, the reduced effective power of Agricultural industry, brought on by the necessity of resorting to inferior soils for additional supplies of raw produce; while, on the contrary, in new or thinly inhabited countries, the main obstacle to prosperity arises from the low effective powers of Manufacturing industry, occasioned by the absence of those divisions of employment, and the want of that extensive machinery, which, in densely peopled regions, reciprocally promote the introduction of each other.

But these obstacles to the accumulation of wealth would in a great measure be removed, by establishing a free intercourse between countries in these opposite situations. If, for example, an expenditure of a given amount of capital and labour would suffice to produce such a quantity of cottons, hardware, &c. at Glasgow or Birmingham, as would exchange for 400 or 500 quarters of Polish or American corn; while, because of the necessity under which we are placed of cultivating soils of a far inferior degree of fertility, the same expenditure, if applied directly to the raising of corn in this country, would not yield more than 200 or 250 quarters, it is obvious, that by exchanging our manufactured goods for foreign corn, we should double the profits of stock, and enable the country indefinitely to advance in the career of improvement. This supposition is not very remote from the truth,—and it shows that we are yet a long way removed from the degree of wealth to which it is in our power to attain before arriving at the stationary state. But if we persist in excluding the raw products of other countries, and consequently force our capitalists to employ their stock in a comparatively disadvantageous production, it requires very little sagacity to foresee that we must continue to languish and decline. Capital will unquestionably be transferred to more favoured situations, and we shall have to contend not only against the difficulties arising from small profits, but also against those occasioned by a diminution of the fund for setting labour in motion, and by whose extent, the extent of the productive industry of the country must always be regulated.

It is self-evident, that a relatively heavy Taxation must also occasion this efflux of capital. If the productive power of capital in Great Britain and France were equal, there could be no inducement to transfer stock from the one to the other. But if, when profits were thus equal, a greater amount of taxes should be imposed in one country, the equilibrium of profit would instantly be deranged; and there would be an immediate inducement, varying in its efficacy according to the relative increase of taxation, to transfer capital from that country in which the government claimed a large share of its profits, to that in which it was satisfied with a smaller share.

From the analysis here attempted of the laws which regulate the rate of return upon productive capital, it is hoped that we may be enabled to trace the causes of the deep distress which has now overspread this once happy country, as well as to ascertain in what degree the schemes of Mr Owen are calculated to revive our drooping industry, and restore employment to our people. Our climate has not changed; our sun is as warm, and our seasons as genial, as heretofore; our admirable machinery for the abridgment and perfecting of labour has in no way deteriorated; and our working classes have, as yet, lost nothing of their wonted industry, energy, and skill, But with all these original sources of wealth unimpaired, there are, in our present circumstances, three several causes combining to suspend prosperity. In the *first* place, we have extended Tillage over lands of a quality so inferior, that, upon any given expenditure, they yield a much less proportional return than the lands under cultivation in any other country in the world. In the *second* place, our *barbarous Restrictions upon Commerce,* deprive us of those continued sources of prosperity which, in the natural course of events, and under a system of free external trade, improvements in manufactures open to a country whose domestic agriculture can be no further extended without a diminished rate of return upon capital. And, in the *third* place, the Tax-gatherer appropriates so large a portion of the surplus produce of industry, already too much diminished by the preceding causes, that in many instances the farmer and manufacturer are left scarcely sufficient to replace their advances. The consequences are, that the productive cost of food and material, as marked by their average prices in the market, are 100 per cent. higher in these than in any neighbouring countries; that from the low rate of profit and of interest, capital either ceases to accumulate at all, or else seeks in foreign investments that beneficial occupation which cannot be obtained at home; and that our labouring classes, though possessed of unequalled energy and skill, are left without employment, and driven upon their parishes for support.

Such are the causes of that widely spread, and we fear deeply seated distress which the proposed establishments of Mr Owen are intended to remove. The means by which he undertakes to accomplish this most desirable end, are, to divide the country into compartments, containing each a thousand acres; to erect on each of these a village in the form of 'a parallelogram, with the requisite enclosures and buildings for carrying on agricultural and manufacturing industry; and to place in each village a thousand inhabitants, who are to cultivate the soil and work up its produce on the principle of combined labour and expenditure; who, from the period of infancy, are to be placed in preparatory schools, and subjected to a regular system of instruction and moral training. Under these arrangements he promises that poverty and crime shall cease, and evil, physical and moral, be utterly banished from the earth! The effective powers of industry are to be so increased, that his villagers shall produce sufficient to pay the rent of the land they occupy, and the interest of the money expended on their first establishment, with their due proportion of taxes; and ultimately, to enable the country to support a greatly augmented population, in ten times the comfort enjoyed at present; while the system of education and moral training is to be rendered so perfect, that every species of useful knowledge shall be infused into the mind, and every selfish and unamiable propensity eradicated from the heart!

Our sincere esteem for the benevolent character and disinterested conduct of Mr Owen, withholds us from expressing any opinion respecting the intellect of the person who seriously proposes to accomplish such ends by such means. We shall merely say, that we have given no inconsiderable portion of attention to Mr Owen's several addresses and publications, but have been unable to discover any conceivable relation or connexion between his premises and his conclusions. His schemes do not touch, nay, they have not the most distant bearing upon, the causes of our present distress. We would appeal to his soberminded consideration, whether dividing the country into districts or farms of a thousand acres each, could improve the quality of those inferior soils to which we are obliged to resort for the supply of food.   We would entreat him to explain in what way the erection of villages in the form of parallelograms, could repeal those enactments against foreign trade which are a disgrace to the age in which we live.   We would demand of him, whether the principle of combined labour and expenditure could charm away the collector of taxes; and we would ask him distinctly to state, whether he has any chance of inducing Mrs Marcet to establish in one of his villages a preparatory school for instructing the members of the Cabinet in the first rudiments of economical science, and for affording them sufficient light to retrace their ignorant and infatuated steps towards bankruptcy and ruin.   Could Mr Owen either increase the quantity of our fertile land, open our commerce, lighten our taxes, or instruct our Rulers, we should be among the foremost to hail him as the deliverer of the people, and the saviour of his country; but so long as he is incapable of accomplishing any one of these things, so long must we continue to regard him in the light of an amiable, but mistaken enthusiast, who, had he the means of executing his plans, would aggravate the evils he dreams he could remove.   This is our deliberate opinion; and we shall proceed to establish its correctness by demonstrating, that it is not in the nature of things that Mr Owen's establishments should increase the effective powers of industry so as to afford beneficial occupation to capital, and adequate reward to labour.

With respect to the powers of agricultural industry, if Mr Owen were to erect his villages on waste lands, inferior in quality to those already under cultivation, it is evident that the re turn upon the capital which he invested in the soil would be less than at present; and that so far from relieving the existing distress of the country, he would bring us a step nearer to that stationary state of society in which, as Adam Smith long ago observed, the condition of the labouring classes becomes wretched in the extreme.   And if Mr Owen, instead of resorting to inferior lands, should seek to obtain a more abundant supply of the necessaries of life, by applying additional portions of capital to lands of good quality, he would, though by a process somewhat different, arrive at an exactly similar result.   It is an ascertained and fundamental principle in political economy, that each additional portion of capital applied to heighten the cultivation of the soil, yields a less proportional return; that is, if 100 quarters of corn, expended in cultivating a field in the ordinary way, will occasion a return of 120 quarters, then a capital of 200 quarters, expended on what is called high farming, will not raise from this field a return of 240 quarters, but some less quantity, as 220. Now, it is necessary for Mr Owen to demonstrate to us, that his villages, with their system of instruction and moral training, are calculated to alter this essential property of the soil, and to enable him to employ upon each of his farms of 1000 acres, additional portions of capital, with an undiminishing ratio of return. Unless he can demonstrate this,—unless his mode of culture increase the produce in the same proportion in which additional capital is employed, every increase of food and material which he obtains will be raised at an additional expense; the surplus of produce above expenditure will become less and less; and, consequently, the means of accumulating capital, and of employing an additional population, will be perpetually *diminishing* in his hands. Mr Owen, indeed, fancies he can overcome all these difficulties by the adoption of spade cultivation; but we will tell him, without fear of contradiction, that spade cultivation, so far from being capable of working the miracles he supposes, is less profitable than cultivation by the plough. Why, in the improved husbandry of this country, has the spade been in so great a degree supplanted by the plough? Only because experience has convinced the farmer that the plough is the cheapest instrument of production, and that, by employing it, he obtains a greater net produce—a larger surplus over and above expenditure. Mr Owen will no doubt contend, that he cares nothing about the net produce; that his plans do not embrace the consideration respecting the proportion in which the return may exceed the expenditure; and that, without regarding what merely concerns the rate of agricultural profit, he rejects the plough, and reduces the number of horses employed in husbandry, in order to obtain a greater gross produce applicable to the maintenance of the productive labourers of his villages. This might perhaps answer tolerably well, if Mr Owen could evade taxation,—if he could obtain land without paying rent,—borrow money without interest,—and persuade his villagers not to increase their numbers. But we must again inform this miscalculating enthusiast, that, with respect to the claims of the tax-gatherer, the rent of the land he occupies, the interest of the money he borrows, and the means of accumulating additional capital for employing a growing population, the net produce, or surplus of return above expenditure, is *the only fund to which he can look*—and that, for these purposes, the gross produce is to be regarded as absolutely nothing. By discarding the plough, and performing the work of husbandry without the aid of horses, Mr Owen might possibly find employment on one of his farms for 1000 instead of for 900 labourers; but though he might thus increase the *gross,* he would infallibly diminish the *net* produce. Assuming, by way of example, that the net produce is reduced from 1000 to 800 quarters of corn, and that the taxes, the rent, and the interest of the money borrowed to erect the village, amounted to 600 quarters, then, that portion of the produce of the soil which is applicable to increase the existing capital, and thus to give employment to additional hands, will be reduced from 400 to 200 quarters. Spade cultivation, therefore, though in the first instance it might allow a greater number of labourers to be engaged on a given surface, would dry up the sources of accumulation and of increased employment; and unless, as we before hinted, Mr Owen could persuade his villagers not to add to their existing numbers, would in a very short time plunge them into *aggravated* misery. For employment can increase only with the increase of capital; and the rapidity with which capital can accumulate, must be in proportion to the degree in which the return exceeds the expenditure by which it is obtained.

But Mr Owen's villages are intended to be manufacturing as well as agricultural establishments; and therefore we must inquire how far his arrangements are calculated to improve the condition of the working classes, by increasing the effective powers of *manufacturing* industry. We understand that, when asked whether the manufactured goods prepared in his villages are intended to be consumed in the places where they are produced, or to be sent out and sold in other markets; Mr Owen replies somewhat ambiguously, and says, that the point will be determined by circumstances. But this vague and indefinite language can avail him nothing. It is a matter of perfect indifference which alternative he may chuse; for, whether his manufactured goods are sent to other markets, or consumed in the villages in which they are fabricated, it is equally impossible that Mr Owen's arrangements should insure increased returns upon manufacturing industry. If he send his wrought goods to find a distant sale, then their prices will occasionally fluctuate with the variations of demand and supply; a brisker flow of commerce will place his villagers in affluent circumstances, while a stagnation or revulsion of trade may not leave them wherewithal to pay their rent and taxes, and may plunge them in bankruptcy and misery. If the whole manufacturing population of England could be placed at once in such establishments as Mr Owen proposes, foreign trade could not be thereby improved, nor the continents of Europe and America enabled to consume an additional yard of our fabrics. As long as the sale of goods, and consequently the employment of the manufacturer, depends upon external sale, it is not in the nature of things that internal training, however conducive to the forming of moral habits, should insure an adequate remuneration to industry, or obviate the recurrence of distress.

But Mr Owen is careful not to pledge himself to any definite mode of proceeding; and, when pressed with the difficulty of glutted markets and suspended demand, he will no doubt endeavour to escape, by saying, that it forms a part of his plan to confine the consumption of manufactured articles to the respective establishments in which they are made. This, however, is escaping from one horn of the dilemma, only to fix himself upon the other. The great cause which increases the powers of manufacturing industry is the division of labour; and the division of labour, as Adam Smith long ago demonstrated, is limited by the extent of the market. In a small village, fabricating within itself whatever it consumed, there could exist no division of labour worthy of the name; each individual would have to follow a multiplicity of occupations; half his time would be wasted in shifting his tools and adjusting his materials; and he would lose the advantage of that miraculous dexterity and quickness which the human hand acquires when confined to one or two simple operations. It is precisely because the effective powers of industry are increased by the division of labour, and because the division of labour is limited by the extent of the market, that roads are constructed, bridges erected, canals opened, and every possible means resorted to, in order to facilitate the intercourse between one district and another. But Mr Owen's discoveries in the science of wealth render all these unnecessary. In as much as his plans extend to make the villages consume within themselves whatever they produce, the division of labour, whether territorial or mechanical, will be superseded; the exchange of commodities between one place and another will cease; and with it all the advantages of commercial intercourse will be lost. What should we think of the person who should propose to increase the wealth of the country, and to give uninterrupted employment to the plough and the loom, by breaking up our roads and destroying our canals, by obstructing our rivers and closing our ports, and by everywhere intersecting the country with impassable mountains? But Mr Owen's project for penning up the population in quadrangular villages, and causing each village to consume its own productions, is in effect the same:—and yet, with the most amusing simplicity and the most undoubting confidence in his own superior wisdom, he gravely proposes it, in the country which gave birth to Adam Smith, and in an age when the

3

discoveries of that great man have been extended by Say, and Malthus, and Ricardo; and rendered familiar to every school girl by an admirable little book, entitled, ' Conversations on Political Economy.' In every human character, in all human affairs, there is a mixture of good and evil; and perfection has no habitation except in the dreams of the enthusiast. The fluctuations of demand and supply, the occasional glutting of markets, and stagnations in trade, are evils which necessarily accompany, and, in some degree, counterpoise the advantages resulting from the division of employment. If Mr Owen retain the division of labour in his establishments, the changes in the state of external markets, and the consequent impossibility of obtaining an uniformly profitable sale for their productions, will occasionally deprive his villagers of the means of paying their rent and taxes, and reduce them to the condition of bankrupts and paupers; and if, to avoid such evils, he discard the divisions of labour, and cause each establishment to consume within itself whatever it supplies, then the great principle which multiplies the effective powers of industry will be thrown out of operation, all the sources of prosperity will be dried up, and universal poverty overspread the land.

In his reasonings, as well as in his plans, Mr Owen shows himself profoundly ignorant of all the laws which regulate the production and distribution of wealth. He tells us, that the distress to which the people of this country are exposed arises from scientific and mechanical power producing more than the existing regulations of society permit to be consumed. This is tantamount to saying, that wealth is poverty, and that the necessaries of life are unattainable, because they exist in excess. The application of scientific power, and the various improvements which have been effected in machinery, instead of being the causes of distress, have counteracted, in a very considerable degree, the effects of our absurd commercial laws, and still accumulating taxes, and have, as yet, averted a national bankruptcy. The steam engine has fought our battles, and pays the interest of our debt. If our improved machinery did not tend to reduce the expense of producing manufactured goods, we could neither sell our fabrics in the foreign market, nor keep our inferior lands under cultivation. The truth of the latter assertion may not be very obvious, but it is quite demonstrable. If a piece of ground will produce 100 quarters of corn, and if the labourers employed upon it expend 50 quarters for seed and food, with clothing and implements which cost 50 quarters more, then it is evident that such land will not be cultivated; and for the plain reason, that its cultivation will afford the farmer no profit. But if improved machinery were to lower the price of manufactured goods, until the farmer could purchase for 30 quarters the same quantity of necessary clothing and implements which formerly cost him 50, then this land would be eagerly sought, for the purpose of tillage; because in this case the diminished expenditure of 30 instead of 50 quarters for the purchase of clothing and implements, would yield the farmer a profit of 25 per cent. A reduction in the value of manufactured goods, which allows lands of an inferior quality to be taken in, also admits of the additional application of capital to our better soils, and promotes that system of high farming for which England is so conspicuous. Were it not for the application of that scientific power and improved machinery, to which Mr Owen erroneously attributes our distress, the whole of our foreign trade would be annihilated, and our tillage reduced one half. Highly as we respect this gentleman for his benevolent intentions, and however we may be disposed to approve his experiments in education and moral training, truth constrains us to declare, that with regard to political economy, and the essential order of society, his principles are radically erroneous, and his projects for relieving the national distress altogether impracticable and absurd.

But as Mr Owen's pretended principle, that the employment of machinery occasions the production of a greater quantity of commodities than the existing arrangements of society permit to be consumed, is at variance with some important and fundamental doctrines of political economy, it seems to demand a stricter examination and more scientific refutation than that contained in the preceding paragraph. The principal difficulty which we have to encounter in performing this new task, arises from the very vague and indefinite language which Mr Owen has employed. ' The existing arrangements of society ' is an expression so extremely general, that it may stand for almost any thing; and it is not very easy to conjecture the precise idea which Mr Owen intended it to represent. Should he by this phraseology mean those barbarous enactments against importation which disgrace our statute book, his proposition must be admitted to be correct. Commerce is the exchange of equivalents,—the bartering between nations of one commodity for another; and that country which refuses to receive the equivalents which her neighbours have to offer, cannot in the nature of things obtain foreign consumers for her goods. In this sense of the phrase, therefore, the use of machinery certainly does enable us to produce more than the existing arrangements of society permit to be consumed. But as the appropriate remedy for this evil is, the gradual abolition of restriction upon foreign trade, and not the erection of quadrangular villages, Mr Owen must attach some other signification to the phrase ' existing regulations of society.' It appears by the context, that he conceives that when competition is unchecked by any artificial regulations, and industry permitted to flow in its natural channels, the use of machinery may increase the supply of the several articles of wealth beyond the demand for them, and, by creating an excess of all commodities, throw the working classes out of employment. This is the position which we hold to be fundamentally erroneous; and as it is strongly insisted on by the celebrated M. de Sismondi in his ' Nouveaux Principes d'Economie Politique, ' * we must entreat the indulgence of our readers while we endeavour to point out its fallacy, and to demonstrate, that the power of consuming necessarily increases with every increase in the power of producing.

Demand and supply are truly correlative and convertible terms. The supply of one set of commodities constitutes the demand for another. Thus, there is a demand for a given quantity of agricultural produce, when a quantity of wrought goods equal thereto in productive cost is offered in exchange for it; and conversely, there is an effectual demand for this quantity of wrought goods, when the supply of agricultural produce which it required the same expense to raise, is presented as its equivalent. As long as commodities are brought to market in such proportions, that the things offered to be bartered against each other are equal in productive cost, and therefore in value, an increase in the supply of one class of goods will afford increased equivalents for the purchase of an increassd supply of another class. Supposing, for the sake of illustration, that a cultivator advanced food and clothing for 100 labourers, who raised for him *food* for 200 ; while a master-manufacturer also advanced food and clothing for 100, who fabricated for him *clothing* for 200; then the farmer, besides replacing the food of his own labourers, would have food for 100 to dispose of; while the manufacturer, after replacing the clothing of his own labourers, would have clothing for 100 to bring to market. In this case, the two articles would be exchanged against each other ; the supply of food constituting the demand for the clothing, and that of the clothing the demand for the food. Now, let us suppose that there are 1000 farmers, *each* of whom advances food and clothing for 100, and obtains in return food for

* Livre VII. ch. 7. De la population rendue superflue par l'invention des machines.

200; and also 1000 master-manufacturers, each of whom, by advancing food and clothing for 100, gets clothing for 200; —In this case, each of the 1000 farmers will feel the same necessity for exchanging his surplus food which the single farmer formerly felt; and each of the 1000 manufacturers the same necessity for exchanging his superfluous clothing. Food and clothing for 100,000 will reciprocally purchase each other, just in the same way that food and clothing for 100 formerly did. The demand for each is increased a thousand fold, because the supply of each is increased a thousand fold. But let us suppose, once more, that in consequence of more skilful applications of labour, and of the introduction of machinery, each of the 1000 farmers, by advancing food and clothing for 100 labourers, obtains a return consisting of ordinary food for 200, together with sugar, grapes and tobacco equal in productive cost to that food; while each of the 1000 master-manufacturers, by advancing clothing and food for 100, obtains a return consisting of ordinary clothing for 200, with ribands, cambrics and lace, equal in productive cost, and therefore in exchangeable value, to that clothing;—In this case, the supply and demand with respect to the food and clothing will remain, it is obvious, exactly as before; while the sugar, grapes and tobacco, which the farmers do not wish to consume themselves, will be offered in exchange for the ribands, cambrics and silks, which the manufacturers do not wish to consume themselves. These different articles, therefore, will be the reciprocal equivalents and purchasers of each other; and there will be an increased demand for commodities, exactly proportional to their increased supply.

It may be objected, perhaps, that on the principle that the demand for commodities increases in the same ratio as their supply, there is no accounting for the gluts and stagnation produced by overtrading. We answer very easily—A glut is an increase in the supply of a particular class of commodities, unaccompanied by a corresponding increase in the supply of those other commodities which should serve as their equivalents. While our 1000 farmers and 1000 master-manufacturers·are exchanging their respective surplus products, and reciprocally affording a market to each other, if 1000 new capitalists were to join their society, employing each 100 labourers in tillage, there would be an immediate glut of agricultural produce;— because in this case there would be no contemporaneous increase in the supply of the manufactured articles which should purchase it. But let one half of the new capitalists become manufacturers, and equivalents in the form of wrought goods will be created for the raw produce raised by the other half: The equilibrium will be restored, and the 1500 farmers and 1500 master-manufacturers will exchange their respective surplus products with exactly the same facility with which the 1000 farmers and 1000 manufacturers formerly exchanged theirs. When an increase takes place in the supply of some particular commodity, or class of commodities, then a glut, or want of sale, is experienced; but when an increase takes place in the supply of commodities in general, the different articles are employed in the purchase of each other,—and augmented supply is identical with extended demand. Let us apply these principles more particularly to Mr Owen's leading doctrine, that the employment of machinery and scientific power, throws the labouring classes out of employment, by producing more wealth than can be consumed.

In the former example, when 1000 farmers and 1000 manufacturers had exchanged their surplus food and clothing with each other, capital was completely replaced; and the sugar, grapes and tobacco of the one class, with the ribands, lace and velvet of the other, remained as net surpluses for immediate enjoyment. Further, as the food and clothing created were equal to each other in cost of production, and the agricultural luxuries equal to the food, and the manufacturing luxuries equal to the clothing, it follows, that all the sugar, grapes and tobacco was equal in productive cost, and should therefore be equal, in exchangeable value, to all the ribands, lace and velvet. Hence, if the farmers were to retain one half of their agricultural luxuries for their own use, and bring the other half to market, they would have the power of purchasing and consuming one half the ribands, lace and velvet, prepared by the manufacturers; while, if the latter retained half their manufactured luxuries for their own use, and brought the other half to market, they would have the power of purchasing and of consuming half the sugar, grapes and tobacco, raised by the class of cultivators. Now, while things are going on in this way, and consumption exactly balances production, let us suppose, that the introduction of improved machinery so increases the effective powers of those branches of manufacturing industry which prepare luxuries; that the 1000 master-manufacturers, without any additional expense, can cause the same number of labourers to fabricate twice the former quantity of ribands, lace and velvet;—Will this increase in the quantity of commodities disturb the previously existing balance between consumption and production? Will the 1000 farmers be unable to purchase, with full equivalents, the additional articles

G

which the 1000 manufacturers present for sale? Certainly not.
With respect to productive cost, and therefore to exchangeable value, the double quantity of manufactured luxuries, now
obtained, is exactly equal to the smaller quantity formerly
obtained. Hence in this, as in the former case, one half
of the sugar, grapes and tobacco which are raised, will be equivalent to one half of the ribands, lace and velvet which are fabricated. The class of cultivators, with the sacrifice of the
same quantity of their unwrought luxuries, will be able to purchase and to consume a double quantity of wrought luxuries,
while the class of master-manufacturers, after purchasing the
same quantity of sugar, grapes and tobacco, will be able to retain and to consume a double quantity of ribands, lace and velvet. Demand will increase in the same ratio with supply, and
the power of consumption keep pace with the power of production.

It is no answer to this reasoning to say, that though the class
of cultivators have the power, they may not have the inclination
to purchase and consume the double quantity of wrought luxuries thrown upon the market by improved machinery. With
the exception of a few insane misers who hoard their treasures,
all persons are desirous of consuming whatever wealth they can
command, either productively with a view to improving their
condition, or else unproductively with a view to immediate enjoyment. The alterations which occasionally take place in the
distribution of industry, may lead to temporary embarrassment; but after the readjustment has been effected, and commodities are brought to market in quantities duly proportioned
to each other, the increased supply will be accompanied by increased demand. Effectual demand is nothing more than the
offering of one commodity in exchange for another. Increased
production, therefore, provided it be general and duly proportioned, is precisely the same thing as extended demand. So long
as the passion for the expenditure or accumulation of wealth
shall actuate the human heart, it will be impossible for the use
of machinery, and the application of scientific power, to increase
the supply of commodities beyond what the regulations of society
permit to be consumed.

The important and fundamental principle, that increased demand is created by increased supply, appears to have been first
noticed by the celebrated M. Say in his *Traité d'Economie Politique*, and by Mr James Mill, in his pamphlet in answer to
Mr Spence, entitled, ' *Commerce Defended.* ' We conceive
that on this subject the reasoning of the latter gentleman is the

most clear and conclusive; and to his able Tract we beg to refer those amongst our readers who, upon questions of this sort, prefer synthetical demonstration from general principles, to that analytical induction from particular cases which we have here attempted to employ. We shall merely add, in this place, that the late glut of British goods in the markets of Europe and America, to which M. de Sismondi refers as a practical proof of his paradox, that poverty may be occasioned by the super-abundance of wealth, furnishes no solid objection to the doctrine that a balance necessarily exists between consumption and production. The present crisis constitutes a case removed by special circumstances from the operation of the general rule. In the *first* place, as we explained in our former Number, the transition from war to peace has caused certain classes of commodities to be less sought for than before, and thus for a time disturbed the due proportion in the quantities of the different articles brought to market, which makes them the reciprocal purchasers of each other, and renders the amount of the supply identical with the extent of the demand. In the *second* place, as commerce is the exchange of equivalents, and demand and supply reciprocal, if our merchants throw goods into foreign markets, under a restrictive system which prevents their bringing back the only articles with which foreigners can purchase them, such goods must necessarily remain unsold; and, in these circumstances, the glut of British goods in foreign markets, instead of militating against our general principle, is a fact which, even prior to experience, that principle would lead us to predict. *Lastly,* taxation counteracts the natural tendency of improved machinery to reduce the cost of production, and consequently prevents that fall in the exchangeable value of our manufactured articles which might otherwise cause the demand for them to extend as their supply increased.

Thus there are, at the present crisis, three special circumstances which account satisfactorily for the existing difficulty in finding a foreign market for British goods, without resorting to the gratuitous, and, as we conceive, absurd assumption, that our distress is created by machinery and scientific power producing more wealth than can be consumed. That part of our distress which has arisen from the transition from war to peace, and from the loss attendant on the transference of capital from one species of employment to another, will in a short time work out its own correction. The other, and *the greater portion of the national suffering, which is produced by fettered trade, and oppressive taxes, will be as permanent as its causes.* Should these be continued, it requires no gift of prophecy to predict, that

England, like Holland, must gradually cease to be a manufacturing and commercial, and consequently a rich and a powerful country. The recent history of our nearest neighbour, holds out to us this awful warning. The republic of Holland, though her commercial system was infinitely superior to ours, yet sunk under taxation comparatively light. In the foreign carrying trade, and in foreign wars, her productive capital glided from beneath the burden which oppressed it. The laws of nature are unchanged; the principles of human action remain the same; and the desire of bettering his condition, continues to exert an influence more or less powerful upon the conduct of every man who lives. Mr Owen will be a potent enchanter, indeed, if, by inscribing productive capital within magic circles, or magic parallelograms, he can prevent its flowing off to seek, in foreign investments, that beneficial occupation which cannot be found at home. *

It has been objected to those who oppose Mr Owen's plans, that they do not themselves suggest any effectual means for the relief of the country. This objection appears to us most extraordinary and unreasonable. Is no one to object to the introduction of absurd and pernicious projects, unless he substitute some project of his own? Is no one to detect and denounce the nostrums of an empiric, unless he pretend to be himself in possession of a panacea? For ourselves, we do not despair of our country; and we have no objection to state what, in our opinion, would restore the kingdom to its once flourishing condition. Give Freedom to Commerce, and lighten the pressure of Taxation, and we shall have no complaining in our streets. As commerce is always an exchange of equivalents, a nation that will not buy, cannot sell; and restrictions upon import, are prohibitory duties upon export. On the contrary, the more we admit the productions of foreign countries, the more extensive becomes their demand for our commodities. Let the absurd system of our Corn Laws be cautiously and gradually abolished, and allow the cheap agricultural produce of the North of Europe, and of the Continents of America and Africa, to be freely introduced, and we shall obtain an unlimited vent for our manufactures; the profits of stock will be restored to their level in other countries; and the consequent accumulation of capital,

---

* We have learned from an intelligent traveller, lately returned from France, that a considerable portion of the lands in Britanny have been purchased by Englishmen, and are now cultivated under their direction. Let the landed proprietors of England, who support the present system, look to this!

will cause the increasing demand for labour to bear a nearer proportion to the increasing supply of labourers. A rigid and effectual system of Retrenchment, would powerfully contribute to these most desirable results. Our advantages, from position, from coal-mines, and from the industry, skill, and energy of our people, are so considerable, that, were it not for unwise laws, and overstrained taxation, England, for ages to come, might continue to be the great workshop and emporium of the world. There is nothing appalling in our situation, except the want of wisdom in our Rulers. This, indeed ' must give us pause.' It is a singular and an alarming fact, that at a period when the questions which come before the Legislature are almost exclusively economical, the Ministers of this country should be ignorant of the leading principles of Economical Science. On the termination of hostilities, and while our influence in Europe was as yet almost supreme, our Foreign Minister abandoned the vital interests of British industry; and, instead of making commercial arrangements for aiding the country in meeting the transition from war to peace, and in supporting the burthens imposed during the Continental quarrel, returned from his mission, declaring that our manufactures and trade had already been carried to an injurious extent, and impeded the exertions of the State! * Our Finance Minister has laid on duties, not with a view to the improvement of the Revenue, but for the express and avowed purpose of diminishing our trade with France. In war, while we were annually borrowing enormous sums, the value of the currency was suffered to sink considerably below that of the coin; and in peace, when extraordinary efforts are required to pay off debt, measures have been adopted for keeping the Bank note at par with gold. And at an awful crisis, when the exhausted nation staggers beneath its load, the Government, instead of reducing, have added three millions to the taxes. These are facts, which the supposition of ignorance alone can scarcely account for, or excuse: And we

---

* See the debate upon the Corn Bill:—When Lord Castlereagh censured the people for their ' ignorant impatience of taxation,' he should have reflected that, in a Statesman, an ' ignorant impatience ' of manufactures and commerce, was an offence which even persons unskilled in Economical Science might consider to be almost as disgraceful as that which he condemned. His Lordship's reasonings, when logically pursued, tend indeed to very original and wonderful conclusions. On the principle that complaints against taxation have their origin in ignorance, and that our manufactures and commerce have been pushed to an injurious extent, it would be easy to demonstrate that we have too little barren, and too much fertile soil.

are sure that it is a mild and mitigated censure to say, that in that important department of the science of legislation which relates to the causes of national wealth and prosperity, the persons who have obtained the management of our affairs, are considerably below the common intellectual level of English gentlemen,—nay, of English ladies. We know one female, at least, fully competent to instruct the Members of our present Cabinet in Political Economy—a branch of knowledge at all times highly important, and, at this difficult crisis, as indispensably necessary to the practical statesman, as anatomy is to the operative surgeon, who undertakes to extract the barbed and venomed steel from a festering and deep-seated wound.

## No. III.

### *The Condition of the Lower Orders.*

THIS is a subject which has been a good deal written upon lately, both directly, and in connexion with various points of internal policy, from the consideration of which a matter so important and so pressing could not be excluded. But though we cannot claim the merit of originality in our subject-matter, we can at all events plead its overwhelming importance, at the present time, in excuse for entering upon its consideration—if, indeed, any apology be necessary for dwelling upon a division of our general subject which is of by far the deepest and most extensive interest of all those which enter into its composition.

We entertain a very special contempt for those, who, in a country like this, pretend to be of no party, and yet meddle in politics; but there are some questions of import so absorbing and universal, that, in the contemplation of them, a thing so comparatively trifling as the triumph of party is forgotten. If our object were to create excitement, or produce effect for a party purpose, we should seek a subject original either in itself, or in the relations in which we should place it; but having in

view nothing but the serious and sober purpose of drawing the public
attention to an evil which is spread
over the whole country, and like a
rising flood threatens general ruin,
unless it can be suppressed, we take
up a subject on which a good deal
has been said already, but which cannot be mentioned too often or too
loudly, until something is devised
respecting it fitting the magnitude of
the occasion.

He must be either a very superficial, or a very inattentive observer
of the present condition of affairs,
who supposes that there is nothing
more in it than has often occurred
before—nothing but the ordinary oc-
currences of a stagnation in trade,
and a harvest of less than average
abundance.  Our condition is the
result of a new form which the industry of the country has assumed,
greatly aggravated, as we must continue to maintain, by a monstrously
erroneous policy with regard to trade
and currency.  This new form of industry, which made such rapid progress during the war, was, in consequence of the peculiar circumstances
attendant on the war, not felt by the
common people, except in the alte-
ration of their employments; but
since the peace, while its progress
has been even more rapid than before, it has indeed been felt by them
in the dreadful and appalling certainty, that as the world goes, it has
no longer any need of them.  The
most important of the old relations
of society have been changed, and
that by a process, which although
rapid, has been sufficiently gradual
to bring the event upon us without
our having taken such notice of it as
would have led to our making due
provision for the change.  When society grew into its present form, of
the few possessing much, and the
many possessing nothing, the multitude dwelt safely, in the security,
that those who had possessions could
not turn them to account without
their aid—that wealth was nothing
except in so far as it gave the power
of accomplishing work—and that
work could not be done without
their assistance.  Natural rights, or
to speak more strictly, their exercise,
were readily abandoned under such
an appearance of things; and for the
purposes of the general well-being
of society, it seemed of little moment

that a few were the store-keepers of
the kingdom's wealth, while such
a guarantee existed for its distribution amongst all the members of the
community who would work.  It was
true that labour was the portion of
one part, while idleness, or at all
events, exemption from bodily exertion, was that of the other; but it was
ever a matter of debate whether labour was, upon the whole, a more
painful condition than that of idleness, and it was cheerfully submitted
to, because it was the sure and always current value for subsistence.
It is no longer thus; and it might
melt the sternest heart to contemplate tne hopeless wretchedness of
thousands, almost millions, of their
fellow-creatures, willing, eager, to
give their labour for bread, and well
able, too, until " sharp misery had
worn them to the bone," who yet
cannot touch a particle of the abundance which teems around them.  In
vain

" They beg their brothers of the earth
To give them leave to toil."

There is a *cheaper* mode of getting
the work done than by employing
them; and there is a certain delirium
reigns at the present time, about this
thing, " cheapness," which having
been taken up as a public principle,
is, without hesitation, used as an excuse for individual selfishness.  In
vain the manufacturing towns throw
off the surplus of their multitudes to
the country—the poor have no land
of their own—the rich, who have
land, think it is very well as it is; and
though they know, or at all events
ought to know, that by a different
system of management, a much more
perfect system of cultivation might
be carried on, and a much greater
number of people be supported thereby, in happy, though laborious, comfort, they are either too forgetful, or
too indifferent about the matter to
bestir themselves, and again the labourer is rejected.

In vain the rural districts and the
provincial towns send the more ad-
venturous of their unemployed numbers to the metropolis, in search of
the casual employment which such
a huge mass of the wealthy might
reasonably be expected to afford.
London itself, with all its gorgeous
show—with all its prodigious reality

of wealth—with all that is magnificent in costliness, and all that is exquisite in art, yet teems with the direst miseries of actual want. Not merely that kind of want which must necessarily be found to some extent in all great cities, where disease and crime get huddled together in dark corners, and even common charity is scared away from those foul recesses in which all that is loathsome in degraded humanity rots and dies, in obscure despair. Not such want as this we speak of; but the decay of laborious decency, the misery of semi-starvation from want of employment of those hands which have never been employed in any thing but honest industry, is even in the metropolis deplorably prevalent. It is so even in the parish of Saint Martin's, in so much that the parish officers, "albeit unused to the melting mood," are thawed into emotion by the dismal sights which their distressing, but necessary duties, bring before them, and it is fearful to think what it must be in less opulent districts, such as Saint Giles's and Clerkenwell, where the poor so much more abound.

Now, apart from all considerations of humanity merely, and those feelings which ought to actuate us as Christian men, it is, as a political question, one of the most interesting that can be made the subject of enquiry—Why such distress should exist, and be in a progressive state of aggravation, *notwithstanding the immense accession which has confessedly been made to our means of producing all those things of which "distress," as we have used the word, signifies the* ABSENCE? Why is it that want, and new and extraordinary means of producing abundance, proceed *pari passu,* and that those improvements which wear the appearance of a general blessing, are fraught with curses to the poor? It is because the process through which the advantages of industry were formerly obtained have undergone a change, and that change has taken away the *necessity* which did exist that the labouring classes should have their share from the capitalists, of all these advantages. The only security which the labourer had at any time for his support was, as has been mentioned, the necessity for his assistance in order to make an advantage of the possessions held by his more fortunate brethren. If these possessions could be turned to profitable account without him, he would have been left to starve; and now that by our "improvements" they can be turned to account without him, or with a great deal less of his assistance than formerly, he is accordingly left to starve. But had these means which are now "improvements," existed from the beginning, society would not have taken the form which it now has; laws would not have been suffered to accumulate one upon another, securing the property to a few, and leaving to the mass nothing but what their power of labouring gave them the command of, if, as now, that power was little or no security for support. If, then, we become satisfied that the great machine of society went on well and smoothly hitherto, only in consequence of a connexion of its parts, formed by necessities and powers which adapted themselves to one another, it is not to be wondered at, that one side of the connexion, namely, the necessitous, being in a great measure worn away, the machine should go out of order, and one part of it work exceedingly to the disadvantage of the other. If the people are to live, if this kingdom is not to become merely the habitation of masters and machinery, with the few necessary to manufacture and attend upon these laborious and long-lived pieces of mechanism, some change must take place in the forms in which property and society are disposed.

If the people are to live, and machines make their labour of so little value to others that they cannot get the means of living in exchange for it, they must be provided with something upon which they can labour for themselves. If the world were all as one family, wherein each individual benefited according to the addition which could, by any means, be made to the common stock, then should we join with the political economists, and rejoice in the freedom of trade, and in every new device by which human labour could be dispensed with in the production of desirable commodities; but as that state of society has not yet come, we must, during the advent of such a happy consummation, resort to means adapted to the selfishness of mankind, and the new powers conferred on that selfishness, by the inventions which dispense with the labour of working men. It is curious to find even the warmest panegyrists of all the effects of machinery admitting that some extraordinary new vent for manufactures, some wonderful extension of trade, is necessary to prevent the country from sinking. China must be crammed with our delf, the whole country of Hindostan be covered with our cotton goods, Japan must have our tin ware, and if that will not suffice, we must freight balloons to the " pale-faced moon," or diving-bells

——" to the bottom of the deep,
Where fathom line could never touch the
  ground,"

in search of new realms to carry off our wondrous stores of manufactures; and all this wonderful extension must take place, ' or else we perish.' Where, then, is the improvement ? Of what advantage *to us* these prodigious means of extending our manufactures without the aid of men, when so many of our own population are thereby left to idleness and starvation, and the profit on the machine-made goods is so small, that nothing but the discovery of a new world to be " saturated" with them, can make the trade worth following ? Our manufacturers have exhausted the world, and then imagined a new, which they have prepared goods to exhaust, if their imagination could be turned into reality ; but who reaps the benefit ?—the people of foreign countries, where they are sold for less than their first cost, while in the midst of the abundance of goods rotting in warehouses, or sent away to be sold at a loss, the English artizan, or he who once was an artizan, shivers in rags, the unhappy victim of modern improvements.

It is high time that the Parliament should look to this matter. Indeed, making all imaginable allowance for the dulness of our representatives to matters of real importance to the country, we cannot think it possible that the ensuing session will pass over without some important measure, adapted, so far as the wisdom of Parliament will go, to the present state of the once working classes. Difficult as it is to force upon the attention of those who live in continual plenty and immoral indulgence

the severe distress of those whom it is a trouble to them to think of, yet they can hardly be blind to the necessity of acting in a matter which the people themselves have taken up in a way extremely novel in this country, and dangerous, or the contrary, according as the Legislature may make it. Multitudes of the common people now see clearly the state they are placed in. They perceive that their labour is valuable, if they had the means of applying it ; but as their former masters have no use for it, they are driven to see whether they cannot use it for their own advantage. Those who have the virtues of thrift and patience, are forming themselves into societies for the purpose of enjoying the benefit of their mutual labour ; and it is impossible to look at their virtuous endeavours to substitute comfortable competence for the horrors of dependence on precarious employment by masters, without wishing them God speed. But it may be worth the while of the politician to look carefully at the effects which such societies, should they become extensive and abundant, may have upon the political state of the community. It is not always well (in a political sense) that the knowledge should be forced upon men, of what they may accomplish by co-operation and union ; and especially it is dangerous in an aristocratical state, where this knowledge is given to men of strong coarse minds, to whom meat, drink, clothes, fire, and the liberty of being governed according to their own views of right, are the *summa bona.*

Without professing much respect for the wisdom generally displayed at extensive meetings of the lower orders, it must be allowed that at several of the many meetings lately held by the working people for discussing the subject of their distress, a rough and vigorous intelligence has been displayed, a readiness of speech and vehemence of expression, which indicate powers of mind that are worthy of some attention. We mean, that they give evidence of the existence of a description of men, who, with sense enough not to rush into a frantic and desperate tumult, can yet keep strongly alive in the minds of their companions the hardships which a state of things, subsisting only by the force of conventional law, entails upon them ; and it is almost needless to add, that no duty of the legislature of a free country is more obvious than to examine, with even deferential attention, any cause of grievance which large bodies of the people firmly and calmly put forth as worthy of redress.

If we be right in the view which we take of the state of the common people in this kingdom at present, there is no subject which can come before Parliament that is not, in comparison with it, insignificant. Again, we say that the people know very well that the means are within the country to make them all comfortable; and let the Parliament beware how it drives them to take their own method of acting upon that knowledge. In the first place, it is expedient that the Parliament should take the earliest means possible of showing the country that the distress of the people is felt, and that they will endeavour to remedy it. This is expedient, in order to satisfy the people during the time which they necessarily must wait before any measure could be sufficiently examined and passed into law. Next, it is absolutely necessary that a measure of relief should pass—a measure to enable the resources of the country to be made available for the comfortable support of the population of the country. The disciples of Mr Malthus are provided with an answer to this, by saying that the country has not resources for the comfortable support of the population, and, moreover, that the law of God is, that the condition of man inevitably leads to an abundance of people beyond the means of support. From the dissemination of such opinions, theological and political, good Lord deliver us! We are content to remark, that, as things are, nearly as much food is raised in these kingdoms as the po-

pulation has need of, and that, with even our present means and knowledge of agriculture, twice as much in England, and thrice as much in Ireland,* could *easily* be raised.

Now the business of Parliament is, to consider *how* the resources of the country may best be made available for the people's support, for that the people have a right to such an application of the country's resources, we hold to be equally agreeable to reason, and to the spirit of the British Constitution. The means of obtaining subsistence in a country, where subsistence can be obtained, if the means were granted, is obviously the very first and most important part of that protection which Blackstone uniformly teaches to be the " right of the people." Allegiance and protection are, he says, reciprocally the rights, as well as duties of the magistrate and the people. " Allegiance is the right of the magistrate, and protection the right of the people."

Having then looked at the actual evil, let us now look at the possible remedy. The evil is, that with respect to large bodies of the people, the means of exerting all beneficial industry are taken away ; they want something *to work upon*, so as to provide for their necessities. Where is this something to be found? Undoubtedly in *the land*. The curse upon fallen man was, that " in the sweat of his brow, he should eat bread;" but it went no further ; it is only by the evil contrivances of men themselves, that even to the sweat of man's brow bread is denied. The changes in the forms of industry having brought it to pass, that the industry of men will not exchange for subsistence in the ordinary traffic of the world, there is no resource, but that men shall be allowed to raise subsistence for themselves, out of the land, and we are firmly of opi-

---

* The population of Ireland is commonly subject, in the harangues of orators, to the grossest exaggeration. Mr Shiel " talks familiarly" of " seven millions Roman Catholics." By the *authentic* census made under the direction of Mr Shaw Mason, the whole population of the kingdom does not amount to that number. The Edinburgh Review lately sneered at this official return, as unworthy of respect. Within these few days the writer of this article has seen an extract from the letter of a public man, whose researches entitle him, beyond all other men in the kingdom, to speak on the subject, and he describes this census as " one of the greatest possible monuments of human industry and comparative accuracy."

nion, that this might be done with great benefit to the present holders of property in land. It is by no means necessary to deprive them of that property, but it does appear necessary, to oblige them to allow it to be more usefully applied, both for themselves and others, than it is at present. It is not necessary for us to go over again the same ground which has been travelled over so recently, and so ably, by the *Quarterly Review*, in the discussion of the " Anti-Pauper System." We refer to that paper for abundant practical instances of what may be done by judicious settlements on lands, which, previously to such settlements, have been wholly unproductive ; and really we cannot conceive how any man, with a heart within his bosom, can read over such a paper, and not glow with an ardent desire to see the squalid and unhappy crowds, the victims of our manufacturing system, settled in the peaceful, virtuous, and happy competence, which such settlements in England might be made to afford. Of all the objects which it can enter into the heart of genuine benevolence to conceive, there is none equal to this, of giving its just reward to peaceful and honest industry, and turning man from that ferocious and reckless savage, which extreme want makes him, to a comfortable, though humble citizen, enjoying the present reward of faithfully discharging his duties as a member of the society to which he belongs, and living in the hope of that reward hereafter, with which the Spirit of God cheers the dwellings of those who mingle religious feeling with the simplicity of that active industry, which gives a certain supply of the necessaries of life.

It is hardly credible, except by those who have had actual experience in the matter, the quantity of subsistence which a small portion of ground may be made to yield, by the application of all the labour which it is capable of receiving with profit. It would fill the public with astonishment if they knew the quantity of vegetable matter, fit for the food of men, or cattle, which the market gardeners around London can raise from an acre of ground, through the application of labour and manure. There is nothing to prevent the

ground in every part of the kingdom from being made as productive of food, if similar means were applied, and instruction given as to the best kind of management.

It appears from one of the Reports of the Commissioners of Woods and Forests, that, having sowed nine and a half acres of ground in the Regent's Park with MangleWurzle, they, in one season, dug up from this small portion of ground 418 tons of vegetable food for cattle—there were 326 tons of root, and 92 tons of leaves ; their expenses were L.146, and the crop sold for L.748. This may give some idea of what might be done, if the people called great men in this country, could be persuaded to turn their attention to subjects of practical, though homely usefulness, instead of dissipating it in extravagant schemes for the extension of foreign trade, and the pushing forward of a feverish energy, for the sake of the vain glory of upholding a system, or of furthering the ends of political jobbing. An excellent suggestion appeared lately in the *Gardener's Magazine* ; that of having extensive gardens annexed (it is not meant locally) to parish poor houses. It is very justly stated, that there is no description of labour, in which all descriptions of persons, young and old, male and female, could so universally be of use, and that with the least irksome of all kinds of toil—the cultivation of a garden is the delight of labour. " God Almighty," says one of the wisest men that ever adorned humanity, " first planted a garden, and indeed it is the purest of human pleasures." It is, moreover, peculiarly favoured in this, that while it is the pleasantest of all descriptions of labour, it is, for the gratification of simple wants, the most profitable also ; and therefore this suggestion of the *Gardener's Magazine*, is a hint which we think may be improved upon with much advantage, in the highest quarters to which the consideration of a provision for our poor extends.

There is, undoubtedly, much to blame in our present system of provision for the poor. The good done is not at all what it ought to be, considering the expense entailed upon the country ; but let it not be thought that any patching of this bad system will answer the end which the present condition of the common people should make the legislature have in view. There is nothing more disgusting than to behold a legislator of the small wisdom school, whose mind could never emancipate itself from the small details of parish laws, and whose soul must be conversant with beadles and with overseers, or with nothing, getting up to stuff some new quirks into the mass of jobbing intricacy which forms the parish poor-laws, and conducting himself with all the gravity of a Solon, while, mole-like, he grubs about in the holes and corners to which his intellectual vision confines him. We hope we shall have no more of this, but that means will be taken for a settlement of the great question which that of the British pauper-system has become, worthy of the British legislature. We cannot see why establishments of agricultural, or horticultural villages, may not be adopted, connected with the parishes, to which the poor may be drafted, and where, under due regulation, they may be made to dwell very much happier than they have hitherto been; and these we would have established on lands already reclaimed and fertile, while the extensive wastes should also be put in a train to become valuable property, and afford employment and subsistence to multitudes unconnected with parish management.

We know it is asserted by many proprietors of wastes, that if they choose to keep their property in that particular condition, for their amusement, they have no right to be interfered with in the government of their own estate. We should recommend such proprietors to consider for a little what it is which makes the estates " their own," and the consideration may perhaps afford them some new light upon this matter. The lord of the manor has no more right than the pauper of the poorhouse, to the land which he undoubtedly does own, except that which the law has given him for the common benefit of the country ; and there will be nothing unconstitutional in the law taking it away, if he be determined to use it adversely to that common benefit. It is monstrous to suppose that any small number of men should be allowed to keep land waste for the amusement of a few weeks shooting, in the year, while that land is wanted for the *support* of the people. Such a proposition needs only to be laid bare, in order to be crushed down by unanimous indignation ; and, however it may be privately entertained, we hope no one will be so rash as to dare openly to put it forth.

But it is not the landholders alone who should be constrained by law to a better provision for the poor, who can no longer live by the exertions of labour in its ordinary channels ;—the fundholders, who can live so much more cheaply, in consequence of the abundance of goods produced by machinery, should be taxed for this especial purpose, until the poor, under good management, begin to maintain themselves, which, we assert, it requires nothing but good management to enable them to do.

The manufacturers also, or the consumers of manufactures, should contribute, by a direct tax on the manufacture, and for this plain reason—the goods are now sold at a profit regulated by wages which the workmen receive during only a part of the year. When periods of stagnation come, the workmen are turned off, and the parish must give them such wretched support as they receive. But it would be just that the consumers of manufactures should entirely support the men who are devoted to a particular condition of life for their convenience; and, therefore, manufactured goods should pay a tax to support the artisans while out of employment.

There is much more to be said on this subject, but we do not like to run our speculations out to too great a length. Our belief is, that some such things as we have mentioned, must be done for the prosperity, if not for the existence, of the state. Who can expect the governed to submit, if the protection which is the bond of their submission be not given them as far as it can be given? Let us then obtain that hold over them which a salutary guardianship will give us.

—— *τυν δ'ορκια πιςα*
*Γινσαμινοι μαχομιοθα τω υ νυ τι κιρδιον ημιν*
*Ελπομαι ιχλιλιιοθαι, ινα μη ριξομιν ωδι.*

This is true, and let the bishops, who at all events will understand the lines, look to it.

J.

# BLACKWOOD'S
# EDINBURGH MAGAZINE.

No. CLXV.      APRIL, 1830.      Vol. XXVII.

### THE INFLUENCE OF FREE TRADE UPON THE CONDITION OF THE LABOURING CLASSES.

THE necessity of providing employment for the multitudes of manufacturing, as well as of agricultural labourers, whom political and social changes have thrown out of work, is become at length so urgent and pressing, that it can no longer be overlooked without seriously affecting the prosperity, or even endangering the peace, of the community. The intensity of the distress which prevails among the industrious classes in this country can be properly estimated by those alone who have personally witnessed its overwhelming pressure. Nor is it of a partial character: it is not confined to those who are employed in any particular species of industry for which the demand has ceased in consequence of a change in their public trade. To this partial degree of suffering every manufacturing community is always liable. When metal buttons or buckles, for instance, went out of fashion, the artisans employed in fabricating these commodities were unavoidably plunged into temporary distress. But while manufacturers of buttons and buckles laboured under difficulties, every other branch of public industry continued to yield its usual returns; some branches of manufacture were even benefitted by the change; the demand for ribband and twist necessarily increased in the proportion in which the use of buckles and metal buttons had been discontinued by the public. There was thus no diminution in the aggregate demand for labour, although it varied in parti-

cular branches; the total amount was the same, although the items which formed it differed. It must likewise be added, that the distress occasioned by a relaxation in the demand for particular commodities, was not only partial in its extent, but also temporary in its duration. The labour and the capital disengaged from the fabrication of metal buttons and buckles, were transferred into the manufacture of ribband and twist; and by this means the rate of wages and profit, momentarily deranged by a change of fashion, was soon restored to its accustomed level. Neither the capitalist nor the labourer was in the end much inconvenienced by this change; the falling off in one branch of manufacture being counterbalanced by an increased activity in some other department of public industry.

But far different appears the character of the depression which has recently fallen upon the industry of this country. It seems to be universal; it extends throughout every district of the country; it affects every interest; it pervades the whole mass of our industrious population; involving in one common ruin the agricultural, the manufacturing, and the trading classes. The records of Parliament will testify that there is scarcely a county—scarcely a parish from Penzance to the Orkneys, which has not petitioned, or at least which is not about to petition, the legislature for relief. The cry in every district is the same—general, overwhelming, intolerable distress. The farming classes are all in a state of absolute insolvency; all incapable of fulfilling the contracts into which they had entered. The landowners have therefore been compelled to compound for their rents, and content themselves with what they can get in lieu of the amount which their tenants had bargained to pay. The farmer, ruined by the fall which has taken place in the price of agricultural produce, is not only unable to pay his rent, but he is likewise deprived of the means necessary to defray the wages of labour; hence the labourers of the country, however able and willing to work, can get no employment. In some parishes they are seen working on the roads, or in gravel pits, at a rate of wages not exceeding two shillings per week; in others, where no labour of any kind is provided for them, they form desperate bands, and rove about in a state of idleness to the great terror of the inhabitants of the district. Some parishes, justly afraid of the consequences which cannot fail to result from this lawless vagrancy, collect their able-bodied labourers once a-week and let them in vestry to the highest bidder. On the fifteenth day of the month of January last, a vestry was held in the parish of Henninghall, in the county of Norfolk, for the purpose of taking into consideration the better employment of the surplus poor; where it was resolved, " That all unemployed labourers shall inform the overseer of their want of work, that their names may be presented by him at the next vestry meeting, to be held on Monday morning in every week, at ten o'clock, that they may be then let at the best price that can be obtained for them for the next week." The same practice has been adopted in the adjoining parish of Winfarthing; and if not speedily arrested, the odious system of putting the labour of human beings up to public auction threatens to spread throughout that part of the kingdom. The gross and pernicious absurdities of the Malthusian school, have inspired the landowners of the country with so much horror of cottages, that the want of that species of accommodation for the labouring poor begins to operate as an intolerable evil in many parts of the country. " I cannot," says the Bishop of Winchester,

in a charge to his clergy, delivered at his primary visitation in the course of last year, " refrain from adverting to an inconvenience unfelt till recently in agricultural parishes, but now beginning to affect them in a manner very prejudicial to the proper habits of the people. I allude to the deficiency of cottages for the accommodation of the poor; arising partly from the excess of population, partly from the natural objection on the part of the landlords, to keep up tenements which are likely to increase the pressure of the poor's rate, but too intolerable already. One parish thus situated, consists of twenty-nine cottages, the inmates of which amount to two hundred and ten persons. By an actual admeasurement of the dimensions of each cottage, it appears that their aggregate contents include an area of three hundred and forty-seven feet in length, by two hundred and eighty-two in breadth; *giving an average space of about twelve feet by ten for each cottage. In many of those tenements no fewer than eight*, and in some instances, *as many as ten persons*, occasionally of different families, are crowded together day and night, *the children literally sleeping under the beds of their parents, without distinction of age or sex*. The consequence of such a state of things to the health and morals of the parishioners, are too obvious to need pointing out; and though in this particular case, local circumstances make it difficult to provide a remedy, I know that a strong desire exists to diminish the evil, and have reason to hope that measures will be taken for this purpose." When Mr Malthus was examined before the Emigration Committee, he suggested, that to render the possession of tenements more difficult to the poor, would prove a salutary measure, by checking population, and preventing too early marriages; he added, that on general principles he saw no objection to the imposition of a tax on a landlord who builds a cottage on his land. The fact stated by the Bishop of Winchester, furnishes an useful commentary on the practical operation of such principles; it seems to operate admirably in destroying the comforts, degrading the character, and deteriorating the morals of the poor: but it appears somewhat doubtful whether it have any effect in preventing improvident marriages, and checking the increase of population. Somehow or other, it would seem that the peasantry of Hampshire contrive to multiply in spite of the pains which have been taken to withhold from them the wicked encouragement of comfortable cottages : it appears that those who cannot command the accommodation of a whole cottage, bring themselves to put up with only a part of a cottage. This conduct on the part of the peasantry, is no doubt very much to be reprehended, as highly inconsistent with the valuable doctrines, dogmas, and suggestions of the Political Economists: these poor and ignorant creatures appear to pay more regard to the law of nature, than to the maxims and warnings of their friends the Political Economists. But whatever may be the motives of their conduct, the effect presents itself in almost every district in England ; from the comfortless character of the cottages into which they are crowded, and low rate of wages which they receive, more especially in the winter season, penitentiaries and houses of correction have become objects of desire rather than of terror to the British peasantry ; they enter them too often with alacrity, and quit them with regret : to be committed for an infringement of the Game Laws, or some other misdemeanour, instead of shunning as a punishment, too many of them court as a reward ; by this means they secure a more comfortable lodging, as well as a more abundant supply of food, than would be furnished them by their parishes or employers.

If we turn from the class engaged in the labours of agriculture, to those employed in manufactures, the scenes which present themselves are equally discouraging: and what renders the distress prevalent in the manufacturing districts of the North of England still more lamentable and alarming, is the fact that it has already subsisted for some years, and yet presents no symptoms of abatement. It commenced, we believe, in the year 1826. In the following year it had, as our readers, no doubt, recollect, become so intense and extensive in its character, that a munificent subscription was raised for the relief of the manufacturers. To prove the intensity of the suffering of our manufacturing population in 1829, we shall quote a passage from the evidence of a witness examined by the Emigration Committee in the spring of that year. Mr Halton, a gentleman of large landed property in Lancashire, and residing twelve miles from Manchester, four south of Bolton, and about ten from Chorley, in the very heart of the manufacturing districts, made then the following statement before the committee. " I have lived at Halton ever since I came of age, and during that time I have never witnessed any thing at all equal to the present distress. I have been regularly visiting, not leaving it to committees, but I have myself visited all the cottages within a large district around my own house. I believe there is scarcely one loom in my own immediate neighbourhood unemployed now, but the state of the families of the poor is certainly much more destitute than it was when a very great number were actually unemployed. The present distress arises from several causes : the bedding and clothes of the poor are totally exhausted. The misery is beginning to work now by the poverty of the small lay payers; for, as has been mentioned by another witness, our farms are generally very small ; they may keep two or three cows; there are exceptions ; but they are generally very small ; and those lay-payers, whose families were employed in the hand-loom weaving, have left their land in a very bad state ; they have generally attended to their loom, now they cannot obtain sufficient to pay their taxes; the consequence is, that the persons to whom their land belongs must suffer. I have ventured to report to the London Committee one or two instances of distress, such as I had not conceived to exist in a civilized country : there is one I have not reported, which was anterior to the last donation we received. Mrs Halton and myself, in visiting the poor, were asked by a person almost starving, to go into a house ; we there found on one side of the fire a very old man, apparently dying, on the other side a young man about eighteen, with a child on his knee, whose mother had just died and been buried :

and evidently both that young man and the child were suffering from want; of course our object was to relieve them, and we were going away from that house, when the woman said, Sir, you have not seen all : we went up stairs, and under some rags we found another young man, the widower, and on turning down the rags, which he was unable to remove himself, we found another man who was dying, and who did die in the course of the day. *I have no doubt that family were actually starving at the time.* We have made a very accurate calculation of the families in that neighbourhood who are on the verge of famine, if not suffering actual famine. In the last township we visited, West Houghton, consisting of rather more than five thousand inhabitants, we found *two thousand five hundred totally destitute of bedding, and nearly so of clothes.* I am positive I am correct, when I say that six per cent are in a state such as that described, a state of famine, or that approaching to it; it is from the papers I have prepared for the committee I deduce that to be an accurate statement. In another case of extreme distress, there was a widow and three children, who had not tasted the meal and water, which is the only thing almost they eat there, for eight and forty hours. I found a young man of sixteen in such a state of exhaustion, that I was obliged to send a cart with a litter to bring him home, and he is now under my own care, and we have hardly been able to sustain him in life; we found many families who have not made one meal in twenty-four hours."

It must, perhaps, be admitted, that at the present moment the condition of the manufacturing classes in the Northern districts, is not quite so wretched as it was at the period above mentioned. Their situation appears to be so far improved, that few of them are altogether destitute of some species of employment; but, from the excessive competition which prevails among them, the wages of labour have sustained so great a reduction, that the earnings of the most industrious workman are scarcely adequate to command a full supply of the meanest and coarsest fare. Various enquiries have been recently made into the circumstances and condition of the working classes in the two great manufacturing counties of York and Lancaster; it is no doubt somewhat difficult to arrive at exactness in an investigation which embraces so wide a field; abundant evidence has, however, been laid before the public, to prove that the wages of manufacturing labour continue ruinously low, and the condition of the workmen incredibly depressed. A keen dispute has recently been carried on between two rival newspapers at Manchester, respecting the amount of wages actually earned by manufacturing labourers in that town and neighbourhood; one of these publications being friendly, and the other hostile, to the present Ministry. The anti-ministerial print asserted, that on a careful enquiry into the circumstances of upwards of two hundred individuals engaged in manufacturing labour, and indiscriminately selected, it was found that, including in the calculation both wages and parochial allowances, the incomings of each individual member of these families did not exceed two shillings per week; while the ministerial print, on the contrary, contended that earnings and parish-pay being included, each of these individuals received for his subsistence three shillings weekly. As we are desirous not to exaggerate the sufferings of the manufacturing classes, we will admit the ministerial statement to be well-founded; but what a dreadful state of things does even this estimate disclose to us—a countless host of industrious workmen, who, after toiling for the space of sixteen hours every day, are unable to earn enough, without parish assistance, to expend fivepence per day upon the lodging, food, and clothing of each member of their families! Surely the prosperity partisans of the Cabinet will not have the effrontery to assert, that the distress prevailing in those districts is only partial? They will not, we should suppose, venture to contend, that as far at least as regards the manufacturing districts of the counties of York and Lancaster, the pressure upon the industrious classes is not overwhelming and universal?

Bad, however, as is the condition of the manufacturers in the North, the state of the clothing districts in the West of England appears infinitely worse; although most inadequately remunerated for their labour, still the working classes in Yorkshire and Lancashire have something to do; but in Somersetshire, Gloucestershire, and Wiltshire, the same classes of workmen are literally without any employment. At Frome, at Shipton-Mallet, at Bradford, and indeed at all the manufacturing towns of the West, the distress of the manufacturers is unprecedentedly overwhelming and appalling. In presenting a petition from the inhabitants of Frome Selwood, complaining of intolerable distress, and praying for relief, the Bishop of Bath and Wells observed, that "nobody except those who had seen the distress could believe the degree to which misery prevailed at present amongst all ranks. He would not say so if the facts had not fallen under his own notice; but he had seen, and he knew that what he said was true. At Wells, where he generally resided, the distress was appalling to humanity—many of the poor creatures had no fuel. At Shipton-Mallet, there was great distress, and so there was at Frome; at various places, the number of persons claiming relief was greater than that of the rate-payers. *He had seen fellow-creatures yoked to carts, which they were dragging through the country.* They were ready to do any thing to obtain the food of which they stood in need; but with all their sufferings, they had displayed no violence, no disposition to turbulence."

At the once flourishing town of Frome, there were about fifty clothiers: of these only sixteen now remain, with scarcely half their former employment. The inevitable consequence is, that the parish contains at this period upwards of 5000 paupers receiving weekly pay. This class consists of able-bodied men, whom the stagnation of trade has entirely deprived of their usual employment. Not long since some of them were considerable manufacturers, and most of them rate-payers; but now they and their families are wholly dependent upon parochial relief. A few of these distressed workmen evince a spirit worthy of their better days, determined to subsist as long as they can upon the proceeds of their own industry, between twenty

and thirty of them, accompanied by their wives, may be seen harnessed to trucks which they draw daily to the coal pits, about nine miles distant. They return the same evening with from three to five hundred weight of coals, which they dispose of (if they can) at about 10d. per hundred weight. By thus performing the functions of beasts of draught, they contrive to maintain themselves and their families without parochial assistance.

Wherever we turn our eyes, the same scenes present themselves—the same overwhelming distress—the same poignant cry of intolerable suffering. To us it appears manifest that things cannot be allowed much longer to go on as they now do, without compromising even the safety of the State. Some vigorous effort must be made to rescue at least the classes which depend upon the earnings of their labour from the poverty, the degradation, and the misery, into which they have been plunged. The wealthier classes, who subsist upon the profits of capital, can perhaps, without incurring utter ruin, wait until the derangement occasioned by the changes effected in our monetary system rectifies itself; but to the operative classes, who are necessarily dependent for subsistence upon what they earn by daily labour, want of employment is want of food. It gives us, therefore, no ordinary degree of satisfaction to find that the condition of the labouring classes is to be specifically pressed upon the attention of Parliament. We sincerely hope, that nothing will occur which may have the effect of preventing the Duke of Richmond from fulfilling the intention which he has announced, of bringing this matter before the consideration of the House of Lords; and we also hope, that his Majesty's Government will not resist the appointment of a select committee to enquire into this most important subject. We are well aware that at different periods committees have been already appointed by both Houses of Parliament to enquire into the condition of the labouring classes: we also know, that although some valuable information has by that means been collected, it has led to no useful or practical result. The different committees have collected evidence and framed reports; and there the matter has been allowed to end. It would, however, be illogical to argue, that because one committee, or a series of committees, has answered no useful purpose, another committee must therefore miscarry. Besides, it appears to us, that the visionary and theoretical views of those who have taken the most active part in these investigations, have greatly contributed to render all their labours abortive. Excited by magnificent plans of foreign colonization, they have spurned with contempt the homespun task of searching into the resources which our home territory may contain for the employment of the people. With the most unfeigned respect for the motives, the perseverance, and the industry of the honourable chairman of the Emigration Committee, we must express our disappointment at the result of his exertions. The reports of that committee contain abundant details with respect to the resources of our North American colonies, and the expenses of emigration—upon these points we are furnished with all the information which appears necessary. We are, however, disposed to think, that by treating the matter in this manner, the committee begin at the wrong end. The first step in the inquiry should be a careful examination of our domestic resources: it should be rendered indisputably clear, that we possess no internal means of furnishing the industrious classes with profitable employment before the public can be brought to sanction the expensive, as well as equivocal, expedient of removing from the country any portion of its industrious population. It is no doubt indispensable, both for the happiness of individuals, and the general welfare of the community at large, that employment should be found for the idle hands which now exhaust the resources of the country; but it by no means follows, that in order to accomplish this object, we must look beyond the limits of our home territory.

That an overproportion of the population of this country is now employed in manufactures is a fact which no person will venture to dispute. The extended use of machi-

nery has displaced a vast amount of manual labour. The inhabitants of other countries are now enabled, by the use of machinery, to supply themselves with the wrought commodities which they had been accustomed to purchase in this country. The use of steam tends likewise to break down that species of manufacturing monopoly which we once enjoyed. Our pre-eminence in manufactures must not be ascribed solely to our national superiority, either in skill, industry, or capital. Much of it arose from the greater abundance, and more convenient distribution, of the water which nature had placed at our disposal. This furnished the British manufacturer with a power which few other countries possessed in an equal degree. But the use of steam, as an impelling power, has greatly diminished the extent of this local superiority. A steam-engine can be erected any where, which renders it perfectly practicable to establish a manufactory in any district or country capable of furnishing the necessary supply of fuel. Hence the use of the steam-engine will have the practical effect of equalizing to a great degree the natural facilities possessed by different countries for manufacturing operations. The only pre-eminence which this country can therefore expect to retain in manufacturing industry is that which may arise from the possession of greater skill or more capital. But even in these respects other nations may be seen treading very closely upon our heels. The French have prohibited the importation of British cotton goods; and the consequence is, that the improvement of their manufacture has been so rapid, that the same calico which in Bonaparte's time, sold for five francs or four shillings and twopence per ell, now sells for twenty sous or tenpence. This rivalry will become more intense, and spread into new regions every year. As other countries improve in industry and skill, they will gradually succeed in supplying their own markets with the wrought commodities which they used to receive from our looms and factories. Hence it seems very probable that the demand for British goods will fall off still more in foreign countries; and as a consequence, the demand for labour in our manufacturing districts may be expected to decline still farther. From these considerations we are led to infer that we have reached a crisis in the history of our national industry. We have an increasing population, while the demand for manufacturing labour is confessedly falling off. Under these circumstances, the prospect before us would indeed be sufficiently gloomy, if we had been left without resource. But fortunately for the country, we possess ample means of absorbing this superabundant population. We have only to adopt the simple and easy expedient of removing a part of our population which now languishes or starves in our decaying manufactories to some neglected portion of our home territory, which, if properly cultivated, would yield an ample return for the labour bestowed upon it, and increase the store, both of human happiness and national wealth. Half the population of Lancashire, for instance, is now pining in indigence, from the low rate at which their labour is remunerated, and half the fields of the same county are nearly in a state of nature from want of tillage. Transplant, at least, some of these people from the cotton mills, in which they now all but starve for want of food, into the corn-fields of the neighbourhood, and they will be able to raise for themselves an abundant subsistence, as well as increased surplus to go into the pockets of the land-owners as rent.

The advocates of the Free Trade system are, in a more especial manner, called upon to use every exertion in facilitating and promoting this transfer of labour from manufacturing operations, where it has become unprofitable, to agriculture, where industry, properly applied, cannot fail to yield the labourer an adequate remuneration. Their grand maxim is, that trade should be left perfectly free and unfettered, and that no branch of manufacture deserves to be upheld which cannot maintain itself without prohibitions and restrictions. Whatever may be thought of this maxim as a guide in commercial legislation, it is manifest that, in the first instance, much individual suffering cannot fail to result from changes in our public policy: when-

ever any manufacture, deprived of the artificial props by which it had been upheld, falls to the ground, the workmen thrown out of employment must, of necessity, become exposed to great distress. Hence the adherents of the Free Trade system are bound by every principle, not only of humanity, but also of policy, to join strenuously in every effort which may be made to open a new source of profitable employment to the industrious labourer, whom the operation of the new system may have thrown out of work. The present condition of the silk manufacture in this country will furnish an apt illustration of this matter. The advocates of Free Trade contend that if this branch of our manufactures cannot sustain itself against foreign rivalry, it is a proof that it is not of a profitable nature with respect to the community at large; and that therefore it ought to be left to its fate. The silk weavers reply, that this may be true as far as the non-productive classes are concerned; and add, that with the declension and fall of the silk trade, their means of subsistence must be greatly diminished, or perhaps entirely fail, when no alternative would be left them except starvation or the work-house. It must, no doubt, be admitted that the opening of the silk trade has not effected the extinction of the silk manufacture in this country; on the contrary, it appears to have increased in extent. But what has been the cause of this extension? The immense fall which has taken place in the rate of wages, and the incredible deterioration which has been brought about in the condition and circumstances of the working classes. The foreign competition which has been let in upon him, forces the British manufacturer to put up with half the remuneration which he had been accustomed to receive for his labour. If he has succeeded in keeping the field against foreign rivalry, it has been done by the application of a double portion of industry; and the fall which has taken place in British silks, to the level of continental prices, is therefore a benefit reaped by the non-productive classes—by those who live on incomes derived from profit, or capital lent out at interest, at the expense of the producing classes—of those classes who subsist solely upon the earnings of manual industry. The wealthy portion of the community is enabled to purchase silks at a diminished price, but, in order that this may be effected, the working classes are obliged either to perform double tasks, or subsist upon a moiety of their usual wages. The Free Traders appeal to the increased importation of the raw material, as evidence both of the extension of the silk manufacture in this country and of the soundness of their principles. If the earnings of the working classes had continued as high as they were before the change, the fact to which they appeal would have been conclusive; but when it is notorious that the working manufacturer is tasked to the utmost pitch of human ability; and that, notwithstanding this extra exertion, under the constant influence of which individuals too frequently fall into a premature grave, this wretched class can command in return for their labour no more than a moiety of their previous means of subsistence; the circumstance which the Economists put forward as the basis of their triumph, is conclusive of nothing except the unfeeling cruelty of their vaunted system. The silk manufacture has no doubt thriven in appearance in spite of foreign competition. The working manufacturer, finding no opening for the transfer of his labour to another branch of industry, has been compelled to stick to his loom, although the remuneration of his labour has been diminished one-half; still half-a-loaf being better than no bread, he is forced to put up with half the reward which he had been accustomed to derive from his labour. From the effect of this reduction in wages, rendered inevitable by foreign competition and consequent deterioration of the condition of the working classes, it is not to be wondered at that the silk manufacture has greatly extended. The fall in the wages of the workmen has now reduced the price of wrought silk so much, that it has to a very great extent been, on account of its cheapness, substituted for other commodities. The persons employed in manufacturing the commodities thus displaced, have in their turn been injured.

They are obliged to work harder, and content themselves with lower wages. The effect of the change has thus extended itself throughout the whole mass of the industrious classes. The changes projected by the Economists benefit the affluent and non-productive classes, by diminishing the cost of the commodities which they consume; but this advantage is purchased solely at the expense of the productive classes, by diminishing their wages, and adding to their toil. This system is admirably calculated to minister to the luxury and enjoyments of the idle and opulent portion of the community; to foster the dissipation, and augment the splendour of the palace and the hall; but the virtuous and hardworking inmate of the cottage it robs of his comforts, and almost of his necessaries. What it adds to the enjoyment of bloated wealth, it takes from the scanty earnings of pining industry. In order that the votary of fashion and extravagance may purchase luxuries at a cheap rate, it trenches with ruthless severity upon the remuneration of productive industry

This, we apprehend, to be the true ground of the opposition which has been offered to the practical application of the principle of Free Trade. The opponent of this system knows well, that the unrestricted admission of foreign silks into our shops, or of foreign ships into our harbours, will enable him to purchase silk goods and foreign commodities at a diminished price. He is not quite such a bumpkin as to doubt, that a foreign weaver, subsisting on chestnuts and water, can fabricate for him a yard of silk at a less cost than an English artisan, who requires to be fed on beef and porter. Although unblessed with the vast intellectual powers of the Economists, he is, notwithstanding, capable of comprehending, that a foreign sailor, content with the coarsest and meanest fare, would carry his tea from China, and his sugar from the West Indies, much more cheaply than a well-fed and jolly British tar. But although he see all this as well, perhaps, as our renowned Economists themselves, he is too generous, too liberal, too honest, to desire to reap these advantages at the expense of fellow-subjects, whom the employment of foreigners would necessarily throw out of work.

In spite of the boasted illumination of the age, we are not ashamed to recommend these principles to the consideration and support of the community. They are honest principles, and appear to reflect credit on those who maintain them. They are considerate and humane principles, which will prevent one man from being benefited at the expense of injuring, and perhaps of ruining, his neighbour. For our own part, we feel no hesitation in avowing, that we would rather wave all the glittering advantages which are held out to us as likely to result from the practical application of the most wonderful discoveries of Political Economy, than consent to reap them at the expense of any class of our fellow-subjects. Pleasant no doubt it is to the eye of the beholder to see the fair forms of our lovely and fascinating countrywomen decked in the elegant productions of foreign looms; or in British productions, perhaps of equal beauty, which our own mechanics and artisans have succeeded in fabricating at an extra cost of labour. But this pleasure is greatly embittered by the reflection, that it is purchased at the expense of much suffering and privation to the industrious classes. A terrible encroachment upon their moderate and necessary enjoyments has been made by Economists for the purpose of adding to the luxuries and superfluities of the affluent and idle portion of the community.

There is indeed nothing in the conduct of the advocates of Free Trade so deserving of reprehension, as the hypocritical pretences with which they attempt to disguise or conceal the real object of their measures. If we credit their professions, this amiable and enlightened tribe of philosophers has nothing in view except the public good, and the improvement of the condition of the industrious classes. There is, however, room to think, that they overestimate the ignorance and blindness of the community in supposing that the mass of our population can be much longer hoodwinked by this flimsy pretence. If the effect of this system had been at any time a matter of doubt, recent and dear-bought experience has taught the working-classes, that the free competition of foreign labour *must* diminish the compensation which they can expect to receive for their toil. The artisans and mechanics of this country have probably by this time become pretty well convinced, that the importation and consumption of the produce of foreign labour has no tendency to ameliorate their condition; and that they at-least form no portion of that public whom the Free Trade system is said to benefit. We must, however, be allowed to assure the labouring and industrious classes, that they constitute no portion of that public, of whom the Whigs and the Economists talk so loudly and so frequently. In the vocabulary of this sect, the personification called "the public" includes only the idle capitalists, the consuming classes, the "fruges consumere nati;" but has no reference whatever to the working portion of the community. The Whig Economists regard this class merely as beasts of burden, as animal machinery produced by nature for the purpose of "hewing wood and drawing water" in the service of the nonproductive and consuming classes. We apprehend, however, that the moment is arriving, when the Free Traders will no longer find shelter from public scorn and indignation, under the hollow and false pretence of intending to benefit the working classes. The time is approaching when they must cease to insult the understandings of those whom they have irreparably injured. Is it not enough, that, by their innovating measures, they have deprived the labouring portion of the community of employment, and their families of bread? Is it necessary that, with an unusual refinement of malice, they should jeer and flout the unhappy classes whom they have robbed and ruined?

The great principle and discriminating characteristics of that honest party in this country, which stands opposed to all speculative innovation is a determination to uphold in all their useful efficiency the institutions, and social arrangements, which, handed down to them by their ancestors, have been subjected to the test of experience; admitting occasionally such moderate and cautious alterations as the lapse of time or change of circumstances may have rendered indispensable. With this party, therefore, adherence to established and tried arrangements is the rule; change or innovation being merely the exception. But the very reverse of this sound principle is the leading characteristic of the Economists. With this party the rule of action is, that, whatever our forefathers established must be wrong; that every old arrangement or institution ought, therefore, to be swept away, in order to clear the ground for the wild experiments of some conceited projector, or crazy constitution-grinder.

Much industry has been employed in heaping obloquy upon those who are desirous to let well alone, and not to tamper with arrangements, which have been found to work well in practice. They are, it is true, firmly opposed to the experiments and crude projects of wild and unprincipled innovators; on this account they are held up as political bigots, wedded to every abuse, merely because it is ancient; and averse from every modern improvement. We must, however, be allowed to state in their behalf, that their attachment for the ancient and established arrangements of the community does not rest, as their calumniators would fain make us believe, upon a blind and superstitious veneration for antiquity, for "the wisdom of their forefathers," although they do not admit that their forefathers were exactly the fools which they are represented to have been by some of our modern luminaries; but upon the conviction, that these arrangements have, from the length of their standing, become so intimately interwoven with the whole fabric of society, that no change can now be carried into practical effect, without at least endangering, and perhaps irreparably injuring the interests and property of some particular class of fellow-subjects. If the community presented a *tabula rasa*, unencumbered with any existing institutions or regulations, then, indeed, would there be an open field, whereon philosophers and economists might be allowed to disport themselves to their heart's content;

producing no injury, they might under these circumstances be permitted to proceed without opposition. But unfortunately this is not the true state of the case. Our stupid ancestors had no philosophers, no economists, no shining lights, no itinerant lecturers, no "schoolmaster" among them; they indulged in no enlarged and magnificent views of general policy; contracted their political horizon within the limits of their own country: limited their care to the interests of this realm alone; and paid little regard to the concerns of other nations, provided the inhabitants of this island exerted their industry, and secured a liberal reward for their labour. In this *perhaps* they were wrong, illiberal, and narrow-minded. But although we should disapprove of the principles on which they acted, still we cannot escape from the consequences which have resulted from them. We may lament the state of things which has grown out of the practical operation of these principles; but we cannot shut our eyes to its existence. Under the shelter of the policy introduced by our ancestors, the arrangements of society had become exceedingly complicated; from time to time various laws of a prohibitory or restrictive character have been passed for the protection and encouragement of particular branches of industry. These laws cannot now be touched, without affecting in a very material degree, or perhaps even annihilating the individual interests which have sprung up under them. That statesman must, therefore, be much more gifted with philosophy than humanity, who can sanction changes in the arrangements of society, which, however beneficial they may in the end prove to the mass of the community, are sure to exhibit their first effects in destroying the property of private individuals, and reducing them and their families to a state of destitution and beggary.

We are inclined, indeed, to an opinion, entertained, we believe, by a considerable and a daily increasing number of our fellow subjects, that in recent times the persons administering the government of this country have evinced rather too great a facility in listening to the suggestions of speculative theorists, and sanctioning alterations affecting in a serious degree the interests and property of particular classes. A judicious Minister will be always extremely slow and cautious in adopting changes, which cannot fail to affect particular interests; a wise and considerate Statesman will oppose all innovation until it has been so generally and so unequivocally demanded by public opinion, that to resist any longer would be inexpedient, if not unsafe; his conduct under such circumstances should put it into his power to say to the injured individual, or class, with an honest conscience, " I have protected your particular interests as long as I could; but I can no longer contend against the united voice of the community: I therefore give you warning, to make the best preparation you can against the moment when the change thus called for must be carried into effect." And in every instance where such a measure may be practicable, ample compensation ought to be made to every individual whose interests or property might be affected by such a change.

For these reasons we are disposed to think, that the promoters of the changes which have been recently effected in our commercial policy, have stopped short of the point at which they ought to have aimed. To the silk-weavers, for instance, they might, and we think should, have addressed the following language:—
" You are now engaged in a manufacture which can be upheld in this country only by high protecting duties and prohibitory restrictions: the public at large can buy silk goods, of foreign manufacture, fifty per cent under the price at which you can afford to sell commodities of the same quality: it appears to us impolitic any longer to prevent the public from having access to this cheaper market. We are aware that this change will be attended with the effect either of driving you altogether from your present employment, or of reducing your wages fifty per cent, in order to compete with your foreign rivals; but we will enable you to embark in a new branch of industry: we will put it in your power to transfer your labour from factories to fields, which,

being fertilised by your industry, will yield from an equal quantity of work a more abundant supply of the necessaries of life than you can secure by continuing your present employment. In this manner the public will enjoy the benefit of cheap silk, while you will derive, from a new and healthy occupation, a full compensation for the losses which you would otherwise have sustained from the change."

If the adherents of Free Trade had reasoned and acted in the manner just suggested, they would have turned aside much of the opposition which their measures have encountered; for the fair opponents of Free Trade ground their objections to the system more, perhaps, upon the effect which it must have upon the social condition and interests of individuals, than upon any general principles of public policy. They have no objection to cheap commodities in themselves; they only object to this advantage to the wealthier classes, when purchased, as it must be, at the expense of the working portion of the community. It may be inconsistent with the theories of the Political Economists, that a rich citizen's wife should be called upon to give a peck of wheat for a yard of silk fabricated in Spitalfields, which she might get from France for half a peck; but if this substitution of French for English silk goods should have the effect either of depriving the Spitalfields weaver altogether of his employment, or cause a reduction of his wages in his own branch of industry, while no opening for his labour should present itself elsewhere, we take upon ourselves to contend, that the admission of foreign silks, when attended with such consequences, is an odious and intolerable act of cruelty. It affords us but little consolation to reflect, that the sleek and pampered citizen should save the value of half a peck of wheat in the purchase of the splendid robe which enfolds her ample frame, when we know that this advantage is obtained at the expense of withholding this quantity of food from the hungry family of the lean and hard-working weaver.

It must, indeed, be conceded to the Free Trade Economists, that the French manufacturer receives only half the food and half the manufactured articles in payment for his labour that the English manufacturer was heretofore accustomed to receive; and hence the article made by this ill-requited workman can be offered cheapest in the market. The wealthy consumer is thus enabled to obtain it at a lower price; but the question is, if, by the demand for labour in England, and by the active employment of every individual, the recompense obtained by the labouring class here is greater than that which is obtained by the same class in France, whether this is to be considered as a benefit or an evil? The rich man, no doubt, pays more,—or, to speak more correctly, before the Free Trade system came into operation, used to pay more,—for the same quantity of labour in England than in France; but we would humbly submit it to the consideration of the Economists, whether this did not produce a great social and political advantage, by promoting the more equal distribution of wealth among all the members of the community. Instead of looking at institutions which affect this object as faulty, we cannot help regarding them as the means of diffusing inestimable blessings among the mass of the people. Is that law wise, is that law humane, is that law friendly to the interests of the industrious poor, which would throw one part of the population out of employment, and produce a glut of labour, and a consequent diminution of the earnings of industry, to enable the rich consumer to purchase more articles of luxury from a foreigner? The truth, however, is, that the self-styled Economists of England regard the poor merely as animals to be driven to death; their aim is to get out of the poor the largest possible quantity of labour for the most scanty remuneration upon which they can be made to subsist. In the vaunted system of those renowned philanthropists, the working classes are set down as animated machines, from the use of which it is sound policy to draw the greatest amount of profit at the least cost. But the real friend of the industrious poor, the enlightened and humane advocate of the lower orders, the man who has the happiness and improvement of his fellow-creatures sincerely at heart, will, as the first

step to civilization, morality, and education, exert all his energy to give employment to the bulk of the people, and insure an adequate reward for their labour. While one human being languishes in inaction and misery, he will stoop to raise him from his abject situation, and do all that lies in his power to give him the means of providing for himself: If he cannot absolutely realise the benevolent and amiable wish of Henry IV., that every peasant may have his chicken in his pot on Sunday, he will at least endeavour to render him independent of the charity of others, and relieve him from absolute want; he will ask, not at how low a money price the luxurious sons of affluence can purchase foreign silks, or pier-glasses, or French wines; but his chief, if not only solicitude, will be, to ascertain whether the loom of the native manufacturer is at work; whether the spade of the labourer is employed in digging the ground; his constant enquiry will be, not whether luxury revels in palaces, but whether plenty and content bless the cottage of the poor?

Whatever obloquy, therefore, may be thrown upon that system under which Great Britain had arrived at a pitch of unexampled prosperity; with whatever contempt the wise statesmen of the present day may speak of these measures, which all tended to foster national industry, the time is not probably far distant when a fatal experience of the evils resulting from an opposite line of policy will produce in the public mind a full conviction of their wisdom and utility. The laws which protected particular manufactures, and prohibited the free importation of corn, gave employment to the general body of the people, and security to the capital which put their industry in motion. These laws gave to every man a full scope for the exertion of his skill, or the application of his property to any pursuit or occupation which held out to him the promise of the greatest return of profit; exacting from him in return no condition, except that he should consent to share his advantages with his fellow-citizens. These laws secured profitable employment to the poor, and restrained the rich from seeking enjoyments to be derived from foreign sources, when these could have been supplied at home. They ministered to the wants of the needy, rather than to the craving desires of the affluent : They protected property and capital engaged in profitable production, as well as the wages of labour. They sacrificed no man or class of individuals to the blind envy of the multitude ; but so long as one human being could be found destitute of the means of providing for his own subsistence, the state, like an affectionate parent, watched over and protected the beginnings of his humble industry. But far different is the course pursued by the Political Economists of the present day ; in the midst of wide-spreading misery and suffering, they persevere, with a callousness of feeling, and a disregard of all warnings, peculiar to themselves, in the prosecution of experiments which threaten to destroy for ever the prosperity of this once happy land.

The Political Economists promised those whom they deluded into the folly of countenancing their experiments, that other nations would be induced to follow the example which we yet set them, and abolish all restrictions upon the importation of foreign commodities. But other nations, blind to the advantages which were held out to them, spurned the suggestions and exhortations of the philosophers. The French, the Dutch, the Prussians, all, in their turn, laughed at the simplicity of the Free Traders, when proposing that foreign commodities should be permitted to compete with the productions of native industry ; nay, the Americans went so far as to establish a prohibitory system at the very moment we were relaxing our own. This is the celebrated reciprocity system, for the introduction of which the statesmen and philosophers of this country claim so much credit. Its advantages, however, are all on one side—We allow foreign industry to come into free competition with that of our own population ; while other nations rigidly exclude all wrought commodities which can be manufactured at home.

In their eagerness to secure to the rich and monied classes the advantage of cheap commodities, the philosophers have felt no scruples in throwing an overwhelming burden upon the shoulders of that class which has vested its capital in the purchase of real property. The thousands of able-bodied workmen whom the new system has thrown out of employment, have necessarily fallen for subsistence upon the poor-rates; nay, so great is the reduction which has taken place in the wages of labour, that a very considerable portion of the maintenance of the workmen constantly employed in the cotton trade is drawn from the parish funds. It is indeed calculated, that in almost every district where the cotton trade has been able to support itself, half the expense of fabricating the wrought commodity is defrayed out of the poor-rates. It thus appears, that an immense tax is levied upon the owners of real property, in order to pay a premium upon the production of cotton goods. No wonder, therefore, that under these circumstances—with wages reduced to a minimum, and one-half of this minimum taken, not out of the capital of the manufacturer, but out of the pockets of the agricultural classes—the cotton manufacture should as yet be able to maintain its ground. The same observation will apply to the silk trade, to the iron trade, and, indeed, to almost every other trade. They are now upheld against foreign competition solely by the bounty which is raised for their support by taxing the owners of real property. In order that the wealthy and monied classes may get their commodities at a cheap rate, half the expense of fabricating them is, in many instances, taken out of the pockets of the owners of real property. A system thus partial and oppressive should by all means be abolished. The agriculturists should, for their own sake, make every effort in their power to withdraw this superabundant population from the factories, in which they are now, at least, partially unproductive, and settle them either as cottagers or colonists in some country district, where they may, by field-labour, replace the whole of the food required for their support.

It will perhaps be said, that, to effect this object, a considerable outlay of capital will be required in the first instance. It will be necessary to build cottages, and provide the means of maintaining their occupants while tilling the ground during one year, at the very least. It may also be urged, that this amount of capital must be withdrawn from the general capital of the country, and that, therefore, the gain in one place will be counterbalanced by an equivalent loss in some other district. A million sterling, for instance, laid out in establishing cottage-farms, or home colonies, must be abstracted from some other branch of national industry in which it is now employed; and, by being thus withdrawn, it will throw out of work as many persons in the district which has lost it, as it would give employment to in that to which it might be transferred. At the first view of the matter, this seems to be a formidable objection to the scheme now recommended; but when closely analysed, it will, we apprehend, entirely vanish. The question to be disposed of, is not, whether it be expedient to transfer a given amount of capital from a branch of industry, in which it is now productive, into some other department; but whether it be expedient to render a certain amount of capital profitable both to the owners and the public, which is now either entirely wasted, or at best yields but an inadequate return of profit. It will at once be perceived, that we speak here of the enormous capital which is annually squandered in this country in the maintenance of able-bodied but unemployed labourers. The food consumed by this class of persons in a state of idleness, is a pure and unalloyed loss to society. Unlike the food consumed by the industrious labourer, no particle of it is replaced: it is consumption without the most trifling reproduction. This wasted capital, if properly applied, would prove amply sufficient to carry into effect the sort of arrangement which is required to give profitable employment to the whole mass of our industrious poor. An able-bodied labourer out of employment necessarily falls upon the parish for support; assume that from this source he draws annually for his maintenance fifty quartern loaves. Being unable to get employment, he consumes this allowance in absolute idleness; hence it unavoid-

ably comes to pass, that at the end of the year not one ounce of the bread which he has eaten is replaced by the fruits of his own industry. With respect to the inhabitants of the parish who maintain this pauper in unproductive idleness, as well as to the community at large, the effect is precisely the same as if these loaves, or, in the language of the Economists, capital, were thrown into the fire. But assume that a different arrangement had been made for the sustenance of this indigent labourer —suppose that the parish had said to him, " We know that ye have no work, and cannot support yourself by the earnings of your ordinary labour; we are also aware that by the obligation of law, and the principles of humanity, we are bound to find you a maintenance ; but upon every principle of honesty and fair dealing, you are equally bound to use your best exertions to replace the food which we advance for your support. We will set apart a small allotment of land for you to cultivate ; by an unremitting and judicious application of your industry to the tillage of this portion of land, you will be able at the proper season to gather a crop which will more than replace the food consumed by you while prosecuting your task."

It should also be always borne in mind, that when a portion of the capital of any country is exhausted by unproductive consumers, the national fund for the employment and reward of productive industry is in an equal ratio diminished ; hence the evil effect of maintaining an able-bodied labourer in a state of unproductiveness becomes doubled. Suppose an able-bodied and unemployed labourer draws from the funds of the parish to which he belongs an allowance equivalent to fifty quartern loaves ; this quantity of food is not only wasted upon a man who does not replace one of the crusts which he consumes, but the amount thus abstracted from the aggregate capital belonging to the inhabitants of the parish, throws another labourer out of employment. Thus it comes to pass, that an unoccupied labourer not only consumes in unproductive idleness the food which he receives from the parish, but by that very act he also deprives another labourer of profitable employment. Hence it is that the evil of pauperism spreads so rapidly and extensively in every country, where, from a defective or vicious organization of society, any considerable portion of the working classes may be unprovided with reproductive employment.

It is very gratifying to find that the system which has recently attracted so much attention,—that of attaching a small allotment of land to the cottage of the industrious labourer, to be cultivated by spade husbandry, spreads so rapidly throughout the country. It would be tedious to specify the various districts into which it has been introduced; it is sufficient to say, that wherever the experiment has been judiciously made, it appears to answer the most sanguine expectations of its advocates; it emancipates the peasant from the condition of a parochial slave, degraded and demoralized by oppression, and places him in a state of comfort and independence. It obtains the countenance not only of the wealthy landowners, but what holds out the promise of making it still more general, the farmers of the country begin likewise to open their eyes to the palpable advantages of the system. The labouring classes evince the utmost eagerness to obtain these small allotments; they are willing and able to pay for them a much higher amount of rent than could be afforded by the ordinary farmer. In a parish not far from Wells, land appropriated to this purpose lets at the enormous rate of eight pounds per acre; it is no doubt of very good quality; and notwithstanding the present depressed state of agriculture, the industrious cottager is enabled to pay this high rent, and at the same time to derive from his allotment a considerable surplus, as a reward for his own labour. The success of these experiments begins to produce its natural effect; landowners begin to see that, by adopting this system, they can derive a much larger revenue from their property, than by letting it to a common farmer; and among the occupiers of extensive farms, the conviction gradually gains ground that nothing short of the general adoption of this plan can prevent the poor-rates from absorbing not only the whole rent of the landlord, but also the whole of the profits of the occupying tenant. Impelled by these considerations, parishes begin to adopt these means of relieving their poor; instead of giving money to support them in idleness, they allot land, to the cultivation of which every hour which the labourer can spare may be applied. The industrious workman is thus provided for by means which do not cost the community a single farthing; for in every instance he pays an adequate, and in many cases even a high rent for his allotment.

This is a subject which appears to deserve the serious attention of the Legislature; every obstacle which may tend to impede its extension ought to be removed. If generally adopted, it could scarcely fail to remove the most crying evil of the present day—the hopeless pauperism of able-bodied labourers. This is the true and only way of relieving the industrious classes in this country from the oppressive influence of the Free Trade system. The superabundant population of the manufacturing districts would be gradually withdrawn; and the wages of the remainder would consequently rise. The condition of the whole working classes would be thus improved, and content and happiness would once more bless this land. The ruin and misery brought upon the labouring poor by the wicked experiments of the Economists would be removed, and we should be no more alarmed by the vapid and absurd declamations about superabundant population. The population of this country is superabundant, merely because our stupid regulations exclude the people from the fields in which their industry would prove highly productive to themselves as well as the community at large. Let the soil of the country be but properly thrown open to the industry of our labouring classes, and we shall hear no more of a surplus population. The cant and nonsense of the pseudo-Economists will sink first into contempt, and then into oblivion. The patience of the public will be no longer teased by absurd schemes for transporting one portion of the community for the benefit of the other portion; and the public feeling will cease to be outraged by horrible suggestions for checking population. Let the people of Britain have but a free trade in land and cottages, and we care not one farthing to what other branches of industry this principle may be extended; we are convinced that the practical result of throwing the soil of the empire open to the industry of our population, would be to create a want of hands, instead of a want of employment. The present competition for *labour* would be changed into a competition for *labourers*, and this would inevitably secure to the workman the full hire of which he is worthy. To us it appears indeed perfectly unaccountable, that some portion of the overflowing capital of this country has not already taken this direction; it could be rendered perfectly clear, that in no way could it be made so productive as by being invested in building cottages upon small allotments of land; and this would the more especially be the case in populous districts. It is well known, that small houses, even now, return a larger profit for the capital expended in building them than more extensive erections; and it cannot be questioned, that a comfortable cottage, with a small allotment of land attached to it, would prove a still more profitable mode of investing capital. An incalculable amount of the accumulated capital of the nation might, in this manner, be disposed of to the great advantage both of individuals and the public. While this mode of investing capital would prove an incalculable blessing to the poor, it would, by diminishing the aggregate of our floating capital, and raising the rate of interest, prove extremely profitable to the rich capitalist.

Art. III.—1. *Minutes of Evidence taken before the Select Committee of the House of Lords, appointed to consider the Poor
Laws.* 1831.
2. *Extracts of Letters from Poor Persons who emigrated last
Year to Canada and the United States.* London. 1831.
3. *The Results of Machinery.* Printed under the Superintendence
of the Society for Promoting Useful Knowledge. 1831.

OF all themes for the meditation of the philosophical statesman, of all topics which can engage the attention of any
reasoning being, the most attractive and deeply interesting beyond comparison, if he possess but the common sympathies of
humanity, is the study of the means of ameliorating the condition of the great body of his fellow-men; who, under the
existing circumstances of most human societies, lead a life of
unceasing toil, rarely remunerated by a sufficiency even of necessaries, and often depressed to unalloyed misery. There are some
                                                          persons

persons who conceive this to be the inevitable lot of the bulk of society. In their opinion the labouring classes are necessarily condemned, not merely to earn their bread by the sweat of their brow, but to earn a very scanty supply of it by the severest exertions: and any expectation of being able to elevate the labourer above this dreary level, is, with them, unreasonable and Quixotic, a rebellion against one of the fixed laws of nature, or rather of nature's great Author, whom they consider to have irremediably prescribed this unhappy state of things.

' Bond damns the poor, and leaves them to the Lord.'

We own ourselves of a very different opinion. So gloomy and hope-forbidding a creed is as irreconcilable with our firm conviction of man's capacity for moral, intellectual, and social improvement, as it is repugnant to our notions of the expansive benevolence of his Creator. That the mass of mankind should ever be able to live without labour, is not only not to be expected, but not to be desired. If this were a possible, it would, perhaps, be the worst of all possible contingencies. The man who has no other object in life but to enjoy himself, is rarely any other than a self-tormenting being; and were this same ' far niente ' ever to become the universal occupation, the evil passions of our nature would probably be developed to a degree which would realize hell upon earth. The true Pandemonium we conceive to be a society of idle and well-fed persons, who tear each other to pieces for want of anything else to do.

But though labour will doubtless always continue to be the condition of human existence, and of human enjoyment also, that the quantity of labour necessary to procure for each individual the means of subsistence should indefinitely diminish, and that the quantity, not of necessaries merely, but of other useful and agreeable objects likewise, procurable by the labour of each individual, should in the same ratio increase, with the advance of knowledge and civilization, seems to us not merely a defensible proposition, but a self-evident truth. Whilst, as in the state of barbarism, man has nothing but his natural resources to depend on, his existence is necessarily precarious; hunger and misery his occasional, perhaps frequent, visiters. But every step that he makes in knowledge and art, in the improvement of his faculties and the enlargement of his resources, ought to remove him farther and farther from the reach of want. And it would be strange, indeed, if after ages spent in successive victories over matter, and in accumulating the means of yet further conquests— after he has not only compelled whole races of the inferior animals to his service, but succeeded in tasking the very elements to do his bidding with superior docility and far less superintendence—

when

when inventions after inventions, one more perfect than the other, have multiplied his powers of production in every branch of industry to a considerable, and in some to an almost incalculable extent, it would be indeed strange if, in spite of all this, he were still unable to escape the grasp of want, still incapacitated from procuring for the larger proportion of his numbers a full sufficiency even of the lowest necessaries on which to maintain life.

If such should indeed be the condition of the population of any country which has made a considerable progress in the arts of production, the simplest reflection will force upon us the conviction that gross mismanagement must prevail either in the direction of its resources or the distribution of its produce.

Perhaps the trite but shallow fallacy will here be objected, that the evil is owing to the increase of numbers outstripping that of the resources for employing and maintaining them. This, however, often as the assertion is repeated with an air of oracular wisdom, is, in a general sense, *impossible.* The effect of *every* improvement in the arts of production is to increase the aggregate means of mankind *in proportion to their numbers*—to increase the average means of every individual man, how many, or how few soever, there may be. To give, therefore, his more or less rapid increase as a reason why the enlarged resources of man have not proportionately improved his condition, is tantamount to declaring, that in a sum of simple multiplication, the increased power of the multiplier has a tendency to diminish the product.

There is, indeed, one circumstance, which, if it had any existence, might account for this anomaly—a deficiency of the natural agents upon which the labour of man is exercised in the gratification of his desires. But are the elements less favourable than heretofore? Is the earth less fruitful? The bright sun less vivifying? Are the seasons more inclement? The genial rains less refreshing? Has the water lost its power of supporting our vessels, or the air of impelling them over its surface? Does fire no longer give forth its usual heat, or are our stores of fuel exhausted? Are the powers of nature, in short, undergoing decay, or is she becoming a niggard of her bounties? On the contrary, every day we are discovering fresh and undreamt of treasures in her yet unexplored recesses. Every hour opens to us new views of her inexhaustible and infinite capacity—new qualities in matter applicable to some purposes of utility. Or is there a deficiency of elbow-room for the increasing numbers of mankind? However we may jostle each other in the Strand or the Toledo, there is clearly space enough and to spare on the pampas and the prairies, in the wilds of Siberia and the deserts—which once were gardens—of Barbary. China of late was believed to be over-peopled to such a degree, in spite of the

' check

'check direct' of infanticide, that space could not be conceded
for roads, and a large part of the population, it was said, are
even obliged to live in boats on the surface of her canals and
rivers, for want of standing room on their banks! It is now
recognized that few countries contain so great an extent of unin-
habited wastes.* We may still then bear a little closer packing
on *terra firma.* And were it otherwise, there would yet remain
the resource attributed to the Chinese. Venice has long ago
proved its practicability. Or, finally, is it that the soils of
the whole globe are so fully occupied and cultivated, that all
their possible produce is already appropriated, and no means left
of raising additional supplies for the increasing number of consumers? How far we are from a deficiency of this nature—in how
minutely fractional a degree the fruitful lap of mother earth has
been yet drained of its deep, and varied, and widely extended
resources for affording nourishment to her children—let those declare who, knowing the numbers that are fed from the native
growth of this one island, and the small proportion that its surface
bears to that of the lands lying within the temperate regions of the
globe, which there is not the least reason for believing inferior to
it in average natural fertility—can calculate the millions which the
latter might support, were the same labour, and skill, and improved processes, applied to their cultivation as to the former. On
another occasion we gave our reasons for presuming that in this
way *at least* a thousand times the actual population of the world
might maintain themselves with facility. It is not worth while to
enter on a detailed calculation in order to verify this supposition.
It is enough for our present purpose to assert, what none will deny,
that there is as yet nothing like a general deficiency of soils from
which to procure an abundance of the food or other raw produce
required for our actual numbers.

How then are we to explain the notorious fact, that in several
civilized countries, and especially in this, where, beyond all others,
invention has prodigiously multiplied the means at our disposal for
the satisfaction of our varied wants, the major part of the labouring
population have in little or no degree profited by these improvements, but remain in a precarious and deplorable condition,
scarcely able to command a sufficiency of mere necessaries in
requital for their toil, and experiencing a growing deficiency in the
demand for their labour, the only commodity they have to offer?
We have already said enough to prove, that this position can be
owing only to a neglect or misdirection of our resources, certainly
in no degree to their deficiency. In what quarter then does the
baneful error lie?

---

* See Sadler on Population, book ii. p. 598., and his authorities.

The

The obvious mode by which to arrive at the solution of this important question, will be to ascertain, first, what is the character of the additional powers of production which the inhabitants of this country have acquired ; and, next, what are the objects which they still continue to be in want of, in spite of these augmented resources.

The inventions which have of late years been, in rapid succession, brought to light in this country, and distinguish it so much from every other, have reference almost exclusively to manufactures—to that branch of industry which supplies its population directly or indirectly by foreign exchange, with clothing, and a variety of objects, which, though they have become from habit more or less accessary to our comfort, cannot be reckoned among the necessary means of subsistence. It is the production of these objects that has been advanced by the spinning-jenny, the power-loom, the stocking-frame, and all the wonderful machinery which that wonderful power, the steam-engine, sets in motion. And, accordingly, there exists an abundance of these things—an abundance notoriously complained of as an evil, under the denomination of *glut*.

But the objects of which, in spite of so many improvements, we experience a *deficiency*, are the necessaries of subsistence, the product of agricultural, not of manufacturing industry. There is an abundance, nay, there is an acknowledged super-abundance, of cottons, and cloths, and cutlery in the country, but there is a sensible want of good wheaten bread, and cheese, and bacon, and fresh meat. The prices of the former objects have fallen in some cases to one-fourth, in others to one-tenth, of what they were half a century ago ; while the prices of the articles of primary subsistence, of the necessaries of life, of *food*, in short (making abstraction of the difference in the general value of money), have very considerably risen during the same period. And as the labouring class cannot live upon calicoes and cutlery, and that the being able to procure clothing and conveniences of better quality than before, is but a poor compensation for an empty stomach, their condition still remains unimproved, but rather, on the contrary, deteriorated, in its essential feature, their command over the means of subsistence. And since, after all, people *must* somehow or other be provided with food, or they will plunder and fight for it ; since too a half-fed labourer is worth little or nothing, and that the price of food, therefore, determines the wages of labour, and that wages enter largely into the cost of all other commodities—the scarcity and dearness of food indirectly, but severely, affect most of the superior classes ; the consumers of other commodities, through their diminished production ; capitalists, through the consequent narrowing

narrowing of their market; and society at large, by the burden it must endure of supporting the unemployed hands, and the insecurity of property which results from the near approach to destitution of a large proportion of its members.

But it will be said that agriculture has not been stationary, but has likewise made very considerable advances. No doubt it has, or we should not be able to support, as we do at present, on the agricultural produce of this country alone, nearly double the population that we did fifty years since. But the improvements of agriculture, and through them the means of extracting an increased produce from the soil of the country, have by no means kept pace with the contemporaneous increase of the population. This, indeed, could scarcely be expected, since that soil is of very limited extent and of various degrees of fertility; and all the best soils having been long since fully cultivated, and none but very inferior qualities remaining yet untilled, the increase of agricultural produce can only take place through the expenditure of continually increasing quantities of labour and capital, either on the old soils, or on those which may be newly taken into culture, for the same return—*unless* contemporaneous improvements in agricultural skill were to diminish the labour and capital required for the growth of fixed quantities of produce, in an equal ratio with the increase of demand caused by the growth of the population. But it is far from probable that agricultural skill should ever improve with such rapidity. The comparative rise of prices we have mentioned, attesting an existing relative deficiency of agricultural produce, shows that it has not done so in fact.

Thus, then, whatever saving has been made, through improved manufacturing skill and power, in the cost of supplying the labouring class with clothing and domestic utensils, has been more than counterbalanced by the daily accruing deficiency in the means of providing them with food. And in this circumstance we have a rational and satisfactory explanation of the fact, at first sight so puzzling, that in spite of the innumerable improvements of the arts of production, both agricultural and manufacturing, but chiefly of the latter, the condition of the bulk of the population has not been proportionately, if at all, bettered. The cause of this, as we have said, does not lie in the mere increase of the population, for *that* ought to have proportionately, or *more than proportionately*, increased the means of supporting them—it lies in the difficulty of procuring increased supplies of food for this increased population, within our own limited territory, by reason of the necessity of having recourse to the outlay of fresh capital or labour, either on the old or on new soils, *with a less proportional return.*

That the population of England has outgrown, and is every day

still

still further outgrowing, the capacity of our home soils for supplying it with food, is, indeed, a fact obvious to the least inquiring capacity; evidenced as well by the gradually increasing importations which we have, however reluctantly, been compelled to admit of late years, as by the number of agricultural labourers who cannot obtain work. Why are these not employed by farmers to raise the desirable quantity of food, and save us from the necessity of importing it? only because the present prices of farm produce will not pay for the further employment of labour on the home soils. Why do prices keep below the height which would remunerate the farmer for raising the desirable quantity of food on the home soils? Those agriculturists whose vision does not extend beyond their own rick-yards, or at best the next market-town, will answer, ' because the duty on imported corn is not high enough, because the law does not prohibit importation.'—They think they have only to prevent importation in order to raise prices to any extent, and to be enabled perhaps ultimately to bring all Dartmoor and Salisbury plain under tillage. This is a dangerous mistake. Are they quite sure that people *must* buy of them at whatever price? Are they not aware that when any commodity rises in relative price, its sale diminishes; that those who cannot afford to buy must and do go without it? Aye, even though that commodity were food. They may help themselves to it by force, or they may come upon the parish, and so get it in that way likewise, without any equivalent; but *buy* they cannot, if they have not the *wherewithal.* We, therefore, keeping in view these very obvious considerations, give as the true answer to the question why prices do not rise sufficiently to remunerate the farmer for increasing the supply of food from the home soils,—*because the other classes of consumers, and particularly their chief customers the manufacturing class, cannot afford, out of the prices which they obtain for their goods in the general market of the world, to pay a higher price for food.*

In a country like this, so great a part of whose population are engaged in trade and manufactures, fabricated in great part for exportation, the prices which those manufactures fetch in the foreign market regulate the home prices, and therefore determine the wages of the manufacturing labourers, and, consequently, the sum they can afford to pay for the food they consume, or the quantity and quality of it at the existing prices. No artificial restrictions, no contrivance whatever, can drive the prices of corn, meat, cheese, &c., higher in this country than what the state of the foreign market will allow the manufacturing population to pay. These, if they cannot get the necessaries they require within that price, must be content with a less quantity, or a worse

quality;

quality; they must sink to a lower scale of living, they must consume bacon instead of fresh meat, and potatoes instead of bread; or, finally, they must starve, or rob, or *come upon the parish— while their former employers carry their capital to establish manufactories in other countries ;*—for that they should give more for their food than the price of their labour will enable them to command, is an evident impossibility; and the attempt to get more from them by preventing importation, or any other contrivance on the part of the agriculturists, must, from the nature of things, not merely prove a signal failure, but just such a failure as that of a certain dog who lost a good bone out of his mouth by catching at the other which he fancied he saw in the water.

This then is the dilemma in which we are placed, and it is essential that it should be well and thoroughly understood. The manufacturing population (whose consumption, owing to their great number, determines the prices of provisions) cannot afford to pay more than the present prices for the food they consume, or to consume a larger quantity at the present prices—*because* they cannot raise the prices of *their* goods and labour beyond the point determined by the increasing competition of the foreign market. The farmers, on their side, can neither increase the quantity of their produce, nor lower its price to suit the diminishing means of the manufacturer,—*because* the soils of this country will not bear any larger quantity without an increased expense, nor the same quantity at a less expense.

Here then we are *at a dead lock.* The hitch is complete and effectual; and as the population, already redundant, is continuing rapidly to increase upon us, (at the rate indeed of above eight hundred *per diem,*) and consequently the competition for labour, and the reduction of wages, and the depression of the labouring class, and finally their demoralization, discontent and disaffection, are all increasing in the same rapid rate of progression,—it is evident that something or other must speedily give way, or the machine of society will go to rack. The great question is, what ought to be made to give way? In what direction is the opening to be safely and wisely broached for our relief from this dangerous state of accumulating pressure?

The opposing barriers which prevent the enlargement of the supply of food to meet the increase of the demand, are, as we have said, but two; the impossibility of raising the prices of the produce of our manufacturers so as to enable them to command more of the produce of our agriculturists; and the impossibility of the agriculturists lowering the price, or increasing the quantity of their produce, so as to enable the manufacturers to consume more. Now the prices of our manufactures in the foreign market are
                                                                    wholly

wholly and absolutely beyond our possible control; they are determined by the comparative skill and resources (which are every day increasing) of the foreign competitors whom we meet there. In this direction therefore relief is *impossible.* Is the other barrier equally insurmountable? Is the difficulty of increasing our supplies of food without raising its price, as those political economists declare who most constantly have it in their mouths, an insuperable one—a cause of decay and declension which must overmatch all the improvements that man can make, and still retain him in the same position, or rather drag him yet lower and lower? Most decidedly we answer *No!* If this difficulty is looked at with an unprejudiced eye, it will be found as capable of removal by wisdom and foresight as any other of the numerous obstacles to his improvement, which, in the progress of civilization, man has encountered and subdued. There are, it is true, no means of increasing the quantity of food *grown in this country* without increasing its price, or of increasing its price without diminishing its consumption and sale, in consequence of the limited extent and fertility of our home soils. *But* are there no *other* soils to which we might have recourse for augmenting the supply of food without any increase of its cost? And if there are, and that they are accessible to us, (as who will venture to deny?) *why,* in the name of common sense, common humanity, and common prudence, should we not avail ourselves of them? Why are we to suppose in theory, or enforce in practice, a limitation for which no necessity exists, and which is so ruinously hurtful in its consequences? If our home soils refuse to afford us additional supplies, except at an increased cost, why not resort—we do not say to foreign soils—though that would be the proper step were there not a preferable alternative—but to the soils, at least, of our colonies, of districts which are an integral portion of the empire, and whose interests are identified with our own? Are those soils in the same predicament? Are they too so fully cultivated, that to raise more food from them will require an increased proportionate outlay of labour and capital? Quite the contrary: their extent is almost boundless; their fertility extraordinary. A very small proportion only of the best quality of the richest vallies has yet been cleared and ploughed at all; and this, though cultivated in a most slovenly and careless manner, is wonderfully productive, and might, by the improved practices which have been adopted in this country, be made to produce, whenever it became necessary, incomparably more than it does at present.

Here then is the obvious remedy for the difficulty experienced by the population of this country in the increasing cost of pro-

curing

curing their supplies of food.　Enlarge the field of their industry. Let them carry their labour and their capital to other soils beyond the narrow geographical boundaries of these islands, but which enjoy nearly the same climate, acknowledge the same government, and are peopled, as far as they are peopled, from the same families,—and the difficulty vanishes at once.　The same labour and capital which, applied here to the production of additional food, will barely reproduce the lowest rate of subsistence for the labourers, and the lowest rate of profit on the capital employed, will there produce food sufficient to maintain the cultivators in plenty, to afford a high profit to the capitalist, and, besides this, to supply our redundant manufacturers at home with subsistence in return for their labour, at such a price as will enable them to command it.　By this one step we should obtain profitable employment for our excess of labour and of capital, both agricultural and manufacturing.　*All* our great productive interests would share in the relief at once.

For it is undeniable, that there is as great a redundancy of capital in the country as of labour.　Capitalists are as anxiously seeking, and as grievously vexed at not being able to discover, a demand for their capital, as are labourers for a demand for their labour.　And to what is this redundancy of capital owing, but to the same cause as the redundancy of labour ; the fact, namely, that enough, and more than enough, of manufactures are already produced, or in course of production, for the existing demand—that they encumber the market—and that the employment of capital in supplying the demand for agricultural produce, where alone the deficiency lies, cannot take place with profit in this country, because of the impossibility of increasing the produce of our limited soil without an increased *proportional* expenditure.

The economical position of Britain possesses, indeed, at this moment, a singular and most anomalous character.　There exists at the same time an excess of capital, that is, of all the artificial auxiliaries to production, causing anxiety and distress among its owners ; and an excess of labour, that is, of the active powers of production, causing the distress of the labourers.　Now there are but three sources of production—land, labour, and capital.　And, since there cannot be any general excess of the means of production, unless we suppose a general falling off in the desire to consume, which is quite repugnant to the most obvious principles of human nature—it follows, as a necessary consequence of the acknowledged excess in this country of the two last sources of production, labour and capital, that there must be a deficiency of the third, namely, of land—of land, that is, sufficiently fertile to repay the employment of labour and capital upon it—that production

has,

has, for this reason, increased of late in an unequal ratio, the increase being nearly confined to objects of secondary importance, whilst the *primary* product of land, labour, and capital, the food upon which human life is sustained—*that species of capital which is by far the most important of all, since without it none other can be set in activity*—has been comparatively stationary,—has not indeed kept pace with the increase of demand for it, caused by the continually enlarging number of consumers.

In confirmation of this view of the real cause of our present position, let us suppose for an instant that the means of enlarging the supply of food *had* advanced as rapidly as the means of supplying clothing and superfluities, either by reason of extraordinary agricultural improvements, rivalling those which have so stimulated our manufacturing industry—or through a miraculous increase of fertility in our soils—or the rapid accession of a large extent of new and rich land to our coasts. It is evident, that in this case none of the evils of our present economical condition could, by possibility, be in existence. The comparative cheapness of food, consequent on its increased production, without any increase in the cost, would not only afford an abundance of the necessaries of subsistence to our whole working population, but enabling them to spare a far larger proportion of their earnings than they can at present for the purchase of clothing and superfluities, would multiply the demand for such objects, and add greatly to the remuneration of both capital and labour employed in manufactures; while this thriving condition of the manufacturers must in turn ensure an equal remuneration to the agriculturists. All our productive interests would be in a state of sound and permanent prosperity.

Now though improvements in agriculture do not occur fast enough to meet the demand of our growing population from our limited home soils, and it is idle to expect any increase in the fertility of those soils, or any considerable accession of rich land to our coasts,—yet the same beneficial consequences which would flow from these hypothetical circumstances, were they possible, must follow from our cultivation of the rich soils that are separated from Britain by the Atlantic, and fully to the same extent as if these soils were attached to our coast, *but for* the single circumstance of the cost of conveying their raw produce across the Atlantic. *This cost, however, is diminishing daily.* Already, within a few years past, the Atlantic has been practically reduced to one-third its width by the establishment of steam navigation. The cost of conveying flour from Quebec to Liverpool or Manchester is scarcely more now than that of its land carriage, a century back, from a distance of fifty miles. And by further improvements

improvements in communication, which are advancing with
greater rapidity than any others, we may reasonably expect our
North American colonies to be every year approaching still nearer
to our great manufacturing districts, and their supply to be shortly
effected from thence with no more difficulty or expense than it
could be from a miraculous accession of rich land along the Norfolk and Essex coast; and effected, let it be remembered, through
the agency of our own shipping and seamen.

Let but our redundant capital and labour take that direction,
and give as free an admission to its produce as if it were really
grown in Norfolk or Essex, and the double object will be answered, of increasing our supplies of food at home, and opening
new avenues for the profitable employment of our surplus labour
and capital, *both agricultural and manufacturing.*

And herein is seen the vast superiority of the trade with a
colony over that with an independent country, though most political economists refuse to open their eyes to it.  Were corn to
be imported freely from Poland or the United States, in exchange
for our manufactures, we not only become dependent for the first
necessaries of life on the caprices of the governments of those
countries, which may, at any time, interfere with our supply, but
we become dependent also upon the rate at which capital, population, and the agricultural arts may chance to advance among
their inhabitants, a rate which we can do nothing to accelerate.
Moreover, though our manufacturing industry may be benefited
by such a trade, our agriculturists do not profit from it in any degree, since there is no correspondent increase of employment for
their labour and capital, but rather a decrease, in case the importation occasion a fall in the prices of their produce.  But the
system of supply *by colonization,* on the contrary, offers a direct
addition to the means of employing our agricultural, as well as
manufacturing population, the skill and capital of our farmers, as
well as of our manufacturers; and thus gives a double stimulus to
the national industry; at the same time that, instead of causing
us to depend for our increased supply of food on the slow increase
of the capital and population and inventive ingenuity of foreign
nations, and on their arbitrary commercial regulations, we at once
employ our own people, with all their known and tried resources
of skill, genius, and enterprise, in its provision, whilst we ourselves regulate the terms of its admission.

If we would but consider a fertile and favourably situated
colony, like the Canadas for example, in the light of an accession
to the territory of Great Britain, which is, in truth, its real character, we should recognize at once its prodigious value as a field
for the utilization of British agricultural labour and capital, and a
                                                                 market

market for British manufactures. The Romans were, in this respect, wiser than the present generation ; they valued their colonies in proportion to the supplies they could obtain from them. Africa and Sicily they esteemed beyond all others as their *granaries*, the source of an abundant provision of the first necessary of life, and it was considered an object of first-rate importance to encourage its production there.

The only arguments that can be urged why a colonial province should not be placed, in this respect, completely on the footing of a home country, rest on its unequal contribution to the expenses of the state, and the possibility of a separation.

The first objection is good at all only as far as relates to the amount of taxation required to pay the interest of the debt, for there can be no reason why a colony should not be taxed to the extent necessary to cover the expenses of its local establishments and defence ; and, abstracting the debt, no portion of the empire pays, or ought to pay, more. Now, the national debt must certainly be exclusively borne by this country, and will as certainly occasion its agriculturists to compete to a disadvantage with the producers of corn in Canada. And the same may be said of other public burthens, with which the agriculture of this country almost exclusively, and most unfairly, is saddled. But the question is not what are the disadvantages under which the home cultivators labour, as compared to the colonial farmers, but whether they can hope to get higher prices, under any circumstances, than the manufacturers can afford to pay ? Whether the existing limitation of the field of agricultural industry is not an evil to our agriculturists themselves ? Whether the productive interests of this country, as a whole, would not be better able to support the weight of the debt and local taxation, if they were encouraged to employ their surplus capital and labour, now lying unproductive, in growing the additional supplies of corn required for our increasing numbers, *in Canada and Nova Scotia*, experience having proved, that a physical impossibility is opposed to their growing them in this country, in the deficiency of fertile soil ? In short, will our debt, and other *insular* burthens, be more willingly or easily paid by a working population, but half-employed and in want of bread, distressed capitalists, and landlords whose rent is eaten up by paupers, than by a people of labourers fully employed and well-fed, and manufacturing and commercial interests in a state of prosperity, which, from the very nature of things, must be shared in by the agriculturists ?

With regard to the second objection, it is clear, that the closer we draw the bonds of union between the parent state and colony, the more completely we identify their interests, and treat the latter as an integral portion of the general empire, rather than as a mere subject dependency, opening our ports freely to its productions, (as we were wise enough to do to those of Ireland, in the beginning of the century,) placing its inhabitants on the footing of fellow-subjects, instead of foreigners, the less chance is there of any desire arising in the colony for a separation. Under such circumstances, we cannot contemplate its possibility.

But for the advantage which Ireland derives in common with this country, from their commercial connexion, *that* union would, in all probability, by this time, have ceased to exist, or would exist only through compulsion, not the voluntary attachment which is founded on a sense of reciprocal benefit. And why may we not, as our population and resources expand, attach *other* provinces as firmly to us, by the same mutually beneficial bonds? Why should not the same facilities be afforded to the application of our agricultural labour, skill, and capital in *their* cultivation, for the supply of the home market, as in that of the Irish, Welsh, or Scotch soils? Why, above all, are we to stint our population in the prime necessaries of life, and keep down the wages of labour and the profits of capital in this country, by confining our redundant capital and labour to the cultivation of our own soils, and our hungry population to their scanty produce, which, through their limited extent and fertility, *cannot* be increased, whilst we have millions of acres of rich soil, courting our ploughs, in our transmarine dependencies; in districts subject to our government, attached to our laws, and asking only to be peopled with the overflow of our population, and to have their vast resources developed for the common advantage, by the profitable application of our redundant capital?

The landowners will not misunderstand our remarks. They proceed from a quarter which has ever distinguished itself by the advocacy of their interests, and which never more strongly supported them than in the line of argument we are now pursuing. Their interest is identified with the general wealth and prosperity of the country; but these must, beyond question, soon give way beneath the pressure of the circumstances we have described; if not by a convulsive explosion, yet, by a rapid, and, when once it has fairly set in, incurable decline. If the extended cultivation of the colonies, and the free introduction of their agricultural produce, were certain to cause a fall of prices and of rents, this would be fully compensated to the landlords by increased security. But a considerable fall of price would, in truth, be compensated to the farmers by the lowering of the poor-rates, consequent on the removal of the surplus population, agricultural as well as manufacturing, which now weighs so heavily upon them, and they would

continue

continue to pay the present rents out of diminished prices. In our opinion, however, prices would not fall materially, since increased production, accompanied by a very slight fall of price, would occasion a proportionately increased consumption. The utmost enlargement that can be contemplated in the produce of our North American colonies, cannot, for a long period to come, do much more than meet the increase of the demand that would follow the enlargement of the market in those countries for our manufactures. But even if rents did fall in consequence, what landlord will venture to say, that it is for the interest of his class that the increasing body of the community shall be reduced to a less and less supply of food—the profits of capital, and the wages of labour continually lessened—the condition, in short, of all the producing classes daily deteriorated, instead of improving, as their numbers, and skill, and productive powers increase? It has been shown in our last number, that the real interests of the proprietors of the soil of any country *cannot* be opposed to, but are indissolubly and completely bound up with those of the rest of the community. He is but a short-sighted politician or political economist, who thinks or says otherwise. The high rents of our landlords, as compared with those of other countries, have grown with, and are wholly dependent on, the success of our manufacturing industry. But our manufacturers cannot continue to thrive, unless they can obtain their supplies of food at a price which the price they obtain for their own products will admit of their paying. They cannot otherwise employ their workmen, who must fall, at once, upon the land for maintenance. The necessary consequence of confining our agricultural industry to our home soils will be the destruction of our manufacturing industry, or rather the migration of our manufacturing capital and machinery to foreign shores, the labouring part of the manufacturing population being left a burden on the estates of the landlords of this country. And this escape of the very blood and sinews of our national wealth is already begun, and whenever the continent is pacified, will continue, with accelerated rapidity, unless measures are, in the meantime, taken to stay the evil.

The root of that evil lies, we think it evident, *in the want of an increase of cultivable territory corresponding to the increase of population and of capital in the United Kingdom;* and the means which we venture to recommend, as fully adequate to its cure, is, that we should carve out that increase from the soil of our most fertile and nearest colonies; that the trade between these dependencies and the mother country should be put upon the footing of the coasting trade; and that an extensive and methodical system of colonization should be organized by govern-

2 B 2                                                             ment,

ment, having for its object to encourage and facilitate the application of the surplus capital and labour of the British isles in the cultivation of those provinces, as the means of producing food, not only for the plentiful subsistence of the emigrants themselves, but also of that part of our remaining population, which, possessing in their coal and iron mines, skill, machinery, and concentration, superior advantages for many peculiar branches of industry to what are to be met with elsewhere, will be able, by occupying themselves in that manner, and exchanging their produce for food, to obtain, in this *indirect* way, a far greater abundance of it, for the same expenditure of labour and capital, than *directly*, by the cultivation of our inferior soils at home.

This, it will be observed, is a very different proposition from the general freedom of trade in agricultural produce urged by that class of writers who are loudest in their opposition to the corn-law. They boldly assert, that any restrictions on commercial intercourse are impolitic ; and, in this respect, they would put a colony and a foreign country on the same footing. It is, on the contrary, because we think a colony is, or may be made, the very opposite, in every respect, to a foreign country—may be incorporated so completely with the parent state, as to form a part of the same in all but its geography—that we are anxious to see our colonial not merely distinguished from our foreign commerce, by a comparative relaxation of duties, but placed on the same footing with our home trade. We need not now enter at large upon the question of the merits or demerits of the protective system. On another occasion, perhaps, we may take it as our theme, and examine the arguments of those, who, on no very stable assumptions, as it appears to us, contend for the unqualified freedom of foreign trade. Our object at present is, to show the advantage of removing entirely from the category of foreign countries, some, at least, of our colonies,—and *thus* obtaining all the advantages derivable from an additional command of fertile land, securing a rise in the *real* wages of our labourers, and in the profits of our capitalists, and rendering the improvements that are, and have for years past been daily occurring in the means of production, agricultural and manufacturing, what they ought to be, and what, but for the mismanagement we have pointed out, they would have always necessarily been, a source of continually increasing improvement in the condition and means of enjoyment of every class of society.

Now, what is actually the condition of the bulk of the population of the British isles, the labouring class, agricultural and manufacturing?—there is no dearth of information on this subject. If little has been yet done to ameliorate their situation, we must

do

do our legislators the justice to declare, that no pains have been spared by them to investigate its nature. Within the last twelve or thirteen years, nearly as many parliamentary committees have sat upon subjects closely connected with this great question; the result of their laboured inquiries is contained in as many voluminous reports; and this result, as far as it affects our topic, may be summed up, alas! in few words. In *Ireland*,—but we will not allow ourselves to recur to that heart-rending and painfully exciting subject,—on a former occasion we drew from the Report of the last Committee on the Irish Poor, the picture of their misery, a misery which, since that time, has been aggravated, as far as it was capable of aggravation, by one of those almost periodical visitations of famine to which the neglected population of that noble country are, under their present system of mismanagement, exposed. We exhibited, too, the obvious, easy, and equitable remedy for this misery, the establishment, namely, of a law of relief; the affording to the Irish peasant some security from being starved in the midst of an abundance which his own labour has created, but which *the law* now permits the owner of the soil to appropriate unconditionally, leaving its famishing producers to be maintained upon *English* charity!

It appears from the reports to which we have alluded, that, in *England*, the agricultural labourer receives, in general, in requital for his labour, a sum totally inadequate to maintain his family, if he have one, and consequently his wages are, by a gross perversion of the poor-law, *supplemented*, throughout the greater part of the kingdom, from the parish rates. The *labourer* is thus necessarily, and in spite of all the struggles he may make to avoid it, in spite too of his full employment in an industrious occupation for the benefit of a private individual, forced to become a *pauper*. He is driven to attend at the parish pay-table for the scanty pittance surlily doled out to him there, upon a scale of relief calculated barely to keep him and his children on bread alone. From 2*d*. to 3½*d*. a-day to each individual in a family, is, it appears, the usual allowance in some of the southern counties; and, *for this*, hard labour, and the degradation of pauperism, are *both* to be incurred, and, *out of this*, lodging, clothing, washing, fuel, and medicine, as well as food, are to be provided!

Are the manufacturing labourers in much better circumstances? In some districts, and during temporary spirts of trade, a part of them receive comparatively high wages; but these halcyon days are succeeded by long intervals of depression, and some classes, as the hand-loom weavers, both in cloth and cotton, whose numbers are very large, have, for many years past, experienced no such fits of prosperity, but endure great and permanent distress,

their

their wages undergoing continual successive reductions, through the increasing competition of the steam-engine. They, too, are wholly unable to maintain themselves without parochial aid, and are thus brought down to the same forlorn level which we have described as the lot of the agricultural labourers—that level of pauperism which the law humanely provides to stop their descent in the ladder of misery, when it enacts that they shall not absolutely starve.

But the case is not much better with the mechanics. Those, at least, who have seen persons of this description crowding for relief, every winter, to the vestries of country parishes, well know that a large number of this class of labourers likewise are in equal distress and redundancy, and driven equally to compete with one another for a scanty and precarious livelihood.

Now let us turn to the condition in which these individuals may be placed by the expenditure of *five* pounds, at the utmost, per head, in transporting them to North America, and especially to Upper Canada. The extracts from letters received from pauper-emigrants, lately exported from some parishes in the west of England, printed in a volume named at the head of this paper, exhibit the reverse of the sad picture we have just been contemplating, drawn by the hand of untaught simplicity, but with the warmth of real feeling, and the force of unsophisticated truth. In those interesting letters we may trace the immense change effected in the common labourer, who, only a few months back, was maintained in his native country on parish pay, in unwilling idleness, if not in crime, a burden to his neighbours, and in a state of suffering himself, by his removal to the colony, at the trifling expense we have mentioned. We see him, immediately on his landing, eagerly hired by a master, in whose house he lives, and *at whose table* he is boarded, upon ‘ beef, mutton, pork, vegetables, pyes, puddings,’ the best, in short, of everything, and from whom he receives, into the bargain, money-wages sufficient to enable him, if he chooses, *at the end of a summer's work, to purchase and stock a farm of his own!* There, a family of children, instead of a reproach and a burden, is a blessing, a credit, and a source of profit. The expressions scattered through these letters of joy and thankfulness to God, and to those friends who assisted them to emigrate, for so great a change in their condition, are truly affecting ; as are also their touching, though homely allusions, to the sufferings from which they have escaped, but which are still endured by their friends and fellow-labourers at home, and their regret that these are not enjoying the same blessed improvement with themselves. But we will let the good folks speak for themselves, premising, that the letters are from emigrants who went
out

out from the parish of Corsley, in the county of Wilts, in the spring of 1830, the greater part of the expense of their passage being paid by the parish :—

'From W. Clements (day-labourer, of Corsley, Wilts), dated Port Talbot, Upper Canada, Oct. 10, 1830.

'My dear Father,—I thank God I am got to the land of liberty and plenty. I arrived here on the 9th of July. I had not a single shilling left when I got here. But I met with good friends that took me in, and I went to work at 6s. per day, and my board, on to this day. And now I am going to work on my own farm of 50 acres, which I bought at 55l., and I have 5 years to pay it in. I have bought me a cow and 5 pigs. And I have sowed 4½ acres of wheat, and I have 2 more to sow. I am going to build me a house this fall, if I live. And if I had staid at Corsley I never should have had nothing. I like the country very much. I am at liberty to shoot turkeys, quail, pigeon, and all kinds of game which I have in my backwood. I have also a sugar bush, that will make me a ton of sugar yearly. The timber is very fine. We sow but one bushel of wheat to an acre, and the increase is about 50. One single grain will bring from 30 to 60 ears. The land in general is black peat and sandy loam. My wife and two sons is all well and happy, and thankful that they are arrived over safe ; and wish father and mother, and all the family, were as well provided for as we be. *If the labouring men did but know the value of their strength, they would never abide contented in the old country.* Cows are worth from 50s. to 3l. 10s. Sheep, large and fat, is worth 10s. 6d. Oxen, from 5l. to 6l. No poor-rate, no taxes, no overseer, no beggars. The wheat that is left in the fields would keep a whole parish. Several of them that came out with us are near, Joseph Silcox within 2 miles, &c.'—pp. 14, 15.

'From James Treasure (shoemaker), Yarmouth, U. C. August 9, 1830.

'All who came over with us like the country very well. There is not a doubt but all who are willing to work would get a plenty, and good pay. Mechanics, they say, are wanted very bad. I have no doubt, but after we are a little more settled, we shall be able to save 30s. a-week. The people here wonder that more do not come. We were told at New York, that 7000 had landed there in about four or five weeks, and 200 families were landed at this creek this summer ; but they are all lost like a drop in a bucket. We are a great deal better, and comfortabler than we expected to be in so short a time. I want to advise you all to come, for here we are all free from anxiety as to getting on. I should be happy to hear that two or three thousand was coming from Frome. It would be the best thing in the world for them. Here would be plenty for them to do, and plenty to eat and drink. In this there is no mistake. I seem now to want to tell this, that, and the other story, about men who came here without a single shilling, but have now good farms of their own, but they would be too numerous. I can only say, that all the good accounts I have heard of America, I now believe to be correct, &c.'—pp. 16, 17.

'From

' From Phillip Annett (day-labourer, of Corsley), Port Talbot, U. C.
May 24th, 1830.

' I think you was better sell your house, and get a little of the
parish, and come to Canada whilst you have a chance. If you don't
come soon it is likely you will starve, and if you don't, your children
will; whilst if you was to come hither with your family, any one would
be glad to take 1 or 2 of them and keep them as their own children,
until of age, and then give them 100 acres of land and some stock
besides. I was agreeably surprised when I came here to see what
a fine country it was. It being excellent land, bearing crops of
wheat and other corn for 20 or 30 years without any dung. Here
you have no rent to pay, no poor-rates, and scarcely any taxes.
Here you can raise every thing of your own that you want to make
use of in your family. You can make your own soap, candles, sugar,
treacle, and vinegar, without paying any duty. Clothing is as cheap
as in England. Wages is high. A man can get two bushels of
wheat for a day's work in harvest time. We have plenty of fruit
here, such as plumbs and grapes, and peaches. Cyder is sold at 5s.
per barrel; it is a land of liberty and plenty. I think no Englishman
can do better than come as soon as possible, if it cost them every
farthing they have, for I would rather be so here, than in England
with 100l. in my pocket. Robert can come, and get a good farm here
in the course of 3 or 4 years at shoemaking, I think he could earn
and save beside keeping himself, 50l. a-year. I am sure he could.
It grieves me concerning you in England, in poverty and hard labour.
A man can earn enough in 3 days to last him all the week. I am
satisfied with the country, and so is Luesa, for we are so much respected here as any of our neighbours, and so would you if you come,
&c.'—pp. 17, 18.

' James Watts, (day-labourer of Corsley) Lancaster, U.C. Oct. 28, 1830.

' We had a middling good passage, and got to Quebec the 6th day
of June, then I set out for Upper Canada to the above place, where I
have been ever since, working at making roads at 8 dollars a month,
or 1l. 16s. of your money (besides board). Will. Singer and Thomas
Singer are along with me upon the same wages, but William Aylsbury left this place on purpose to go home to his wife and family.
Whether he will get home I don't know, but if he should, you will
get all the news better than I can write. As far as I can learn and
as far as I have seen, it is a good country, for any industrious man
coming to this country; and if he can bring some money he will get
land upon very reasonable terms, and in the course of a few years may
make a very comfortable living.'

The William Aylsbury mentioned in this letter, it appears, returned last winter to his parish, Corsley, where he had left his wife
and children. His intention was to persuade them to return with
him, which the wife, however, refuses to do. This man saved a
sum

sum of money (nearly 7*l.*) out of his summer's wages, on the roads in Upper Canada, sufficient to pay all his expenses home: a fact which speaks strongly for the possibility of obtaining repayment of the costs of emigration, indirectly out of the labourer's earnings in the colony.

' From Thomas Hunt, (day-labourer of Chapmanslade in the parish of Corsley), dated Nelson, U. C. Nov. 14th, 1830.

' We are in a good country for poor folks ; we have plenty of good fire and grog. Wheat 4*s.* per bushel, good boiling peas 3*s. 6d.* Rye 3*s.* Buck wheat 2*s. 6d.* Indian corn 2*s. 6d.* Oats 2*s.* Potatoes 1*s. 3d.* Rum 10*d.* per quart. Good whiskey 7½*d.* Brandy 9*d.* per quart. Port Wine 1*s. 3d.* Tea 3*s. 6d.* per pound. We make our own sugar, our own soap, candles, and bake good light bread. Beef and mutton 2*d.* per pound, &c. Fat geese 1*s. 6d.* Best fowls 1*s. 3d.* per couple. Wages 3*l.* per month and our keep. We dine with our masters. Women 2*s. 6d.* a day and good keep. Good apples 1*s.* per bushel, &c. The price of land is about 1*l.* per acre near the roads, some way back it is cheaper. No poor-rates, nor taxes of any consequence. I see in the paper great lamentations for our departure from Chapmanslade. *More need to rejoice.** We three brothers have bought 200 acres of land at 12*s. 6d.* per acre. We have paid 25*l.*, and have 100*l.* to pay in five years, that is, 20*l.* a year, between three, that is 6*l.* 13*s.* 4*d.* each. It is in Nelson, District of Gore, about five miles from Street, with a pretty good road to our lot. Only nine miles to lake Ontario, a good sale for all grain. A grist mill and a saw mill within 25 chains, which is a great advantage. A good river runs right through our lot of land, and good springs rise on it. We shall never want for water nor timber. We have several adjoining houses, chiefly English people. We can raise up a good house in a little while at little expense. We have thousands of tons of timber, and good stone for building. · It is called the healthiest place in Upper Canada. We have no sickness since we have been here. Stouter than we was in England. Sarah wishes to see all her friends here. We expect to clear 20 acres by next harvest. We cut the trees about 3 feet above ground, and put fire to it, and burn it root and branch. We are about 700 miles from Quebec. That is but little here. Sarah Hunt and her five children is all well ; she was confined on the river St. Lawrence. She had a very good time. She and all is very stout, never wishing to return to England, but rather all friends was here, for here is plenty of work, and plenty to eat and drink. *Thank God*

---

* This is the emigrant's pithy reproof of the maudlin sentimentalities of those persons who so pathetically deprecate the ' tearing away of our peasantry from their homes—the snapping asunder the ties of country, kindred, &c.,' and who wax indignant at what they call ' the atrocious cruelty ' of the advocates of emigration. Mighty cruelty, to be sure, the assisting families, whose labour will not keep them from pauperism and misery in this country, to remove to another part of the British dominions, where they may command all the comforts and many of the luxuries of life, and look forward to still higher prospects. Great cause of grief and lamentation this ! ' More need to rejoice,' as Thomas Hunt says.

*we*

*we are here. We all wish that our fathers, and mothers, and brothers, and sisters was here, for here is plenty of room for all there is in England.* They that think to work may do well. But if our fathers and mothers was here, they should never be obliged to do a hard day's work, for we would keep them without work if they were not able. But if any of you should come, they must make up their minds not to be faint-hearted. You may expect rocking, but I don't fear the raging seas. For more may come as safe as we, for the God that rules the land rules the sea. There is some come this year turned back before they knew whether 'tis good or bad. But I thank my God that we are here. Thomas Hunt, James Hunt, Jeremiah Hunt.'

'From William Snelgrove (day-labourer of Corsley), Dundas, U. C. Sept. 3d, 1830.

' Dear Friends,—This comes with my kind love to you, hoping it will find you in good health, as it leaves us at present. Thanks be to God for it. Health is a beautiful thing ; and it depends upon God alone to give it. Was it in the hands of man, health would decline, as many other things have in England, as labour and victualling, which, if the good God give us our health, is as plentifully with us as the scarcity is with you. We have plenty of good beef, and mutton, and pork, and flour, fish, fowl, and butter ; and I'm happy to state that by one day's work, a man can supply himself with sufficient of all these necessaries for 3 days. *You have a good many cold bellies to go to bed with, I know, or things is greatly altered from the state that it was when I was with you. But if you were with us, if you liked, for three half-pence your belly would be so warm that you would not know the way to bed.* With regard to work, harvest work is one dollar a day and board, other work is three-fourths of a dollar and a pint of whiskey. Wheat is from 3s. 9d. to 5s. per bushel. Butcher's meat 2d. to 3d. per lb. Cousin Henry, you may depend that all is here said is true, so that you see here is all the chance in the world for a poor man to live, &c.'

The accounts of the change in the condition of the emigrant weavers, shoemakers, brickmakers, and other mechanics and artisans, are equally striking and delightful. Delightful we say, indeed, for what a resource is here opened to us in our difficulties, —what a well-spring of joy and hope is found to bubble up in the wilderness for the relief of our parched and thirsty population. Think of the change to a man from parish allowance, just enough to keep life in himself and his family upon a potato diet, to one of meat three times a day, tea, bread, butter, vegetables, with whiskey, brandy, and tobacco *ad libitum*, and wages into the bargain, out of which he may put by from 30l. to 50l. per annum, and with this sum may purchase, if he think fit, the fee-simple of a rich farm of twice as many acres! And what is to prevent more, many more, nay the *whole* of our redundant population, from being removed to such an earthly paradise? Is it the trifling cost
of

of their conveyance thither—the 3*l*. or 4*l*. per head which must be laid out to remove a human being—a fellow-subject—ay, one whose *rights* to the regard and paternal care of the common government are as sacred and as strong as those of the highest and wealthiest of the land—to remove him from a situation of great and undeserved suffering, which he cannot of himself escape, to one where it will be in his power to live, and bring up a family in industry, plenty, independence, and virtue,—a life than which there is none happier under the face of heaven?

How cheaply, then, may we now purchase the pleasure of making the happiness of a fellow-creature! Here is a new and poignant luxury for our epicurean felicity-hunters. For *twenty pounds* a whole family may be removed from the depths of misery to a state of certain and permanent prosperity,—as far as anything human is certain and permanent—themselves and their descendants! That the judicious benevolence of our nobles and wealthy landowners has already, indeed, begun to take this direction, we are pleased to perceive, from the little tract we have just quoted, as well as from other sources. We have heard with pleasure that there is a prospect of the formation of an Emigration Society, having for its charitable object to assist the unemployed poor to transfer themselves to the colonies. But individual benevolence is not enough—is not the proper mode of effecting the end in view. Is there no party whose express duty it is to take whatever available steps present themselves, for mitigating the distress and ameliorating the circumstances of our people? Is *the government* of a country justifiable in remaining inactive, while its labouring population is reduced to extreme want, and a practicable, nay an easy and simple and all-effectual remedy is in its power? Even if the paltry expense we have mentioned as the average cost of emigration to Canada were necessarily a sacrifice, a complete loss, to the party providing it, surely it would be a most legitimate, most justifiable application of the national resources. The government of this country expends upwards of fifty millions a year in providing for the necessities of the state. But is there any one end of government more necessary, any one interest of society more pressing, than the protection of the mass of the people from want, and the degradation and wretchedness of a life of pauperism? If the expenditure of *a million or two* yearly, in facilitating the emigration of our surplus labourers, could accomplish this great object, will any one say it would not be cheaply purchased, or that the money were not as well laid out on this, as on any one of the various items of the national expenditure? Nothing, however, can be easier, than to show that, in a purely pecuniary point of view, such an outlay would be a wise measure of economy, a saving of expenses, other-

wise

wise unavoidable and of far greater amount, both to the nation at large, and to the particular parishes who are, by law in Britain, and where not by law, as in Ireland, ( *proh pudor !* ) yet by the compulsion of charity and *prudence,* obliged to support this excess of the labouring population in unproductive inactivity.  But even this is not all.  If we look to the small amount of the necessary expense of emigration, as compared with the immense *profits* resulting from it, we shall see that it cannot be difficult to devise means of obtaining the reimbursement of that expense out of those profits. The great difference between the value of a labourer, as an instrument of production, here and in the colonies, is represented by, and indeed, consists of the difference between his wages here and there.  It is, therefore, out of this difference, out of the increase of wages which a labourer gains by his removal from this country to the colony, that the cost of his removal should in perfect equity be taken.  There can be no reasonable ground whatever, for objecting to make the labourer himself responsible for the repayment from his increased wages, of the necessary expense of the process by which alone he has been enabled to obtain them.  And the labourers themselves will, without doubt, see the justice of this, and willingly consent to it, especially as the deduction from their wages required for this purpose, will bear but a small proportion to the total increase consequent on their removal.  It is not, however, from the emigrants themselves, that we would recommend, in all cases, the collection of these payments, which might be found irksome in practice, but from their employers in the first instance, so long as they remain in the condition of labourers.

The plan which, on these grounds, we would propose is, that labourers wishing to emigrate by aid of government, should enter into a contract to serve the colonial government, or any employers to whom they may be transferred by that government, for a term, say of three or four years, if the expenses of their passage are not sooner repaid, and for a stipulated rate of money-wages, beyond their board, calculated at not more than one-half the wages current in the colony.  The labourers, on their arrival, would be registered at the proper office, the cost of their passage being debited to them individually, and then allowed to engage with any employers who may be willing to hire them *as yearly servants,* and undertake to pay certain monthly instalments, towards liquidating the debt due by the labourer to government.  The scale of repayment might b : something as follows :—

6*l.* per annum, or 10*s.* per month, for every single male above fifteen years.

9*l.*      ,,      or 15*s.* per month, for a man and wife.

3*l.*      ,,      or 5*s.* mouthly, for every unmarried female or male under fifteen years.

The

The competition of the masters would naturally induce them to engage each labourer at the current wages of the colony *minus* this monthly payment to government, a deduction which the labourer will hardly feel, in a country where wages are from 40s. to 60s. per month, besides board; and which he will scarcely grudge, knowing that it goes to liquidate a debt justly due by him to government, for the cost of his removal from a state of want in the mother country, to one of full employment at comparatively high wages in the colony. He would have the prospect of being free, at the end of a year or two at farthest, even from this engagement. He should also be encouraged to pay off the debt himself, at a still earlier period, from the savings of his wages, by a liberal remission of interest.

The master should be bound not to discharge his labourer without the sanction of the nearest justice of peace or government agent, whether at the end of the yearly hiring or before, and the labourer should be bound by his contract to put himself, whenever discharged, at the disposal of the same officer. When not hired, the labourers would be employed, according to the terms of their contract, on the government roads and other works, and distributed through the colony for this purpose. The comparatively low rate of wages they would receive in this employment would make them extremely desirous of entering into the service of private individuals, and dispose them to exert themselves to please their masters and retain their situations. The English law of hiring and service introduced into the colonies, if, as we believe, it is not already in force there, would be sufficient to enforce the fulfilment of the contract by both servant and master, with the addition of such regulations as may be required for the contract of the latter with the government on hiring one of the emigrant labourers. It was the opinion, indeed, of Commissioners Bigge and Colebrook, as given to the Emigration Committee in 1826,—

' that the law at present in force in the colonies would be fully effectual for securing the fulfilment of such contracts, which they strongly recommend, as a means of obtaining repayment of the expenses of emigration that can be attended with neither inconvenience or difficulty to the government, nor with any hardship to the emigrant labourers.'—*Report of Emigration Committee,* 1826.

On a former occasion, in proposing the adoption of a system of colonization on this principle, we spoke of it as applicable solely to our Australian colonies and the Cape, and not to those of North America, owing to the contiguity to the latter of the United States, into which labourers might pass in order to void their contracts, and escape the repayment of their debt to government in any shape. This circumstance we still consider an effectual

tual bar to the re-imbursement of the costs of emigration out of the wages of the emigrants, as far as those colonies are concerned. But when we recollect the trifling comparative expense of the passage across the Atlantic, averaging, in all probability, under judicious and systematic arrangements, not above 3*l.* per head*, while that to New South Wales or Van Diemen's Land amounts to 12*l.*, we are of opinion that *other* resources are at the disposal of government fully sufficient to cover this expense.

We think it may be fairly presumed that the introduction of every able-bodied labourer will occasion the purchase, within a moderate lapse of time, of at least fifty acres of land, whether by himself or by a capitalist-settler desirous of employing him, but who, without the certainty of obtaining labourers, would not make such purchase. The sale of these fifty acres by government, at but the *minimum* price of 5*s.* per acre, will bring in a sum of 12*l.* 10*s.*, quite enough to cover the cost of importing the labourer and his wife, with interest on the advance up to the time of payment of the purchase-money; and the demand which the family of this couple will eventually occasion remains to cover whatever deficiencies may occur through casualties.

But it will be said that the government is not by any means the only party who have lands in the market for sale. The most profuse grants have been made within a few years past to individuals and companies. Upwards of three millions of acres have been in this way disposed of in our North American colonies, the owners of which have an equal chance with the government of profiting by whatever demand for land the increased importation of emigrant labourers may occasion. And if it were impossible to obviate this objection, we think, as we have formerly said in discussing the scheme of the Colonization Society, it would be fatal to the proposal of obtaining repayment of the cost of emigration by the sale of land. But there is a simple mode of preserving to government a part, at least, of the additional value which the waste lands in the hands of companies or private individuals must acquire in consequence of the importation by government of emigrant labourers. We think this might be easily, and with perfect equity, accomplished by a moderate *tax on the sale of waste land* in the colony. This, in fact, is the only step left for redeeming the error of former colonial administrations, in putting such immense tracts out of the power of government; it would place the government, and those who have obtained these large grants,

---

* Mr. Richards, the gentleman employed by government to ascertain, by personal examination, the facilities to emigration offered by our North American colonies, estimates the price of conveyance to Quebec (including provisions) at from 3*l.* 5*s.* to 4*l.* 15*s.* for adults, and one-half for children.

not

not for cultivation, but on speculation for re-sale, on something like an equal footing. Nor can it be objected to by the latter as a hardship, much less as an injustice, so long as the proceeds of the tax are strictly expended in the importation of emigrants, which must cause a demand for, and a rise in, the value of land fully proportionate to the tax, and proceeding from a cause which the owners of these grants could not have contemplated at the time of their original contract with government.

Upon the strength of the income to be derived from these resources, namely, the sale of government lands at an upset price of 5s. per acre, and a moderate tax on the sale of all other lands, government might proceed to expend any sum which may be required for introducing emigrant labour to our North American colonies, with a certainty of the expense being ultimately repaid by the due appropriation to that purpose of these two funds. It must be remembered that the revenue arising from the sale of land will increase in a rapid ratio as the country becomes further settled, and its population grows by birth and immigration together. The government of the United States derives an annual revenue of *about a million sterling* from this source ; and under the impulse which a plentiful and regular supply of labour would give to the cultivation of our colonies by British capitalists, there can be little doubt that the process would go on to the full as rapidly there as in the neighbouring states. Hence we do not hesitate to recommend that the operation should be *commenced* on a large scale, it being certain that the means of eventual repayment will increase in proportion to the liberality and spirit with which colonization is from the first encouraged.

We have abstained from discussing the plans for locating labourers immediately upon land at the cost of government, which was the particular mode of emigration recommended by Sir Robert Wilmot Horton, because we conceive it to be at present generally recognised, that so long as private capitalists are to be found in the colonies willing to *hire labourers* at high wages, government should confine itself to supplying their demand by merely undertaking the transport of the labourer from this country to the spot where he is wanted. The establishment of the labourer as a settler is treble the expense of his mere passage, is unnecessary, and will be far better accomplished by the man himself, if he has a taste for it, out of the savings of his wages, in the course of a year or two's service in his accustomed and proper capacity of a labourer, during which he is learning, what he arrives totally ignorant of, the business of ' wilderness-farming' and the habits of the country, both indispensable for his success as a ' settler.'

Were this plan to be acted upon, government would, of course,
only

only remove gratuitously those labourers who were proved to be destitute of the means of supporting themselves here, or of paying their own passage to the colony; no doubt many to whom assistance was refused, through their not being in this predicament, would, as now, emigrate upon their own resources; and it should be made a part of the duty of the agents appointed by government in the colonies to assist these persons, when they arrive at the ports of debarkation in a state of destitution,—to superintend their distribution through the colony to those points where labour is most wanted, and employ on public works those among them who, after these precautions, may be unable immediately to procure other employment. Public provision should likewise be made for widows, orphans, the sick, and the crippled. In the United States, every town has a poor-house appropriated for the relief of such persons, and supported by the township; nor can any state be fairly designated as civilized and Christian where no such refuge is provided for those whom casualty has reduced to destitution.

We proceed to consider the objections we have been able to meet with. The first, and that most generally advanced, is, the presumed inadequacy of the remedy to meet the evil; that it will be hopeless to get rid of our actual and constantly accruing redundancy, except at an outlay of capital, such as cannot be spared. Now, to this it might be sufficient to answer, that a remedy in a desperate case is not the less worth taking, though it may not be capable of effecting a perfect cure, but only materially mitigate the disorder. But we have no scruple in declaring our opinion that such a permanent scheme of colonization might be carried into execution by government as would effectually take off our actual redundancy within a few years, and wholly prevent it for the future; and this not only at no sacrifice to this country, but to her infinite profit, and to the vast increase of her resources. In the first place, it should be remembered that a small excess of labourers will make itself felt in a grievous reduction of wages. The actual numerical excess is much smaller than is usually supposed, and will no doubt be greatly diminished by certain improvements that cannot be much longer delayed in the internal economy of the empire, to which we shall presently advert, and which must be expected to give a considerable stimulus to the employment of labour. Secondly,—It is a common but a gross mistake to imagine that the whole annual increase of our population, which exceeds three hundred thousand individuals, must be annually exported in order to prevent any future redundancy. This is to suppose that the resources of the country for maintaining its inhabitants are to remain stationary! It is forgotten that they are continually increasing

creasing at the same time with the population, though not quite in an equal ratio, and that the annual addition to the *redundancy* of the latter consists merely of that fractional part of the annual increase by which it exceeds the contemporary increase of the means of employment. Thirdly,—It has been fairly shown, upon a calculation which we have not seen impugned, that by a judicious selection of young couples in the prime of life only, for emigration, as considerable a reduction can be made in the rate of increase at home, as if eight times the number were taken promiscuously at all ages.\* And, fourthly,—It must be recollected that the new demand upon the industry of our manufacturers, which the exported labourers will themselves create as soon as they get out, and the very expenditure of capital in taking them out (upon our shipping, stores, &c.) will yet further diminish the redundancy of unemployed labour at home.

A second objection is, that the removal of capital from this country, whether it be employed in transporting emigrants to the colonies or in cultivating their soils, would diminish, *pro tanto*, the means of employing the remainder of our population at home, whose condition could therefore be in no degree bettered. In the first place, however, it is notorious that monied capital is in this country in as complete a state of plethora as labour; and that the lowness of profit, and the difficulty of employing it to advantage, both check the accumulation of capital, and drive much of that which is already accumulated into foreign investments. The demand that would be created for capital in England by the opening of a profitable avenue for its employment in the colonies, would in no degree be supplied from that which is already engaged in the employment of labour in any shape here. It would flow back from its present engagement abroad, particularly from the foreign funds, which, through the general character of the European stock-market, form as ready a receptacle as our own for the deposit of spare monied capital when no opportunity is afforded for its active occupation. If the vacuum were not filled up in this way, it would at all events be almost immediately supplied by *new accumulations,* the increase of which, through the known *elasticity* of capital, is accelerated by the opening of any fresh prospect for its profitable employment. But even if this were not thought enough, it would be easy to show that the capital which would be profitably employed in carrying out emigrants would amount to but a very few years' purchase of the sum now annually

---

\* Statement of the Principles and Objects of the National Colonization Society. Ridgway. 1830.

*wasted*

*wasted* in their maintenance here in idle and unproductive pauperism.

In fact, however, the result of this measure would be but a momentary consumption, followed speedily by the rapid *creation* of capital,—of *that kind* of capital which is alone at present deficient, and causes, by its deficiency, the redundancy of all other kinds,—namely, of *food,* the grand desideratum—the capital of capitals—whose relative scarcity, by raising the money wages of labour in this country, (though without improving the circumstances of the labourer,) renders it unprofitable to employ him in utilizing the other classes of capital. The rapid increase of this kind of capital is a necessary consequence of the fertility of the soil on which the expenditure would take place, and which is known to produce at least four times the necessary subsistence of the labourers who cultivate it.

A third class of objectors are afraid, that, however abundantly the emigrants might raise corn and other raw produce upon their settlements in the colonies, it would not be possible for them to turn this into *money,* wherewith to repay to government the cost of their emigration. It is, however, *not money, but raw produce,* that we stand in need of in this country. The object of the scheme we are advocating, is quite as much to create an addition to our supplies of corn and other raw agricultural produce from the colonies, in requital of the labour of our ill-fed manufacturing population, as to remove the excess of our agricultural population. The coin in which alone the emigrants will be able to pay us, is exactly that which it is most desirable for us to receive.

The last objection which remains to be noticed, is, that the colonies will not take the numbers we have to dispose of; that though they may be beneficially irrigated by the stream of emigration, they are liable to be injuriously inundated by too large an overflow. We have shown that the numbers which it is generally supposed desirable to remove, are very greatly overestimated: let us now see what space there is for their reception. Those of our dependencies which are open to us for this purpose, are the provinces of Nova Scotia, New Brunswick, Cape Breton, Prince Edward's Island, Newfoundland, and Upper and Lower Canada, in North America; the Cape, the eastern as well as the western coast of New South Wales, and Van Diemen's Land. We have Mr. Uniacke's opinion given before the Committee of 1827, that Nova Scotia alone could at that period absorb from fifteen to twenty thousand emigrants annually. If we suppose New Brunswick, Cape Breton, Newfoundland, and Prince Edward's Island, each to take only half as many, and the Canadas but

but twice that number,\* it will appear that from seventy-five to one hundred thousand might be annually disposed of in our North American colonies; and it is surely not too much to calculate that the Cape, with all our Australian settlements, would provide for the employment of as many more; making in all from one hundred and fifty to two hundred thousand emigrants for whom room may be found,—a larger number, perhaps, than we should find it desirable to remove in any one year. We are, indeed, told that the emigration which is already spontaneously taking place, though not reaching to that extent, produces great inconveniences at the places where the new-comers disembark. No doubt it does. But because the ports of Quebec and Montreal are molested by crowds of pennyless and famishing wanderers, landed from speculating passage-vessels, (no better mode of conveyance being provided for them,) and destitute of the means of finding their way up to the more distant parts of the colony, where they would meet with instant employment, is there any reason for presuming that similar results would follow from the landing of even ten times the present number, under the care and direction of public agents, who would take charge of and distribute them up the country wherever labourers were most wanted, or employ them on the government roads, canals, and clearings, until such opportunity presented itself?

There exists, indeed, a simple test, by which it may be seen at any time whether the immigration into a colony is really going too far or not—in the *current rates of wages.* Until these are reduced by the competition of immigrants to something like the wages of the mother-country, we may be sure that the process which has for its object to bring the demand and supply of labour in the two countries to a level, is not proceeding too fast. At this moment, when the wages of a common day-labourer average, in all the colonies we have enumerated, 4s. 6d. a day, and those of a mechanic 9s.,—which, reckoned in provisions, according to their prices there and here, is equivalent to three times that sum in England, or about *ten* times the real wages of the mechanics and labourers of this country, and more than *twenty* times the wages of Ireland,—it is preposterous to talk of the imminent or probable risk of over-stocking the labour-market of those colonies by any number of emigrants we can contemplate pouring into them.

It is not merely in cultivation that labour is required, but for

---

\* That these assumptions are by much too moderate is proved by the fact, for which we have the best authority, that during the last summer upwards of fifty thousand emigrants landed at Quebec and Montreal alone, and have been wholly *absorbed* (that is, taken into employment through the country) without perceptibly diminishing the eager demand for labourers in both Upper and Lower Canada, or reducing the high current rate of wages.

clearing

clearing land of its timber, building houses, barns, fences, &c., and making roads and other communications. As the population of a newly-settled district increases, the division of labour proceeds, and the several trades establish themselves; and, with the advance of its wealth, the wants of the inhabitants become enlarged, and give occasion to the employment of additional labour in their gratification. We do not, in truth, perceive what possible limit there is, other than the extent of fertile soil, to the numbers which a country situated like Canada may be brought to receive, so that they are introduced with due preparation, and distributed in a methodical manner, and on the supposition of her surplus agricultural produce being received free of duty here. At least, it is evident that until the mother country is fully supplied with food, and the real wages of her labouring class consequently brought to approach to the high level of those which indicate the value of labour in her colonies, it will continue to be profitable to her to employ her surplus labour on soils, though distant, which produce fourfold the consumption of the cultivators, and to the colonies to receive the influx of that labour, and to exchange its produce for that of her manufacturers.

We are writing in ignorance of the intentions of government as to the re-introduction of the Emigration Bill of last year. We do, however, sincerely trust that this valuable measure will not be allowed to fall to the ground, but be persisted in and passed in the present session of Parliament, in time to enable parishes to avail themselves of its provisions for removing a part of their surplus labour to the Canadas in the spring of 1832. The coldness with which the bill was received in the House of Commons, and the partial opposition it met with from some landowners, we have always attributed to the unaccountably high calculation made by Lord Howick, in his introductory speech, of the expense of sending out a labourer's family: this he reckoned at about 57*l.* Now Mr. Richards's estimate, and it is confirmed by many facts within our knowledge, is but 3*l.* per head for adults, and half for children, that is, 10*l.* 10*s.* for a family of five. This is the expense of the voyage only (including provisions), and we do not see the necessity of making any further allowance, since every able-bodied man may be *profitably* employed at fair wages by the government, from the moment of his landing, until engaged by some private employer. But add 30*s.* for the expense of taking care, for a short time, of the family on that side the water, the total will then be 12*l.*, and this sum may be repaid to government by the man's parish, with interest, in annual instalments of 3*l.* only for five years—being an immediate saving to the parish of from three-fourths to nine-tenths

of

of the actual cost of this pauper family, and, after five years, of the whole! If such a boon as *this* were held out by the bill to the owners and occupiers of land, there need be no fears of its refusal by *them ;* and we have too good an opinion of the enlightened and benevolent persons who advocate the employment of our poor in this country, to suppose that any predilection for their own plans will lead them to oppose the giving at least a fair trial to a measure having the same ultimate object in view, and which will work in perfect harmony alongside of their own. We have all along done our best to promote their views also; indeed Lord Braybrooke gives us the credit of having originally put the scheme of cottage allotments into the heads of most that have of late years been trying it. Let parishes and the poor, we say now as we have for years been saying, have the choice of both home and foreign colonization, and leave it to experience to determine their comparative advantages.

Let us now advert to the remedies usually recommended by writers on political economy for the acknowledged derangement of the equilibrium between the supply and demand of labour. That which has been most prominently brought forward, and is still insisted on by we believe we may say the whole sect, is the inculcating among labourers a prudential foresight, which may induce them to lessen their own numbers by greater abstinence from marriage. But, in the first place, if we could persuade them to endure this privation, the remedy is too slow to be effectual, since a whole generation must elapse before abstinence from marriage, carried to any extent now, could begin to make a sensible difference in the number of adult competitors for employment. In the second place, there is no probability of any persuasions that may be adopted having much influence in opposition to the primary instincts of nature. Stop the increase of population by lectures on prudence! we might as well attempt to dry up the ocean with blotting-paper. But, thirdly, and we might have been content with this argument alone, if the increase *could* be stopped, *why should it,* when by simply removing the surplus of labourers, as fast as it shows itself, to the colonies, they can be placed in a situation to command all the comforts and even the conveniences of life, and the aggregate of human happiness thereby proportionately augmented?

There is another remedy recommended by the author of a little tract called ' The Results of Machinery,' and printed under the superintendence of the Society for the Diffusion of Useful Knowledge, which deserves notice, if only for its singular infelicity. Addressing himself to the labourers, he tells them, that when there is a glut of workmen in the market, and wages inclining to fall,
their

their remedy is ' to go out of the market.' That they may be able to do this, he recommends them to *become capitalists*, to lay by a proportion of their earnings in a Savings' Bank; not for their support in sickness, old age, infirmity—not to enable them to improve their circumstances by employing their savings productively, (which employment indeed would alone give them a just title to the denomination of capitalists,) but that they may, whenever wages fall, withdraw themselves from the market for labour, and live in idleness upon their savings, until the demand for labour rises once more to a fair remuneration.    And *this* is seriously proposed as a complete remedy for the falling off in the demand for labour which follows improvements in machinery! Nothing, however, can be clearer than that if this writer's recommendation were generally adopted, the improvement he expects in wages would never take place. The benefits of machinery are, as he elsewhere himself informs us, that, by effecting a given result with a less expenditure of labour, it releases a certain quantity of labour which may be beneficially employed in producing something else, and this increased general production, by multiplying the number of consumers, will ultimately augment the general demand for labour. But if, as he recommends, the labour that is released by any improvement of machinery which causes a temporary fall of wages be *suspended*, instead of seeking some other channel of employment, production will not increase, (indeed it must be specially with a view to prevent its increase that the suspension of labour is recommended,) and, consequently, the demand for labour will be equally stationary. The workmen who have taken this wise advice may therefore eat up the last sixpence of their hard-earned savings, without seeing the smallest symptom of any reviving demand for their labour; the improved machinery supplying the market by means of the smaller number of hands to about the same extent as before, and at very little less than the same cost; and no cause existing to alter this state of things, or bring about any increase of employment.

But the great remedy of all which is to include those just mentioned, and every other, in the opinion of this writer, and of all the school to which he belongs, is the acquisition of ' *knowledge*' by the labourers.   Now we will not give place to any in sincere anxiety for the general spread of education, moral, religious, and intellectual.   We are anxious for it, because we expect the lower classes to derive from thence, and thence only, an improvement in their tastes and habits, desires elevated above the pot-house and skittle-ground, greater refinement of manners, more peaceful and orderly conduct, a more virtuous course of action, a more rational piety, and higher mental happiness.   It is further to be hoped, that by by giving an elementary education to *all*, the opportunity would be afforded to all upon whom nature had bestowed the fitting qualifications, for advancing themselves, and for adorning or benefiting the world;—that no ' mute inglorious Miltons'—no Raphaels innocent of pen or pencil—no Newtons limited to calculating with their fingers—no Watts or Wedgewoods with undeveloped organs of constructiveness, would, in this case, ' waste their sweetness on the desert air' of their native villages. But here our list of the benefits to be expected from general education is exhausted. We are not such zealots in the cause as to believe or assert that it is to do everything for the poor, or enable them to do everything for themselves. We do not believe that any education which it is possible to give them will ever render the working classes capable of thoroughly understanding, and, consequently, of being trusted with the regulation of their own interests, so as to relieve their superiors from the duty of guiding and protecting them. And we think the instance just given will justify our scruples. Here is a treatise put forth, at a most momentous crisis, by the Society for promoting Useful Knowledge, a society comprehending many of the most learned men of the day, and yet its author and editors fall into and propagate a dangerous error, the very reverse of right, upon a most important practical question relating to the conduct of the labouring class. Is it, we ask, to be expected that the bulk of that class will ever, by any degree of education which we may contemplate for them, be secured from falling into equal errors on equally important questions? And if not, how absurd to hold out the acquisition of knowledge, such knowledge as is likely ever to be within their reach, as the certain means of enabling them, through their own efforts, to effect the improvement of their economical condition!

That improvement must be the work of their superiors—of those who, possessing the leisure which will enable them to give their exclusive attention to such subjects, gifted with more than the average share of intellectual capacity, enjoying more extensive information, and raised above the petty details connected with the subject, are able to bring to its consideration powers of a far higher order than the ordinary mechanic or labourer can ever possess. Individually even these are liable, no doubt, to frequent error, but from their discussions much truth must be elicited, much fallacy eliminated, and the result of their deliberations must, at all events, be a far nearer approximation to real wisdom than the opinions which the labouring classes themselves, however educated, can be expected to form.

The little work to which we have referred has had, we believe, a very considerable sale, and may have been, in spite
of

of its many blemishes, productive of good, by setting before the public, and the working classes especially, the great general advantages of machinery, and the hopelessness and folly of any attempts to check its improvements. But though it is well to endeavour to remove the prejudices of the ignorant against machinery, it will not do to be content with this. Convince, as much as you please, a body of labourers thrown out of work by any improvement in machinery, that the change is productive of a *general* benefit : yet may they not justly continue to urge that, with all its advantages to the public at large, it is a grievous source of suffering to *them*, and that the instinct of self-defence prompts them to prevent or put it down ? What can be replied to this ? Can we hope that all such bodies will exhibit the exemplary patience of the so often quoted Joseph Forster and the other Glasgow hand-loom weavers, who continued struggling *for twenty years* against the competition of the power-loom, losing ground constantly, and becoming daily more and more depressed, till their wages of 20s. a week for easy work had fallen to 7s. only for the most severe and unremitting ? What was it *to them* that the community, or rather the civilized world at large, was all that time profiting by the growing cheapness of cottons, caused as much by the gradual lowering of their wages, as by the improvements in the power-loom ? They were probably told, by some such writer as the one we are reviewing, that ' the results of every improvement in machinery is *ultimately* to increase the demand for labour ;' and, believing it, they resigned themselves to privation and poverty, continuing to hope, ('the hope deferred which maketh the heart sick') that every fresh fall in the amount of their earnings was the last, and would be the herald of the reaction they were led to expect. Who can paint the agonies of that fearful struggle, protracted through an entire generation,—the vain efforts to compensate by redoubled toil for its diminished reward—the transient advantages obtained at intervals by ingenuity or increased exertion,—and the frightful strides with which their giant competitor almost immediately overtook and left them far behind ? But at length a climax of suffering was reached which forbade endurance. Hope was worn out, and the unfortunate weavers threw themselves on the compassion of the legislature, and earnestly petitioned to be assisted to leave a country which denied them bread in requital for their honest industry. Would that we could add that their prayer was granted !

This is a remarkable and most meritorious example of patient forbearance. It is likewise, and must, from the principles of human nature, necessarily be, a *rare* one. If we wish to prevent
sufferings

sufferings like these from producing their *natural* results, namely, combinations, and violent attacks on machinery, it is not enough for us to call such proceedings ignorant and mistaken, and to preach up the *general* advantage of machinery. It is not enough to educate or reason with the sufferers. The highest degree of knowledge in the Glasgow hand-loom weavers could not teach them that *they individually* were not injured by the power-loom, and would not be benefited if they could prevent its use. But it might teach them another lesson—it might lead them to inquire whether they competed on equal terms with their unhungering rival—whether machinery was *taxed* to the same extent as themselves—whether, in a comparative exemption from taxation, an unfair legislative bounty was not given to its employment in preference to theirs—whether the owners of coal-mines and iron mines were not enriching themselves at their expense—whether the right of an individual to subsistence in exchange for his labour is not quite as sacred as the right of property itself? These are questions not touched upon in ' The Results of Machinery.' But they will serve to show that it is not quite enough to prove the *general* advantages of such improvements, to reconcile individuals to changes which press so severely upon *them*. And even if that argument were far more cogent than we can allow it to be, there is a proverb we should do well to bear in mind, ' Ventre affamée n'a point d'oreilles ;' and a fearful couplet, still more to the purpose, has been already sung in our streets—

' Hungry guts and empty purse
May be better, can't be worse.'

Well has it been observed to be an awful state of society, when large masses become musical in this metre.

The true method of preventing attacks on machinery is obviously to prevent the sufferings which tend to make poor men desperate. Appeals to the reason and good feelings of the displaced operatives may be of use as a lenitive ; but in order to get rid of the disease we must attack it in its source ; we must open new channels for the employment of those who are no longer wanted in their accustomed business, and assist them to remove to those points where their labour is in effectual demand, instead of encouraging them by illegal aids from the poor-rate to continue engaged in a desperate and dangerous struggle, or contenting ourselves with telling them that their case is hopeless, and that resistance will not better it. Far different things are from week to week re-urged on them, in language admirably calculated for their taste and comprehension, by writers, whose desire to excite a wide-spread bloody *jacquerie*, and thence a real ' radical reform,' that is to say, a revolution of property in England, is hardly veiled, and universally understood :
and

and it behoves every one interested in the continuance of tranquillity and the security of property, to forestall the necessary consequences of such preachments, and step forward voluntarily to remedy that state of things which, by thrusting large masses of the people into unmerited sufferings, renders them the willing disciples of ferocious and cowardly demagogues, and thus endangers, not merely the peace, but the very existence of society.

The political economists have one sophism still in reserve. ' Capital and labour (they say) are free to move wherever they are most wanted. Why have they not removed to the colonies, if it be true that such opportunities exist there for their profitable employment ? ' The answer is clear. The labourers cannot go for want of means. It is only the pressure of poverty which will lead them to abandon their homes and native country, — and this very poverty is an effectual bar to their unassisted emigration. The capitalists, who can do nothing in the colonies without labourers, will not make the advance necessary for carrying them out, because they can obtain no security for its repayment. All their attempts to bind emigrants by indentures, or other private engagements, have hitherto failed. This, in truth, has been the simple but insurmountable obstacle to spontaneous emigration. But for this, the demand both for capital and labour in this country and her colonies, would probably long since have put itself in equilibrio. As it is, government only has the power of effecting this great object, and of ensuring the repayment of the cost of removing the labourer out of the profits arising from the transaction.

Though, however, we look to colonization as the principal and permanent remedy for the evils of our economical condition, yet we are far from denying that those evils have been greatly aggravated by the injudicious interference of the legislature with the spontaneous direction of industry, or that the removal of such impediments, so far as the complicated nature of society in this country will allow of it, should be made to accompany any measure for facilitating emigration, and will materially assist in stimulating the home demand for labour and capital. The opinions we have long entertained, and repeatedly enforced on these points, have been fortified by a perusal of the minutes of evidence taken before the Select Committee of the House of Lords appointed in the spring of 1831 to consider the Poor Laws: a mass of evidence, rude and undigested to be sure, and exhibiting few profound or very enlarged views of the subject, but containing several useful statements of facts, and some valuable opinions from persons of great practical experience and judgment—such as Messrs. Becher, Slaney, Bacon, Whately, &c. We do not wish at present

to

to go into these subsidiary measures in detail, but shall merely glance at a few of the most important of them: and

1. We adhere to the opinion we have so often expressed, that, first and foremost, England ought to have *freedom of banking,* or, at least, as near an approach to it as is enjoyed by Scotland. Had the experiment never been tried, the question between freedom and restriction would be undoubtedly decided by abstract reasoning in favour of the former; but when a long course of experience has accumulated an irresistible mass of facts on the same side of the argument—when we see *freedom* in one part of Great Britain giving rise to a sound, cheap, and sufficient currency, with which a thriving trade and *unrivalled* agricultural improvements have been carried on, unchecked by any reverses attributable to the state of their own money-market—while *interference,* in another division of the same country, has brought in its train constant fluctuations in prices, uncertainty in all productive occupations, general want of confidence, alternations of extreme scarcity and dangerous abundance of money, a depressed agriculture, and multiplied bankruptcies in trade, together with the occasional failure of some sixty or seventy banks in a fortnight, followed by a crash of credit, threatening the subversion of all the existing arrangements of society—in presence of these practical proofs of the relative advantages of the two systems, it does appear strange that any reasonable person, however averse to confuse himself with the theories of either, should hesitate between the two. What is there in the character of Englishmen that unfits them for being trusted *to trust each other* to the same extent as the Scotch? Time and dearly-bought experience must surely by this time have opened the eyes of all to the enormous mischiefs of our narrow, fettered, and monopoly-crippled banking system; and the same sure test has proved the security and efficiency of the open, free, and broad principle on which banks in the north are allowed to establish themselves. Through this Scotland has enjoyed a regular and abundant supply of the circulating medium in all its transactions, and in its remotest districts. The banker there is allowed to deal in a cheaper article than gold, and the profit that he obtains enables him to give a salutary credit to those around him. There is no farmer in Scotland, at all respectable in character and connexion, who cannot obtain a bank credit to some amount, which precludes the necessity of disposing of his produce at an unfavourable period, or of turning off his labourers till he has some grain fit to carry to market. All his surplus cash, too, as he collects it, to meet his rent-day or any other payment, instead of being unprofitably, and perhaps insecurely, locked up in his own desk, is deposited in perfect safety in the bank, whence he receives it when wanted, with the

the addition of interest. Give the English farmer the same opportunity, and he will be able to employ more labour and cultivate his farm far more thoroughly than at present. Most of the witnesses before the Lords' Committee, acquainted with agricultural business, declared their opinions that the greater number of farms in England are imperfectly cultivated, and the labourers unemployed for want of sufficient capital among the farmers ; and that even at the prices of the last three or four years, much additional labour might, and would be profitably laid out on the land, if the farmers could command the money necessary for paying the men on the Saturday night. How is it that agriculturists experience a deficiency of money for these purposes? Because the facilities which the banks once afforded them have been withdrawn, through the effect of the existing restrictions on the circulation. A farmer in England is now obliged to have a *double* capital—one fixed in his stock and crops, the other floating in money, with which to pay his labourers' wages and his rent. In Scotland the farmer pays his outgoings for rent and wages with the notes which the banker lends him *on the credit of his stock,* crops, and securities : so that farming capital in Scotland will go nearly twice as far as in England ; and it is not too much to say, that the establishment of a similar system of banking in England would almost double the efficiency of every respectable farmer's capital—and, in consequence, afford a vast stimulus to the employment of agricultural labourers.

2. We need scarcely repeat in this place the arguments we have so long urged in proof of the urgent necessity for a thorough reform in the vicious mode of *administering the poor-laws in the southern counties.* We must bring back the law of relief to the simple and wise statute of Elizabeth.

3. We must have a *General Inclosure Act,* which should enable the majority, or a certain proportion of the persons interested, to obtain an inclosure of a part, or the whole of the waste land of any parish, by application to the court of Quarter Sessions; this would, it cannot be doubted, occasion the cultivation of many strips and patches of land now lying waste, because, though they might repay the cost of inclosure and cultivation, they are neither sufficiently fertile nor extensive to repay that, and the 600*l.* or 700*l.* which an act of parliament costs, into the bargain. Under such an act, numerous spots of waste land would probably be very soon lotted out, and brought into the market ; and it would be highly desirable that parish vestries should be allowed the power of purchasing and locating upon such spots of land any of their able-bodied labourers for whom they cannot find employment. Such is the desire to become possessed of land, that we are confident arrangements might be made by the overseers with paupers of this

description

description for the ultimate repayment, by instalments, of the expenses of their location, the debt remaining as a lien on the land until paid off. We do not share the fears of those who expect families located in this way to multiply and deteriorate in condition till they resemble the Irish cottiers., In the first place, we consider multiplication to be in itself no evil at all, since the excess may, by precautionary measures of the simplest character, be always directed to spots where they can maintain themselves in comfort;—in the next, we are quite certain that the English pauper, who is paid for his children at per head, marries and multiplies *now* much faster than he is likely to do when placed in circumstances of industrious independence, in which caution and foresight will be for his immediate interest.

4. In spite of all Professor Senior's ingenuities (of which more anon) we must have *an Irish Poor-Law.*

But in conjunction with these several important measures, we repeat that *a permanent and general scheme of colonization* is necessary to allow this country to avail itself to the full of the vast resources which are at its disposal for the maintenance of its increasing population. Nothing, we are persuaded, is wanting but candid and patient enquiry to remove the prejudices and air of ridicule with which this subject has been unfortunately surrounded, and to convince the public of its paramount importance to the interests of individuals, of communities, and of mankind at large. *Magna est veritas et prævalebit.* The clouds we have alluded to are fast clearing away, and we look forward with sanguine hope to the time when the noble scheme of a systematic emigration from all the over-peopled parts of the earth to the under-peopled, preserving health to the mother countries by moderate depletion, and invigorating infant colonies by the infusion of full-grown labour, will be carried into general adoption by all civilized states; when no European writer on *population* will think of choosing such a motto as we have recently met with:

> ' O voice, once heard
> Delightfully, *increase and multiply!*
> Now death to hear! for what can *we* increase
> Or multiply, but *penury, woe, and crime?*'—*Par. Lost.*

and when, with reference to the state and prospects of our own land, no meditative Coleridge shall be tempted to quote with prophetic melancholy the awful words of Holy Writ:—' The burden of the valley of vision, even the burden upon the crowned isle, whose merchants are princes, whose traffickers the honourable of the earth ; who stretcheth out her hand over the sea, and she is the mart of nations.' *

---

* Isaiah xxiii. See Coleridge on Church and State, (Second Edition, 1830,) p. 73.

---

Art. VIII.—1. *The Moral and Physical Condition of the Working Classes in Manchester.* By James Phillips Kay, M.D. Second Edition, enlarged.—Ridgway. pp. 120.

2. *An Address to the Higher Classes on the Present State of Public Feeling among the Working Classes.*—Whittaker, Treacher and Co.

THE various orders of society are mutually dependent; their interests are interwoven with a complexity which cannot be unravelled; and natural connexions tend to diffuse throughout the mass the happiness or misery suffered by any particular portion. Evils which affect one class, poison the sources of well-being in another; and the sensation created by ills endured, is propagated by a chain of most subtle sensibility. Artificial causes indeed, sometimes benumb the feeling of society, and render it torpid and inert under the pressure of social calamities, and certain orders may for a time be protected from the influence of events that produce misery in others; but the tendency is still the same. The true interest of each is the happiness of all. The security of no class can be permanently attained at the prejudice of any other. A narrow, partial policy necessarily issues in the injury of the order for which it was framed. All philosophy is finally found defective, which is not so enlarged as to include the happiness of the aggregate.

The best test of social institutions, is the condition of the community subjected to their influence. Temporary prosperity may certainly be attained, even under imperfect forms of government, from the influence of external circumstances, which control for a time the natural tendency of such institutions to produce physical and moral degradation among the mass of the people; and in any analysis of the causes of their condition, the influence of these external agencies should be carefully separated from the natural effects of internal misrule. But the process of deterioration and decay will in the end prevail. The blessings which flow from without, will at last, in such states, like a stagnant stream, cease to fertilize the barren wastes of an ignorant people; and may add to the pestilential influences of a continually increasing moral debasement.

Certain orders of society may be protected by artificial barriers, which may, for a time, resist the efforts of misrule. Secured from actual dangers, not tortured by the goad of continual toil, unpursued by the hounds of want, being able to wait the law's delay or to resist the oppressor's wrong, even if some encroachments be made on the extent of their possessions, and the mound which resists the invasion of actual suffering be weakened and undermined ; the consciousness of present ease is too apt to induce apathy concerning future dangers,—to lull them in the lap of refined pleasures,—and even to cheat them with dreams of the happiness of the whole people, at the very moment when the hoarse voice of popular discontent is sounding in their ears.

The effects of misgovernment are first experienced by the weak and unprotected ; by those who have no hoard of wealth to consume, but whose daily labour produces their daily supply. The prudence and morality of a people may for a time enable them to maintain a manly struggle with the multitude of evils, which arise from imperfect and partial laws ; or external circumstances may postpone the day when these laws will produce their natural results ; but, at length, the moral and physical character of the population will be degraded. The absence of proper intellectual and moral culture ; impediments to the spread of knowledge ; oppressive taxation ; restrictions on the natural tendencies of trade and civilization, and their results the privations and toil of the working classes, exchanged only for reckless dissipation ; boons for the increase of a superabundant population, in the guise of remedies for impending calamities, and their consequence the destruction of forethought and economy ; the combined effects of ignorance, vice, and want, evinced in the alienation of the natural charities and the growth of domestic and social discontent ; all these evils, a monstrous growth from the same poisoned root, tend to produce a state of society too fearful to be contemplated, possessing a restless and anarchical energy, which if not counteracted would speedily issue in the destruction of all the cohesive properties of the social constitution. To correct legislation, nothing is more necessary than minute and constant information concerning the actual condition of the people. In the absence of this, the influence of laws on the happiness and morals of the mass, and on the prosperity of the empire, cannot be traced ; no comparison can be instituted between the state of the population under different systems of policy ; and evils of the most frightful magnitude may be permitted silently to grow, especially among the labouring classes of society, unnoticed by their superiors, denied by their oppressors, and unknown to the government, until the state is shaken by some frightful convulsion. But even the ordinary and daily purposes of legislation cannot be accomplished without these data on which to found its conclusions.

Yet in this country there is no organised system for obtaining statistical returns. Even the registers of marriages, births, and deaths, are kept in an extremely imperfect manner. When particular emergencies render a special inquiry necessary, general evidence is presented by the parties interested in some projected change, before a Committee of the House of Commons. The evidence thus adduced, consists too frequently of what is merely *ex parte;* statements which contradict and neutralise each other, and often so vague and general in character, as to be almost useless to the support of any practical conclusion. Even the existence of commissioners appointed to make specific inquiries, demonstrates that there is an absence of information on the most important subjects of legislation, at the very period when a crisis demanding the decision of government has arrived. The labours of any private individuals placed in circumstances which favour the acquisition of correct information, are therefore peculiarly valuable in the absence of a universal statistical system ; especially when the results of their investigations are recorded with impartiality, and reduced as much as possible to a statistical form.

The rapid progress of our manufactures and commerce has accumulated great masses of population, in which society has assumed new relations amongst its several classes. The invention of the steam-engine, and the mechanical improvements introduced into all manufacturing processes, have increased in an extraordinary degree the power of supplying articles of exchange. The enterprize of our merchants, the vast extent of our colonies with which a peaceful though a restricted trade is secured ; the extraordinary stimulus given to our industry by the late war, which for a time almost extinguished the manufactures and commerce of the continent; our natural resources in the facilities of internal communication, and mines of mineral and coal; the extent of the national capital, and the energy of the national character; all these combined causes have occasioned a developement of the manufacturing and commercial power of the nation, unexampled in the history of the world.

' Visiting Manchester, the metropolis of the commercial system, a stranger regards with wonder the ingenuity and comprehensive capacity, which, in the short space of half a century, have here established the staple manufacture of this kingdom. He beholds with astonishment the establishments of its merchants—monuments of fertile genius and successful design :—the masses of capital which have been accumulated by those who crowd upon its mart, and the restless but sagacious spirit which has made every part of the known world the scene of their enterprise. The sudden creation of the mighty system of commercial organization which covers this country, and stretches its arms to the most distant seas, attests the power and the dignity of man. Commerce, it appears to such a spectator, here gathers in her storehouses the productions of every clime, that she may minister to the happiness of a favoured race.'

'When he turns from the great capitalists, he contemplates the fearful strength only of that multitude of the labouring population, which lies like a slumbering giant at their feet. He has heard of the turbulent riots of the people—of machine breaking—of the secret and sullen organization which has suddenly lit the torch of incendiarism, or well nigh uplifted the arm of rebellion in the land. He remembers that political desperadoes have ever loved to tempt this population to the hazards of the swindling game of revolution, and have scarcely failed. In the midst of so much opulence, however, he has disbelieved the cry of need.'

'Believing that the natural tendency of unrestricted commerce, (unchecked by the prevailing want of education, and the incentives afforded by imperfect laws to improvidence and vice,) is to develope the energies of society, to increase the comforts and luxuries of life, and to *elevate the physical condition* of every member of the social body, we have exposed, with a faithful, though a friendly hand, the condition of the lower orders connected with the manufactures of this town, because we conceive that the evils affecting them result *from foreign and accidental causes.* A system, which promotes the advance of civilization, and diffuses it over the world—which promises to maintain the peace of nations, by establishing a permanent international law, founded on the benefits of commercial association, cannot be inconsistent with the happiness of the *great mass of the people.* There are men who believe that the labouring classes are condemned for ever, by an inexorable fate, to the unmitigated curse of toil, scarcely rewarded by the bare necessaries of existence, and often visited by the horrors of hunger and disease—that the heritage of ignorance, labour, and misery, is entailed upon them as an eternal doom. Such an opinion might appear to receive a gloomy confirmation, were we content with the evidence of fact, derived only from the history of uncivilized races, and of feudal institutions. No modern Rousseau now rhapsodises on the happiness of the state of nature. Moral and physical degradation are inseparable from barbarism. The unsheltered, naked savage, starving on food common to the denizens of the wilderness, never knew the comforts contained in the most wretched cabin of our poor.'

' Civilization, to which feudality is inimical, but which is most powerfully promoted by commerce, surrounds man with innumerable inventions. It has thus a constant tendency to multiply, without limit, the comforts of existence, and that by an amount of labour, at all times undergoing an indefinite diminution. It continually expands the sphere of his relations, from a dependance on his own limited resources, until it has combined into one mighty league, alike the members of communities, and the powers of the most distant regions. The cultivation of the faculties, the extension of knowledge, the improvement of the arts, enable man to extend his dominion over matter, and to minister, not merely to all the exigencies, but to the capricious tastes and the imaginary appetites of his nature. When, therefore, every zone has contributed its most precious stores—science has revealed her secret laws—genius has applied the mightiest powers of nature to familiar use, making matter the patient and silent slave of the will of man—if want prey upon the heart of the people, we may strongly presume that, besides the effects of existing manners, some accidental barrier exists, arresting their natural and rightful supply.'

' The evils affecting the working classes, *so far from being the necessary results of the commercial system, furnish evidence of a disease which impairs its energies, if it does not threaten its vitality.'*—Moral and Physical Condition of the Working Classes in Manchester. p. 76.

The increase of wealth, and the spread of enterprize have indeed received severe checks in later years. The nation reels beneath the enormous burthens imposed on it by the profligate expenditure of the late war. Taxation has been pushed to its utmost limit. The powers of supply have overtaken and surpassed the effectual demand ; and restrictions and monopolies fetter the enterprize which would open new sources of exchange for the industry of the country. Our powers of successfully rivalling the manufactures of other nations, are reduced by a tax on the staple commodity of life, which thus increases the cost of production in a ratio constantly accumulating with the amount of labour employed, in every successive process necessary to the completion of the article to be exchanged. While the demand for labour is thus diminished, our poor-laws stimulate the increase of an uneducated, toilworn, and ignorant working class. We have a vindictive criminal code, which is so abhorrent to common sense, that juries modify their verdicts to elude its vengeance, and judges interfere between the victim and the law, to solicit the mercy of the crown. Our system of secondary punishments is neither exemplary nor corrective ; it neither conveys terror and warning to the people, nor does it improve the mind and elevate the habits of the criminal. Crime is often committed and confessed, in order that the criminal may enjoy the boon which the law offers for

offences. In the provinces, there is no preventive police. The
excise-laws promote the increase of the haunts of intemperance,
and foster the reckless sensuality of the lowest class. Our
gaols, though improved, are still schools of vice, where the
novice is initiated in the more subtle secrets of chicanery and
fraud; where the sensibilities of the young offender are seared,
and, with a callous heart, his passions are prepared for deeds of
violence, and scenes of rapine. Add to all this, that there is
no system of national education for the people. Imperfect
means of acquiring knowledge are partially distributed by the
spontaneous efforts of individuals; but useful knowledge is not
diffused. An abortive philanthropy cultivates the minds of
the working classes, just so far as to render them capable of
receiving right instruction, and then abandons them to the
tender mercies of blind chance, or to the mischievous teaching
of restless and perverted spirits; it prepares the soil with all
the diligence of the careful husbandman, and then leaves it to
be sown with thistles by the wind, or with tares by the enemy.
The people are taught by their own miseries, that they
suffer grievous wrongs; they feel that they have been depressed by the expenditure of an impolitic war, by the lavish
patronage of government, by an ignorance on the part of their
rulers of the principles of trade and the sources of national
wealth, and that they have been thus deprived of the just rewards
of their labour. But from the want of a sound acquaintance
with the sciences of political economy and legislation, they are
liable to be deluded into an implicit reliance on the patent
schemes of political nostrum-mongers. A wise government would
provide institutions of the most liberal and popular character,
for the political instruction of the people; and taxes would no
longer shackle the diffusion of sound principles amongst the
masses. While the labouring population is oppressed by toil,
goaded by misery, deluded by the designing, tempted by sensuality, and debased by the law itself whose imperfections
seduce to vice and impel to crime; the state should tremble,
lest the great basis of society, its strength being destroyed,
should crumble beneath the weight of the superincumbent
mass, or be so agitated that the mighty structure it supports
should be shaken into an utter and irreparable ruin.

   These reflections are natural deductions from the details of
the pamphlet which presents a picture of the moral and
physical condition of the working classes in the largest manufacturing town in the empire. The natural tendency of trade
is, as there shown, to diffuse wealth and happiness through
the various orders of society, and to cultivate the intelligence,

the industry, and the virtue of the middle and lower ranks. It is contended that commerce will issue in greater individual and national happiness than any other form of social organization yet developed; but, being in a great manufacturing town, and daily brought into contact with evils which affect the well-being of great portions of the community, the author portrays the revolting features which deform society, and then endeavours to trace their origin and suggest the means of their removal. It is grateful to perceive how the general principle adduced concerning the tendencies of trade, is supported by an array of statistical evidence, by which is shown that the evils exposed may be legitimately attributed to the temporary influence of causes capable of being removed by timely and judicious legislation. These facts are, moreover, not exhibited as evidence of the existence of an insulated exception to the prosperity of the working classes throughout the kingdom, but rather to attract public attention to an investigation of their condition in other communities, with the melancholy conviction, that similar inquiries will, elsewhere, issue in the discovery of similar evils. This foreboding is justly founded, and in entering into a slight analysis of the facts contained in this work, chords will be touched whose vibration will awaken feelings of interest in the most remote portions of the country.

The extraordinary progress of commercial prosperity during the close of the last and the commencement of the present century, occasioned the colonization of extensive districts. Some counties were suddenly crowded with inhabitants. The most remote and sequestered vallies, where streams of water and supplies of fuel and of minerals existed, became the scene of manufacturing enterprize and ingenuity, and the towns increased with an unexampled rapidity. Public attention was absorbed in the application of capital to these great and bold schemes. For in the progress of endeavours to invent and improve machinery,—in the erection of manufactories, and the constant attention required for the success of these establishments,—in the working of mines and quarries, and the multiplication of roads and canals, so perfect an abstraction of the public mind from other pursuits was produced, that the police of towns was, for a considerable period, neglected, and municipal evils were permittec to accumulate. In erecting towns, land was let by proprietors, for the most part non-resident, to speculators who unrestrained by any police regulations, built houses for the poorer inhabitants, often destitute of the conveniences which minister to comfort and cleanliness— huddled together in confused groups, separated only by narrow streets, and intersected by close courts, alleys, and avenues, where filth was permitted to accumulate. The streets not being subjected to the influence of any police laws, were permitted to remain unpaved, were unscavengered, and consequently became the receptacles of the most disgusting offal. From investigations made by the Board of Health at Manchester previously to the invasion of Cholera, it appeared that out of 687 streets inspected in the township of Manchester, 248 were unpaved, 53 partially paved, 112 ill ventilated, and 352 contained heaps of refuse, stagnant pools, ordure &c. The report of the state of the houses in the same township was that out of 6951 houses inspected, 2565 required whitewashing, 960 needed repair, of 939 the soughs required repair, 1135 were reported to be damp, 452 ill ventilated, and 2221 were destitute of privies.

' The state of the streets powerfully affects the health of their inhabitants. Sporadic cases of typhus chiefly appear in those which are narrow, ill ventilated, unpaved, or which contain heaps of refuse, or stagnant pools. The confined air and noxious exhalations, which abound in such places, depress the health of the people, and on this account contagious diseases are also most rapidly propagated there. The operation of these causes is exceedingly promoted by their reflex influence on the manners. The houses, in such situations, are uncleanly, ill provided with furniture ; an air of discomfort if not of squalid and loathsome wretchedness pervades them, they are often dilapidated, badly drained, damp : and the habits of their tenants are gross—they are ill fed; ill clothed, and uneconomical—at once spend-thrifts and destitute—denying themselves the comforts of life, in order that they may wallow in the unrestrained licence of animal appetite. An intimate connexion subsists, among the poor, between the cleanliness of the street and that of the house and person. Uneconomical habits, and dissipation are almost inseparably allied ; and they are so frequently connected with uncleanliness, that we cannot consider their concomitance as altogether accidental. The first step to reck-lessness may often be traced in a neglect of that self-respect, and of the love of domestic enjoyments, which are indicated by personal slovenliness, and discomfort of the habitation. Hence, the importance of providing by police regulations or general enactment, against those fertile sources alike of disease and demoralization, presented by the gross neglect of the streets and habitations of the poor. When the health is depressed by the concurrence of these causes, contagious diseases spread with a fatal malignancy among the population subjected to their influence. The records of the Fever Hospital of Manchester, prove that typhus *prevails almost exclusively* in such situations.' —*Id.* p. 28.

The Boards of Health recently established in conformity with the Orders in Council should be constituted permanent organized centres of medical police, where municipal powers should be directed by scientific men to remove and prevent the accumulation of those agencies which most powerfully depress the physical condition of the inhabitants. Besides this suggestion, Dr. Kay regrets that commissioners were not appointed many years ago, and invested with authority to regulate the laying out of building land within the precincts of Manchester.

' Private rights ought not to be exercised so as to produce a public injury. The law, which describes and punishes offences against the person and property of the subject, should extend its authority by establishing a social code, in which the rights of communities should be protected from the assaults of partial interests. By exercising its functions in the former case, it does not wantonly interfere with the liberty of the subject, nor in the latter, would it violate the reverence due to the sacred security of property.'

The powers obtained by the recent changes in the police act of Manchester are retrospective, and exclusively refer to the removal of existing evils : their application must also necessarily be slow. We conceive that special police regulations should be framed for the purpose of preventing the recurrence of that gross neglect of decency and violation of order, whose effects we have described.'

Streets should be built according to plans determined (after a conference with the owners) by a body of commissioners, specially elected for the purpose—their width should bear a certain relation to the size and elevation of the houses erected. Landlords should be compelled, on the erection of any house, to provide sufficient means of drainage, and each to pave his respective area of the street. Each habitation should be provided with a due receptacle for every kind of refuse, and the owner should be obliged to white-wash the house, at least once every year. Inspectors of the state of houses should be appointed : and the repair of all those reported to be in a state inconsistent with the health of the inhabitants, should be enforced at the expense of the landlords. If the rents of houses are not sufficient to remunerate the owners for this repair, their situation must in general be such, or their dilapidation so extreme, as to render them so undesirable to the comfort, or so prejudicial to the health of the tenants that they ought to be no longer inhabited.'—*Id.* p. 105.

The great demand for workmen required by the sudden increase of manufacturing establishments, rapidly absorbed all the labourers of the district in which such changes occurred. Capitalists therefore encouraged colonization from distant parts of the kingdom, and crowds of Irish flocked into the country. In Manchester out of a population of 220,000 people it is calculated that there are 50,000 Irish. The settlement of this latter class has had a most important influence on the condition of the people. An immediate effect is the rapid increase of the poor-rate. As it would be worse than useless to re-transport a pauper to Ireland who would immediately return to be again a burthen to the parish, the claims of the Irish are admitted before they have obtained a legal settlement. Hence, notwithstanding the utmost jealousy on the part of the overseers and the most zealous administration of the law, the number of Irish who become burthensome to the parish without having obtained settlements, augments with great rapidity.

In the months of November, December, January, and February of 1827—8, the number of Irish cases without settlements, relieved in the township of Manchester, was 3671, and of English and Irish having settlements, 27,046. In the same months of 1830—31, the Irish cases without settlements, had increased to 9,892, and the English and Irish cases having settlements, were 35,950. But the effects of this immigration on the physical comfort, the morals, and happiness of the people, are much more remarkable. In employments requiring great skill, the effects of the competition were little felt ; but, in some in which no skill is required, and in others where it is easily attained, the competition of the redundant labour of the Irish, combined with the constantly accumulating embarrassments of a restricted commerce, reduced the rewards of labour to the lowest degree in the scale. In this state, the example of the Irish spread with the rapidity of contagion. The English population, too frequently overborne by toil and a constant strife with necessity, rapidly learned the habits of their neighbours. Their houses became squalid ; the pittance procured by labour was not economized ; once having tasted the luckless charity of the law, they relied on its support for the future. Forethought, frugality, cleanliness, and method were banished from their habitations. The toil of the day was too great to permit them either to learn lessons from the past, or to provide for the future. Uneducated, starved, toilworn, apparently abandoned to their hard fate, without any to instruct or cheer them, they too often yielded also to the seductions offered by the haunts of vice, and spent the wretched earnings of their wearisome labour, or even the paltry stipend doled out to them by the executor of the law, at the tavern, seeking to drown the remembrance of their misery in the delirium of intoxication.

Unremitted labour is in itself debasing. The abstraction of intellectual and moral stimuli leaves the mind in a state of torpid inertness. If no provision be made to introduce the grateful relief of variety of occupåtion, but the workman be constantly subjected to the same dull routine of ceaseless drudgery ; if little or no leisure be permitted to him ; and if during that leisure his wearied energies be neither refreshed by gentle amusements, nor his mind by more elevated pursuits, his tastes will sink to the level of the brutes, to which by the process he is assimilated. A more frightful fate could scarcely be contemplated than this, of which the only relief would be its brief respites of profound forgetfulness.

For the degree of labour which is demanded from the working classes, and the meagreness of the remuneration which most of them receive, thanks may be given to the opponents of free trade, and the partisans of monopoly. The increase of population, though it has been little subjected to the wholesome control of moral restraint, has never been so rapid as the augmentation of the resources of the country might have been, had its commerce been unrestricted. But devoid of education, rendered reckless by want and extreme toil, and tempted by the boon practically offered by the law for the increase of the population, the most wretched of the working classes have married at the earliest period ; and while commerce has overtaken the limits prescribed to it by the law, the population has surpassed all that under such limitation is consistent with the due reward of the labourer.

The effects of the Poor laws are thus described by Dr. Kay.

' A rate levied on property for the support of indigence is, in a great degree, a tax on the capital from whose employment are derived the incentives of industry and the rewards of the frugal, ingenious, and virtuous poor. If the only test of the application of this fund be *indigence*, without reference to *desert*—be *want,* irrespective of *character*—motives to frugality, self controul and industry are at once removed, and the strong barrier which nature had itself erected to prevent the moral lapse of the entire population is wantonly destroyed. The tax acts as a new burden on the *industrious* poor, already suffering from an enormous pressure, and not only drags within the limits of pauperism unwilling victims, but paralyses with despair the efforts of those whose exertions might otherwise have prolonged their struggle with adversity. The wages of the worthy are often given to encourage the sluggard, the drunkard, and the man whose imprudence entails on the community the precocious burden of his meagre and neglected offspring.'

' The feeble obstacle raised in the *country* to the propagation of a pauper population, by making the indigent chargeable on the estates of the land-owners, is even there rendered almost entirely inefficacious by the too frequent non-residence of the gentry, or the indifference with which this apparently inevitable evil is regarded. In the South of England the fatal error has been committed of paying a certain portion of the wages of able-bodied labourers out of the fund obtained by the poor-rates ; and a population is thus created, bound like slaves to toil, and having also, like them, a right to be maintained. But, in the large towns, the feeble check to the increase of pauperism which thus exists in some rural districts, is entirely removed.  The land is let to speculators who build cottages, the rents of which are collected weekly, a commutation for the rates being often paid by the landlord when they are demanded, which seldom occurs in the lowest description of houses.  A married man having thus by law an unquestioned right to a maintenance proportioned to the number of his family, direct encouragement is afforded to improvident marriages.  The most destitute and immoral marry to increase their claim on the stipend appointed for them by law, which thus acts as a bounty on the increase of a squalid and debilitated race, who inherit from their parents disease, sometimes deformity, often vice, and always beggary.'

' The number of labourers thus created diminishes the already scanty wages of that portion of the population still content to endeavour by precarious toil to maintain their honest independence.  Desperate is the struggle by which, under such a system, the upright labourer procures for his family the comforts of existence.  Many are dragged by the accidents of life to an unwilling acceptance of this legalized pension of the profligate, and some, over informed by misfortune in the treachery of their own hearts, are seduced to palter with temptation, and at length to capitulate with their apparent fate.'

' Fearful demoralization attends an impost whose distribution diminishes the incentives to prudence and virtue.  When reckless of the future, the intelligence of man is confined to the narrow limits of the present.  He thus debases himself beneath the animals whose instincts teach them to lay up stores for the season of need.  The gains of the pauper are, in prosperity, frequently squandered in taverns, whilst his family exists in hungered and ragged misery, and few sympathies with the sufferings of his aged relatives or neighbours enter his cold heart, since he knows they have an equal claim with himself, on that pittance which the law awards.  The superfluities which nature would prompt him in a season of abundance to hoard for the accidents of the future, are wasted with reckless profusion ; because *the law takes care of the future.*  Selfish profligacy usurps the seat of the household virtues of the English labourer.'

' Charity once extended an invisible chain of sympathy between the higher and lower ranks of society, which has been destroyed by the luckless pseudo-philanthropy of the law.  Few aged or decrepid pensioners now gratefully receive the visits of the higher classes—few of the poor seek the counsel, the admonitions, and assistance of the rich in the period of the inevitable accidents of life.  The bar of the overseer is however crowded with the sturdy applicants for a legalized relief, who regard the distributor of this bounty as their stern and merciless oppressor, instructed by the compassionless rich to reduce to the lowest possible amount the alms which the law wrings from their reluctant hands.  This disruption of the natural ties has created a wide gulf between the higher and lower orders of the community, across which, the scowl of hatred banishes the smile of charity and love.'—*Id.* p. 45.

One fact connected with the state of the population which is mentioned by the author, is too remarkable to be omitted. 'The average annual number of births attended by the officers of the lying-in charity in Manchester, is four thousand three hundred, and the number of births to the population, may be assumed as one in twenty-eight inhabitants. This annual average of births represents therefore a population of 124,000, and assuming that of Manchester and the environs to be 230,000, more than one half of its inhabitants are either so destitute or so degraded, as to require the assistance of public charity in bringing their offspring into the world.'

Unremitted exertions are requisite to prevent the growth of the jealousy which divides the capitalists and the labouring classes. The embarrassed state of commerce has constantly tended to reduce the wages of labour. To resist undue encroachments, and to maintain a general standard of remuneration, the working classes have combined in associations for mutual protection, which have not unfrequently been engaged in impolitic, useless, and vexatious contests with their employers. Leaders not sufficiently acquainted with the principles regulating the rate of wages, have misled the people; some unprincipled men, whose element is the agitation created by public feuds, have at times influenced their passions; and in seasons of commercial perplexity, a wide-spread spirit of discontent has thus been fostered, which has occasionally issued in the commission of acts of licentious violence. Many of the most enlightened of the working classes repudiate these excesses. The objects to which the efforts of such associations have been directed, have seldom been attained, though the struggle has been prolonged with remarkable obstinacy. The trade of certain districts has received material injury, in the loss of the confidence necessary to the investment of capital. The operatives have suffered severely during the contest, certain of their leaders have embezzled their funds, and they have had sufficing evidence of the absurdity of the projects into which they have been plunged. But during the 'turn out,' lamentable disassociation has been effected between the higher and lower orders of society.

The manufacturing capitalists of the large towns comprize many enlightened, high-minded, and generous men, foremost in every struggle for the liberty and prosperity of the country, and earnest advocates of all that can conduce to the elevation of the people. To such men it belongs to break down the barrier which separates the rich from the poor, and by measures equally benevolent, sagacious, and energetic, to accomplish a more cordial association between the higher and lower orders of society.

' The people are every where easily governed by any one who will take the necessary means to possess himself of their confidence. You may acquire influence over them yet more extensive than that of the demagogues they now confide in. For you have wealth, and power, and *character*, as well as talent ; and they are accustomed to pay deference to all these attributes. But this influence can never be acquired, if you stand aloof in indolent security or arrogant contempt. You cannot guide them without mingling with them. " You cannot live *for* men, without living *with* them."* But, first, you must gain the esteem and confidence of the lower classes : without this you can do little. Shew them that you are as ardent an advocate of liberal principles as themselves, and that the ends you aim at are the same, though the means you would employ to gain them may be different. Shew them that you have their interests at heart, and are willing to sacrifice and suffer much for them ; and have no private objects of your own to serve. They are naturally disposed to respect and obey those who are above them in rank, and wealth, and education ; and by care and conduct you may cultivate this disposition to almost any extent.' —*Address to the Higher Classes, &c.* p. 7.

How great soever may be the prosperity which the skill, industry, and enterprize of the great manufacturing towns may attain, the apparent well-being of these communities will be fallacious and transitory, in the absence of expedients to maintain a high moral tone in all classes, and a cordial association of the several orders of society. If the relations of the wealthy with the poor, be merely those created by the exchange of labour for wages, the association is heartless and degrading. To regard the workman solely as necessary to a certain process of labour, to limit all intercourse with him to the contract for the animal power which he has to sell, is practically to debase him to the level of a machine, and even to remove him to a greater distance from the thoughts of his employer, inasmuch as the machine is an integral portion of his capital, in the successful employment of which he has a more immediate interest than he can have in the health or moral elevation of the animal power, for whose use he has made only a temporary bargain. On the other hand, if the workman discover that his connexion with the capitalist is limited to the contract for his labour, all feelings which might have associated him with his employer are severed, and in their stead arise jealousy of the power of his superior, a constant suspicious watchfulness lest he should enjoy more than his rightful share of the accumulated profits,

* Sir James Mackintosh.

sometimes envy of his success, resistance to his rightful authority, moody discontent, and deeply seated animosity.

How frightful a picture would a vast manufacturing town exhibit, of which it should be asserted, that a wide, untraversed gulph, separated the wealthy classes and the poor! That the workman rose before the sun to his daily toil, and pursued it until night, with brief intervals of respite, sufficient only to satisfy the absolute necessities of his nature. That during the day he encountered only the overseer of his employment, and received at the close of the week, from a subaltern agent, the wages of his exertions. That after twelve hours spent in actual labour, and two in proceeding to and from his habitation and taking the necessary refreshment, seven being subtracted for sleep, he should have three of leisure, which from his precedent toil, he would rather be disposed to spend at the tavern, than in gentle amusements, or in occupations which might elevate his mind and refine his tastes ; and that during these three hours, he was visited by no friend of the instruction of the people, but that his power of resisting the seductions of sensuality being diminished by the inevitable results of toil, he was abandoned to struggle alone with his fate. That when the day of rest came round, nothing appeared to rouse him from the apathy into which, in the absence of all moral and intellectual stimuli, he was plunged, or to rescue him from the debasing indulgences with which he supplied the want of innocent and ennobling excitement.

The engagements of capitalists, especially in the present state of commerce, are such as to preclude the possibility of their personally maintaining a useful intercourse with the whole body of the workmen in their employ. It is also true that, if evils at all resembling those described exist in any of our great manufacturing towns, they have arisen gradually from the influence of circumstances over which no individual had any control, and that their existence has only of late become apparent to these communities. Considered as a whole, such misery is too great to be wrestled with by any single strength, and the habit of thus regarding it has induced despair of its removal. Thus, the great masses of habitations, closely peopled by the lowest and least moral of the poor, which, in almost all great cities, threaten ultimately to surround and bury in their bosoms the dwellings of the rich and the refined, are too frequently regarded by the benevolent, as hideous moral wastes in which lurk those maladies of society which mock all the expedients of social and legislative interference.

The labouring population is, when only numerically considered, so vast a power, that the policy which should dare to neglect its interests would be bold even to madness. But on contemplating the energies of this mighty multitude,— what strength of endurance, and what desperation to resist might be awakened in each member of this mass;—and, on the other hand, what impulse each of these minds when culti- vated is capable of giving to the progress of civilization;—the importance of this arm of the national power swells to a magnitude which the mind fails to comprehend.

' If a period ever existed, when public peace was secured by refusing knowledge to the population, that epoch has lapsed. The policy of governments may have been little able to bear the scrutiny of the people. This may be the reason why the fountains of English literature have been sealed—and the works of our reformers, our patriots, and our con- fessors—the exhaustless sources of all that is pure and holy, and of good report, amongst us—*have not been made accessible and familiar to the poor.* Yet, literature of this order is destined to determine the structure of our social constitution, and to become the mould of our national character; and they who would dam up the flood of truth from the lower ground, cannot prevent its silent transudation. A little knowledge is thus inevitable, and it is proverbially a dangerous thing. Alarming disturbances of social order generally commence with *a people only partially instructed.* The preservation of *internal peace,* not less than the improvement of our national institutions, depends on the education of the working classes.'

' Government unsupported by popular opinion, is deprived of its true strength, and can only retain its power by the hateful expedients of despotism. Laws which obtain not general consent are dead letters, or obedience to them must be purchased by blood. But ignorance perpetuates the prejudices and errors which contend with the just exercise of a legitimate authority, and makes the people the victims of those ill-founded panics which convulse society, or seduces them to those tumults which disgrace the movements of a deluded populace. Unacquainted with the real sources of their own distress, misled by the artful misrepresentations of men whose element is disorder, and whose food faction can alone supply, the people have too frequently neglected the constitutional expedients by which redress ought only to have been sought, and have brought obloquy on their just cause, by the blind ferocity of those insurrectionary movements, in which they have assaulted the institutions of society. That good government may be stable, the people must be so instructed, that they may love that *which they know to be right.*'—Moral and Physical Condition &c. p. 91.

The great means of promoting temperance, and of elevating the moral condition of the people, is the introduction of habits of cleanliness and forethought into their habitations. The wages of the poor discreetly employed, would often purchase double the amount of comforts which they now obtain; and a clean house, a wife neither a slattern nor exhausted with toil, but capable of welcoming her husband to a cheerful supper, might win even the vicious, from the excitement of the tavern. Where there are infant children in the family, (who when the mother works, are put out to nurse at considerable expense,) it is more than probable that, when the husband and others of the family are fully employed, the loss of the woman's wages would be almost saved by the effects of her household management.

The tendency of this article will perhaps be received as proof of a desire to extenuate no evil, and screen no abuse ; the greater confidence is therefore felt of obtaining credit to the affirmation, that if the statements recently published in the public journals, from the evidence given before a Committee of the House of Commons, are adduced as proofs of the general physical condition of the children of the manufacturing poor, they are utter and groundless exaggerations. The depression of health among the manufacturing population results more from municipal, social, domestic, and moral evils, than from the nature of their employment. The collecting of the cases where health has been depressed by the combined influence of these and accidental causes, and exhibiting the exceptions as evidence against the rule, was an obvious measure to one so versed in political tactics as the late member for Newark. In the country, under judicious management, Dr. Kay proves, by a reference to some interesting statistical evidence relative to the works of Mr. Thomas Ashton of Hyde, that ' the present hours of labour do not injure the health of a population *otherwise favourably situated*, but that when evil results ensue, they must chiefly be ascribed to the combination of this *with other causes of moral and physical depression.*'

The hours of labour in mills are, especially in towns, hostile to the improvement of the moral and physical condition of the working classes. The just inference from which is, that the whole laws of trade must speedily be subjected to so thorough a revision, that our manufactures may be successfully conducted, without demands being made on the labour of the working classes which are inconsistent with their permanent well-being.

The present hours of labour in the manufacturing districts have been gradually introduced, as the pressure of the several restrictions and burthens upon commerce was felt. The tax in support of West-Indian slavery added one portion to the hours of infant labour, —the East India monopoly another,—the Corn Laws ran up the total to fifteen ;—yet so dull is the manufacturer's perception, so gullible the English animal, that this very fact is pounced upon by the supporters of these abuses as what shall be made to aid their purpose. The direct and visible object of the inventor and mover of the Factory Bill, was to run his Bill against Parliamentary Reform, Slave Emancipation, and the removal of the Corn Laws; and the Mirror of Parliament is there to prove it. Yet the manufacturing population run headlong into the snare, and support the schemes of their oppressors for the beggarly boon of being directed how many hours their children may work to escape the artificial famine the same men are making for them. Profits have been gradually diminished,—the rapidity of production, transmission, and return have constantly increased,—the most persevering industry and the most subtle sagacity have been racked for expedients to maintain the contest. The question presented has been whether our manufacturers would be able to meet their foreign competitors in the market; and the alternative, the loss of their capital, and the ultimate non-employment and destitution of the population dependent upon them. In these struggles the hours of labour have been gradually increased. The cotton trade is even now in a critical position; and the only way to relieve the workmen from the evils of oppressive toil, is to remove the burthens which render that toil necessary to the support of the commercial portion of the country, and consequently to the continuance of employment and subsistence to the people.

Our vaunted advantage in machinery is declining. The latest machines introduced into the cotton trade are of foreign invention; and even in the remotest part of the Continent, machinery on the English plan is invariably employed. The chance of gaining and keeping the manufacture for the Continent of Europe, was thrown away the day it was determined, that none but a landholder should sit in the British parliament.

The following is a rapid survey of the state of the cotton trade in various countries of the Continent.

1. *France.*—In 1831, 74,000,000lbs. of cotton were consumed, and produced 63,000,000lbs. of yarn. The population employed in this manufacture is about 200,000. The average wages paid are 5s. 8d. a week. The hours of labour are generally twelve; and fourteen in Alsace. Power looms have not made much way in France, but in Alsace their number is increasing fast and they succeed well. In 1830, France exported, in cotton goods, 5,174,400lbs. equal in value to 2,192,240l.—Of this 3,194,240lbs. were printed cottons of the value of 1,483,640l.

2. *Switzerland.*—In 1831, the consumption of cotton was

56,000 bales, or 18,816,000lbs. The population employed in the cotton manufacture is at least 28,000, and
children are admitted into the factories at ten years
of age. The hours of labour average eighty per week,
and are often fourteen a day. The average wages paid
are 4s. 5d.; and No. 40. twist can be produced, every
thing included, at 14½d. per lb. when the raw material
cost 8⅗d. In England, with cotton at the same price,
it costs 14d. These data will serve for points of comparison. As nearly as can be calculated, the average
wages in an English *Coarse* Mill, are 8s. 4d.

Switzerland has been an exporting country for many
years; and the Swiss goods, particularly fine twills and
the better description of prints, have successfully competed with British goods of the same kinds in the Medi-
terranean markets, and lately in South America. There
is no duty on the raw material in Switzerland, nor, of
course, any drawback on exports. The population engaged
in the cotton manufacture is generally well off, and the
people happy.

3. *Prussia* and the *Rhenish Provinces.*—Here the production is
rapidly increasing, though as yet it has not reached any
considerable extent. In 1830, the consumption of raw
cotton was 35,000 bales, or 7,000,000lbs. The number
of persons employed in spinning alone is 7,000. They
work sometimes twelve, but oftener fifteen or sixteen
hours a day. As high as No. 34, they can successfully
compete with English manufacture. The average wages
have not been ascertained. Power looms have been
successfully introduced into the Rhenish provinces.

4. *Saxony.*—In this country, chiefly in the neighbourhood of
Elberfeld, the cotton manufacture is just commencing,
and promises a rapid increase and eminent success.
The yearly consumption may be reckoned to amount
to 1,200,000lbs.; and is fast augmenting. Children are
admitted at six or seven years of age, and the hours of
labour are twelve a day. The average wages paid are
about 3s. 6d. a week. They can compete successfully
with English yarn as high as No. 50. for warp, and
No. 80. for weft.

5. *Lombardy.*—The yearly consumption in Lombardy is about
12,000 bales, or 4,000,000lbs of cotton; but the wages
paid and the number of hands employed have not
been ascertained. They work twelve hours a day.

6. *Austria.*—The cotton manufacture flourishes, and is rapidly

advancing, in Hungary, Austria Proper, and the Tyrol. It is, however, of recent growth. In 1831, the cotton consumed in the Empire was 12,000,000lbs.; the yarn spun in Austria Proper was 4,750,000lbs. Children enter the mills at eight years of age. The newest machinery is employed, chiefly of Swiss manufacture, and the factories in general are remarkably well managed. In the Tyrol, the average wages are 3s. 9d.; and they can produce No. 40. Twist at 15½d. per lb. when the raw material is 8⅔d.

7. *India.*—Spinning manufactories are only just commencing their existence; but the vicinity of the raw material, and the excessive cheapness of labour, will give them great advantages. There is a mill containing the best machinery, and 20,000 spindles, lately established about twelve miles from Calcutta. They work seven days in the week, and eleven hours a day in winter, and thirteen or fourteen in summer, averaging about ninety-one a week. They spin No. 20. and No. 40. twist, chiefly. A spinner who attends to one mule gets 7s. a month. A piecer, (of which there are three to a mule) gets 3s. to 4s. Spinners in England obtain from 5l. to 7l. a month, and piecers from 16s. to 28s. per month.

In the year 1831, from a Report * made by a Committee appointed by Congress in the spring of the year 1832 to inquire into the progress of the spinning and manufacturing of cotton in the United States, it appears that in twelve States there were 795 mills, 1,246,503 spindles, and 33,506 looms. The weight of cotton consumed was 77,557,316 lbs; and allowing two ounces per pound for loss, the total weight of yarn produced was 67,862,652 lbs., the average weekly produce of each spindle being 16¾ ounces. The number of males employed in the cotton-spinning and manufacturing was 18,539, and of females, 38,927; total, 57,466. The amount paid for wages in the year was 10,294,444 dollars, or 2,144,780l., being 42,895l. per week, averaging 14s. 11d. for each person thus employed. The average wages in a cotton mill in England are about 10s. for all ages, and when many power-looms are employed, about 12s. On considering, therefore, the expenses attending the transport of cotton from America, the duty of three farthings per pound (10 per cent) to which it is subjected in our custom-houses, the cost of the transmission of the manufactured produce to the United States, and the duties which are imposed on

---

* See Burn's Commercial Glance.

our manufactures, even by the tariff which has been recently introduced, it will be seen what chance our manufacturers have of entering into competition with the Americans in their own markets; and if we continue to shackle our trade with fresh restrictive regulations, what hopes we may entertain concerning our future success in the markets of other nations.

The preceding details demonstrate how rapidly commercial competitors are rising up, unencumbered by duties on the raw material, or restrictions on the hours of labour, but having, for the most part, the advantages of cheap labour and food. Certainly these statements afford no argument to those who, before any relief from our commercial burthens is obtained, would add to the difficulties already experienced in maintaining the commercial position of the country, by arbitrary regulations affecting the internal economy of trade.

It is a principle in political philosophy, seldom announced, but never contradicted, and which contains a sound and sober wisdom attested by centuries of bitter and calamitous experience, that he legislates best who legislates least;—that laws in their best estate are only necessary evils, and that nothing but necessity can justify their fabrication. Restrictive laws, interfering with the internal regulations of commerce, may prevent the recurrence of some specific evils which they are intended to remove, but they effect this by ultimately occasioning extensive embarrassment to trade, and consequently inflicting serious ills on the working classes. Hence, nothing but the strongest necessity can justify legislative interference with commercial concerns; and the whole onus of the proof of that necessity, lies with those who propose the violation of a great general principle.

The Bill introduced into Parliament by Mr. Sadler, strikes at the root of none of the evils which affect the poor. The opponent of almost every other measure which has been advocated for promoting the elevation of the people;—content to leave them still uneducated, and uninstructed in domestic economy;—horror-stricken at the thought of their being politically enlightened;—the advocate of their improvident marriages;—the protector of the poor laws;—and the champion of restrictions on trade;—he would add, to the benefactions of his microscopic benevolence, the paltry boon of reducing the hours of the labour of the ill-paid poor, thus making them still poorer.

This law would be extremely defective in its practical operation. No restriction of the hours of labour can be extended to all branches of trade, and unless extended to all, it would be unequal and unfair to impose it on any. The best general measure which could be devised to restrict the hours of labour, would be partial in its practical operation. Where manufactories are most subjected to public inspection, and therefore to the influence of public opinion, and where they are consequently best regulated, restrictive laws would, from similar causes, act with the greatest force; but in remote districts, where the present laws are infringed because there public opinion has little power, all future laws would be equally inoperative. Those manufactories which are therefore least amenable to the control of public principles, and are consequently worst managed, would have their sinister advantages increased to the prejudice of superior establishments. Even if the restriction were placed on the moving power, an extent of interference which few would probably be prepared to support, the enactment would be evaded, as all others have been, by mutual consent of master and workman, because it is inimical to the obvious interests of both. Unless a special preventive police were established to enforce the law, it would be disobeyed, as the present law is, by an agreement on the part of the workmen to indemnify the master for any penalty to which he might be subjected for disobedience. This statement supersedes all commentary. Legislature, in the depth of its wisdom, enacts, that under an artificial scarcity of that legislature's own creation, you shall not work a man's children above twelve hours per day, lest their health should be injured; and the man himself, preferring not to starve, guarantees you against penalties inflicted upon you for evading the law passed for the protection of his children.

How will such an enactment, supposing it to be efficient, affect the operatives themselves? One of three events must occur. Either all children under the prohibited age (eighteen), will be immediately dismissed, and their places supplied by adults who will be worked thirteen or fourteen hours per day; or all mills will work ten hours, and the production be consequently one-sixth less than at present, and proportionally more costly;—or the masters will contrive, by employing machinery instead of men, by stimulating their workmen to greater exertions, by increasing the speed of their machinery, to render the law nugatory by producing as much in ten hours as they do in twelve.

Suppose all children under eighteen years of age to be dismissed. The number of individuals now employed in cotton factories in England is about 170,000, of which about 70,000 are children under the prescribed age. The loss to the industrious classes of the community from their non-employment, would be about equal to 15,700*l.* in weekly wages. If the limitation extended to cotton factories alone, many of those dismissed might find employment in woollen, flax, silk, and other establishments; but the result would be a reduction of the general remunerating price of all labour which could be performed by adolescents, in consequence of the immensely increased competition. On the other hand, if, as impartiality would dictate, the restrictive law were extended to all factories, the number dismissed from employment would be far greater than has been above calculated, and they would be unable to find any other occupation, but would be sent adrift to drain the bitter cup of poverty and destitution, or to cultivate every vicious propensity in the school of idleness.

It might be supposed, by those ignorant of the practical regulations of trade, that an equal number of adults would be employed to supply the places of these dismissed children. An adult would, however, frequently be expected and obliged to do the work of two children, and he would not receive, even then, much higher wages, for the profits of trade would not admit of such increase in his remuneration. On the other hand, adults would be obliged to purchase any augmentation of their wages which might occur, by an increase in the quantity and the duration of their labour, in comparison with which the present system is an easy burthen.

According to the second alternative, all mills would work ten hours instead of twelve; the production would be diminished one-sixth; the wages would, after a short interval, be reduced in proportion; more mills would be built to compensate for the diminished supply from those already in operation; a larger number of workmen would thus become dependent on the manufacturer; and, after a certain period of feverish excitement, the market of the trade would be reduced within narrower limits by the increased cost of production, and the wages of the augmented population would be seriously reduced. To what extent this diminution in the reward of labour might proceed, would be determined by the power we might still possess of entering into competition with foreign manufacturers. The injury resulting from restrictions on trade, accumulates however in a rapid ratio, and is especially felt when the danger of the success of foreign rivals is imminent. When the balance is wavering, feathers turn the scale.

Lastly, masters would employ machinery in operations where they now employ men. The limitation of the hours of labour would introduce the self-acting mule throughout the trade, and many thousands of the most highly paid hands would be dismissed from employment.

Or masters would introduce improvements by which they would be enabled to 'speed' their machinery; by which measure, *cæteris paribus*, much greater exertion and attention would be required from the operative. The number of threads which used to break some years ago in certain operations, was thirteen per cent; it is now reduced to three per cent; and other improvements by which the speed of machinery might be increased without a deterioration in the quality of the yarn, would naturally ensue in a season of commercial embarrassment. Thus Throstle spindles used to run 4500 turns per minute; they now run in many cases 5400 turns, and mule spindles have been 'speeded' in a similar proportion. The American throstles have been introduced, which run 7500 turns per minute. Other machinery has also been 'speeded' from ten to twenty per cent. If the Factory Bill occasions the working of machinery at an increased speed, an intensity of application will be required from the operatives, which will at least balance any advantages arising from the diminution of the hours of labour.

Has legislation no better remedy for the evils suffered by the working classes, than this new restrictive blunder! Are we still to continue the slaves of the pernicious school which has manacled our commerce from head to foot? What have the opponents of retrenchment, reform, and free trade to do with the interests of the working classes? Long ago have they proved how ignorant they were of even the elementary principles concerned in the advancement of the social state, and after this bill has caused a reduction of wages,—an increase of mills, and consequently of population,—a 'speeding' of machinery, and a substitution of machinery for men,—will they even then be content to abandon their measure; will they not rather favour us with some new restrictive nostrum for the evils their short-sighted policy has entailed upon the people;— fresh bleeding and more warm water? What remedy would they propose, when necessity had compelled the resumption of the hours of labour;—when production had still further surpassed the demand;—when prices had fallen,—profits were reduced,— wages diminished,—extensive failures had occurred,—multitudes had been dismissed from employment,—and the poor-rates had become more oppressive than ever;—what panacea would they find for these evils;—how would they allay general dismay, discontent, turbulence, and crime?

Are the miseries which have been exposed, to be tolerated without any effort being made for their removal? By no means. Remove the Corn Laws; and as a preliminary, let Mr. Sadler be brought as evidence before a Committee of the House of

Commons to prove their consequences.  A woeful day was it for his employers, when he bethought himself of raking into the consequences of their legislation.  Evils undoubtedly there are, though they have been exaggerated ; and they must be mended at the right time.  But two inferences will force themselves on all whose powers of thought are above the lowest standard. First, that *every man is either dishonest or the victim of dishonesty*, who when one reform is demanded, thrusts forward the absence of another as a reason for refusing it ; and Secondly, that when the two nuisances have been abated which the Factory Bill was brought forward as the stalking-horse to cover and protect,—the Corn Laws and West-Indian slavery,—then and not till then, the government should take the Factory question in hand, and give the country the measure of its talent, by the judgment and despatch with which it applies the remedy.

# PRESENT CONDITION OF THE PEOPLE.

## BY THE AUTHOR OF " OLD BAILEY EXPERIENCE."

### CLASS I. LABOURERS IN CITIES AND TOWNS.

LABOURERS, literally so understood, are contradistinguished from mechanics and artisans. Many of the former are employed in large towns, to fetch and carry materials for the use of the latter ; others in repairing the highways, or as excavators, labourers on the wharfs, coal-whippers, coal-heavers, carters, and those who work the craft on the river ; besides a numerous body of persons, of both sexes, called costermongers, who traverse the town over, and its vicinity, with various articles of common use for sale : among whom is included a considerable body of thieves.

These are the characters which come properly under the meaning of the lower classes in the metropolis. We must, however, include some ten thousand jobbing porters, whose everyday's subsistence is found in casual employment : the whole number of the very lowest class, not including the actual inmates of the workhouse, may be estimated from 250,000 to 300,000.

Never besides themselves on the surface of the globe has existed so many human beings constituting a body characterised for reckless improvidence, for the lowest depravity and profligacy, and so utterly wretched. They perform the most laborious and disgusting offices of the community ; many of them earn good pay, most of which is carried to the gin and beer-shops, or spent in the lowest public-house tap-rooms. They are a distinct class, having, nor professing to have, any fear of God or man ; they are without an idea of religion or morality. Among themselves, it is deemed a reproach to acknowledge or respect a superior ; in their orgies they ridicule the controlling authorities, denying their right to rule : their common cry is, " Let us have a general clearance at once ! down with the parsons ! no places— no pensions—no taxes ! " Anarchy, spoliation, and plunder, are topics which occupy their idle thoughts by day and their dreams by night. I do not mean to say, as was said in a *brochure* lately published, that the better classes are in any immediate danger

from these men ; they are too besotted, too deficient in energy, and want skill to perpetrate any mischief, in a political sense. Should, however, an emergency arise in trade, or any other cause of national excitement transpire, which might break down the dikes and mounds which held them in check, the remembrance of the horrors of the French revolution would be lost in scenes of much greater atrocity, notwithstanding the absence of any immediate danger from this body, or indeed at any time, so long as the middling classes are true to themselves. Our rulers, say they, will watch and put them down ; it is devoutly to be wished they may : but if an opportunity occurs for them to shew their strength, they would be found more formidable than our government considers them. At present, they are only dangerous in a political view, as disaffected ; or we may look upon them as a powder-magazine, which only waits the ignition of the train to explode. Economically contemplated, they are a prodigious nuisance to the inhabitants of London ; were it not for their existence, the metropolitan police might be reduced to one-tenth of its present establishment : the brutality, however, of the lower orders, and their proneness to insult all persons of respectable exterior, makes it absolutely necessary that in every quarter there should be a protecting force. In a moral point of view, whether we consider the anomaly of the existence of such a body in a highly-civilised and polished metropolis, or contemplate them as true Christians and philanthropists, it becomes a question of the first importance to all who love their country or mankind.

If with a standing army, a few thousands or millions of discontented and desperately-disposed subjects be objects of no terror, either to the aristocracy or the middle orders, it may be inquired if we ought not, on other grounds, to endeavour at the tranquillisation and improvement of their minds, by finding out and remedying the cause of their debasement.

Some writers have advised, that the shopkeepers should provide themselves with fire-arms, and prepare to shoot the lower classes, as wolves were in ancient times, when they infested this country. We cannot but suspect those who put themselves forward to give this advice to have sinister motives to gratify; perhaps they think that an armed shopkeeper may, at no very distant period, be induced to attack the more wealthy classes, and let them in for a share of the plunder. Certain it is, that no real friend to good order could be found to set one class wantonly in battle-array against another. A more humane and just policy is open to our rulers — one which it is my ardent desire to press on their attention —a *real* and not *spurious* education for the lowest classes. I am the more anxious and sanguine on this head, because we have two very important facts before us; viz. that there is, quite unconnected with political party-feeling, a genuine and serious intention on the part of rulers to afford every facility for the education of the poor. Secondly, that even now we should have been spared these painful remarks, as they would have been educated, were it not that an infatuation for an erroneous and false system has disappointed our hopes; a fatal error in the plan has frustrated the consummation of the benevolent and politic intentions of the country.

Man educated will ever make a better subject than one in a state of ignorance; every reasonable creature should be rendered capable of considering and reflecting on what relates to himself and the social rights of his fellow-men. It is not necessary that he should be taught foreign languages or abstruse sciences; he may be instructed to know his place in society, and the duties annexed to it, without being made a learned man. Let him be taught that his happiness depends on honest and moral conduct — on the cordial performance of his duties in a civilised and well-regulated country. Some few there are who imagine that any mental cultivation is incompatible with a state which fits men for hard labour; I refer those who hold this doctrine to the improved moral condition of the mechanic and artisan, whose physical toils are in no way short of the common labourer's: a few years only have elapsed since these men were in a simi-

lar state of mental degradation, and I request it may be borne in mind that no class, all circumstances considered, can now vie with the regular mechanic. I am aware that this is not a received opinion with the upper classes—it is nevertheless true; evidence of which has been offered before a committee of the House of Commons, by those who best know their character, and feel an interest in national reputation.

The causes which have wrought this reformation are most important in the history of mankind, and will be discussed in their proper place. We must now proceed to the consideration of the lower class: how it is, in a country replete with establishments for gratuitous education, and abounding in societies for the promotion of moral and Christian knowledge, that such a large number of beings lead such abandoned lives.

He takes upon himself an ungracious task who impugns the judgment of many, and it requires some moral courage to become the first in attempting to convince a whole nation of error. A disastrous one, however, has been committed in the system of education adopted for the poor in this country. If ever any perversion of terms was glaring and palpable, it is unquestionably so in this misnamed national education for the poor. Better would it have been for the poor, and society at large, had they been left in total ignorance of the alphabet, if they were to receive no other instruction; a duty which has hitherto been wholly neglected. Here is the error: teaching the letters and words of a language has been mistaken for education, whereas it is only the means by which it may be obtained. Thus we have rushed into the evil we sought to avoid — we have placed in the hands of children loaded fire-arms, and neglected to teach them their use. Mental suicide has followed.

In the national schools no effort is made to improve the boy's mind, or to prepare him for the purposes of life; nor is there any approximation to an improved and expanded judgment. The manner in which the scholars learn words is calculated to stultify rather than to enlarge the intellect; the method in which they acquire the art of reading is so mechanical, that any good feelings which may be latent in a boy are blunted.

The quick and ready boys are always

at the head of their classes, where an off-hand manner is held in greater estimation than a reflective and sound judgment. When quickness is made the test by which approbation is bestowed, the slow but strong boys give up the race in disgust and despair to the lighter breed; the short and often violent efforts made under the system of emulation, tend to destroy all real love for what is morally and intellectually good. Boys should be made to like that which is good; in a large school, for every one whose improvement is promoted by the emulatory plan, fifty are retarded. Under a private tutor, if two or more pupils can be put together of equal age and mental powers, no system answers so well; but then it requires skill in matching them, as a good coachman would say, when selecting four horses of equal courage and paces, that they may not overwork each other.

The question before us is one of unbounded importance—education for the lower classes. In the most flourishing days of Rome, we are told, its inhabitants were declining; and the reason assigned is, that science and learning introduced refinement and luxury, which have ever been the forerunner of ruin: but it must be remembered, that while the Roman aristocracy were wholly engaged in voluptuous and refined enjoyments, that the other classes became debased and immoral in the extreme. Had a wise policy actuated the rulers in that day, it is more than probable that the heart of the populace might have been preserved whole; if, instead of degrading the commonalty, they had educated them and taught them to value themselves, the moral and physical force of the country might have risen with the exigencies of the state, and been preserved to oppose its enemies in times of peril and danger. This country is peculiarly happy in the desire evinced by all to avert a similar calamity, but at the same time unfortunate in having mistaken the means.

The boys taught at the national schools cannot read, with even tolerable facility, in any book, however simple, if it be not their own; and not one out of ten can, at twelve or fourteen years of age, tell the title of the book they read in (excepting the Old and New Testaments), unless when they are asked the question, they have

the book to refer to. A very large majority cannot read at all without their school-book, and in their own class, so peculiar and injurious is the system. Further, it is scarcely possible to find one out of a hundred who can, under the most accommodating examiner, put two ideas together, and draw any kind of inference of a rational kind therefrom. They can all say their church-catechism, without having the least notion of God or a devil, or of any respect "*for those put in authority over them,*" or the nature of self-responsibility; they can repeat the multiplication-table, without possessing any ideas of the combination of numbers; they can, when standing in their class (which position serves greatly to aid their associations), answer to set interrogatories respecting the historical and biographical incidents in the Scriptures, without attaching any meaning in their own minds as to the bearing or object of the questions: and all this, without the consciousness of having either been asked the questions or of having answered them; so mechanically have the ear and the mouth been brought to act in concert, without troubling the power of reflection.

Those boys who are the most *au fait* at their answers when in school, are always (in London) those who earliest find their way to prison (and there is a good reason for this), where their parents come with a prize Bible obtained at the national school, the names of their sons, with an account of their merits, being inscribed on the fly-leaf: they then urge the propriety of so good a boy being let off on very merciful terms of punishment, although he has picked a pocket.

The best security a state can have against its moral degradation, is that all its members should feel they cannot live without the respect of their neighbours — a feeling which is the main compact of society with all who have in it a place to lose. But a class uneducated have no value in themselves, and understand not the high importance of character; nor will the stultification of the mental powers effect these desiderata. The knowledge of the art of reading only exposes them to the designs of the vilest of men — the writers of cheap, obscene, lewd publications, and low political ballads, in which their betters are held up to ridicule and contempt; slang songs, laudatory of crime and vice in every form; biographies of courtesans and desperadoes, &c.; the vices and the crimes of the clergy; political penny papers, in which they are told that levelism is the law of God, and that the rich are their oppressors. Through the influence of these works, all the sharp and best-reading boys are early diverted from regular habits, and abandon themselves to idleness and debauchery, which leads to crime; the expansion of body precedes the development of judgment, sent out into the world as they are untaught, without rudder or compass. Many hundred boys and girls in this metropolis, under twelve years of age, pair themselves and live together; continence after fourteen, is very rare. Such is the influence of these publications, association, and want of proper instruction. At a more advanced age, the *Poor Man's Guardian* and the *Cosmopolite* take them up, and complete their education; with the assistance of the itinerant speechifying politicians, who, for a draught of heavy wet and a few halfpence, nightly harangue them from the tap-room table. Three of these I have heard, within this last fortnight, who entirely subsist by stirring up the bad passions of the poor. However well or ill-founded the doctrines they teach may be, I will not stop here to discuss; suffice it to say, that the mischief is on the increase, and that nothing but an early inculcation of moral maxims, with an improved judgment, can avail for the salvation of the poor man. It is also a part of the tact of those wretches who cater for his reading faculty, to furnish him with songs extolling the pleasures of drinking and a jolly life; and at the same time palliate the vice, by holding out that the habits of the rich, and the ministers of the church, are the most abandoned of all classes.

The full extent to which this mischief is carried is not known, and when stated, is scarcely credited. In their perambulations, respectable persons avoid low neighbourhoods, and rarely heed if they pass a ragged vagabond, with a bundle of papers under his arm; hundreds of whom are daily traversing the town, spreading pestilence and poisoning the minds of the lower class in every dirty street, lane, and alley. At the head of the first paper is a rude wood-cut of the cloven-footed gentleman running away with the ministers of state on a pitchfork; on the second is the same personage busily engaged in sawing down the pillars of the church; the third exhibits to your view a palace in flames, with numerous crówned heads in the midst of it, while our educated lower orders are huzzaing and throwing up their caps on the glorious occasion.

The first salutations among the gentlemen of the hod and pickaxe of a morning are now accompanied with inquiries whether there be any thing new of the devil's works among the tyrants; and very few hours pass any day without their being gratified with the sight of some such trash opposite their own door, where stands a man (perhaps two or three) bawling out its contents to a crowd of ragged children in the street, whilst the parents suspend all domestic operations to hear its recital from the window.

The publication of a painted daub of a wood-cut, or the singing a few doggerel lines in the street, may be considered by those who look only upon the surface of affairs, and indulge in generals more than particulars, as of trifling importance; but it is universally allowed, that the songs of the celebrated Dibdin contributed much in exciting and forming the character of our seamen during the late war.

In high life and in low, the human mind is never wholly stagnant — every day it is either engaged in imbibing prejudices, or in disabusing itself of them; and it is certain, that poetry affects the highly-cultivated and the most ignorant minds more than the middling classes. This is verified by a comparison of the nationality of all the lower classes in every country with their ballads and tales in rhyme, however rude òr unrefined. It may be said, that the style is adapted to their tastes, and not to form it; but those who know the English populace are aware, that a few stirring songs will, if well circulated, and effectively sung in houses of entertainment, in a few weeks produce a political revolution in their minds: and I am not certain whether the anthem of *God save the King*, and the national song of *Rule Britannia*, have not been the sheet-anchor of the nation throughout the last war. In this day, the poor man finds his Bible in the street-ballads and rhymes, which become his book of morals and rule of life. Go the round of public-houses in low neighbourhoods, and you will find that the poor labourers know no other language; all their aphorisms, apologues, political and religious creeds, are derived from these publications: the exordium, argument, and peroration of all their subjects of discussion, consist in *" as the song says."* It is a melancholy consideration, that the happiness of many hundred thousands of our fellow-creatures should hang on so slender a thread, under the influence of some half-dozen scribblers, divested of principle or shame.

The question then is, how we are to disenthral and emancipate them from the slavery of those who conspire against youth and ignorance. Not by any attempt to shackle the press; such a measure would not only be impolitic but futile, bringing, by an increase of sale, more writers into the market, unless all hawked printed papers were prohibited; the success of which experiment would still be very doubtful. We have, then, but one path open to us — to cultivate the minds of the people to a point above their mental dictators; until this be done, there will always be found a party of wicked men to collude and actuate a large portion of the moral and physical materials of the nation to mischief. The schools which ought to counteract the dissemination of atheism, democratic fanaticism, and immorality, are erected in every parish, and the money is subscribed for their support; it therefore needs only an efficiently improved system to bring about an entire change, to give another tone to the character of the poor man, and, in the philosophical analysis of society, in a short time, to rank him among the number of rational beings. Good morals have existed among no people on the face of the earth, it will be said; but the reason is plainly this, that none have had good laws — rulers will not descend to *minutiæ*: society naturally divides itself into classes; the aid of government is only required to prevent any strong lines of demarcation being drawn between any of the grades in proximity to each other. Society should be like a gentle declivity, that none, with common prudence, need fall rapidly; while the ascent, by perseverance, may be both gradual and attainable: and this is the actual state of the commu-

nity in this country, excepting only the lowest class, whose immeasurable distance in the rear of the mechanic (mentally considered) leaves them without hope.

In the investigation of the merits of the national school system, here is an irrefragable proof of its mischievous effects. No mechanic, if he can possibly pay 7s. or 10s. per quarter, will allow his son to join a national establishment; but the labouring men's children, who do attend them, have regularly retrograded in intellect and morals, while the mechanic, in an inverse ratio, has improved : his conduct and his demeanour have undergone a marked and decided change for the better, and he is rewarded by being in possession of more personal and family comforts. Weak and timid apprehensions are entertained by many lest an effective education of the poor should endanger the welfare of the state; to such I say, examine the political feeling of the two classes above contrasted in morality: the mechanic is reasonable, and passively bent on obtaining what he conceives his rights, constitutionally, through his moral powers; the other is ferocious, and determined, whenever the opportunity can be found, to sate himself with blood and plunder. Here is a practical illustration, that rational education is the only infallible remedy for brutality and debasement— the only panacea to convert bad into good subjects. If the present national system of education be incapable of amendment, it behoves us to abolish it, rather than it should make men worse (which it does) than if found in a state of nature : improved, however, it can be. Do away with the iterative and reiterative plan altogether, and substitute an intellectual one adapted to their condition; make attendance, under certain conditions, compulsory; think less of dogmas and rote tuition; strengthen the understanding by daily exercise, and constantly bring the judgment into activity. Let moral ideas and moral conduct, elicited by frequent examinations, be the subjects of praise and rewards, rather than bestow them on those boys whose vociferous lungs enable them to be the loudest and longest in calling out "twelve times twelve make a hundred and forty-four," &c.

Anxious for the education of all classes, I was a strenuous supporter of the national schools when they were first instituted ; but for upwards of twenty years I have suspected that they were doing mischief. With this impression, I have never missed an opportunity to inform myself on the subject; and it has, in a most fortuitous and remarkable manner, fallen to my lot to have had peculiar and uncommon opportunities to pursue my inquiries. My own experience also in tuition gives me some claim, under several systems, to an attentive and assiduous interest in the development of the youthful mind. I have for several years made it my especial duty to visit the national schools from time to time, and also to collect around me as many boys as I could induce to give me attention after their school-hours, for the purpose of ascertaining and noting their improvement and state of mind. The result of my observations, accompanied with the most serious reflection I have been able to give them, are as follows:—That I never found a boy who exhibited any mental improvement which could legitimately be claimed as the effect of any national-school tuition ; and I hesitate not most unequivocally to add, *that all boys, more or less, under the present system, are stultified,* to a degree which will astonish all interested in the study of man.

This, it will be said, is a broad assertion ; but should I be found mistaken, I know not which we shall have cause most to lament, the truth or error of what I state : for if I am wrong, there is no hope for the amendment of our species in this or any future generation ; but if I am right in saying that the national schools have occasioned the deterioration of our species, then we may cheer ourselves with the anticipation of the most splendid results, by abrogating the whole system and beginning *de novo.*

The more forcibly to impress on my readers that this is not a crude and hastily given opinion, I beg to state, that I have been at the trouble of seeking out more than sixty boys, in low neighbourhoods, who were totally unacquainted with their letters, never having been at any school, but brought up wholly with their parents. My object in this was, the better to satisfy myself whether the general uniform stolid state in which I always found the national-school boys, was the result

of low parentage and habits, or occasioned by the system of tuition. The experiment fully justifies me in denouncing the national system altogether. I found that the reasoning faculties of those untaught, in all save what they received by association with the world and their parents, far to excel any of the boys educated in the national schools. These are facts, the proofs of which are within the reach of all persons really disposed to separate truth from falsehood.

Independently of the hands the poor man's child falls into after he has acquired the art of reading, some other causes must be sought to account satisfactorily for the general ignorance of the pupils when at school, and the universal debasement of all when grown up to manhood. With a view to give this subject the fullest consideration, I have daily, within this last month, attended at some national school, in order, if possible, to penetrate the defects of the system. I asked myself, What is the use of education ? To improve the mental and thereby the moral condition of man— to raise man above his animal propensities — to teach him his social duties here on earth, and to fit him for another state of existence. Have the national schools, then, accomplished any of these objects ? I then contemplated the wretched state of mind in which all those are found who come out of their hands — I thought of the prisons filled with those whom they have taught — I looked at the gin and beershops all over the metropolis, and thought of this passage, *by the fruit shall the tree be known.*

The faculty of uttering words can be of no benefit to any individual — they serve not to convey ideas to the mind. All acquire a sufficient number of words, and the ideas of which they are the signs, to enable them to express their wants, their pleasures, and their pains, in some way intelligible to their fellow-men : mere words, then, for the performances of the common offices of life and labour, desires and wants, are obtained by oral intercommunication, whilst living in a social state of existence. Education, in the common acceptation of the term, for this purpose, then, is not required ; yet this is all the national schools profess to do : and it was thought a new revelation had fallen on us when one boy was brought to teach another to read and spell ; the light, however, so dazzled us, that we did not then perceive that the practical introduction of this discovery not only taught the boys plain words, but subsequently to live without thinking; transforming beings designed for rational uses into mere animal machines, all but leaving the grosser passions under their own control, which is little less than converting the noblest work of God into a brute. That the national schools do inflict this injury on society, will be apparent to any intelligent and unprejudiced man who will seriously and thoroughly undertake an investigation of the subject. For instance, select one or more boys, children of the lower classes, seven or eight years of age ; let them be totally uneducated ; submit them to the examination of persons competent to judge, from a series of questions constructed for the purpose, of the range of intellect the boys possessed, as developed in the replies to the questions propounded to them. It might be as well to select some remarkable for their acuteness, others for their stupidity, and some of middling capacity ; only let the degrees of talent they shew at the time be well ascertained ; then let them be sent to the national schools for the usual routine of instruction. Neither the boys, their parents, nor their teacher, must know any thing of the nature of the experiment; but after every three or six months, during a period of two or three years, let them be brought up for examination, and their mental capacity again noted and registered, making reasonable allowance for their advance in age. Now, if such an experiment were properly conducted, and an impartial jury impanelled, I think, on this particular subject, that I possess prescience enough to foretell, that the boys would, if there were a hundred under trial, be found to have retrograded progressively in mental powers; and, what is still more conclusive, that the longer the experiment was prolonged, the more striking would be mental deterioration. Education for the lower classes should comprise daily instruction in what is good for man to do, and what for him to leave undone ; to inform them that they are moral agents, and that they may themselves know right from wrong, if they will exercise their reflection, and consult a certain innate

feeling, which will be their guide through life under all circumstances of difficulty and doubt; that they have duties to perform, through which only can they obtain happiness, and which, if neglected, will inevitably lead to misery. The nature of virtue and vice, and their effects, should be expounded and illustrated every day by numerous examples from real life. Their acquirement in reading would then be a blessing instead of a curse to them.

Under the present system we have seen that the result is stultification, drunkenness, and demoralisation,—irreligion, political discontent, and a general deterioration of the human species, as far as regards the poor of England. When a boy enters a national school, he joins a class ; in the same room are many other classes, which are all at one and the same time calling out with all the strength of their lungs certain words and figures, amidst the utmost confusion ; and only exceeded by the noise of some extensive coppersmith's, where fifty men are engaged in hammering at one time. I have ever considered that silence was absolutely necessary in a place of study, and that very strong adult minds find it no small difficulty to collect their thoughts in noisy and stormy scenes ; hence it is that peacefulness and quiet are so congenial to a refined and cultivated mind, while the reverse is the enjoyment of those who are uneducated. Let every one capable of reflection apply the case to himself, and then inquire what can be expected from a mind in a state of incipient development placed to learn words under such circumstances. If it be tender, excitable, and susceptible, will it not very soon become confused, irresolute, and in a short time callous and indisposed to all action ? Will a boy so treated ever be able to form a syllogism — to collect two ideas, and out of them to extract a third ? Mr. R. Owen, in his *rational system of education*, very zealously endeavours to enforce, that the character of man is formed under peculiarities of organisation, combined with the external circumstances to which he has been subjected in the course of his existence. Out of this question springs another of equal importance, viz. if organisation and circumstances form the character of man, do not circumstances alone materially affect the organisation and general conformation of man ? If so, we can at all times improve the physical man, as far as we can control the circumstances which surround him ; and we know that, to a certain extent, exercise strengthens all the members of the body. The sailor sees the coming storm ; the African distinguishes objects beyond the reach of an European eye, and knows his friend from his enemy at a very considerable distance, even in the dark, by means of his exquisite sense of smelling ; and the blacksmith's arm enlarges by the use of the hammer ;—so does mental exercise enlarge, expand, and strengthen the reasoning faculties,—hence the importance of its being kept in moderate activity. The national-school boy, however, is placed, at the most critical period of his life, in a situation which renders it impossible for him to think ; and the manner in which he is employed makes it unnecessary that he should exercise any of the mental faculties. The boy is clay in a soft state, ready to take any print or impression ; but as soon as he comes under the system he is in a kiln, and is soon converted into a hard substance which can never again assume its original malleability. It is generally considered that a numerous school is favourable to the improvement of the scholars ; without doubt it is, being an epitome of the great world, bringing their members early into mental and physical conflict with each other ; but it must be remembered, in respectable establishments, that the boys converse with each other, and hourly discuss questions which are laid before them ; the genius of one assists and generates ideas for another, whilst the whole are pursuing progressive studies suited to their years and various capabilities. In establishments of this nature the labours of the teacher are lightened by the assiduity and eagerness of his pupils for knowledge ; in the national school, the master soon becomes as dull and dead to thought as his boys,— both are tied down to a set of movements, similar to the sergeant and his recruits on the parade. If the scheme were good for any thing, it might be made available to teach the factory children while at work. If the young can be so instructed, some modern Stentors should be placed on pedestals in the workshops, to repeat the multiplication-table, or bawl out a half column of spelling throughout the ten hours of their labour. After a few days, however, as it is at the schools, the children not only would cease to hear their teachers, but be unconscious of their presence ; as it is said of a gentleman, who, on bargaining for a lodging, told the landlady that he had but one objection to the place, which was, that, from the tolling of a melancholy bell (the sounds from which just then fell upon his tympanum), he had discovered that his intended dormitory was in close contact with the church. " Oh, sir !" said the shrewd woman, " that's what all the neighbours complain about, and at last it is to be taken down, which order will be carried into effect next week." " Very well," said the gentleman, " if it be only for so short a period I am to be annoyed, I can endure it." Ten days after, the landlady inquired if he heard the bell. " Pooh !" said he, " how could I, you know it's taken down." The bell, however, was still there, but custom had rendered him deaf to it. Carefully notice the countenances of the boys in their classes at the national schools, and it will be evident to any acute observer, that all their duty is performed with unconsciousness : mark the deadness of the eye, the want of animation in every feature — all strongly denoting the absence of thought ; the motion of the lips indicates that the words they are told by the monitor to repeat drop still-born to the ground — none feel an interest in what is going on or passing before them. Like a squirrel in his cage, who spins it round without being conscious that the bars which afford him amusement constitute his cage.

All men now admit the efficacy of education in the exaltation of the human species ; its high value is universally admitted ; but there is one of far greater importance, viz. the manner of it. In estimating the value of any matter learnt, we must consider the mode in which it has been conveyed to the mind. On the manner in which instruction is imparted, and the time employed in comprehending a subject, depends not only the abiding properties, but its appreciation by the judgment, and consequently its value to the learner. Not to understand the application of knowledge to the purposes of our existence is to be without it. " *Whoso loveth instruction loveth knowledge.*" The boy, however, who is never taught the use and value of knowledge, never can love instruction, seeing not the end and meaning thereof; in this consists all the difference between the national schools and all others. Every schoolmaster more or less feels it his duty to induce reflection, except the national teacher, whose avocations partake more of the office of the parish-beadle than a schoolmaster; his functions call upon him to walk about the room, and see that the boys stand true to the chalked line, scream out in their turn, and that no time is allowed for reflection. When a boy enters one of these classes, however predisposed he may be to ruminate and chew the cud of reflection, it is all over with him as a mental being. I defy the most determined and practised thinker to make any use of his mind in such a scene. What then must become of young minds who have yet to learn to think?

Reason has three general assistants, thought, memory, and opinion; besides various other helpers. Thought conceives and calls in the idea; memory forms and retains complex ideas; opinion then confirms by their mutual cooperation, and supports conception: reason only can decide. Reason, which is the organ for judging, is either science or opinion: the principle of one is intellection, the principle of the other is sense. So says Plato. Considered primevally, it is restraint on the passions, a check to vice, and an incentive to virtue. The system for the education of the poor rejects all these considerations: it is a delusion, a mere subterfuge, an excuse for neglecting to educate—it is hypocrisy and cheatery, or foolery. The object of education is the stimulation of the reasoning faculties, the incitement to thought, by which reflection may be superinduced, and the eye of inquiry reflected into the inward man, prompting him to examine his innate sensations, and to adapt himself advantageously to the external circumstances and things of this world. Nothing shews the weakness of those who control the movements of the present system more than the parade and importance attached to the getting up a small book from which young children are to be taught to read in these schools. Committees are formed in every part of the kingdom, comprising bishops, doctors of divinity, and examining masters from the uni-

versities, to discuss the merits of a rudimental small reading-book for the junior classes at a charity-school; every chapter, section, sentence, and phrase, is put to the vote, contested, and as warmly debated as if the fate of nations depended on their decisions. In the categories of the party politician, the construction of a sentence in one of these books will determine whether the reader (or stammerer in it) shall be a future Radical or a Tory; and the ecclesiastic imagines that on the same pivot turns the question whether the world shall henceforth be occupied by saints or atheists. Then, because Lord Brougham's Useful Knowledge Society disclaimed any interference with sectarianism, the Society for the diffusion of Christian Knowledge must establish another called the Society for the Diffusion of Knowledge, the avowed object of which is to supply the world with books calculated to promote religion; as if all real knowledge did not tend to make man more sensible of a first cause, of a ruling power to which all must be amenable—the primary elements of all religions. But, say these quidnuncs, we will have religion taught to the poor in the abstract, independently of all other knowledge, because it comprehends *all other knowledge in itself*. Why do the divines who reason thus labour so anxiously to procure for their own sons every kind of knowledge appertaining to this world? Why do they, regarding their own offspring, take more concern for secular than spiritual matters, and in the case of the poor man affect to be concerned altogether for his immortal part? It is a sickness of the soul to wish for things impossible. The ignorant man may for a time, under peculiar circumstances and frame of mind, be taught mechanically to profess any creed. But religion is apart from profession; it must be felt. Our Christian Society people have hitherto accomplished nothing but their own delusion. They aim at that which is impossible, and from its nature impracticable, viz. to implant true religion on an untaught mind. It never yet did happen that an ignorant and unreflective person long held fast to any doctrine received through the agency of man, unaided by intellectual conviction. Hence it is that so many characters, who were at one time remarkable for their religious enthusiasm, suddenly become the greatest reprobates and scoffers at religion. Hence also it is that the progeny of Puritans, who make religion a bugbear to their children, turn out generally contemners of all religions. The only soil on which religion can flourish and bring forth fruit is an intellectual one. Cultivate and manure the ground, then sow your seeds (if they do not spring up spontaneously)— let religion reach the heart through the judgment, seasoned by reflection, not merely through the ears—let it have a natural, an indigenous growth; if it be reared in a hot-bed, and made an exotic, it will droop and die when exposed to the blast. Locke says, "That God should make a creature to whom the knowledge of himself was necessary, and yet only impart that knowledge by the channel through which all manner of error comes into the mind; a channel much more likely to let in falsehoods than truths—since nobody can doubt, from the contradictions and strangeness of opinions concerning God and religion in this world, that men are more likely to have frenzies than inspirations." Certain it is that, in the art of teaching, those for whom such large sums have been subscribed have not had inspired masters. "Some oracle must rectify their knowledge."

It appears, from a recent report, that 1,097,099 boys and girls are educated in England and Wales at the National and Sunday schools, and that in London there are 100,000 who are not educated, and in all England 500,000. Whether the number which are educated (as the phrase is) be deteriorated or improved as human beings, is the point now at issue. What a consideration for the philanthropist! As far as my experience and judgment can penetrate the question, I feel myself under an obligation to declare that none are benefited—most are losers—and that a very considerable number are every day, under the national-school system, rendered permanently incapable of improvement. The main causes of which may be stated as follow :—1. That all systems of education must be bad which have not for their object the exercise and drawing out the reasoning faculties; 2. That the national schools essay not an attempt at this desideratum; 3. That there is in all minds, when unassisted by human art, a spontaneous and natural development of the reasoning

powers, aided by the ideas elicited through the natural and physical scenes which surround us; 4. That the time employed in the national schools is all a total loss to a boy, because he is deprived of the advantages offered him in the scenes of nature and commerce with the world, without receiving any compensating equivalents from those who profess to render him mental assistance ; on the contrary, he is engaged in a manner positively calculated to repress and crush all thought, however active the predisposition to it on entering his class ; his employment varying little in effect from that of a boy shut up all day with a hammer in his hand to beat strokes against the wall for his amusement ; 5. That all persons disqualified, through the weakness of their reasoning powers, to distinguish right from wrong, in the general sense of these words, should not, if taught to read, be allowed, if it be possible to avoid it, to peruse any writings but those of the purest and simplest kind ; 6. That the rising generation of the poorer classes are both stultified and taught to read, the two heaviest misfortunes which can befall a human being in this age of cheap scribbling and cheap publications ; thus causing their victims to be plunged deep into the dark error of night, through the vitiating influence of a degraded race of dissentients to all moral and political restraints.

The ultimate remedy for these errors in the education of the poor consists in adopting a system which shall cause those who are to be taught to think. Every new principle, every new idea, is knowledge and wisdom. Repetition of mere words avails nothing in the improvement of man. It is not the abundance of words which is needed, but of things —

" Good teaching from good knowledge
        springs ;
Words will make haste to follow things."

They must reflect and compare the merits and demerits of every question brought under consideration. It is well asked by a writer, " What is the use of imagery or facts without mental comment ? A story once told, and its *dénouement* known, who will read it a second time ? The interest is gone ; there is nothing to cite or refer to ; there is no general truth ; nothing applicable to any other combination of circumstances. What is a riddle when it is known?—dead and evaporated! Moral and psychological knowledge is conveyed by comments, not by facts." The boy who reads under the national-school system, would, if there long enough, go through the whole range of science, as written in books, and be in the end as ignorant of the matter he had read as one who was never taught the use of his letters. The encumbering the memory with external facts exercises not the reasoning powers. Dr. Johnson remarked, that some men would learn more whilst stepping over a gutter, than others did by many times crossing the Atlantic Ocean.

In a national school let a competent master be engaged, and let him try the experiment with a class of boys in reading history. Suppose the subject to be Nero's cruelties. When the boys have concluded, let the master say, in a familiar manner, " Well, lads, what think you of this Nero? How should you like such a man for your king?" In their present condition the boys would all stare at him, and evince a total want of thought on the subject; as much so as if they had not read a line from the book. Let the master now rouse them, and continue to say, " What! not notice the abominably cruel conduct of this monster! Come, we must read this again." The probability is, that some would, after the second reading, have something to say condemnatory of Nero's conduct. Now let the master inform them, that the next time they were called up to read he would point out to their notice an opposite character; when he should expect them to give their opinion on the merits of the two, and which was most likely to find favour in the eyes of God. This mode of proceeding (simple as the case is put) would, if followed up, prompt the boys to reflection; and if tact and perseverance were used, more good (as regards making rational beings of them) would be accomplished in one month, than under the present system is performed during the whole time they are under tuition. And here let me hint to the general schoolmaster, that it is not he who retains the most facts in his memory, but he who reasons on them with most discrimination, to whom the meed of praise should be awarded. Schoolmasters of all ranks may cogitate on this hint. There can be no education

without comment, especially for the poor; because they have not the advantages of parental assistance to enable them to turn the eye of inquiry into themselves. School acquirement, in the common acceptation of the term, is of secondary consideration, compared to the exercise of the mind here intended to be pointed out.

In many of the higher schools there are erroneous notions on this head, and the extraordinary disparity of intellect exhibited by boys, at different establishments, is wholly attributable to the modes adopted in exciting the intellectual endowments to reflect, compare, and comment. With a view of furthering this object, a multiplicity of school-books have been constructed, on the principle of question and answer, which have defeated themselves. The teacher gives them to the pupils, out of which lessons are to be learned; of course, both questions and answers are committed to the memory, and the object of the Socratic method of mental employment is lost in the mechanical system of tuition by rote. In all schools where there is an intelligent teacher these books are now excluded—they have been tried and found wanting; all questions for the improvement of the pupil must emanate from the master. One of the most celebrated and expensive works of this kind is Mangnal's *Questions.* The book commences with historical queries, and ends with an account of gamboge, gum, ginger, and nutmegs, &c. &c.; to which is added, a catalogue of constellations, and some of the principal stars. If the contents of this book be committed to memory, only conceive the immense time which must be devoted to it, and how much better it would have been if the same time had been employed in reasoning on only one dozen of the facts contained in it, were it only for the sake of habit. A book describing the actual position of all the mile-stones in the country, would equally well answer the purpose for the abstract consideration of exercising the memory, which, at best, is but a wretched substitute for substantial employment of the mind. The truth, however, is, and it cannot be too generally known, that Pinnock's *Catechisms,* and the whole tribe of such trash, met with success only because it enabled any washer-woman's daughter who could read, and from a book ask questions, to open an

" Establishment for the Education of Young Ladies." There is not, in any part of society, so great and extensive a system of quackery practised, as in the school-business of this country. Asking, the other day, a French lady who had been engaged in several schools as teacher, her opinion of the English system of education, she replied, " Fine clothes and fine houses are the only system in this country."

Schools in and about London (especially for females) have their fashions in education, as in dress. No study is agreeable unless it possesses the charm of novelty; merits of a work, or of style in painting, &c., are no considerations with a governess who has an expensive establishment to uphold. Is it novel? will it attract the attention of the pupils? and will the introduction of it into my school increase the half-yearly bills? These are the questions all prudent ladies ask themselves, when planning a scheme to give a fillip and a new impulse to overcome the *ennui* which so frequently obtrudes itself into English female seminaries.

About ten years since, when the Society for the Diffusion of Useful Knowledge published their abstract of the sciences in sixpenny numbers, natural, moral, and physical philosophy had their turn, when masters were in great request. At this period, and subsequently, I attended, from first to last, some two hundred schools, in and about London, for the purpose of amusing them with experimental natural philosophy. I say amusing them, for as they never intended to learn any thing but a smattering of the subjects brought before their notice, it would have been displeasing had any attempt been made to task their mental faculties : all they want in such cases is to learn only through the eyes, and to express surprise and delight as the various experiments are exhibited to their notice. During this mania, I had an opportunity of penetrating into the arcana of not a few of these places of learning. About one-tenth part only is in the proprietorship of persons qualified to perform the functions : many boys' schools are kept by men who have been servants in gentlemen's families, and some of the most respectable ladies' schools have at their head a *ci-devant* lady's-maid, whose only accomplishments are the art of bustle, dress, and assurance. I knew one

female who had been a housekeeper for upwards of twenty years, that subsequently kept one of the largest and most dashing establishments for the education of young ladies, in which she made a fortune. She would destroy half a quire of note-paper before she could correctly write six lines, with the help of a dictionary, a private study, and three hours' devotion of time; yet did this woman sit down in her school-room, with all the confidence and assurance of the most accomplished and recondite scholar, and through the aid of the books containing pages of questions and answers, she interrogated and scolded her pupils for negligence, and passed for an excellent teacher.

About seven years since, the Rev. Mr. S***h came from Ireland, hired a horse and chaise in London, and drove up with an air of great consequence to the doors of several ladies' establishments, offering to lecture (by way of great favour) on a new principle of pneumonics, of which he was the inventor; stating, that unless they availed themselves of his services on that morning, they would inevitably lose the benefit of his important discovery, which, from the extraordinary facility it gave pupils in the acquirement of all kinds of knowledge, would render their school celebrated and conspicuously noticed above all others. In one week he realised upwards of 100*l.*, purchased a horse and chaise for himself and son (who accompanied him), and took the whole round of schools in the vicinity of London, making, for many months, not less than 30*l.* per day, as he himself informed me; after which he travelled through England, with great success, on the same scheme. His lecture was given at per head for each pupil, in one class, which occupied about one hour in delivering; after which he sold each a book, containing the principles of his discovery, for 2*s.* 6*d.* The extraordinary gullibility of the wisest English heads, is strikingly exemplified in this individual's career; he carried with him testimonials, obtained within the short space of one month, of the efficacy and the utility of his system, from all the first-rate classical schools within twenty miles of the metropolis, including the genuine signatures of the most celebrated men now known in the art of classical tuition. A short time before he quitted England, he called on a gentleman who kept a large scholastic establishment, and proposed to advance a sum of money for his brother, if the gentleman would admit him a partner. As the proprietor of the school had, on a former occasion, spoken very disparagingly of this Irish charlatan, he expressed his surprise that he should have selected him for such an intended favour. " That," said the Irish adventurer, " is answered by telling you, that I have a very high opinion of your good sense in seeing through my humbug; and also a favourable impression of your integrity, because, when I offered you a liberal allowance out of the money to be charged to the pupils, you refused to allow me to waste their time." Voltaire said, when in England, that nothing surprised him so much as to learn that any of the natives were afflicted with disease: being asked why, " Because," he replied, " I observe you have a certain cure for all maladies." This was a pointed sarcasm on English credulity. In this day, his astonishment would be excited to find any lacking wisdom, seeing academies and seminaries in large letters on every tenth house; besides the host of super-enlightened men who are going about to perfect pupils in all languages, in twelve lessons, &c. &c. I repeat, that there is not in any trade, calling, or art, so much trickery and swindling as in the school-business of this country.

Education for all classes should be a consideration of the government, and every subject who can afford to pay for the tuition of his children, ought to have a certain rate of education secured to them, according to the sum paid. Independently of the important question of education, the more legitimate, fair, and upright all transactions are between man and man, the nearer shall we approach to a state of perfect morality. The proximate cause of a laxity of principle, now so marked among our middling classes, is the general cupidity of mankind, and the facility and impunity with which tricks in trade are allowed to pass unnoticed. There is, however, an easy way of remedying the evil now under consideration. Men who undertake either the *cure* of the body or soul are obliged to submit to an examination; and, under prescribed forms, are constrained to prove their qualification for the performance of their duties, or they

are prohibited under penalties from assuming and following their calling. Now, when it is considered that, in a measure, the *cure* both of a man's soul and body depends on an efficient education — at least, that cure which he who is most interested in the question is enabled to give it — does it not raise a wonder in the mind, that no legislative enactment should secure to the public competent and qualified instructors for all classes ? It is a stale adage, that prevention is better than cure; it ought, therefore, to be our policy so to teach men generally that fewer parsons and doctors may be needed every generation. As sentiments of freedom and universal liberty become prevalent, it is natural for men to feel a repugnance to restrictive enactments; hence the cry for breaking down the monopoly of the church establishment, and the manifold complaints against the colleges of physicians and surgeons, and the company of apothecaries: yet all advocates of rational liberty will discriminate between the use and the abuse of power. There is a tyranny of democracy; but if the public weal alone is to influence the measures of governments, nothing more imperiously demands their attention than the state of our scholastic establishments throughout the empire. I propose that the teaching profession be divided into four classes, and that a course of examination for each be instituted; on their passing which they may receive licenses, according to their qualifications, to set up as schoolmasters and mistresses, having printed on their prospectuses first, second, third, or fourth class.

This division would include accommodation for all the grades of society, in proportion to their means, and secure those who embarked in the profession against the intrusion of quacks; every man, on the one hand, would receive a payment for his labour in accordance with his talent, and on the other, every parent would have a guarantee that his offspring would receive value for the stipend paid. This measure would place the teachers on a respectable footing, and insure them a position in society which the arduous duties they have to perform demand. There are no people so apparently acute in worldly affairs as your London tradesman, and yet none are more credulous and gullible. Accustomed themselves to deceive the world by outward show and tinsel decoration, they fall the first into their own trap. Hear them talk to each other on the eligibility of a school for their children : " Fine house!—well furnished!—beautiful view!—only four miles from town ! —coaches pass every hour !—only a Sunday walk !—plenty of food !—and the master a devilish hearty fellow !" Not one out of a hundred will speak of that which is the most essential; viz. the qualifications of the master to teach that which is promised on the face of his prospectus.

These remarks on schools in general have incidentally obtruded themselves; the subject is one of national importance, and on which there is great room for amplification : suffice it to say, that if teachers were called upon to undergo an examination, nine out of ten of those now engaged in tuition must abandon their profession. It is natural to expect, that the intelligence of the people should be in proportion to the capital expended on the cultivation of the public mind; preparatory, however, to the fulfilment of this just expectation, the masters who are employed must be in advance of their scholars in the acquirement of knowledge. The reputation and the interest of the country demand that it should be so ; which, however, can only be effected through the examinatory and licensing system.

But this savours somewhat of a digression, my subject confining me to the evils arising out of the Lancasterian plan of education for the poor in large towns — a body as decidedly reclaimable as any other in society, if properly treated at the proper period. It will be urged, that the whole number of poor children cannot be even taught to read under any other system. Suppose, however, we divide the school-rooms now built into two parts, upper and lower, continuing the present plan for the junior boys only, until they are able to read in their first book ; after which, let them be removed to the upper school, where the whole system shall be an intellectual one, under a competent master to hear them read, and comment and question thereon. One half the day should be spent in this way—one hour in writing and ciphering, that they may not be wholly uninformed on these heads, although of secondary consideration for a poor man who is doomed to wield the spade

and pickaxe. The remaining hours should be employed in committing to memory such matter as may be deemed desirable and profitable in promoting the great object of reflection. Moral axioms and trite rules of life are the best lessons for the poor—they are fond of the terse ; and a stock of concise sentences and sayings would be armour to defend them against their enemies, the writers of immoral and licentious publications. It is desirable that they should be drilled, and made perfect in a small but good work of this kind. Dr. Franklin justly appreciated this style of conveying knowledge to the untaught man, when he wrote his *Poor Richard*, and other similar works. In this arrangement, it would be desirable that not a larger number than fifty boys should be under one master ; yet if the Perryian system were adopted, a hundred or more might be managed without confusion, their lessons heard, and all the pupils prepared every hour, if found necessary, for a general examination of the master. Of all the systems ever yet invented, that of Mr. Perry, for wholesale tuition, outstrips any other yet known. Rapid modes of teaching, however, are at all times, and under all circumstances, objectionable. It is very evident that the poor cannot (even were it desirable) be thoroughly educated ; it becomes us, therefore, not only to select that which is useful and suited to their conditions, but also that we should be careful that that which they are taught should be done in a way to make a lasting impression — that it should have a pre-occupation of the mind, and take precedence of all other matter likely to be thrown in their way, as they pass from boyhood up to man's estate. Some will exclaim, You want to fill their minds with prejudices — the idols of the den ! Certainly I do, if those prejudices favour the cause of virtue, and will work the redemption of a million of our fellow-creatures from a state of wretchedness and debasement of mind ; for, notwithstanding all that is said about first filling the belly before you think of *learning*, vicious habits and improvidence of conduct are the parents of ninety-nine hundred parts of the distress and misery which pervade this metropolis.

In London there are so many ways in which every person, whose habits of dissipation do not interfere with industrious resolutions of obtaining a living, that few need want who will remain sober. If it could be ascertained, I have not the slightest doubt but that 200,000 persons (or whatever number there may be in the metropolis and its vicinity)— labourers, huxters, sweepers of street-crossings, &c. &c.— obtain more money in the course of the year than the same number of regular mechanics who have been brought up to trades, and find constant employmen?. Many families among the poor who attend markets of all kinds, on the speculation of a glut of any commodity of food, will oftentimes realise in one day 2*l.* or 3*l.*; and this I have known happen several times in one week : even the women who sell fruit in the streets will occasionally have their lucky days; the average profits of these stalls is from 3*s.* to 5*s.* per diem ; but I have myself more than fifty times heard a day's reckoning of profits cast up by fruitwomen which amounted to 1*l.* and upwards, besides the extra drains taken on these occasions. We hear a great outcry about the poverty of this class, but they are only poor through improvidence; as a proof of which, I may adduce the fact, that among the mechanics in 1831 there were 4117 friendly societies established, consisting of one and a half million of members; and that, with the most diligent inquiry, I cannot in the whole metropolis find one provident society instituted by the class now under our consideration : yet I do not write unadvisedly or without data, when I affirm, that as a body, in proportion to their numbers, they not only obtain more money than the mechanic, but carry on their predatory callings to a greater advantage than the small tradesman, who has to struggle with the payment of house-rent and taxes, and the maintenance of a decent appearance in the world. Among the lower classes it is the want of self-respect, and a total disregard of habiliments and cleanliness, which stains and defaces the population of the metropolis, giving more the semblance than the reality of poverty. Without doubt, many of their families are every day in want of the necessaries of life; the same may be said of an equal or a greater number of families in the more respectable classes, where it is less apparent, every effort being exerted to disguise straitened circum-

stances, when a decent pride prevails over the mind ; on the other hand, the low man, being without shame, often complains of poverty with plenty of money in his pocket. It is not long since that upwards of 7*l.* were found on an Irishwoman, who, together with her husband, were applying for relief at St. Marylebone workhouse ; but, in most cases of actual distress among the working lower class, it is brought on themselves by drunkenness and other indiscretions.

The disease is in their state of mind, their disregard of character and contempt of the world's opinion — *contemptá famá, contemptá virtute.* No physical or moral power with which man is endowed can now make these men Christians, or transform them into rational creatures. The Society may pour down tracts and homilies till they lie as thick as Alpine snow — nothing can avail — it is a hopeless case, which all men, if they have not private ends of their own to warp their judgment, and are acquainted with mankind, will acknowledge. Our hopes and all our means should now be directed to their offspring ; we must aim, through a proper mode of instruction, to dispel the darkness of the mind, and let in the pure light of reason — the only guide that God ever intended for man. We must labour to engraft on the rising generation a decent pride, and give them a taste for real domestic comforts ; they must be taught that the sums of money which their parents spend in destroying health, may be made available for bettering the condition of themselves and their families, when they are called upon to support one.

In their present state, the working poor are conscious of a distinctness of character, and of an unfitness for any society but their own ; they are outcasts in a world full of persons of their own natures. No other class is in this predicament ; none are without hope of rising in society save the lowest; all think themselves qualified to sustain a station higher than that which they occupy among men : here are recognised the incentives to industry and virtue. But the poor man is out of the race ; bring him near enough by instruction to participate in the prospect of the general benefits of society, and, like other men, he will become a candidate for a good name. It is the mental breach which occasions that yawning chasm which there is between the poor man and all the rest of society — it is a gulf over which he knows he cannot pass; the hope of rising and the fear of falling are both alike unknown to him; his only resource is in abandoning himself to the gratification of his appetite. Despondency and hope alternately possess the lovers of mankind, when contemplating the probability of the universal reign of virtue : there is, however, no reason why we should despair, if we observe the powerful restraining causes which operate, even now, in the preservation of virtue and repression of vice, on all who have a caste to lose. If we are not in an actual morally improved state, as compared to any former age, yet it is very evident that we have advanced one step towards it in the almost universal desire evinced by men *" to assume a virtue, if they have it not."* It is past dispute that character is held in higher estimation than heretofore, and also palpable to the sense of every man who keeps his eye upon society, how peculiarly careful all are to disguise their failings, and to stand fair with their neighbours. I remember the time when all young men were ambitious to be thought drunkards and libertines — even Virtue then fell into the fashion, and assumed the garb of Vice; now it is reversed : loose principles are as prevalent, but none will exhibit them gratuitously. We have achieved something; we have put a check of reprobation for immoral conduct on all the links of society, excepting only the lower one, which is like a recently amputated limb, having no sympathies or sensations with the other members but those which cause pain, and, by superirritation, derangement of the system : they have none of the amenities of civilised men even among themselves — sordidness and brute passions fill up their span of life.

Whatever may be the state or condition of man, on the adaptation and fitment of his mind to the external circumstances which surround him depend his happiness. In an uncivilised state of existence, he in a wonderful manner adapts and accommodates himself to climate and privations ; but in an artificial society, with all the conveniences and luxuries for the enjoyment of life every hour full in his view, the poor man cannot so facilely bend his nature to his fate. With all other men the good things of this life are the prizes held out to them as incentives to virtue, whilst we shut the wretched out of the race, and still demand as much exertion from him as if the reward were before his eyes. Besides, a man without knowledge, or the desire for it, can have no prospects beyond those of every day's gratification of the animal passions, his whole time being spent either in providing for the exigencies of the moment or in drunkenness. How is he to become possessed of any moral maxims, or rules of life, if not inculcated in early days, before he is called upon to perform his part as a man ? Some say, meddle not officiously with society. So every sensible man would say. It will assort itself, and find its own level, if you organise and reorganise it to the end of time : the gradations of power and property will and ought to have their weight ; but then we should give an equal chance to all. Man uneducated is little better than a brute. Do we then reverence the commands of God, who sent his Son into the world for the salvation of mankind, in keeping some hundreds of thousands of our fellow-creatures in a state of brutality, with the means in our hands of redeeming them ? We have the power (knowledge), and the great lever is at work ; but from the mechanism which it propels there is no hitcher on the poor man's wheel to bring him within the range of its influence. It is a disgrace to our pseudo-religionists and hyper-professors, to whom the benevolent and truly good have intrusted their money, that the poor should daily be deteriorating as moral agents and human beings,

" Fit for the mountains, and the barbarous caves,
Where manners ne'er were preach'd."

PRESENT CONDITION OF THE PEOPLE.

BY THE AUTHOR OF " OLD BAILEY EXPERIENCE."

## CLASS II.

### LOWER METROPOLITAN TRADESMEN.

THE provincial petty shopkeeper is generally a man of industry, and one of usefulness to his neighbour; in the metropolis they are of an opposite character, being a predatory, moving body, who for the most part live, in various ways, by chicanery and plunder.

A very large number, however, of chandlers' shops, and other petty dealers, are kept by the wives of mechanics and minor clerks, who form an exception to this general denunciation. A small shop of business in London very rarely supports itself honestly; full one-third are opened as a blind, while the principals are engaged in callings more profitable, but less regular. I once marked out twenty small shops, which stood from year to year as steadily as if a very lucrative trade were attached to them, although I never could see a customer in them. Prompted by curiosity, I took infinite pains to penetrate into the secret. Out of the twenty I at first selected for my experiment, I found two belonged to smugglers, or venders of contraband goods, whose depôt was at any place rather than their home; four were receivers of stolen goods, who carried on their business at places of rendezvous; five were waiters, or groom-porters, at gaming-houses; two were sham-ringers, or passers of base coin; three E. O. and *une deux-cinque table* keepers, who travelled the country to visit races in the season; one, I have every reason to believe, belonged to a gang of wealthy housebreakers; another, clerk to a money-lending swindling party; another, such as is called " a modest brothel," viz. a milliner's shop;* and the other, as it subsequently turned out from the detection and prosecution, a house where a private still was car-

ried on. All men who live upon the cross (practices contrary to law), and are liable to appear every day before a magistrate, find it to their account to have some ostensible or apparent calling on which they can fall back, and put forward as the means of their living. Many small shopkeepers subsist entirely upon giving false bail; that is, coming forward for a douceur when wanted, to swear themselves worth any sum of money for which security may be required to be given. We need not wonder at men making a calling of giving bail, when we see it encouraged by the judges who sit at Sergeants' Inn. A few days previous to the law-return days these men come in flocks to solicit employment: one can scarcely enter the inn for their pressing importunities. Through this body the judges pass, in the way from their carriages to the chambers, having a full knowledge of the purpose for which they are assembled. It is true that they are called men of straw, two sticks, &c. &c., and used only at this place for a temporary purpose; yet such useless practices and legal fictions should be abolished; it is a bad example, and none who have a beginning here with a half-a-crown fee ever stopped short of open perjury, for any purpose, in proportion to the bribe offered. A very considerable number of small shopkeepers are supported by letting their lodgings to females, where prostitution is carried on with less offence to public decency than in open and avowed brothels.

I do not diverge from the point of truth in affirming, that nearly another fourth of all the small shopkeepers in and about town live by moving from place to place, and running away when

* As in all other trades, without doubt, there are many milliners in this metropolis whose respectability is unquestionable; and also many who are employed by the middling classes in this calling, that maintain industrious and unblemished characters. But if the truth regarding London deceptions may be told, there is none equal to the practice of alluring young men into snares, under the pretext of carrying on this business. I believe that I could, in a few hours any morning, point out two hundred milliners' and dress-makers' shops, or parlours, not one of which is kept by persons who would thank a female to enter, either to make a purchase or give orders for making up goods.

getting into debt. The extent of this practice is known to landlords. This will be thought too astounding for credence, and illiberally unjust as to extent. In reply I say, that in sitting down to describe society, I can only state facts as I find them; and that I have not turned to the right hand or the left, nor been influenced by any desire to astonish and deal in hyperboles. I have observed and written only what I believe to be true, and have in most part seen, or had confirmed by the experience of others. The several classes are sufficiently illiberal towards each other; lookers-on ought not, therefore, to libel any. He who has spent a life in chicanery and trickery, when his pouch is full and the game of trade-play over, takes up with honour and honesty, and denounces abuse in others. Men who once palliated their own crimes in the defence of others of the same caste, now unblushingly sit in judgment, and consign others to the gallows for practices not less dishonest than those by which they rose into importance; they will not say,

" Let wretches loaded hard with guilt as
    I am,
Bow with the weight, and groan beneath
    the burden,
Before the footstool of that Heaven I've
    injured."

Men read life as they read their Bible, according to the circumstances of their environment and commercial purposes.

The labourer is a useful member, but a demoralised one for want of tuition, and poor only (in London) because improvident.

Without the mechanic, civilisation would be a chimera; he erects the edifice which protects us from the inclemencies of the seasons; he makes in a desert a comfortable home, and embellishes it with all the luxuries of superfluous wants; he has at length seen his own usefulness, and now feels his importance in society; he is temperate because intellectual, and independent because industrious; his avocations are those of art, which lift him above mere physical labours or matters of petty exchange. The minor tradesman, as the political economist would say, has but one property—that of *consumption. He produces nothing;* some little he *distributes;* but it would be better for his neighbours, in the majority of cases, if he left this work unperformed. Imposition and roguery mark his progress in all transactions. False weights and measures are the curse of the poor; the annoyance-juries are no annoyance to the petty trader, who sets them at defiance. The poor are cheated of weight in every article they purchase, unless they are wise enough to go to a respectable shop; but, in most cases, their improvidence precludes them from this privilege.

I would not be understood to include in these strictures many little tradesmen, who, beginning with small capitals, endeavour through industry and fair dealing to rise to a more substantial trade, for the laudable purpose of supporting a family. The nefarious tricks, however, of most of the small shopkeepers are very enormous, and should be exposed; the petty shops are so numerous that many return, in money, scarcely enough to pay the bare rent of the premises they occupy: how insignificant, then, must be the profits under a fair system of trade? The little general shopkeepers in London are supplied with their goods by persons who manufacture and prepare articles expressly for the petty dealer. Thus there are bakers who manufacture bread of an inferior quality and light weight, who confine themselves exclusively to serving chandlers' shops. There are grocery adulterers, who vend articles at half the usual cost. Coal-merchants, who mix up large quantities of inferior qualities with a small portion of the better sort, making this commodity pay, with short weight, cent per cent; which is a pressing hardship upon the poor: even bundles of fire-wood are made up of a particular size for this trade. In fact the poor man, in one way or another, pays nearly thirty per cent more than the rich for the necessaries of life. There is, perhaps, no remedy for these impositions but to make the poor, through early tuition, more provident and better informed on the subject of economy. There is not much honesty, of a genuine nature, extant in any of the walks of society; but want of a moral principle peculiarly characterises this class —I speak generally. As before said, one-fourth of them roll or float over the metropolis, and its vicinity, on speculating schemes of cheating the neighbourhood where they settle. Many make a false shew of business

—manufacture bills and receipts of goods bought from week to week, during the occupation of their shop, then advertise it for sale, and take in some unwary newly-married couple, for whom they represent it as peculiarly adapted; obtaining fifty or a hundred pounds premium for good-will, &c. &c. They then move to some other quarter, and conjure up another profitable concern; all of which they are only induced to part with *in consequence of going into the country to carry on a concern bequeathed them by a relative, recently gathered to his fathers.*

Many hundreds have for years found this a profitable pursuit; and I question whether there are not more than one thousand families, in this present year, who have no other means of subsistence, and perhaps have no wish to try any other, finding it sufficiently lucrative for their purposes.

The larger number of those now under consideration are, however, fly-by-night birds (to use their own phraseology); that is, persons who live entirely upon credit, staying in one neighbourhood until it is too hot for them, when they resort to another — removing their goods at night, technically called *shooting the moon.* This practice is somewhat lessened, in consequence of the police commissioners having issued orders that their officers shall take the name and number of all vans and carts they see engaged in removing household goods, so that they may be traced. Although this precaution has lessened the practice of nocturnal flights, yet it has not decreased the number of rovers on the town: unity and confederacy surmount this difficulty. They do not all in one party want to remove on the same day; one therefore conveys his goods to the house of another, and the next day carries them to his new residence, and thus secures a safe retreat. Men of one caste, particularly those who live upon the expedients of the day, associate, and have a fellow-feeling for each other.

It is the object of this floating body to contract debts in every neighbourhood they honour with their presence; for which purpose they often take shops, and when an accumulation of debts presses them hard, and they can no longer resist the law, they take the benefit of a whitewash, and at it again, as they say, for another five-mile heat.

The number which subsist in the metropolis of London upon this systematic course exceeds the belief of those who see no more of men than that which lies within their own immediate sphere of action. The Arab or the gipsy does not live a more predatory life than this body; only as one roves over a dense population, while the other takes to the plains and wood, both living upon exiguous resources from hour to hour and day to day, like the *feræ naturæ*, the harder they are pressed the more daring they become.

This class, unlike regular robbers and swindlers, have no special characteristic, but are a mixed body, comprehending all trades and assumptions: they not only vary their locality with the changes of the moon, but their callings, existing not altogether by any defined legal or illegal fraud, make business subservient to dishonesty. They are bound up in little bands and knots for mutual defence; when discovered and arrested, they have all the advantages of honest but unfortunate tradesmen, although they never for one moment contemplated the payment of their engagements, representing themselves as unfortunates who have struggled hard against the adverse fate of mishaps. Society has especial cause to deplore the toleration of this body, whose progeny cannot but be familiarised with trickery and chicanery: they must also be devoid of education, and, through the force of example, unprincipled and bred in idleness.

We shall, perhaps, be not far from the truth, if we attribute to the Insolvent Debtors' Court the existence of this class as a systematic body. Our law of debtor and creditor is founded upon injustice, which must ever work evils in the community. The honest but unfortunate debtor is involved in the same fate with the swindler and the rogue: both are imprisoned alike, unconvicted of any crime.

Three-fourths of the inmates of every debtors' prison are comprised of men whose whole study it is to live upon their wits, and to avoid labour; when, therefore, in a state of despondency, an honest but unfortunate ruined man is for months associated with these characters, he becomes disgusted with the injustice of the laws, feels himself disgraced, and imbibes a sentiment of resentment; and in this frame of mind listens to schemes and tales which teach him how to make reprisals on the world. Penury and the desertion of his former friends come in to aid in breaking down his principles; he feels himself injured, and abandons himself to schemes of retaliation. In the course of his incarceration he learns all the modes of obtaining credit in multifarious trades, and how, by the aid of confederates, the public may be taxed for his support.

At first he proposes to himself, that having lost his credit among his former connexions, he may try to regain his former position in society in another quarter, and embark in a fresh calling; for this purpose, he greedily collects all the information he can of the ways of the world from his prison companions. In this state of mind he is again ushered on the stage of life, still unwilling to allow a whisper from conscience that he is contaminated, and that the barriers of principle are broken down. On his appearance in the world he meets with a chilling reception from his former companions, and finds himself without capital and surrounded by a family in want of every necessary; whilst he occasionally meets with some of his prison-associates in the streets, whose appearance denotes flourishing circumstances, and who seem to reproach him with want of ability. He now throws aside his timidity, and after a time is offered a reference by some of his former associates, who are already settled in shops; which induces him to boldly venture upon taking one himself, not for the purpose of plodding on as heretofore, but to possess himself of money, by obtaining goods without the slightest prospect of payment. He is now constrained to make false statements, and desperately push for credit; he is taught the art of making a show out of nothing, by putting dummies upon his shelves, &c. &c.; gives and receives cross-acceptances, to offer as security for goods; sells at a loss to outdo his neighbours, obtain ready money to make first payments, and procure larger credit: in fine, he is now nothing less than a legalised swindler, by the law of debtor and creditor.

" Let never man be bold enough to say,
Thus and no farther shall my passions
    stray;
The first crime past compels us into more,
And guilt grows *fate* that was but *chance*
    before."

In a few months, seeing that he cannot stand his ground, nor again take the benefit of the act, but dreading poverty, he contrives to put 50*l.* or 100*l.* into his pocket, and abandon his premises; then sends the key by one of his associates to the landlord, with threats that, unless he consents to take it, and forego the rent, he will keep him out of possession until his premises are dilapidated. In ninety-nine cases out of a hundred this is agreed to, the landlord wisely considering that the first loss is the best. The success of this adventure, after a short seclusion in idleness, and perhaps debauchery, encourages him to follow up the same system; and thus out of an honest man a prison has made a rogue, and involved a large family in sinister practices for the remainder of their lives, and, perhaps, for generations to come.

Remember, this is an every-day event, while the government is looking on, and wondering what it is that demoralises society.

It would be thought that such practices, from their frequent occurrence, would be generally known and guarded against by every prudent tradesman; but it is forgotten, that every year the monster Death removes a large portion of the experienced and wary, whose places are filled up by novices. The mischief lies in the system—in the indiscriminate *imprisonment for debt.* If, however, it were possible to make all men cautious, the evil could not end here; when once the principles and character are gone, if men cannot cheat they will rob, and swell to a fearful extent our criminal calendar: as it is, many of this class do annually fall under penal sentences, and it is astonishing that rulers should be so blindly fatuitous and pertinacious in upholding a system so fraught with mischievous results.

Many of the men engaged in this warfare keep a regular ledger, in which they insert the names and residences of all persons with whom they have in the course of their career had dealings, and honoured with a call, that they may not tread the same path twice over. As their dupes die, fail in trade, or retire from business, they are marked off in the book; but many, through constant practice, know the whole body of London traders, as persons are known to each other in small market-towns—

large numbers, of experience, having been in prison a dozen times, and taken the benefit of the insolvent debtors' act every five years, or oftener, since it passed into a law.

If we inquire into the nature of the Insolvent Debtors' Court, and its effects upon society, we shall see that it works all ill, having not one redeeming feature in the system. The bill emanated from the House of Lords, whose knowledge of the affairs of trade, and of society in general, is picked up from lawyers and a few city merchants, who are occasionally consulted on questions of commercial polity. Lawyers are better at expounding and evading than making laws, unless it be to increase their own practice; and merchants, although well acquainted with business upon a larger scale, and the nature of foreign trade, know but little of the details of the common trading class. Moreover, when legislators have the fullest and the very best evidence upon any subject, they always mar their measures by the introduction of isolated abstract opinions of their own, setting up theories against practice, calling themselves lookers-on, and therefore more competent to judge; hence timidity and indecision characterise all their movements in regard to the internal policy of the country: they fear to repair, lest they should have to rebuild. Besides, in all questions connected with laws for particular classes of society, there are a number of interests to be considered, which is the reason why bad laws and abuses of all kinds find their supporters. It is the sin of our government, that in all their legislative remedial measures for the benefit of the public they endeavour to amalgamate and accommodate all these conflicting parties; to enact laws which shall serve both the abusers and the abused; to harmonise and reconcile opposite principles in nature, and effect a happy state of society, as we make punch by a mixture of sweets and acids. In the vain hope of legislating at some period for the interests of the people at large, and at the same time conciliate the ambitious views of the rich and powerful, no question is fairly placed before the legislature, discussed, or grappled with, in the way the subject demands.

In a country so enlightened as this, we have a right to expect equal justice meted out to both high and low; not that one man, who contracts debts by thousands which he is unable to pay, shall have immunity from imprisonment, while the poor debtor for a few shillings is consigned to a gaol. The following instance, which recently came to my knowledge, is peculiarly striking, and illustrates this species of injustice of the law.

A very respectably connected young man, a musician, was taken in execution, upon a summons issued from the Court of Requests in the borough, for 18*s.* Being out of employment and unable to pay, he was taken to Horsemonger Lane Gaol, and confined in a loathsome dungeon used for felons, where he was fed after the same manner: viz., one day, gruel and soup; and the next, six ounces of boiled fresh neck of beef, carried round in a pail, which was thrown to him by the keeper as if feeding a yard-dog. A few days subsequently to his caption, a friend, hearing of his misfortunes, went to the prison with an intention of paying the debt: the prisoner, however, although suffering from ill-treatment, would not allow him to do so; saying, that his cruel usage was sufficient payment, and that, rather than the plaintiff should have his money, he would remain in prison until his death.

Thus was a young man disgraced like a felon — his character blasted — all the worst passions engendered — familiarised with a prison — rendered desperate, and exasperated against the laws of his country — irritated to the highest degree with society altogether, for tamely submitting to the infliction of such shocking injustice upon one of its members; and all this is occasioned by an honest man being out of employment for a short time, and owing 18*s.* for lodgings, which at the moment he was unable to pay.

Talk of monstrosities, and savage life! no circumnavigator ever brought home a tale of horrible cruelty and injustice to compare with this. But the worst is not told. In another part of the prison, where there were comforts allowed, debtors for larger amounts were confined, and permitted to purchase every luxury their funds could afford them. One man, who was known to be a notorious swindler, having money, obtained a private room, and lived in the first style, taking every day his bottle of wine, &c. Our hero's friend, seeing the cruel situation of the young man, conferred with the gaoler upon the subject of his removal to the debtors' yard, and the means of affording him other sustenance than that allowed in the prison; but was informed that, it being a small debt (under forty shillings), he must remain in the dungeon, and be fed only upon prison allowance: and that, as an expiation for the offence of not owing forty-one shillings, or more, no money could purchase him even a pint of porter during the several weeks he must be imprisoned. Whilst the prisoner's friend was meditating upon this specimen of English legal justice, a waiter passed him with a dinner-tray, upon which was a roasted duck with the et cæteras, and a bottle of wine; which, on inquiry, he learned was going to his highness the notorious swindler, who was in debt something more than forty shillings by several thousand pounds, and therefore not punishable in the eye of our superexcellent laws in the same manner as one who had the wickedness not to pay eighteen shillings, although without money.

Seriously, unless we take special care to have these matters well attested, and registered in the archives of the country, posterity will not believe them. I know that I should have suspected the veracity of a man who were to bring me the tale from another land, however uncivilised its inhabitants might be.

The reader must not suppose that this judicious discrimination in the punishment of crime and misfortune is peculiar to one gaol, or to the county of Surrey. In all prisons for debt, the want of accommodation (that is, the punishment) is inversely to the magnitude of the debt; which, of course, in these cases of imprisonment, is the crime. It is for this reason that men who are guilty of the crime of being in debt, when in prison, taking the same view of delinquency as our equitable laws do, always make themselves out as innocent as they can, by magnifying the number and amount of their debts, and assuming airs of consequence over their more guilty but petty fellow-debtors, in proportion as their debts can be made to appear large.

In Mr. Charles Mott's evidence, given before the commissioners on the administration and operation of the poor-laws, we have an opinion of some value on this subject. He says, at p. **322,** " I am well informed that credit is given to the poor people, on the knowledge on the part of the creditors that they have a sort of security on the parish-rates. They know, that when the head of a family appears likely to be thrown into prison, on the judgment of one of the small-debt courts, the wife and family immediately apply to the parish for relief; and the parish-officers too often assist in paying the debt, in order to get rid of the burden of his wife and family. I can hardly trust myself to express my feelings with relation to what I have heard, and the instances I know of the oppression and cruelty practised by these small courts, where the judges are *small shopkeepers, directly interested in the decisions.*"

In the year 1829, there were 932 committed to Horsemonger Lane prison, on process out of Courts of Request, and confined during periods of from one to one hundred days; the aggregate amount of these debts were 1900*l.*, and the costs 574*l.* During the same year, 1563 persons were confined in Whitecross Street prison for similar periods; and the total amount of their debts was 2071*l.*, and the costs 746*l.* The return from this prison states, that there are upon an average about 75 prisoners on process out of the Courts of Request constantly in the above prison; and their food, firing, bedding, medicine, &c. are estimated to cost annually 422*l.* 14*s.* 4*d.*

The tally shops and chandlers' shops, forming by far the larger proportion of the business of these courts, have effected much mischief, in fostering habits of improvidence among the poorer classes. The apology for these courts has ever been their cheapness; yet it is seen by the returns that the costs are little less than one third of the money sought to be recovered. Every plan which is calculated to settle the disputes of men equitably, cheaply, and promptly, will meet with universal praise and support; but none of these objects are attainable in the London petty courts. One who walks through the metropolis for the purpose of hearing the opinions of men cannot but be struck with the very general disapprobation expressed by all men of intelligence of the machinery of our petty courts for the recovery of small debts; and he will find few days pass without

580 *Present Condition of the People.* [May,

some flagrant act of injustice told and generally condemned by respectable and thinking tradesmen. Not one of the least evils of the system is the permitting the plaintiff to make an affidavit of the justness of his claim, and then adjudicating in his favour in the absence of collateral evidence; this practice has generated perjury to a frightful and unknown extent. Whole families among the poor, after a long run of success, have been detected in making a living by this practice—four instances of which have come to my knowledge from sources not to be questioned. These will establish the actual practice as a system, besides the knowledge of many others suspicious in their nature, but of a strong presumptive character of guilt. One case of recent occurrence will illustrate the course of perjury and robbery adopted.

Mr. White, a salesman and potatoe-dealer, James Street, Covent Garden, was summoned by an Irishwoman for payment of twenty shillings under the following circumstances: Mr. White carried on a considerable business as a wholesale potatoe-dealer, and served many of the poor in St. Giles's, in quantities of not less than one quarter of a hundred weight. It would often happen that many customers were in the warehouse at the same time: to prevent mistakes, therefore, Mrs. White was stationed in one spot to receive the money after the customers were served. The woman in question caused herself to be served with a hundred weight of potatoes; then turning round to Mrs. White, said, " Now for my *chainge hout* of the *soveran*," with a true countenance of Irish brass. The attempt was so flagrant and bared-faced, that the man who served her compelled her to turn out the potatoes from her sack upon the spot, and then pushed her from the shop-door. Subsequently a summons was brought from the Court of Requests to recover twenty shillings from Mr. White. It happened that on the day on which it was to be answered, I was at the house. On hearing the story, I advised that the evidence of all who could be spared from the warehouse, and had witnessed the transaction, should be taken to the court to rebut, and if possible punish, the party who had the wickedness and audacity to make such an attempt at robbery. Mr. White, two porters, and myself, went to the court. The com-

missioners heard the woman's story, and asked if she would swear to having given Mrs. White the sovereign; this she did forthwith, and Mr. White was ordered to pay her twenty shillings with costs, without being permitted to call any witnesses—the commissioners saying they could not allow one party to swear against the other, when it was apparent that one party must be perjured. Mr. White paid the money, with this request: " Gentlemen, if you should ever again issue a summons against me, I request the favour of you to desire your officer to wait for the money and expenses when he brings it, because it will be always better for me to pay it at once than lose my time in coming to this misnamed court of justice to pay it; for, after the specimen I have had of your legal profundity, I shall never think it worth while to defend any imposition to which you may lend yourselves, or practise upon me."

Since the occurrence of this case, and the appointment of a barrister to preside at this court (Kingsgate Street), oaths are taken all round, very frequently in such a way as that it is certain, however the case may go, that many must leave the court with wilful and corrupt perjury upon their consciences. This is demoralising and bad enough in cases where a few shillings only are at issue; but the greatest extent of mischief is to be traced to the imprisonment of the person for such small sums. I cannot forbear to give an instance of the danger there is in arming a creditor even for a shilling with the power of dealing with his debtor as his own feeling may dictate. The case may be relied upon, as it occurred near to my own residence, and was well known to the whole neighbourhood.

A young man, having a wife and two children, was, in consequence of being involved in security, constrained to leave his home until his affairs could be arranged. During his absence, a brutal fellow who had a summons out for twenty-five shillings against him obtained a judgment upon it: when this occurred, the unfortunate wife was in ill health, far advanced in pregnancy, and in a desponding condition, having been delicately brought up, and unused to buffet with the world. One day, at seven o'clock in the morning, this creditor for twenty-five shillings came with two officers, entered the house, and penetrated in the most brutal manner into her bedroom, also into the bedrooms of some very respectable female lodgers — declaring he would have the villain dead or alive. After abusing the females in the very worst style of language, they took their station at the door for several hours; and subsequently the creditor spent the whole day in going from one public-house to another throughout the neighbourhood, in treating the officers whom he had brought out on this occasion — making known their business in every parlour and tap-room they entered—until evening came, when the creditor was too intoxicated to pursue his vindictiveness further than to declare that it was not for the money but revenge he had come out—that he did not regard the two or three pounds the men had cost him, besides loss of time. The debtor's wife miscarried in consequence of this brutal conduct, and a very protracted illness followed; to which may be added the total ruin of the family. The husband shortly returned, having settled his affairs, but his credit and respectability with his neighbours were gone; he was therefore compelled, after all his struggles and those of his friends to meet his engagements, to abandon a connexion which had cost him so much time and capital to establish.

Now that any man, for twenty-five shillings, should have the power, under the sanction of the law, to inflict so much misery upon a whole family is contrary to all sound principles of justice, humanity, and national polity. These courts certainly ought to be limited in power, if they are to be permitted to issue judgment against the goods, without touching the person: it is more than they should be trusted with, constituted as they are. It would, however, among the labouring classes, be much better if no sum under forty shillings were recoverable; such a measure would not interfere with the general credit of trade, whilst the honest and industrious man would receive accommodation upon honour to as great an extent as he has been in the habit of receiving, or could require, under the supposed check of the law.

All transactions in the commercial world, legally considered, should be divided under two heads, viz., those of the fair and fraudulent trader; all the debtors of the former character should

be treated alike, and not permit one insolvent who owes thousands to throw away a hundred or more pounds of his creditor's money for the protection of his person, while the petty debtor who owes only five pounds is imprisoned for three or four months, dragged through the streets like a felon, and exposed the whole day in a public court to the gaze of the tender-hearted multitude.

It is not many weeks since a poor man took the benefit of the act for 4*l.* 10*s.*, being the only debt he owed in the world. The precise nature of the case I have not been able to ascertain; but, from the circumstance of its being his only debt, we cannot presume that he was much prone to contract debts. He was in prison nearly four months, during which time his family was supported by the parish. The expenses of his liberation amounted to something more than the debt, which was defrayed by subscription. This is an extreme case, it is true; but numerous others are of daily occurrence, wherein the amount of debts upon the schedule filed are comparatively trifling. Good laws, the legislature should always bear in mind, will never make the dishonest man honest; but bad laws will make honest men rogues and bad men worse.

It would be difficult to find a reason why the poor honest debtor, who is generally without friends, should be imprisoned, and his family, for want of his exertions, reduced to beggary; while his tools and little all are sold to obtain bread during months of constrained indolence; and, on the other hand, why the large debtor, generally rich in friends (as regards a few months' support in prison), should be privileged under the bankrupt laws to walk at large. Another incongruity here offers itself to our notice, which it would be equally difficult to reconcile upon any principle of known justice. The bankrupt, who damnifies his creditors to the amount of ten thousand pounds, or more, is exonerated from all future claims, while the petty debtor's property is ever afterwards made liable for his debts. It may be said that, in the case of the bankrupt, it is the creditor's own act which frees the debtor, by signing his certificate; but be it remembered, that it is only the signature of a portion of the creditors that the law requires; and the whole may be passed over by petition to the lord chancellor, and the certificate granted them without, if he deems the creditors harsh and contumacious. Few, however, are driven to this appeal; most bankrupts prepare the way for a grant of their certificates, by sending in as many friendly proofs of debt as will ensure this last favour.

The frauds committed even under the present amended system of bankrupt laws are not only greater in amount but more ramified, and easier to practise, than any in the Insolvent Debtors' Court.

The following is a striking case of city honesty and honour. A young man, highly connected in the city, embarked in mercantile transactions, and in a few years found himself upwards of eleven thousand pounds in debt. When the state of his affairs became known to his family and relations, a consultation was held upon the propriety of advancing a sum of money for his relief. All the relatives were persons of considerable possessions and ready capital : in the party was an old wary city tactitian, uncle to the involved young man ; he was the Nestor of this assembled coterie, and, after hearing the opinion of others, he spake as follows :—" I tell thee what, Bob will never succeed in any business ; he'd better marry the girl he has courted so long, and settle in the country, and not throw away good money after bad ; he'll never recover himself. She will bring him ten thousand pounds, and you (addressing himself to the father) may as well settle the same sum of money upon him ; he must have it all, you know, in the end : upon the interest of this, with frugality, they may for the present live comfortably enough." " But what is to be done with his debts," said the father ?" " Make him a bankrupt," rejoined the uncle.

In a few days afterwards, a docket was struck, the commission worked ; and in two or three months a certificate obtained. This story was related to me by one of the creditors, who, after the marriage of the parties, was made acquainted with a history of the affair, through a friend who was intimate with the family. There is no place in the world where so many nefarious barefaced robberies have been committed as in Guildhall ; and the same scenes are now re-enacting in the New Court, Basinghall Street, but with more decent external appearances of legal proceedings.

Advertisements in the public papers used formerly to be common, offering to carry men through a commission of bankruptcy, which meant that those who were criminally involved in debt, and could not face their creditors upon equal terms before the authorities of the law, might, upon the payment of a certain sum of money, be provided with a fictitious petitioning creditor to strike a docket, and a sufficient number of proofs of debt to secure the assigneeship and certificate, in defiance of all the bankrupt's *boná fide* creditors. The parties engaged in this calling have agents, who visit the debtors' prisons to solicit employment.

I know an instance, last year, of a perfect stranger waiting upon a person in the King's Bench prison who had petitioned the Insolvent Debtor's Court. He was addressed something after the following manner :— " Sir, I have been told that your's is a crooked case, and that you anticipate a remand ; I come, therefore, to offer you assistance. Your only alternative is a bankruptcy. Be under no concern about your creditors. If you pay my employers the sum of fifty pounds they will undertake to do all the business, and obtain you a certificate within a week after you have passed your last examination ; which they also guarantee you shall do without any trouble or inconvenience to yourself." Let Lord Brougham and the other strenuous reformers of the law rely upon the truth of this anecdote, and reflect thereon. The misuses of the bankrupts' law, although often practised, are not, however, of so frequent occurrence in this way as among the citizens of London, who daily contrive to make them subservient to the purposes of robbing each other. Many of the most flagrant and swindling nature are known to all who have any great practice in these courts, or knowledge of the nature of such nefarious transactions among men. One, the particulars of which in detail is known to me, I will therefore succinctly relate. There is a large party of tradesmen in the city who had an interest in the affair, and used great exertions to obtain for themselves justice without effect. As this story may not be lost upon them, I shall use the initials of all concerned in it.

In the year 1827, Messrs. W. and B., Manchester warehousemen, engaged two young men (linendrapers) to open a shop in a city about seventy miles from London, where a dashing display of business was made in the names of the two young men (Messrs. H. and E.). The object of the wholesale men, Messrs. W. and B. in putting these young men into the shop was to force a vent for an over-stock of unsaleable goods at that time lying in their warehouse, not two hundred yards from Bow Church. This scheme had for a long time been practised by them, and some few others in the city, working infinite mischief to society in many ways, on which, under its proper head (trade) I shall have occasion to dilate. If the shops opened upon this plan succeed, so much the better for all parties, and no harm is done; but not one in a hundred stand their ground for any length of time, and the reason why they fail is obvious. The warehousemen, who are the *boná fide* speculators in these nefarious transactions, have in view, first, the opening new markets for old stock, and general extension of their business; secondly, to obtain larger (and in most instances they do) inordinate profits upon the goods sent in to their agents, or tools; and yet at the same time run little or no risk, which is accomplished in the following manner. The first stock to furnish the shop, of course, is sent in by the *honest* wholesale speculator, who previously obtains the lease of the premises, and a warrant of attorney for an amount sufficiently large to cover any probable debt he may have against the party; who, as it would appear to the world, is going into business upon his own account, and in consequence of his stock and show is presumed to have capital; and thus paves the way in the incipiency of his business for future credit. The wholesale man, with a legal instrument of this nature, can at any time enter up judgment and re-possess himself of his own property, and that of other persons, which may at the time be in the possession of their *protégées.* From the commencement of the business they take especial care to have upon the premises a relation, or confidential spy, in the capacity of shopman or shopgirl (in this case girl) to report, *sub rosá,* the proceedings of the parties. Further, to guard against all contingencies of risk,

weekly **returns of sales made,** with the **cash taken,** are remitted : this stipulation is rigidly enforced.

As soon as the trade begins to work, it is the immediate object of the wholesale projector to induce other houses to offer the beginner credit, more especially in those particular articles of the trade which are not directly in their own line — in this case haberdashery, silks, &c. For this purpose all references are made to the house of the cunning speculator, who, when applied to by his neighbour and fellow-tradesman, affects to have the greatest confidence in the party, and promptly opens his ledger to shew the extent of it, by referring to the amount of goods sold ; and thus they thrust the young men upon the market of credit, whilst every pound's worth of goods sent in goes to secure the payment of their own debt. By degrees, and as policy may dictate, suggested by the success and profits of the trade, the original speculator either continues to force his own goods at an unfair profit, or to withhold, and at once shift the burden upon his neighbours, who, not being in the secret — behind the wicket — continue to supply goods up to the moment of a stop, which is always postponed until the original projector of the scheme is paid.

It will at once be seen, that the interest of the parties put into business (as it is called) never enters into the wholesale man's calculation ; yet they are seduced from a situation to become apparent masters, and find themselves, from the first, less independent than when serving behind a counter at a salary of 20*l.* per annum, besides having before them, in a very short period, the prospect of a bankruptcy, or a jail, —sometimes both ; when, towards the close of the adventure, they live in hourly expectation of an execution coming upon the premises to sweep away every vestige of property out of their hands, leaving them penyless to the mercy of a hungry set of irritated and justly incensed creditors. This short statement must not be deemed episodical : my readers, understanding the general practice, will comprehend the particular case before us (to which I now proceed) with some facility.

Messrs. H. and E. had now been in business, and managed to keep up appearances, between two and three years, at which period they had, through the recommendations of Messrs. W. and B., become considerably in debt; but as the trade fell off, it was deemed advisable by the latter to wind up their affairs in the concern, they having still left a debt of 12,000*l.* against the parties whom they out of their goodness had helped into trade.

In this instance, however, the precise nick of time for drawing in had been miscalculated; for other creditors also stopped; and it became evident that the firm of H. and E. must soon be defunct. How then was the 12,000*l.* to be got out of the fire? It was ascertained that there were ample assets upon the premises to pay under the warrant of attorney, if entered up; but for the house of Messrs. W. and B. to go in and sweep away the whole property, only a few days subsequently to having given them several recommendations with a view of bolstering up their credit, was too barefaced;* and, moreover, liable, under a commission of bankruptcy, to be brought to that most objectionable of all funds —refund. In this dilemma the following plan of action was determined upon: first, that the young men (the insolvents) should be secured to their interest, by promises solemnly made that, if they would favour all measures adopted to indemnify Messrs. W. and B. from loss, after a bankruptcy, they should be again reinstated in business in some other country town; and, secondly, that a relation of one of the parties in debt, a Mr. T***e, a tailor resident in London, should have a fresh warrant of attorney of sufficient amount to cover the whole stock, about 2,500*l.*;† and that he (the tailor) should, under this instrument, sell all, and put the proceeds into his pocket; first having given joint bills of exchange with the insolvents to Messrs. W. and B. (the wholesale men) for the 12,000*l.* due to them, which should give them a claim upon the tailor, and justify him in entering up judgment upon the warrant of attorney. Now

all this was excellently well concocted to keep Messrs. W. and B. in the background, while it secured them their money. Yet, under a commission of bankruptcy, with honest and independent assignees, the whole might be overthrown; it then, therefore, became necessary to create a petitioning creditor and assignees, bound to their especial interest, which was done in the following manner. A country linen-draper, a Mr. W. B., who was kept in requisition for such emergencies, was ordered to repair to the insolvent's premises, and manufacture trading documents of fictitious transactions, which should make him appear a creditor competent to strike a docket against the insolvents; and, lastly, that the bills of exchange given, together with others drawn for the purpose, should be negociated among a party selected for that purpose, who should outvote the real creditors in the choice of assignees. This plan was carried into effect, and succeeded to the top of their wishes. Subsequently, however, the creditors, when they saw themselves cheated, and several thousand pounds minus by the sacrifice of the bankrupts' property under a sale by auction, and the payment of one in full, to their prejudice, they impugned one of the assignees' debt, a holder of a thousand pound bill, who, unconscious of the foul plot, was made a cat's-paw in the affair. Unwilling, however, either to expose himself or those with whom he had become connected, he stood his ground, and after much legal controversy and expenditure of money, succeeded in maintaining his position as assignee. Those who abandon themselves to a love of gain are rarely free from guilt. In this instance, when the question of assigneeship was under litigation, the primary movers of the affair, Messrs. W. and B., in order to go boldly through with the transaction, plunged into the commission of the grossest and most barefaced perjury; they were, however, victors, and pock-

---

* In these cases, when a recommendation for credit is given, which, if not cautiously managed, might involve the responsibility of payment, the parties have a trick of saying to the applicant, "The best and only answer to your inquiry will be for me to shew you my ledger: there you will see the extent of our confidence in the house; and shall only add, that we shall continue to serve them with goods so long as they are willing to deal with us." This artifice evades the law of implied responsibility, or the giving a false character; but has the desired effect of transferring a confidence to other wholesale houses.

† It sold, under the sheriff, for upwards of 1600*l.*

eted the money, while the residue of the 1,600*l.* was divided, after the expenses were paid between the petitioning creditor and the tailor, as a compensation for their trouble. The poor are happy compared to the rich, when made so by the means of crime. One of the partners, Mr. W., shortly after the termination of the business, departed to his account; his place was filled by another who took an active part in this robbery, and he also died within a few months; the tailor became a bankrupt; and the petitioning creditor failed; leaving only one to receive his punishment, J. B., who, having connected himself with other partners, is, for the present, in the plenitude of success. I will only add, that the bankrupts were deserted and deceived by those whom they encumbered their consciences to serve; and two *bonâ fide* creditors who voted in the choice of assignees, under a promise of a payment of their debts, were also betrayed, after having been made instruments in their own loss. This is but a short history of one nefarious case of swindling under our law of debtor and creditor.

If any approximation to an equitable adjustment between those who take and those who give credit were brought about in law, debtors would always find their interest in adopting an honest course: under the present law, no man (if honest) can do justice to himself and family, and at the same time to his creditors.

Facts of the above nature are of hourly occurrence, and could be cited, if practical knowledge and facts weighed aught with our law-makers, who have latterly adopted the theory, that theorists are the best qualified to make laws, because they are learned, and unprejudiced by the knowledge of any one peculiar or insulated species of practical information. The history of the world is but the history of error,

most of which have in all ages originated with the learned, who render it more mischievous in its effects and duration, because they are the best capable of defending it; and from this source have arisen the many damnable heresies. Learning may strengthen the inherent powers of ratiocination, and fortify the judgment so as to repel the vigorous efforts of opposition; but it cannot be denied, that refined learning has a direct tendency to render the participant not only aspiring in his views, but vain, and regardless of the rights of others: hence it is rather in the way of law-making, distracting the mind from inductive knowledge, and filling it with scholastic prejudices; as the ages pass and destroy one string of categories, the learned introduce others equally false in their application to the state and wants of man. All hints in legislating for the commonalty should be taken from the most intelligent in the common walks of life.

Learning is by no means requisite to make an honest man wise or virtuous — good subjects or good members of society; practical knowledge is the best for a legislator; ornamental decoration and rhetorical figures are not essential; they may adorn and beautify error, but assist not in the discovery of truth. The maxim that the best things are perverted to the worst purposes was never better illustrated than in the application of learning to the enactment of laws. Subtle lawyers are conscious of this, and are constantly heard to say, that they defy our classical legislative body to frame a single clause in an act of parliament that they cannot make a hole in large enough for a man on horseback to leap through.

" The toils of law —what dark insidious men
Have cumbrous added to perplex the truth,
And lengthen simple justice to a trade."

## Art. IX.

### DOMESTIC ARRANGEMENTS OF THE WORKING CLASSES.

IT is recorded in Scripture, that when Adam was expelled from Paradise sentence was pronounced on him that he should 'earn his bread by the sweat of his brow.' This sentence has commonly been interpreted to mean 'a curse.' We, however, read the sentence differently. Man was originally maintained in Paradise without any exertion on his own part; and when he sought the 'knowledge of good and evil,' his only punishment was to be cast upon his own resources, with Reason for his guide, whereby to tread the difficult paths of experience. The 'sweat of the brow' must be held to represent the working of the brain within the brow. When the brain works aright, the man earns bread easily—not only for himself, but for his fellows; but when the brain lies fallow, little indeed is it that the hands can accomplish. Those whose hands work under the direction of their own brains are commonly in a condition of great physical comfort: those whose brains direct the hands of others are not less so, and in many cases more so. But those who use their hands alone, without brains to direct them, are the class who usually feel, in its full bitterness, the true curse—the appalling curse of POVERTY.

Poverty, in its widest sense, must be understood to mean, the privation of anything tending to physical, moral, or intellectual advancement; but our present purpose is to consider poverty principally in a physical point of view—the form in which it is most feared by those who suffer under its effects. We do not belong to that class of alarmists who avail themselves of misery as a stimulant, and delight themselves and distress others by declaiming on the 'increase of poverty and immorality;' on the contrary, we know full well that poverty is constantly lessening in amount, and that intemperance diminishes: the very splendour of the 'gin-palaces' being a proof that the poor require something more than gin—that taste, though of a barbaric kind, is putting forth its germs amongst them. But we know that the progress from poverty to comfort is slower than is necessary, and that the change might be made rapid by proper guidance: in short, that Poverty is only another name for Ignorance; while Intelligence may be regarded as the synonyme of Comfort.

There are various conditions of physical poverty amongst nations which are called uncivilized; but the most demoralizing and deteriorating of all poverty is that which exists amongst civilized nations, and more especially in large towns. Some hold that the condition of the Irish hovel-dwellers—where the father, mother, children, and a pig, live in common in one shed, and the children are emulous which shall sleep nearest the pig, for the sake of the warmth—some hold that this is the worst condition; but we are of a different opinion. The crowded lanes, courts, and alleys of a large town, whose every house is one unseemly den of squalid hunger, strife, envy, hatred, malice, and all uncharitableness—these are the abodes in which poverty appears in her most fearful garb, surrounded by vice and every variety of misery. And even this condition is rendered worse when any peculiar circumstances afford the chance of occasional debauchery. The various improvements which have taken place in London have swept away huge dens of misery, and more especially two which still dwell in our memory: we allude to the labyrinth of courts and alleys which formerly occupied the site of St. Catherine's Docks, and that between Chandos-street and the Strand. Whoever calls to mind that London was once almost wholly composed of such miserable dwellings, will not doubt that poverty is gradually departing. There are still similar dens to be found, in which human beings are born only to suffer, or to escape suffering only through the torpidity of their senses. An accurate historian would describe the birth, life, and death of one of these beings somewhat as follows :—

'The child was one of nine, the eldest of whom had been born on the ground-floor of a house situated in a row, in a long dark alley, where the sun was never seen save at mid-day, and then only occasionally during the summer's heat. The father had originally been a decent mechanic, earning from twenty-five to thirty shillings a-week; and when his first child was born, there were few men in his station so happy as he, for all his wants were well supplied. His wife was an industrious, cheerful partner; and the gloominess of their abode was unheeded, relieved as it was by their weekly walk in the green fields. Still more prosperous times came ; and the earnings of the husband being increased, he was enabled to occupy both the rooms of the first floor. Three more children were born ; and the necessity for a larger supply of food obliged them to encroach on their rent. The first floor was exchanged for the second ;—the family was increased by two other members, and all removed to the garrets. For some years the weekly walk in the fields had been discontinued by the woman; and the garments of the husband having become unsightly, he also had ceased to seek the free air : the whole of his time was taken up with providing the food necessary for his children, and his wife was wholly occupied in looking after them, and contriving to keep together the rags which covered them. Two more children were born; and all were confined to a single back garret, where, the wages of the husband being insufficient to appease their hunger, the wife endeavoured to eke them out by washing for their neighbours, some of whom were not quite so poor as themselves. It was a scene of misery, from which the elder children were glad to escape, and play upon the staircase, or in the court before the house, becoming early inured to disputes and quarrels among themselves and with other children, every room in the house being occupied by a separate family. In the midst of this, the man's wages happened to be reduced; and after long bearing up against misery, he at last yielded to the habit of intoxication—partly to appease the cravings of unsatisfied hunger, and partly to get rid of thought. His wife still struggled, and worked harder, but only to procure food, for all other considerations were now disregarded. In this condition her ninth child was born; and charity alone—the charity of misery to still greater misery—saved them from starving. But the woman was changed: she had become reckless through suffering, and the sight of her youngest child only served to remind her that an additional weight of misery had fallen on her. *She* also took to intoxication as a refuge from pain : the coin which was inadequate to supply food was yet sufficient to produce a temporary oblivion of the want of it. The frequent hunger and pain which the child experienced were alleviated in the same manner;—none smiled on its young eyes when they opened, and almost the only sensation of pleasure it could experience was in gazing vacantly on the rays of sunlight which at some few intervals penetrated the apartment. Mother and father were now frequently away from home for hours, and sometimes days together; and remarkable in a sickly infant was the tenacity of life, which would not suffer it to perish. How the other children lived, was a mystery to all but those in a similar condition : they had no daily meals, nor even sat down to food. Like dogs or wolves, they had a great capacity for endurance : having no labour to perform, they could exist for days on the smallest possible quantity of food, and they were ever on the alert to beg, snatch, or steal. One feeling alone was uppermost in their minds, which gave room to no other—the pain of unsatisfied hunger. Their dreams, during the scanty time of sleep, were of eating; and when they awakened, it was to seek the means of eating. The elder children took by force from the younger any scraps of food they found with them; and the younger resorted to cunning to devour them in private. If chance threw in their way a larger booty than ordinary, it was devoured in haste, and in quantity, which left them in the condition of the torpid boa—a prey to the pangs and helplessness of over-repletion.

'Gloomy was the daily scene on which the young child gazed when his faculties began to awaken. During the summer he would crawl towards the miserable casement, and look upwards through the interstices of surrounding stacks of chimneys, to gaze upon the light; but when winter came, he shrunk shivering, huddled up in his rags, towards the fireplace, which rarely contained a fire, and when by chance it did, volumes of smoke filled the apartment, and clouded over the wretched fragments called furniture, which only remained unsold by the parents because they were worth no one's purchase. Ere the child was old enough to descend the stairs, to follow the pursuits of his brothers and sisters, the whole family were ejected from their miserable abode, to one still more wretched—they were driven to the cellar. It was in the autumn, and the damp of the place soon made a fearful change. Ere they had been a week in it, the whole of them were laid prostrate by typhus fever. The father, the two eldest boys, and the youngest, alone survived to endure farther suffering. They might even then have become worthy members of society, had the father retained strength of purpose or moral feeling, for the disposition of the eldest boy was naturally kind and benevolent, ere it had been hardened by want and misery. But it was now too late; and the intellect of the boy only served to make him a skilful thief. The whole family were maintained by the provisions which he, and his brother under his directions, contrived to pilfer. Occasionally they were committed to prison, to pursue the same course when again enlarged. The magistrates lectured them, and warned them to change their course, knowing at the same time that if they ceased to steal they must starve, or go on the parish, for they knew no other means of earning a living: they lived in the belief that thieving was their proper trade, and those who punished them for it, tyrants, whose only right was might. The heart of the eldest boy, which yearned for affection, expanded towards the young child, who was accustomed to look for his return home as his only source of pleasure; and when the father died of disease and debauchery, he took him for his protégé, and removed to a more healthy abode. The other brother disappeared, no one knew whither; and when the youngest attained the age of seven years, his only friend, his only protector, the only being who loved him, was taken from him by a sentence of transportation. Left alone in the world, he became a thief at that early age; and ere he attained eight years, he became acquainted with the interior of a prison. Harshly treated by all, he grew fierce and reckless; and as his intellect expanded, he became a fearful spoiler of his kind. He loved no one, and trusted no one;—sensual excitement was his only pleasure, his only wish, and he revelled in every kind of debauchery. His natural energy was divided between the pursuit of robbery and the dissipation of the gains acquired by it. His intelligence succeeded in putting off to a distant period the retribution with which he knew society would sooner or later visit him; and he had attained twenty-three years of age ere he was convicted of felony, and transported to a penal colony. His career was then short. On the voyage he planned a mutiny, which failed of success by the treachery of an intended accomplice; and on landing, the punishment inflicted on him was of a kind which would have destroyed every spark of humanity in him had any remained. He escaped, and became a leader of bush-rangers; his hands were made familiar with human blood; and after going through scenes of the most disgusting horrors, he was shot, like a wild beast in his lair, by those who feared to approach him from terror of his untameable ferocity. Yet this being was once a gentle infant, smiling in innocence.'

Those reasoners who are accustomed to think that the shortest cut to reconcile difficulties is the best, sometimes allege, that as some classes of the community have too much, while others have too little, the easy process is to make the poorer class happy with the superfluity of the richer one, by giving share and share alike to all. Now this would be specious enough, if the amount of superfluity were equal to the amount of want—if the numbers of the very rich were equal to the numbers of the very poor. But it is not so; the rich *seem* many, because their position causes them to stand prominently out from the crowd, while the large numbers of the poor are comparatively little noticed in their obscurity. To take away from the rich anything which is absolutely superfluous, would, it is true, inflict no positive evil on them; but neither would it confer any positive good on the poor—rather an evil, of the same nature as that of bestowing casual charity on habitual beggars, and thus preventing them from superseding the necessity of charity by the exertion of industrious energy. To mingle the property of the rich and poor in one common stock, and reduce all to equal rations, would certainly reduce the rich to great misery, and ultimately destroy their lives prematurely, by exposure to hardships to which they had not been trained; but it would have no more effect in alleviating the distresses of the poor, than would the solitary rations of the captain of a war-ship in augmenting the stock of his crew ;—and if it would, all rational persons in all ages have seen that the alleviation would only be temporary.

Supposing that, in a newly-discovered island, the division of the whole land were to take place among the whole community, each family according to its numbers ; such a division could not be lasting in its effects—no, not even if the thinness of the population afforded at first to every individual a considerable lot. One would cultivate well ; another would breed cattle well ; but it would inevitably happen that numbers would neither do one nor the other. These would not be able to procure food from their land : as a consequence, they would sell their allotments, or hire them out to those who knew how to turn them to account—and receive food in return. Thus, piece by piece, the whole land would eventually centre in the rich and intelligent minority, and the poor majority would serve them as herdsmen and cultivators, soldiers, retainers, and labourers. In a low state of civilization, the worst evils attributed to inequality of property would inevitably follow. Civil commotion would make men scarce, and leave land plentiful ; the owners of the land would endeavour to force labourers into their service, and poor men would be kidnapped and made slaves. The necessity of protection would make every poor man dependent ; and each would attach himself to a superior, whose interest it would become to protect him. Every unattached man would then be immediately marked and persecuted till he chose his chief—and thus would arise a feudal system. While men were scarce, the profits accruing from their labour would be considerably greater than the expense occasioned by the obligation of maintaining them ; but growing peaceable habits would soon tend to the increase of population ; and as population would probably increase faster than the means of support, men would gradually cease to become a valuable commodity as working slaves, and would in lieu thereof be considered useless and troublesome dependants. Their feudal superiors would then throw them off as quickly as possible, and the feudal system would be ended. New arts and new discoveries would from time to time absorb portions of the disengaged labour ; but in an uncivilized—i. e., an uneducated community—there would always be a large surplus of unemployed labourers ; and the labourers must be fed, if not killed off. They would have a claim on the land on which they were born, which claim nothing but death could abrogate. Though they possessed no share in the land by legal title, they would possess a moral title to a share of the food produced on it, which no legal enactment could defeat. Improved methods of producing food would soon increase its quantity, and one man would produce as much as several could eat. Fresh labour would thus constantly be liberated, which, as invention advanced, would be directed to the creation of new species of wealth. But the progress of improvements in production could not always continue to keep pace with the probable increase of population; and many poor people would therefore exist in a condition of misery, produced by constant dread of starvation, or in an unimproving condition, caused by apathy arising from hopelessness. This is precisely the condition of many amongst the poorer classes in England and Ireland at the present day.

The remedy for this is not in reducing the rich, but in raising the poor. If equality of fortunes—which, under existing circumstances, would be only another word for equality of poverty—could be introduced, and what is far more difficult, maintained, the poor would in no respect be better off. And one evil, of no small magnitude, would assuredly be effected: there would be taken from before the eyes of the poor the example of better things than they themselves possessed—the general standard of physical comfort, which all should strive to elevate, would be lowered.

The poor man may not benefit physically by the abundance of the rich one, but if his mind be rightly constituted, he must benefit morally. Beholding a higher standard of comfort than he himself enjoys, his reason will set to work—not enviously, to reduce the rich man to his own level—but hopefully, to devise means of raising himself to the level of the rich man. He will see that from riches springs leisure, and that leisure enables the benevolent man more efficiently to work for the benefit of others. He will then ask himself the question—'How came that man to be rich?' Other questions will succeed, and at last will come the important one—'Are wealth and poverty conditions of human nature within human control, or are they the result of accident, or of invincible necessity?—and if they be within human control, is not the desirable condition, wealth, attainable by all? or at least, is not the objectionable condition, poverty, avoidable by all?'

Food, and all other things constituting physical wealth, are the results of human labour. Improved methods of applying human labour may increase the amount of wealth; and if that wealth be produced much faster than it is consumed, it will form an accumulated stock, constituting what in common language is termed *riches*. By this means numerous individuals in a community do become rich. By due precaution and industry, may not all become so? If by the term *rich* be understood the possession by a few of a greater amount of physical wealth than the many, all cannot be rich; but what we mean by the term rich, is that condition in which all the physical wants are abundantly supplied.

It is evident that the essential condition to the accumulation of wealth is, that it shall be produced in greater abundance than it be consumed; in other words, that labour shall be profitable, and earn more than its own maintenance. This can mostly be done by skilled labourers, but rarely by unskilled ones. The rich men of Greece and Rome acquired their riches by the labour of slaves, who were scantily fed and hard worked; in other words, their superfluities were gained by subtracting from the necessities of their poorer fellows. The many toiled, and their lives were shortened, that the few might riot in luxury.

But, fortunately for mankind, a labourer has now been discovered, who requires no food fit for human nutriment, and who will work day and night untiring, without rest—we allude to steam. Steam either actually does, or could perform, the whole drudgery of the whole community,—it could furnish a greater amount of mere power than the whole race of human beings combined. But it does more than this: it has long been a skilled labourer; art has taught it to spin and to weave, and to perform most mechanical processes. With the superintendence of one man, it can provide garments for a hundred. It creates wealth with the assistance of mere human *exercise*, and without human *labour*. It fulfils the condition of accumulating wealth (of many varieties) in greater abundance than it can be consumed.

' But,' say the working mechanics, ' steam is our enemy; it is the servant of the rich man, and does nothing to serve us, but, on the contrary, throws us out of work by giving its labour at a cheaper rate.' This we believe is the common argument of the uninstructed, but it is a very fallacious one. It is owing to steam alone that they are enabled to enjoy what comforts they have in the shape of dwellings and garments. Where would be their fuel but for steam? where would be the fabrics which clothe them? where would be the very tools they use in their various trades? where the materials on which they exercise their arts? What would become of the countless iron trades, were steam excluded from the preparation of the material? With respect to the supposed supersession of human labour, it is, in the first place, to be remarked, that the transition from manual to steam labour is always gradual, and meanwhile new inventions are continually raising a demand for fresh labour; and lastly, the claim of unemployed mechanics to maintenance is as strong against the owners of steam engines, as that of unemployed agricultural labourers against the owners of land. ' But,' the labouring people, the mere unskilled toilers, will say, ' if steam continues to make progress, the time will come when manual labour will cease altogether to be required.' We can only reply to this that we devoutly hope, we may almost say believe, that that time will come. We love our race too well to be content while we behold the immense majority condemned to a life of drudgery. Most gladly would we hail the extinction of all labour which is felt as uninteresting toil. We would have the unskilled labourers cease to exist as labourers, but not as men; we would give them leisure to cultivate their minds, by freeing their bodies from their shackles.

We are not about to enter at present into the consideration, by what means that deplorable poverty, which we depicted in the commencement of this article, may be rooted out from the whole world. We shall have other opportunities for discussing the causes of high and of low wages. Our present observations are destined, not for the absolutely poor, but for those who are not so rich as they might be; for that portion of the working people (happily very numerous) who want only a more skilful employment of their earnings to render machinery a valuable servant to be employed by them, instead of an obnoxious rival to be destroyed by them; who have the means, if they knew how, for availing themselves of its powers to increase in an indefinite degree their physical and mental enjoyments, and to relieve themselves *even now* from much of the drudgery of their existence.

' But how can poor men become proprietors of machinery without capital?' some mechanics will ask. The answer is plain —by saving, as others have done. ' Our earnings are barely sufficient for us to live upon,' the poor men will reply. Let us analyze this.

The wages of a working carpenter, bricklayer, and many similar trades, average five shillings per day, or thirty shillings per week. There are working men, of athletic appearance, who earn less than two-thirds of that sum, and maintain families healthily upon it. Now it is a known fact that working men pay dearer than any other class for the provisions and necessaries they consume. The reason is, that they purchase every thing by retail in very small portions. They buy their meat by the single pound, their potatoes by the amount of the single meal's consumption, their cheese and butter by the quarter of a pound, their tea and sugar by the ounce, and their beer by the pint. This process makes the work of distribution, which is performed by the shopkeeper, a very troublesome one. To sell an ounce of tea is to him as much labour as to sell a pound would be, and he must have a much greater per centage on the transaction. And not only does the mechanic buy in small quantities, but he very commonly has the bad habit of taking a week's credit. For these two reasons, the shopkeeper commonly lays a profit of thirty-three per cent. on all he sells to him. The shopkeeper has him, in the technical phrase, ' under his thumb.' He cannot deal with another, who might be disposed to sell cheaper, for he cannot get together the amount of money necessary to pay his debts; his weekly wages are mortgaged to one who makes him pay a heavy interest at his own pleasure. It is not too much to affirm that twenty-five per cent. is weekly abstracted from the working man's wages, without any benefit accruing to him. In this is a double evil; the working man loses a large portion of his hardly earned wages, and the distributor gains it, if not by a process of chicanery, at least by services which, in a well arranged state of society, would scarcely be necessary. The business which, under a good arrangement, might be well performed by one man, is badly done by twenty. A green-grocer or chandler with a capital of a few score pounds, will make an income of a hundred per annum, in a shop of a few feet square. What is there to hinder the customers whom he profits by from arranging such matters for themselves, and putting by their savings?

The chandler's profits arise from buying wholesale and selling retail. Time has something to do with the consideration of a dealer's transactions. A merchant can sell a chest of tea in the same time the retailer can sell an ounce, and supposing them both ready-money transactions, the former will be content with a profit of two per cent., when the latter requires ten, twenty, or thirty. Now what is there to prevent a body of mechanics from joining together to buy the chest of tea from the merchant, as many wealthy private individuals do. The answer is twofold; they lack mutual confidence, and they lack convenient and well-arranged dwellings. With every thing they consume it is the same; even the fuel they use is brought to them on men's backs, in amounts of half a day's consumption. Every thing the working people consume, instead of coming to them direct from the producer, who would be content with a moderate profit, passes through so many hands, each of which adds something to the cost, that it reaches the poor consumer at a double price. Persons who live at hotels and inns live at a far greater expense than those who live in private houses, because they buy all things in small portions as they consume them; the uncertainty of trade also contributes to high prices: the hotel-keeper keeps his house open twelve months, six of which are probably barren of guests; he is therefore necessitated to exact double profit. To get rid of these disadvantages, large numbers of people, of various classes, have joined together to institute what are called club-houses, where, their provisions being purchased in quantities by their own agents, they can consume them at little unnecessary expense. The defect of the club-houses is, that they are not dwellings, but merely places for eating and for reading. The principle upon which the members eat their provisions cheaply, might be applied to all the wants of life. It might form a bond of union, not merely amongst a number of unmarried men, but amongst a number of families.

Generally speaking, no class of people are so ill-lodged as the working-people. Their dwellings are rarely built purposely for them: they are commonly houses which have served other purposes, and having fallen into disuse, are converted into inconvenient lodging-houses, in which each family occupies an apartment at a high rate of payment. Even in houses built on purpose for them, their conveniences are little attended to. They have been accustomed to nothing better, and they submit. And wealthy are they sure to be who supply the wants of the poor on a large scale. Where the builder makes five or seven per cent. by the dwellings of the rich, he makes twenty-five by the dwellings of the poor. Where one fortune is accumulated by selling wine to the rich, fifty are gathered together by selling gin to the poor, and all their other wants afford the same proportion of profit.

That the working-people generally have a perception that the misery they endure is not a necessity, but merely a circumstance within human control, is proved by the fact of their strong exertions to maintain Trades' Unions, for the purpose of permanently raising the standard of wages. It is clear that trades' unions must fail to do this in the mode they propose, because the rate of wages depends on the supply of labour which is brought into the market, and not upon the arbitrary regulations of either masters or men. Competition is a principle existing throughout organized nature, whenever production is too rapid. The forest trees compete with each other when too thick, and numbers of them perish, naturally, if they are not artificially removed by man. The field which is too thickly sown with wheat will produce little save straw, unless it be artificially thinned. And thus when workmen are too numerous the rate of wages diminishes, and they have no remedy unless they use their reason to reduce the supply, at least, to the level of the demand. For their own sake they should reduce it rather lower, in order to maintain an assured equality with their employers, because the capital of the employers is a fund which will sustain them for a time without business, whereas the workmen, having no capital, cannot forego their work. But whenever the amount of labour is rather below the demand, the competition of the employers will work beneficially for the workmen.

The principle set forth by the trades' unions, that no man should work at more than one trade, and only at that in case of having served an apprenticeship to it, is most monstrous, and only excusable by the reflection that it arises from ignorance—ignorance of which we have ample patterns in the absurd laws which have crowded our statute books. The statutes have usually been framed with a regard to the interests of the rich, at the expense of the poor; and now the trades' unions are endeavouring, by similar means, to uphold the unskilful workmen at the expense of the skilful. If such absurd purposes could be accomplished, they would reduce the working people of England to a condition resembling that of the East Indian *castes*, and effectually place a bar upon all improvement. It is a curious thing that while the spirit of the age is totally averse to monopoly in all its customary channels, such strenuous efforts should be made to create monopolies in every branch of mechanical art; and to give a compulsory sanction to what is called the ' division of labour,' which, to the extent to which it is now carried, tends more than any other thing to prevent the expansion of intellect in what regards the common arts of life.*

* It is quite true that a man's pursuits may be so diffusive as to produce a result in none, but as practical science is divided into branches, it is quite clear that an individual who knows the general principles of each, will bring a more grasping intellect to bear on his own particular branch, than he will who only studies a particular portion of a particular branch. The mechanical arts are all conversant with one single subject,—the artificial forms of matter. Whether that matter be animal, vegetable, or mineral, is immaterial to the argument. It is the business of the working mechanic to convert it into various geometric forms, with such tools as are fitted to operate upon it. Some operations may be particularly delicate, as the finer varieties of ivory work, the mechanism of watches, or jewellers' work; and delicately skilful hands may be required for them. This then would form one class of work. The operations of the builder, the carpenter, the joiner, the cabinet-maker, the coach builder, the wheelwright, the millwright, and various others, would form another class. The engineer, the smith, the machinist, the founder, and metal-workers generally, would form another class. In preparing youths for the mechanical arts,

That the workmen who compose the trades' unions have not discovered this, and have acted on principles diametrically opposite, is no proof that trades' unions are mischievous institutions. It merely proves that the workmen composing the trades' unions are in a state of ignorance ; and this ignorance is more likely to be removed by the existence of unions, than by any other circumstance. Workmen who join unions are incited to discussion, which produces habits of thinking, and thus truth is gradually elicited, and errors disappear.

But trades' unions are far from being the most advantageous kinds of unions which can be established; several evils attend them. The meetings are held principally at public houses, and thus a tendency to drinking is encouraged. They are also meetings of separate trades, except on extraordinary occasions, and the interchange of discourse is thereby limited in its useful effects. And lastly, the men are taken from their families during those hours of leisure which should be employed in cultivating the domestic affections, and giving moral instruction to children. This disadvantage is probably increased by the time expended in walking to and from the place of meeting. We have understood that, in consequence, the wives of the trades' unionists frequently look upon the unions with an unfavourable eye. But, as unions are in themselves desirable, the question is, how to attain their advantages without their customary evils. We think that it will be no hard task to show how the working people may enjoy the benefits of unions without these evils, and with many other advantages which the present unions give no hope of.

In effecting a revolution for the better in the general condition of the working classes, it is evident that, before all things, it is necessary that they should enjoy physical ease; in other words, that they should be free from painful bodily sensations.

---

the rule should be to set them at work first on the softer materials, such as wood, that the hand might become accustomed to accuracy as well as the eye, by meeting little comparative resistance; and this accuracy once acquired, would be continued when the more stubborn materials, such as metals, became the subjects of operation. The free circulation of labour would enable all to choose the work for which they might possess the greatest liking, and consequently in which they would achieve the greatest excellence. To the separate classes above mentioned, the greater portion of the workmen would confine themselves; but others would be found of superior skill, who would go through the whole variety of mechanical arts, and the general body would thus acquire an amount of skill, energy, and intelligence, which at present we do not dream of. Change of employment relieves monotony of the body, as much as change of books relieves the monotony of the mind. It stimulates invention, and gives a great variety of circumstances, many of which must operate beneficially, and the mind of the workman becomes enlarged, and habituated to find resources in difficulties.

To accomplish this, they require an abundant supply of food, clothing, warmth, and shelter. We have before shown, that there exist a considerable number of working men earning wages sufficient for their comfortable maintenance, but who nevertheless do not reap the full benefit of their earnings, as these are dissipated in the payment of heavy rents for wretched lodgings, and exorbitant profits on retail purchases from day to day; and beyond this, there is a still larger waste of fuel and time, from which last loss no one can possibly reap benefit— either consumer or distributor. Now what we propose is, to enable these producers to reap the whole benefit of their own earnings, instead of contributing a large portion of them to maintain a host of retail shopkeepers, and to pay the high rents of builders, ignorant of the superior economy of a more social life. It may perhaps be objected, that if the retail shopkeepers lose their trade, they will lose their livelihood—that the advantage of the producers will be their loss. This is true; but it is our business to concern ourselves with that portion of society which possesses the means of improvement. It is better that the producers should be permanently bettered in their condition than that an artificial class should be kept up in perpetuity, on the earnings of others. The distributors who might no longer be needed, in consequence of new social arrangements, would emigrate, or be absorbed in other employments.

In order to reduce our proposition to a definite shape, we will suppose two hundred working men of the skilled class, earning on the average 2l. weekly. Supposing each man and his family to occupy two rooms, and bare decency will not admit of less, for the various purposes of dwelling, cooking, eating, sleeping, and depositing fuel and provisions—his rent for these rooms will amount to, at least, 7s. per week, or about 18l. per annum. Setting aside all consideration of locality, the prime cost of two such rooms at the present rate of building materials cannot exceed 50l.; and, were they built in quantities, and with every possible regard to economy, as manufactories are erected, 40l. would probably be sufficient; the profits therefore are enormous, supposing the rents regularly paid. But this is not the case: the landlords exact a large rent from those who do pay, in order to make up for those who do not pay. If a landlord were certain of his payment, he would be glad to lower his rents; a rent of seven and a half per cent. upon the capital laid out in building would remunerate him, and ten per cent. would be an inducement which would produce amongst capitalists an active competition.

The cheapest class of buildings which can be erected, where

accommodation is needed for numerous occupants, is that in the barrack form—say a quadrangle, with an open space in the interior. We propose, therefore, to erect a quadrangle, with fifty dwellings on each side; each dwelling consisting of a sitting apartment on the ground-floor, and two bed-rooms above it. As our proposed plan precludes the necessity for chimneys, fire-places, or kitchens, within the dwellings, the cost of the erection would not exceed 60*l.* for each dwelling, or 12,000*l.* for the whole. At a rental of ten per cent. on the capital, the rent for each dwelling would be 6*l.* per annum, and say 2*l.* for ground-rent. The tenants might have them, taxes included, for 10*l.* In the centre of the quadrangle we propose to erect a building consisting of a basement, a ground-floor, and a story: the basement to contain a steam-engine, an apparatus for pumping cold and hot water into pipes circulating through the whole of the dwellings, and a gasometer. The open space between the dwellings and the central buildings might contain cellars for coals and durable provisions. The basement story is to be a kitchen, fitted with apparatus for cooking plain provisions of all kinds adapted to the supply of the two hundred families. The room above that would be adapted for a dining-room for such of the community as might choose to dine together; the remainder would carry their provisions to their own apartments. The dwellings would be warmed in winter by the hot-water pipes, which, under a certain pressure, would supply heat enough to boil milk or coffee, or for other similar purposes, by a proper arrangement; and cocks might be placed in the pipes at proper intervals to supply warm water for washing. The gas could be placed in lanterns in the walls of the dwellings—thus lighting the inside and outside at once, and preventing any offensive odour from entering the apartments. In addition to the other conveniences, there should be provided a sufficient number of warm and cold baths, and also a laundry and wash-house.

Taking the expense of the central building, machinery, and piping into consideration, we may estimate the whole at about 8,000*l.* At a rental of ten per cent. this would amount to 800*l.* per annum, or 4*l.* more for each family—making their rents 14*l.* per annum each, or 4*l.* less than we have estimated their present expense. But in return for this they have three rooms instead of two; and, the essential requisite of heat being supplied from a joint stock, one-third of the fuel will suffice to keep them in a state of comfortable warmth. They may also buy their provisions in large quantities, and save probably one-third of their present cost. There are two ways of doing this: they may either appoint some of their own number as their agents, or they may put a contract up to auction stipulating for quality, as is the case with the army and navy; but, probably, the owner of the building would find it worth his while to save them the trouble. The total income of the two hundred men we estimate at 20,000*l.* per annum. Reckoning the rent of each at 14*l.*, and clothing and pocket-money at 26*l.*, there is a balance of 60*l.* to be expended on food and other necessaries. Supposing, therefore, that the proprietor kept the kitchen, shop, and baths, in his own hands, and secured the custom of two hundred families—by selling better commodities and at a cheaper rate than the retail shopkeepers, which his facilities would enable him to do—he would make a return of 12,000*l.* per annum, ten per cent. profit on which would be 12,00*l.* a year; and, as all would be ready-money transactions, a very small capital would be required. Thus the judicious employment of 25,000*l.* capital would realize an annual income of 4,000*l.*, and, we apprehend, with a less degree of risk than almost any business that could be named. The advantages, the mere physical advantages, to be reaped by the workmen from dwelling in such an establishment are so obvious, that no fear could be entertained of the dwellings lying idle. So far from such being the case, they would be found willing to pay their rents weekly, and in advance, in order to secure a preference. So large a profit, of course, could not be maintained for a very long period. The first speculators would have the advantage; but when the speculation was found profitable, fresh capital would be embarked in it, until the rate of profit reached the level of all similar undertakings of equal risk. Two hundred working men, who had saved 125*l.* each, might invest their capital in such a speculation, and divide the 4,000*l.* per annum amongst them—thus putting the profits and interest into their own pockets.

The liberation of the wives and daughters of these working men from drudgery in cooking, scrubbing, cleaning, water-carrying, and numerous other things, would give them a large amount of leisure for the cultivation of their own intelligence and taste, and the training of the children. The men also, after the labour of the day was over, would come to cleanly homes and cheerful conversation : the gin-shop and the public house would be alike abandoned. The means of cleanliness would be easy and abundant as regarded their persons, and their health would be improved. So much as regards physical comfort ; but in respect to facilities for the cultivation of the mind, the advantages would be very great indeed. The large room in the centre, serving as a dining-room at mid-day, might serve at other times for other purposes : it might be provided with a library of books, periodicals, and newspapers ; it might serve as a school-room morning and afternoon, and in the evening as a reading-room, lecture-room, and mechanics' institute. If necessary, another story might be raised above it, in order to provide for an infant-school, hospital, or nursery. A popular lecturer could scarcely desire a better audience than he would find in such an institution, both of men and women ; for, as there would be no necessity for going away from home, women as well as men might attend without loss of time. The moral and intellectual benefits which would be wrought in the characters of such a body of men, women, and children. are almost incalculable. Vice would be ashamed to show its face, just as poor people dislike to appear on Sunday in their soiled working garments, amongst their decently-clad fellows. And as such institutions increased in number, there would arise amongst them a generous emulation in improvement: they would be like fields separated by hedges, in which the relative excellence of the crops could be ascertained, and experiments usefully tried. They would form a general bond of union amongst the working classes, based on their true interests, and would teach them how to co-operate usefully for commercial and productive as well as social purposes.

Earnestly do we wish that capitalists may see this plan in the same light as we do, and in making their own interest go hand in hand with the working-men's welfare, teach them to REGARD CAPITAL AND MACHINERY AS THE MOST EFFICIENT PROMOTERS OF THE INDEPENDENCE OF THE WORKING CLASSES.

J. R.

## THE WHIGS—THE RADICALS—THE MIDDLE CLASSES—AND THE PEOPLE.

THE social revolution with quickening step pursues its career, gaining from each concession, extorted from fear, or proffered as the sordid calculations of place and pay, force and velocity, ever on the increase, as the impetuous career of the Alpine avalanche in its downward course is accelerated co-equally with its massy and ever-gathering proportions, until it precipitates itself upon the happy vale, and confounds man and nature in one shapeless wreck of death and desolation.  Principles and institutions are dealt with, carved, mangled, or overthrown, with lack of measure so reckless on the part of administrators, and with hands so destructive on that of legislators, that with after ages it will be a question whether asylums have not been ransacked both for members of Parliament and Ministers of the monarchy ; and of the two species of insanity, which is best calculated to effect the downfal of a state,—the idiot who, half maliciously, half stupidly, sets the house on fire, or the stark-staring maniac who, with demoniacal laughter, heaps faggot upon flame.  Changes have been multiplied until change for its own sake alone has become the craving of a distempered appetite.  The love of change to-day ferments into the fever of revolution to-morrow, and we laugh to scorn the wisdom of our ancestors, of whom Bacon was one, who bid us take heed that it be " the necessity which provoke the change, and not the desire of change which pretendeth the reformation."  Politically, as physically, one member of the body cannot long be diseased, without affecting through all its ramifications the whole system.  Occipital excitement and derangement is not slow to communicate, with corresponding symptoms, to the central organ of life, and the dispensing recipient of the vital store.  The action of the heart and the stomach, unnaturally stimulated, induces a deceptive plethora and an accelerated circulation of the blood, which, with its customary accompaniment of boisterous yet uneasy gaiety, imposes for some time as the rude robustness of health and the natural exuberance of animal spirits.  The exhaustion and revulsion consequent arrive and reveal the existence and the causes of the malady, but inflammatory tendencies are then only the more alarmingly exhibited, and the more difficult to be subdued, from the physical debility and prostrate powers of the patient.  So is it now in the political world.  Material prosperity had been advancing with sure and measured pace up to the period when political agitation and revolution became the order of the day.  The stagnation of industry in France and Belgium, and subsequently in Spain, attendant upon civil war and national convulsions, imparted an additional impetus to the gigantic and productive energies of this country.  The vacuum of supply created by the temporary secession of those nations from the field of competition, could only be supplied from hence ; but since the return and concurrence of the two former, we have been so far from yielding back the share which devolved to us by fortuitous incidents, that speculation has been rashly pushed beyond all legitimate bounds, and markets have only the more been inundated.  To this may be added the restless, unsatisfied, and eager aspirations after some distant and undefinable El Dorados, mystically shadowed out in ministerial harangues, and the infatuated pursuit of which was fanned into flame by continuous declamation about Whig prosperity.  From the comfortless contemplation and the turmoil of faction, selfishly fomented by the Government at home, the industrial interests sought refuge and consolation in the counteracting influences of commercial enterprise abroad.  From these divers and co-operating causes have resulted a fury of overtrading.  Prices have been in excess—wealth, fictitious and illusory, has been apparently accumulated, only afterwards to mock the grasp.  The lurid and plague-fraught glare of the meteor, misinterpreted by official astronomers for the sun of national aggrandisement, is now fast overspreading with the gloom of the coming tornado.  The tale of its mid-day glories has been duly sung in lofty strains by placemen and pensioners in Parliament or before constituencies, and zealously commemorated in a venal press ; to the London Gazette is now consigned the task of enumerating, with pomp lugubrious, the lengthening tail of its parched-up victims, for the due celebration of whose funeral rites a weekly supplemental sheet is found indispensable.

Thus a commercial crisis is in presence and in daily developement to complicate the embarrassments and enhance the perils of the social struggle. The cape has to be doubled, at whose headlands opposing tempests meet and howl and mingle in terrific confusion; where counter-currents and contending seas mix and mount in foam and fury to the heavens, in seeming deadly strife for mastery; and where all these elementary horrors combine, as if by tacit accord, to assail and engulf the luckless vessel betrayed through false reckoning into the vortex. With stout hearts and skilled hands at the helm, the good ship might yet ride out the raging storm and right herself, with timbers sound in the main, and, albeit damaged in rigging, still able to make headway under easy sail, sporting her royals, and flying her glorious union-jack. But at this moment of double peril, with a majority of one, and the strongest branch of the legislature, applauding measures which threaten the civil and religious institutions of the state with utter disorganization—one moiety of which, constituting a faction apart, confident, if not commanding, does not scruple to avow its determination of pressing to a final and irretrievable overthrow—and when the material interests of the empire are in the incipient stages of an awful crisis, the results of which no man can foresee, although the boldest may quail at the mere contemplation;—at such a moment, we repeat, despondency must fill the mind of every reflecting man as he turns his regards to the centre of action, and takes measure of the steersmen in charge. The thoroughpaced revolutionist, indeed, derives additional boldness from the contemptuous survey of the pusillanimity ostensibly arrayed against him, but ever receding before him; his strength increases in proportion to the weakness which yields upon pressure; accordingly, republicanism is seen to rear its brazen front with greater audacity each succeeding day, and during the present session of the Commons' House, its representatives fearlessly take the lead in debate, at one

moment proclaiming " unmingled horror for the Irish," and for the Protestant Church at large, concluding with a howl for the repeal of the Union; at another, preaching open rebellion to the Franco-Canadians, or urging our brethren of Upper Canada to shake off the " baneful domination of the mother country ;" and ever by speech and act hallooing on to organic change and the work of destruction ; whilst the sworn servants of the King and the Constitution, with trembling or treacherous souls, sit listening by, or with false hearts and coward lips, where open defiance is the part of duty and manhood, seek pitifully to propitiate, whilst by implication they commit themselves to participation in the *quasi* treason, with deferential salaams to the " profound and comprehensive reasoning," the "admirable and luminous speeches" of people intellectually so shallow, and politically so worthless, that nothing less than a complete inversion of the natural order of society could have raised them to the surface of the troublous stream on which they float, and where, side by side almost with the genius and virtue of the land, the ignoble refuse, amidst the caresses of depraved officials, may well be tempted in self-satisfied companionship to exclaim, " See how we apples swim !"

No more heavy curse could be visited on a nation than, with revolution in progress, and with an industrial crash imminent, to have men in the supreme direction of affairs mentally, morally, physically moreover, incapable of rising, not above only, but to the level of the circumstances which surround them. We have a Premier, amiable, doubtless, in all the relations of private life, and a lover of literature, but who, in the best of his bygone days, exhibited nothing more remarkable than the degree of talent which soars not beyond the art of pleasing, and provokes not, by the lofty and uncompromising advocacy of principles, or the towering pretensions of genius, to command either envy or hostility in any quarter. A life of luxurious ease, with all the goods of fortune in possession, has wasted whatever of vigour might once have been his in the hey-day of the blood ; contradiction makes him querulous, but it is not in his nature to be energetic. Too high-minded, if not too conscientious, to join the revolutionary pack, whose designs, nevertheless, do not baffle his penetration, he is too indolent to counterwork them—he is impotent for opposition. We may take him at his word, that to the solemn league and covenant of Lichfield-House between ex-officials, agitators, and republicans, he was no party, and shunned all contact with it. We may believe that he reassumed his former post, partly from pique at an unceremonious, too ungracious, because, on his part, not specially provoked dismissal, and partly, also, from the urgency of colleagues and followers, to whom, as the ostensible leader of a party, he may fairly be said to have been bound on the point of honour. Lord Melbourne has no family exigencies to satisfy ; he is not one of the younger sons of a numerous brood, and of a house historically voracious. His estate is ample and unencumbered ; he is without sons whose fame or advancement he has to care for. Personally, therefore, from sordid imputations he may be acquitted ; of great personal ambition at his years, and with his habits, we are not disposed to challenge him strongly in tempestuous days like the present, however the seductions, the love of power and patronage in other and more tranquil seasons, might have tempted. His is a character compounded of negatives. There is nothing about him positively good to command respect, or great to admire, or absolutely vicious to denounce— and in this is the danger, for he is no more than the slave of a party, of which he exhibits as the leader, whose necessities, urgent and imperious, he must provide for, and the more pronounced section of which hold him in tutelage. Too inert for reflection, he resigns himself to the dictation of colleagues of more active habits and determined mould, but whose intellectual capacity no man estimates more truly, or holds in more sovereign contempt than himself. The language and the sentiments of the Prime Minister in one House are unscrupulously repudiated by his subordinates in the other, and he condescends to propose measures, of the motives or the merits of which he is no further cognizant than the notes of instructions transmitted to him by the heads of departments for their vindication. What better instrument can the revolutionist desire than a Premier buried in aristocratic sloth, who dreads the annoy-

ance of thinking, and begs only not to be *derangé !*

However deficient in the higher attributes of the statesman, Lord Melbourne is withal an accomplished gentleman—not contemptible for talents and acquirements—personally disinterested—liberal-minded, frank, generous and sincere. What proportion of this praise can truly be accorded to the small person of the Abbey (for small in every sense he is), by whom he is bestridden and tormented ? Lord John Russell is one of the younger scions of a family great alone by territorial possessions ; which, from the dawn obscure of its rise unto this present noontide of its splendour, has never yet gratefully presented the state, as some equivalent for transcendent value received, with one offshoot whose name adorns, or is worthy to adorn the page of history—save one. By some freak of nature or caprice of womankind, there chances an exception to the rule, but even Lord William Russell is more celebrated for the virtues of constancy, and the sufferings of martyrdom, than for commanding powers of mind, or service of high national import. He might indeed have been gifted in the one sense, and shone in the other—had fate and Popery permitted the developement. Otherwise the trophies emblazoned of the house of Bedford, must be sought, not in the annals of Great Britain, but in the pages of Junius and Burke. Of Lord John himself, the present hero of our pen, may be repeated what Burke said of one of his progenitors,—" he was swathed, rocked, and dandled into a legislator." Of the cunning which alone made, and still remains hereditary in the family, he is the very type — the " child and champion." Cunning is the essence of small minds, and not unfrequently the characteristic of men of small stature. If any record could exist of so insignificant a personage as the Russell of Henry the Eighth, the first of the known name, and the man who slily inveigled out of the capricious tyrant the spoils of a fallen church, in some of those fitful and lavish moments, upon which he servilely waited, it would perhaps be found that he was some dwarfish pimp to royal fantasy—for popular caprice there was then none worth administering to. The family tree is still notorious for the same fruit—centuries have not sufficed to scour the taint from the blood,—the passage of nearly two thousand years finds the children of the money-changers of the Temple, money-changers still. The descendant of the first Russell, faithful to the traditions of his race, has ever been, and will remain a waiter upon Providence, and a timeserver of ascendency, until the day fast coming, but not foreseen—for wisdom only is foresighted for to-morrow—the tiny optics of cunning pierce not beyond the hour—when the people of whom he has been the pioneer to level the way shall decree the reassumption of national domains, with which his minions were so prodigally endowed by the reckless despot—when the vast possessions of the house of Bedford shall revert to their former and, since the revocation of poor law rights, rightful owners. Thus Lord John lauded the old Constitution with all its blemishes so long as it was popular, but when a change came over the spirit of the land, the object of his veneration was pitilessly abandoned to its fate, and a new one concocted — he bowed the knee before Old Sarum first, and after broke his idol in pieces. The ancient Russell forsook the falling church of his age, and out of its ruins founded the future dukedom ; the modern patriot aids likewise to undermine what he believes the falling church of his day, so that the timely claim of gratitude may be established in the event of scramble or repartition of another wreck hereafter. For the petty details of intrigue and for mischief the Secretary of the Home Office seems gifted with capacity just sufficient, and no more. The grasp of his mind may be estimated from the conclusion solemnly meditated in his closet, and published to an astonished world, that the corruption of the ancient noblesse, and their devotion to the refined sensualities and Heliogabalan luxuries of the *cuisine,* was a chief cause of that mighty outbreak, the first French Revolution. By a parity of logic, the Reform Bill, and the revolution now working here under the pretext of Reform, are not attributable, as vulgarly believed, to Lord John Russell and the Whig lust of power and place, but to the epicurean extravagances of Crockford's and the enervating *potages, soufflés* and *entremets* of that prince of artistes, Monsieur Ude. Of a piece with this profound discovery,

was the pitiful exhibition of fright and feebleness on the introduction and opening dissection of his misshapen Reform bantling, when Lord John fled the withering sarcasm of opponents, and the contemptuous condolence of friends, in the Commons' House in dismay, and took to a bed of sickness (as is yet his wont when difficulties perplex, and his faculties are bewildered), devolving upon the brawny shoulders of Lord Althorp the burden of defending his unsightly cub, and licking it into shape. As a speaker the language of the Secretary corresponds with the commonplace character of his intellect. He never, by any accident, digresses into eloquence—his pedantic pretension of manner cannot disguise the poverty of ideas—he is heavy without matter, verbose without logic, diffuse without clearness, pompous without elevation, solemn but not impressive. Imagination he has none ; he is heard rather than listened to, concludes without producing conviction, and but for social position and official station, would scarcely be tolerated beyond a colloquy in committee or a turnpike bill debate. Such is the colleague in chief, and the *imperium in imperio* of the government over which Lord Melbourne presides in appearance but not in reality. The subaltern leads his commander, because ever cunningly a march in advance—his cry is always *en avant marchons,* and following freebooters eager for foray and spoil, cluster preferentially round the standard that floats in the van. Upon the other adjuncts of the cabinet, it were profitless to waste words—they are but the makeshifts of one, and the cast-offs of another party. There is but one whose talents soar above mediocrity, and he listlessly content to serve where most qualified to command—Lord Glenelg barters acknowledged powers for a life of ease and license to doze away an official existence.

The attempt were bootless to canvass or classify the merits or pretensions of the Ultra-Radical section which have followed in the wake, and now head and hurry the march of the more lagging Ministerialists. Among themselves they own no chief, because superior mind amongst them there is none. They are a striking exemplification of a perfect democracy—an equality of capacities with a certain unity of action, but with no common bond of conviction. For here are amongst them republicans pure, and republicans *quasi*, and republicans turn-about; men who hate the hereditary principle in King and Lords—men who would stop short of the Monarch—men who, for a price, would be staunch to one or both. All these diverse people talk now and then of universal suffrage by way of popularizing themselves; some few would sincerely go the length of household suffrage; the generality prefer the sovereignty one and indivisible of the middle classes, could they, by sacrifices of consistency and principle, however base, acquire their confidence. Of these various fractions of a faction, with and without principle, Mr Joseph Hume is the finished Iago. Now he distils wormwood into the ears of the credulous and impetuous Othello—anon, makes drunk with flattery mine " ancient "—and next excites the easy idiot Roderigo. Honest Joseph sides and sails with all and each—whoever sinks, his bark he resolves shall not founder. If now he swear by Lord John, to-morrow he will fasten upon Mr Grote, and the next day proffer his adorations to Sir William, or go the whole hog with Carlile himself. Obtuse of intellect, in a ratio commensurate with his powers of matchless effrontery, Mr Hume does not the less largely and lengthily deal with every variety of subject, expounding none, because none comprehending; the sole description of philosophy in which he is at home being that of the breeches pocket. Accordingly, no man ever besieged the public offices more audaciously, or practised among them more successfully. From a commissionership down to a policeman—from contracts in grand to contracts for a half share in the supply of police clothing—no place or job to be made or given away has been beyond the aspiration, or beneath the notice, or escaped the clutches of Joseph Hume, Esq., M. P. for the Metropolitan county, or Messrs Hume and Cŏ., army-clothiers and police tailors. It was so in the times of Tory ascendency, let it be said with shame—so it is even now in the halcyon days of Whiggery; we could quote the very terms of scorn and loathing in which more than one Whig functionary has reprobated a nuisance which they cannot, or dare not abate. But the

disinterested patriot is never liberal to others, without an eye to interest or business. The suppliant for patronage must make out his qualifications; he must show credentials of Hume clanship—a bar sinister, moral or heraldic, counting for nothing—or his rate-receipts and testimonials to command of votes in Middlesex or Aberdeen, which is the ex-candidate's *pis aller*, or other places for which sit his creatures, more mean than the meanest of patrons, as we are told below the deeps there is a deeper still. These only are the sterling coins of claim and merit current at the Hume Office; all else are rejected as counterfeit. You exclaim, as well you may, against the possible or the probable of such cormorant rapacity, ever fed and still hungering, because you see, and have seen, votes recorded against Whig friends and Tory foes indiscriminately, and read speeches, so far as words go, bitter against both. So reasons the simplicity and common sense of mankind; the fact of votes and speeches is there printed and published; but of votes, motions, annoyance—jobbed, compromised, or stultified—there is and can exist no tangible record or glossary. The late Admiral Harvey, M.P. for Essex, used to answer applications of friends for army influence with the Government of the day, " If you want favour at the Horse Guards, go to Sir Ronald Ferguson." The name of Sir Ronald, as every one knows, was never seen except on the Whig lists of opposition. One must be behind the curtain to comprehend the working of the machinery. There are two systems: that of the Tories was to neglect and spit upon their friends—their opponents they delighted to honour and reward. The Whigs have adopted a *mezzo termine*, and, it must be owned, a better calculated if not more equitable policy. In Ireland they gorge their foes to repletion, and so silence them; in England, rather than postpone the claims of friends, they manufacture places express, and find sops abundant wherewithal to soothe the cravings of importunate croakers like Mr Hume.

In contemplating the character and judging the capacities of the two parties, one of which wields the government, and both combined constitute the parliamentary majority of the Commons' House, it is impossible that the mind should not be carried back to those phases of the first French Revolution which reflect men and things in parallel positions, and with the outlines of parties and individual characteristics not dissimilar to those of the present day in this country. In order to ensure the overthrow of Royalists and Constitutionalists, the two factions of the Gironde and the Mountain were banded one and indivisible, so far as the special object in view; each in all other respects marching under its distinctive banner, and urging its separate theories. In the ranks of neither body were to be found the great names of the Revolution, but indisputably the ablest as the most respectable innovators were those of the Gironde. Now, an impartial scrutiny must satisfy the most partial of the extraordinary inferiority in talents and acquirements of the Whigs and Whig-Radicals, with scarcely an exception, to the Girondists, with whom from position and circumstances they naturally enter into comparison. Register the Ministerial benches, and where shall we meet with the brilliant and burning eloquence of Vergniaud, the more cool and subtle reasoning of Brissot, the philosophical elevation of the scientific Condorçet? These were men, however, not distinguished beyond many, and barely above a large proportion of their colleagues of the same colour of opinion. No sane person would certainly think of elevating Lord John Russell to the unattainable standard of Brissot, or of comparing the intellectual budget of Mr Spring Rice with that of Condorçet, or collating the polished diction, exuberantly overlaying paucity of matter, of Lord

Glenelg, with the "thoughts that breathe and words that burn" in the orations of Vergniaud. The member who nearest approaches to a Brissotin by the qualities of his mind and his oratory is perhaps Mr Grote, if we may accept his recent speech upon the Ballot as a fair specimen of both. It is unquestionably a vast improvement upon his former efforts, however false its conclusions, and none the worse for the absence of that affected display of classical reference which on a former occasion subjected him justly to the imputation of an ambitious pretension to scholarship which superficially only he could possess, inasmuch as he had evidently misread or misapprehended, and assuredly misrepresented, his authorities. Mr Grote ranks, however, in common acceptation, as a Radical pure, and certainly not as a Whig. If the section of Radicals pure, or philosophical Radicals, as with ludicrous self-laudation they love to style themselves, be weighed against the men of the Mountain, the process exhibits the like results. The distance is almost measureless from Barrère,[*] Robespierre, and St Just, down to Buller, Hume, and Roebuck. Beside the keen wit, the learning and fluency of Barrère, the powers of argumentation of Robespierre, and the rhetorical ability of St Just, to judge only by what remains of them, how inefficient, marrowless, and unreasoning appear the senatorial performances of the British trio, who, so far as principles, seem emulous to tread in their footsteps! When those principles are once triumphant—when the institutions of the state and the altar are laid prostrate, and the Goddess of Reason en-

---

[*] The hoary revolutionist still lives—at least he was alive and made his appearance in Paris after the Revolution of July. Some time after that event, he was found out, and a large party invited by an old acquaintance of other days to meet him. Of course all the world was there to see and hear one of the great monsters of the Revolution. The lion made all the *frais* of the conversation, and his powers of wit and repartee were found as brilliant as ever. One of the company present was M. de . . . . . . himself no mean proficient in revolutionary lore, whose father, a Court banker of Louis XVI., was guillotined in the times of Robespierre. Barrère, as president of the Revolutionary Tribunal, presided at the execution, and as usual, seasoned the deed of blood with a pun. As the head of the victim was being severed from the body, he exclaimed to a friend, in allusion to the money-dealing pursuits of the sufferer, *c'est battre de la monnaie*—this is coining. M. de . . . . . . . the son, being asked, subsequently to the party alluded to, his impression of Barrère, ingenuously and unconcernedly answered—*c'est un homme extraordinaire, mais il a tué mon père!* Undoubtedly none but a Frenchman born and bred to revolutions, could have done or said the like.

throned, monsters will not long be wanting to carry them out practically to all their sanguinary consequences here as it was in France—consequences at the bare reflection upon the possibility of which, those deeply sinning, but still we hope well-intentioned Radicals, must start with horror and affright. Robespierre himself, whose capacity, from a just abhorrence of his atrocities, has been exceedingly underrated, betrayed no indications originally of those ferocious instincts which successful ambition and the acquisition of power unlimited subsequently so fearfully developed. The Gironde initiated him in the taste for blood, and fell almost the first victims to the latent carnivorous propensities which they had aroused and feasted.

The mediocrity of talent in the leaders is commonly assigned as the first cause of the sanguinary anarchy which accompanied the march of the French Revolution, and the failure of the republic which they aimed at constructing out of the ruins of the monarchy. The mediocrities here being more signal still, the revolution can terminate only in the same results of destruction to life and property. When the masses become agitated, feebleness in the governing power is the surest symptom, and the forerunner of violence and anarchy. What M. Chevalier profoundly and philosophically observes of France, specially in his work on the United States, may be usefully applied here. " Weakness," says he, " is what the people tolerate least in their rulers. The mediocrity men (*hommes mediocres*), who in their ridiculous vanity dare aspire to preside over the destinies of thirty-three millions of men, and who, once invested, degrade power to their own level, and allow it to be dismantled, would they not deserve to be accused of conspiracy against social order, equally with frantic revolutionists or crazy counter revolutionists? Do they not compromise equally one and the other the public tranquillity—do they not undermine the foundations of the prosperity and safety of the country ?" Counter revolutionists there are none here, because there is yet no revolution finally accomplished to provoke combination. To the Reform Bill, announced by Reformers as a " final measure," the great Conservative body has long yielded an unanimous adhesion, and none are more

zealous in upholding the law than those who have ever been accustomed to obey with cheerfulness, and most rarely to violate it. The property and intelligent classes have themselves so deep a stake in the conservation of this final adjustment, intact from invasion, that no danger need be apprehended, provided a Government, strong by the concentration of talent, firmness, and patriotism, with its foundations based on such a rock, existed to represent and enforce their opinions and resolves. The only conspirators hitherto declared against the Reform Bill are to be found among its authors and abettors ; the only propositions to change or subvert it have emanated from those who most loudly demanded, and most solemnly accepted it, as satisfaction in full of all demands. But there can be no question, that by the working classes, it is far from being regarded with that enthusiasm with which on its appearance it was hailed, under the prevalence of which, and of the unpardonable impostures practised upon them to that end, those physical demonstrations were resorted to which contributed so largely to decide the fiercely disputed point of its acceptation by the Legislature. Excitement over, they have not failed to discover, that under the old Constitution, anomalous, complex, and corrupt in parts as it was, they still enjoyed a voice in the national representation ; that if the mass was not privileged, component portions of that mass, identical in feelings, opinions, and interests, were. Freemen, potwallopers, and those who voted in right of a smoke, all formed part of the operative classes, and had a controlling power in the elections of various cities, towns, and boroughs. Thus, through a sort of delegation of the order, the people, commonly so called, had a direct and influential action upon the representation—a distinct, and no mean share in the representative body. To these descriptions of electors, a life-lease of their privileges was secured by the Conservatives, after a struggle, under the Reform Bill ; but, in most cases, their force is swamped already by the overwhelming numbers of the ten-pound franchise electors; the body is wasting away annually in the course of nature, so that in a few years not a vestige of rights and power so strictly popular will remain. This did not, at the time, escape the penetration of

Cobbett and Hunt,* whose remedy, indeed, was to the most thoroughgoing extent; but the masses, inflamed to the wildest fury, rushed blindly on under other and more artful leaders, and neither bargained to retain the powers they had, nor to secure an equivalent for an extension of them. The freemen might be, and to a certain extent were doubtless corrupt, but not more so than the ten-pounders in the smaller communities are rapidly becoming, and will become within a short period. Alarmed even at the prospect of the moral or physical agency which the people non-entitled may still exert over the qualified electors, the Reformers are hotly urging on the ballot, with the more special object of depriving them even of the shadow of control, although this same "moral" and indirect agency was largely insisted upon, during the discussions on the Reform, by its supporters, as one of its most unquestionable and desirable results, by enlarging the sphere of popular influence, and bringing it more directly to bear upon the proceedings of the Legislature. Mr Grote, doubtless, desires to lay the axe to the root of aristocratic and county influences and dictation, and to act upon the relations of landlord and tenant; but he deceives himself wofully, if he thinks to throw dust in the eyes of the public by this pretext alone as to other ulterior views, more cogent although less salient. He would, we opine, have no disinclination to compromise with aristocracy, and leave the counties alone, if the towns might be surrendered to the ballot. Not that Mr Grote hates the aristocracy less, but that he dreads the workies more. The theories of Whig and Radical governments, so far as they have been developed, are not altogether of the most popular complexion, nor, as they come to be practically applied, do they promise to improve in that sense upon further acquaintance. Anti-popular votes, such as those for the abolition of the old Poor Law, that palladium of the poor man's social rights, and for the enactment of that barefaced imposture miscalled the Poor Law Amendment Act, are not calculated to curry favour with those who are both insult-

ed and agrieved thereby. The return of Radicals, no less than of Whigs, to Parliament will be endangered, unless the popular action upon the electors be neutralized or destroyed. The votes of the ten-pounders, whose pockets are spared in the payment of poor's rates are, it is selfishly calculated, safe and sure in grateful behalf of their rate-saving representatives, provided that through the process of secret voting the people are shut out from knowledge or interference direct or indirect. However the electors, in their own case, and for their own convenience, may relish this guarantee for the unrestricted exercise of a more free volition, it may be doubted whether they will be so readily satisfied with the application of the ballot to the regulations of the honourable House itself; whether they will consent that the votes of their delegates shall be equally unshackled and shrouded in darkness quoad those who depute them, as their own with the ballot would be quoad the non-privileged and unrepresented of their countrymen. For in the one case, as in the other, despite fine-drawn and cob-web distinctions, it is a simple affair of trusteeship, in the one expressed, but in the other understood only; the powers in trust with which the ten-pounders are invested by the nation, being again, and by virtue of the trust-authorization, committed into fewer and more selected hands, with the reservation of certain obligations and responsibilities, direct and special, from representatives towards the constituency, but from the electors to the non-electors implied and moral only. With the ballot once in the House of Commons, the mode in which it will work is already familiarized to us by the example of the French Chamber of Deputies. In that assembly it not unfrequently occurs, upon a disputed popular question, that on the first scrutiny, which is by *assis* and *levés,* by one party rising and the other remaining seated, or open voting, the result is a majority on the popular side; but on the demand for the application of the ballot, or secret vote, by which the publicity of the member's opinion is avoided, the reverse takes place; the majority, swayed by

* Nor we believe of Mr Bell, of the True Sun then, but of the London Mercury now.

an occult influence, be it royal or aristocratic, it may be in the exercise of an impartial judgment, no longer coerced by the fear of public odium, is found to be arrayed against the open vote and popular decision. To this complexion the ballot, once adopted for the constituency, will come at last. The argument, if worth any thing, is irresistible in the one application as the other ; the representative will urge his title to protection against the electoral body, on the indisputable plea that they on their part have been withdrawn, and secured from the popular jurisdiction. Let the constituency beware how they give into the trap, for if the robbery of the remnant of popular rights be countenanced in the spirit of encroachment or tyranny by them, they will be fleeced in return, and their own arbitrary inclinations retributively retorted upon them.

What valid objection, moreover, can be urged against extending the scope of the ballot to the House of Peers, and thus withdrawing that body from the control and coercion of public opinion ? The House of Commons is a reflected and dependent power only ; but the Lords represent a fixed, hereditary, and independent principle *per se* in their own persons, and the hereditary principle equally resides in the property qualification, which is the basis of the electoral right. The elector may be disfranchised by the accidents of life, but the property never ; so the peer may die, but the peerage never, save by default of heirs in the right line. The Commons are a delegation direct, with powers as to persons revocable periodically. The Lords are seized of power in their own right as a branch of the constitution, and coeval with it—the constituency is a delegation permanent, with faculties non-revocable. The two latter alone are legally, that is, constitutionally irresponsible. There exists no tribunal to which they are amenable, save the moral force of public opinion. The Lords politically, as numerically the weaker, as against Commons and constituency, and therefore the more exposed to lose its independence of action, may feasibly urge their stronger pretensions to the protection of the ballot ; it would be gross injustice and oppression to invest either Commons or constituency, or both, with it to their exclusion. If conce-

ded to the Commons, it annuls their direct responsibility to the constituency ; if to the constituency and the Lords, it vitiates the agency, slow, indirect, but irresistible, of public opinion ; it sweeps away the last relic of the rights of the people. If to the constituency alone, it clothes a class apart with all the awful attributes of an Inquisition invisible though absolute. The masses are enslaved by a despot, with whom, because unseen, they cannot grapple—the monarchy is undermined by a hidden foe, whom it cannot counteract.

In the convulsion forthcoming of the industrial world, to aggravate the perils of the political crisis, what claim, we ask, has the Whig-Radical Government to the confidence or the gratitude of the masses, who will be the chief sufferers and the most dangerous complainants ? Let them answer it with the Factory Bill, and the Workhouse system, and the Central Police system in hand—for no one doubts that a Central Police system was already concocted, prim, perfect, and absolute in all its parts before the Board of Commissioners was formed, or one single leading query of the trashy circular traced in ink. Let us begin with the Factory Bill and the Factory system.

It is not our intention to recapitulate any portion of the horrors of that system unregulated by law. There are the committees of 1816, 1818, and 1819, before the Houses of Lords and Commons, with their folios of appalling evidence arrayed in judgment against it. The Lords, more especially, devoted two sessions to the duties of humanity. There is also the committee of the Commons in 1832, most reluctantly conceded by the Whigs to the late lamented philanthropist, Mr Sadler, as the former were due to that good and able man the late Sir Robert Peel, and the untiring energies of that eminent benefactor of the working classes, the late Mr Nathaniel Gould of Manchester. These three gentlemen were all Tories ; for, by a fatality almost incredible, we never hear of a Whig or a philosophical Radical active and prominent in works of benevolence—devoting unostentatiously the powers of mind and body to soothe the miseries or add to the sum of comforts of those in humble life.

The factory system passes for being the creation of modern times—for having sprung from the loins, as it were, of the splendid inventions of Arkwright. The mistake is singular, and shows the carelessness or the want of research in writers who have descanted so largely upon those industrial interests interwoven with it. Neither M'Culloch, Dr Ure, nor Mr Baines, in their several publications upon the cotton manufacture, seem to have been aware of the fact that the Factory System, such almost as we have seen it in years past, such in its leading features as it exists at present, such, unchecked by legislative interference, as in times of pressure, low prices, falling wages, and the application of the screw it might and would become hereafter, had, centuries ago, flourished in all its rank luxuriance in South America, fostered, if not planted, under the genial auspices of Spanish avarice and Spanish despotism. As an ample justification for the exercise of the superintendence, ever-watchful, of a wise authority over the health and wellbeing of the labouring classes, no less than as a warning to merchants and master manufacturers, of the revolting cruelties which a lust for gold renders possible, and which might come to be perpetrated in after times under the Factory System, abandoned to the caprice or cupidity of future administrators—cruelties, from the commission of which they would recoil, as from the mere perspective they will with horror—we shall conclude with one extract from the *Noticias Secretas de America*, descriptive of the Factory System in the cotton and wool manufacturing districts of the provinces of Quito and Caxamarca (now forming part of the new Republic of the Ecuador), and generally applicable to all those of Peru and New Granada in the former part of the last century. These *noticias* are official reports, drawn up for the private information of the Government, from personal survey, by Don Jorje Juan, and the justly celebrated Don Antonio de Ulloa, by the latter chiefly, in conformity with special instructions to examine into the administration of authority and the situation of the people, in that portion of South America seated on the Pacific. The Inquisition was commenced on the termination of that scientific mission for measuring a degree upon the Equator, on which those two functionaries, no less eminent for learning than for their humanity, had been deputed to accompany and assist the French astronomers, Godin, Bouger, and La Condamine, in the year 1735.

" The labours of the manufactory commence," says Ulloa, "before daybreak, when each Indian (the factory workmen were all Indians) hastens to the room appointed for his class of work, where their task portion of the day is distributed to them ; which done, the master fastens the door and leaves them incarcerated. At noon, the door is opened for the women (the wives or other female relatives), who bring their poor and scanty rations of food. The meal consumes little time, and they remain again imprisoned as before. When the darkness no longer permits them to labour, the master manufacturer comes to collect the work ; those who have not been able to finish the allotted quantity are, without listening to reason or excuse, castigated with a cruelty that is incredible ; and, turned into unfeeling brutes, these impious men discharge upon the miserable Indians stripes by hundreds,* for in no other manner do they know how to count them ; and for conclusion of the chastisement, they are left locked up in the prison-room (although all the building is no better), fettered and placed in the stocks. There is a particular place set apart for punishing them with greater *indignities* † than would

* The instrument of punishment is thus described :—" Este instrumento de tortura consiste en un cabo, como de una vara de largo y un dedo de gruesso, o poco menos, hecho de cuero de vaca torcido à la manera de un bordon."—A kind of rope's-end about a yard long and a finger thick, made of ox-hide, and twisted like a pilgrim's staff.

† The mode of punishment thus :—" Se le manda (the Indian) tender en el suelo boca abaxo, se le quitan los ligeros calzoncillos, que es todo su ropage, y los azotar con el ramal, haciendole contar los latigazos que descargan sobre el hasta completar el número de la sentencia." After which the poor wretch was suffered to rise, and on his

be done with the most guilty slaves. During the day the master, his assistant, and the overlooker, visit every room various times ; the Indian who has been the least remiss is instantly chastised in the same manner with stripes, and then returns to his work until the hour of leaving off, when the punishment is repeated."

Such was the Report of an upright Spanish *Commissioner.* The local government were conscious of the habitual practice of their enormities, without the power to remedy. The Viceroys of Peru had before, as Ulloa testifies, despatched commissioners to enquire, and armed with full powers to call the masters to account, and inflict condign retribution. In vain ; the commissioners, who on their arrival in a district would neither be bribed nor feasted * by the masters, were insulted and abused, and were finally too happy to escape threatened assassination, by a precipitate departure and abandonment of their mission. Few were, however, so honest and scrupulous as not to barter conscience and compound with crime for the sake of ease and profit.

Let no man lay the flattering unction to his soul that monstrosities such as described by Ulloa of America could never obtain and be tolerated in this more enlightened era—in this more civilized land. Extremes meet —as imperial Rome advanced in refinement, more gladiators and hosts of slaves were slaughtered at her festivals—the amphitheatre overflowed with gore amidst the enthusiastic plaudits of ravished assemblages of the most advanced people of the earth. The Factory System, in some of its leading features, is the same in England as in Peru—the differences are of degree only. The oppression which crushes childhood first may hereafter lay its iron hand upon manhood— upon manhood depressed and spiritless from times and circumstances, from the competition of supply in the labour market and the paucity of demand, from receding wages and insufficiency of employ—for tyranny grows with the consciousness of power, and the cravings of the demon of avarice become more insatiate as hecatombs of victims are multiplied. Children and young women form the majority of the factory population already—ere long adult co-operation may be wholly displaced, and children only remain the subordinate agents of the steam-engine, the self-acting mule, and the power-loom. The strap and the billy-roller are but other names for the *cabo de cuero de vaca*—the scandal of the South American discipline upon children would be less gross, less repugnant in form, although more pitiless towards the helpless sufferers. But for legislative intervention all the evils of the parent—of the South American —factory system might be realized here to the fullest extent. They who doubt it have never consulted the Parliamentary evidence, not even that collected by one-sided Whig commissioners. Our humble and impartial testimony has never been wanting in the cause ; but to those who are still incredulous we advise a perusal of " the Evils of the Factory System," † a masterly compendium of that evidence, and of the Parliamentary debates upon the question, preceded by a rationale so forbearing, so free from personality where personality is almost a virtue, so excellently, philosophically, and humanely reasoned, that we know not which is most to be admired in the author, the goodness of his heart or the soundness of his understanding.

In the cause of the factory children and the factory population we have seen that Whig-Radicals and Radicals philosophical were not only not zealous, not only not neutral and quiescent, but they were outrageously and indecently arrayed against them. All the manœuvres of Government and of faction were played off, and success-

---

knees forced to return thanks, and invoke the blessing of the Almighty on his inhuman flagellator. Women and children, who also were employed in the factories, were indiscriminately subjected to the same barbarous as indecent discipline.

* Mr Drinkwater Bethune, the Leeds Factory Commissioner, would do well to consult Ulloa as to the mode in which the tribe were feasted in Peru one hundred years ago—human nature is the same it appears in all ages.

† " Evils of the Factory System, demonstrated by Parliamentary Evidence." By Charles Wing, surgeon to the Royal Metropolitan Hospital for Children, &c. London : Dedicated most appropriately to Lord Ashley.

fully, to defeat their claims—the claims of humanity. In this Lord John Russell and Mr Hume, Mr P. Thomson and Mr Gisborne, displayed an unanimity reprehensible, if not surprising. When, from the evidence of facts irresistible—of facts forced upon them by their own specially instructed and delegated tools—farther resistance was impossible, with the malice prepense of the great father of evil in the like dilemma, what could no longer be openly opposed was, with the wile of the serpent, insidiously countervailed. They who had vociferously maintained the healthy aptitudes of the child for twelve hours of toil continuous and daily, with a revulsion of opinion too sudden to be conscientious, as boisterously asserted that eight hours was the physical limit of endurance. The Factory Bill prepared in accordance was, with a fiendish ingenuity in its provisions, so drawn up as to be impracticable—so conceived that the operatives themselves should be the first to complain of its pressure upon their interests, demand its repeal, and prefer to hug once more the chains of former oppression. The bait has indeed not taken, and so the President of the Trade Board has been reduced to the necessity of recording the abortive result of Ministerial delinquency, by moving the Commons'* House to stultify itself and rescind the act of Whig-humanity quackery. That he failed only adds dishonour to the contempt before felt for the governing power. Under the *regime* of the Ballot and secret voting it had been far otherwise. But it needs no Delphic priestess to tell that the sunshine of Whig and Radical patronage was withheld from factory operatives, because they had no votes, and their opponents had. The factory operatives are, however, but one section of the working classes ; let us see if the general body have been treated with more mercy, and how social rights have been interpreted with respect to all, and justice administered. The party now in power have for the last fifty years been at the head, and the apologists of every popular movement—the patrons of all popular discontent. They have humbled themselves to the people—cajoled them— pandered to their passions, their excesses, their vices in every shape—no adulation has been too gross—no subserviency too degrading. On the

shoulders, and amid the acclamations of the populace, they were carried into office, and there maintained. The grateful return has been the Poor-Law Abolition Bill, in the enactment of which, and animated by the same motives, the Radical Utilitarians, who for twenty years have been contesting the race of popularity with them, have been the most zealous as the most heartless co-operators. Why ? Because the poor have no votes, and rate-payers have. The people are trampled on because no longer useful. The old poor-laws were abused, because mal-administered. But the tree is not rotten or in decay because in autumn its foliage grows yellow and dies off. The system was still sound at the core ; it was founded in natural rights, and had been consecrated by social covenants ; humanity presided at its birth—by consummate wisdom it was fostered into strength and fair proportions. The nation had waxed great, the middle classes prospered, the poor were contented under it. But as the Whig-Radicals changed the constitution to gain votes, so they conspired against poor-laws because the poor had none—*point d'argent, point de Suisse.* The fate of the old poor-laws was foredoomed in the composition of the preliminary Board for enquiry—in the selection of the assistant tools for procuring and moulding evidence wherewith to bolster up a foregone conclusion. The Grand Inquisition, with its familiars, was the veritable incarnation of the barbarous political economy of the day. The satellites sallied forth under banners emblazoned with the hideous spectre of redundant population—their mission was to survey the land, and cut down the excess. Merciless as Procrustes himself, their theory was unstretching and unaccommodating as his bed. The mass was measured, and the superabundant victims adjusted by it. At one end they were lopped off by the premium on infanticide, and at the other by the workhouse system ;— the axe of the one was whetted by bastardy clauses, of the others sharpened by starvation-diet and the horrors of imprisonment. Such was the origin, such the parents, such the intents, such the achievements, of the new Poor-Law Abolition Bill. Not one friendly voice represented in the Commission the interests or feelings of the poor—none was found to cry,

God bless them. A case was got up to justify oppression by means of garbled testimony and one-sided depositions. The assistant or touring Commissioner was officially instructed to *use his own discretion* as to the places which appear to be most deserving of investigation, and *as to the points of enquiry* which may be most successfully investigated." The license was used in all its latitude. Lawyers real and lawyers nominal,* of the class of lacklanders, who had studied the poor only in the assize calendar or in police courts,† transformed paupers into felons, and presented poverty as crime. The Grand Inquest of the nation found a true bill upon the *ex-parte* allegations of witnesses so partial and corrupt. Corrupt and partial they were, for the prize of place and salary was contingent on the case to be got up— a prospective premium was held out for the most varied and apposite collection of distorted facts and the boldest perversion of reasoning. The competition was great, for golden was the reward; so exceptions were hunted out and multiplied sufficient to pass muster for the rule—reports were manufactured to establish, in conformity,

a general principle—finally the pains of parturition concluded with that monstrous birth of Whig-Radical legislation most comprehensively understood as the Workhouse System.

Into the practical working of this atrocious system it is not within our province now to enter, nor is it necessary. Volumes of heart-rending evidence have already been published to illustrate it—every journal in the kingdom teems daily with the most revolting details of it. It is now submitted to the process of Parliamentary investigation — a consummation achieved through the dauntless energies of that friend of the people, the member for Berkshire, but from the result we have no anticipations of justice ; a packed ministerial committee will labour to suppress, not elucidate truth. He who can rise from the perusal of Mr Walter's masterly exposure of the grinding tyranny and remorseless havoc, which, true as the dial to the sun, reflect the progress of the workhouse system with soul unmoved and unappalled, may boast the human form divine, but of humanity otherwise, no more than if he had been bred in the

---

* Of the genus distinguished as "lawyers nominal," the public are not, perhaps, generally aware. The fact is, that numbers of the gentlemen who delight to place "barrister" after their names, have never held a brief, or worn a wig, or studied a statute. What is more, some have been and are incapacitated by want of previous education, others disabled by want of means, many from disinclination, want of ambition, and the possession of a competent fortune. The rank of barrister is, however, to all socially a convenience, and easily attainable. For a man has only to enter himself of an Inn of Court, eat his commons in term time with punctuality for a probationary period, and he is admitted as a matter of course, without examination into his legal attainments, provided no objection be stated against his moral character. He thus gains a *settlement* in society, and takes rank, without question, as a gentleman, something in the same way that a pauper qualifies for a parish *settlement*, and a claim upon the poors' rate.

† It is commonly reported, but the thing is incredible, that one of the functionaries of the new Poor-Law Board is himself the offspring of an agricultural labourer. Far be it from us to allude to the fact, if fact it be, otherwise than as redounding the more to his honour in his elevation, provided that elevation were purchased by no sacrifices of principle—no truckling subserviency to the dark laid designs and nefarious conspiracies of those in high station against the poor. We have, however, read portions of the Report of an Assistant Commissioner, now officially known under another designation, with feelings mingled of disgust and contempt. The reasoning about "independent labourers and paupers,"—the "means by which the fund for their subsistence is to be reproduced," &c. &c., is just as trashy as might be expected in a penny *a*-liner; and the spirit which seasons the whole savours strongly of conclusions drawn from the habit of witnessing and recording the scenes of gin-drinking broils, petty larcenies, squalor, filth, and pauper misery daily exhibited at Bow Street or the Mansion House. That sort of experience would seem greatly to ministerial taste, as may be gathered from the lists of Poor-Law Commissioners, Factory Commissioners, and Rural Police Commissioners, in which certain names invariably recur. The hardest taskmasters are usually those of the order to be oppressed—the most callous of nigger drivers is the nigger himself. Does Lord John recognise the policy of the slavery system?

jungles of India, and sucked the dugs of tigers. By Whigs and Radicals conjointly he was assailed, interrupted, and insulted, all to stifle the expression of hateful facts, and drown the voice of the speaker—happily in vain. " The interruptions," said the fearless orator, " within the walls of that house—even if they amount to the howlings with which the neighbourhood rung two nights ago, shall not prevent me from making known the cries of the poor out of it." (He alluded to the disgraceful yells with which the ministerial pack had saluted Lord Lyndhurst.) One Captain D. Dundas, a nominee and retainer of Lord Lansdowne's, we believe, whom nobody ever hears of, except for braggart and bullying airs in Berks or St Stephen's towards Mr Walter, took umbrage, it seems (as Joe Miller would say, what other place has the man of war taken ?) about the " accusation of howling," from which it may be inferred either that he was himself one of the beagles, or felt sore at being coupled by the speaker among so degenerate a breed of mongrel curs. And what reply did Lord John Russell make to the dreadful enumeration of " large families starving," wretched children without other disease than " prostration of strength from want of food,"—deaths (murders would be the proper term) of the poor and aged from absolute want and relief denied—representations, that in certain parishes the poor were " dying in great numbers, and die they will, sooner than go into the bastile, as they call it, as did the poor woman," &c.,—"that in these bastiles, " if a man is dying, his wife cannot see him, if she be an inmate," so stern the separation of husband from wife, of parent from child ! What, we repeat, was the answer of Lord John to all the array of hideous examples cited, with names, dates, times, and circumstances, furnished and vouched for by honourable men, clergymen, and magistrates ? Why, Lord John informed the House, and rested his justification of the Workhouse system on the proof of the decrease " in the amounts of the poor rates." He enumerated places where the savings reached 30, 40, 50 per cent and more, as if the economy of

starvation were denied. It is, however, well that the mask is cast off, and that the great principle of the workhouse system is now avowed to be that of pounds shillings and pence alone, in other words, the gaol and hunger. The expenditure of poor's rate, Lord John exults in stating, has been wondrously diminished. In

| | |
|---|---|
| 1834 it was . . . | L.6,700,000 |
| 1835 . . . . . | 5,500,000 |
| 1836 down to . . | 4,360,000 |

and he charitably opines they may and ought to be reduced within the compass of L.4,000,000. Why four millions ? Why four pounds ? Why stop short of one of the clauses of the original bill, as carried by himself and Lord Althorp through the Commons, but mercifully rejected by the Lords, for fixing the date when all poor relief should cease and determine ? But whilst poor's rates have been lessened, and paupers have been ground down in their allowances, the higher order of paupers, the commissioners, flourish in all the chubby freshness of absolute plethora. Their salaries have been raised in the ratio of pauper allowance cut down, thus—

Chief Commissioners from L.1000 to L.2000 per annum.

Assistant Commissioners L.800 to L.1500 do.

By the Workhouse bill the number was restricted to nine ; there are now twenty-five. Even the saving, as Lord John put it, is a fraudulent assumption. He allows nothing for the constantly increasing absorption of labour during years past through a course of trading prosperity almost unparalleled, through extensive building speculations, through railroads numberless, and the improved prospects of agriculture. The cry is and has been that poor's rates and paupers are on the increase, that they are evils " every year and every day becoming more overwhelming in magnitude, and less susceptible of cure ;" and Lord Brougham went the length of asserting that all property would be swallowed up by them. Let us note the progression of this plague, pestilence, and famine, from the tables of Mr Nimmo. (*Parl. Papers,* 1830.)

| Years. | Relieved. | Population. | Ratio. |
|---|---|---|---|
| 1688, | 563,964 | 5,300,000 | 9.4 |
| 1766, | 695,177 | 7,728,000 | 11.3 |
| 1792, | 955,326 | 8,695,000 | 9.7 |

| Years. | Relieved. | Population. | Ratio. |
|---|---|---|---|
| 1803, | 1,040,716 | 9,168,000 | 8.0 |
| 1813, | 1,361,903 | 11,028,425 | 8.0 |
| 1821, | ———— | 11,977,663 | 9.3 |
| 1831, | 1,275,974 | 12,300,000 | 9.6 |

Relatively to the population, therefore, it is evident that pauperism has not been on the increase, but rather the reverse, the numbers relieved having varied only between 8 and 12 in 100 during a period of 140 years. The increase per cent of the cost of the poor's maintenance, in quarters of wheat, Winchester measure, which,

in 1820, as compared with 1803, was 47 per cent, was no more in 1830, as contrasted with 1820, then two one-seventh per cent. In the mean time, it may be useful to note the progress of national wealth, as measured only by the exportations of produce and manufactures, home and colonial. From

| | | | | | | |
|---|---|---|---|---|---|---|
| 1698 to 1701 the medium of exports was (official value) | | | | | | L.6,500,000 |
| 1802 | . | . | . | . | . | 41,500,000 |
| 1820 | . | . | . | . | . | 43,000,000 |
| 1830 | . | . | . | . | . | 66,000,000 |

The official values are taken, because no formal records of declared values exist before 1779. But as the export of 1698 was doubtless according to the ascertained, that is, " the declared " as well as official rates of values then current, it may be fairly compared with the " declared " values of British produce and official values of colonial exported in 1830, which were nearly L.46,000,000. Thus, whilst population and pauperism have little more than doubled in 140 years, national industry, even in the restricted view thus exhibited, has augmented sevenfold, and national wealth, did the enquiry fall within our limits, would be found to exhibit a much more considerable developement.

We shall not dwell on the frauds practised by the Commissioners, or, as we are loath to suspect men of respectable antecedents, of their subordinate officials, to impose upon public credulity with pretended abuses of the old, and forged or strained eulogiums of the new system. Among others, the parish of Cholesbury figured in the reports of the ambulant tribe, and in the speeches of Lord John, as damning proof of the property-swallowing qualities of the act of Elizabeth—" All the farms in the parish, we were warned with impressive repetition and awful solemnity, had gone out of cultivation under the old system." This darling and selected parish, it turns out, consists of 110 acres only, with two farms of 50 acres each! " The clerk of the Petworth Union states the M. P. for Berkshire

wrote a letter to the Commissioners, stating, as may be seen in their Report, that the people were much more orderly than heretofore." All this was true, so far as it went, and the Board ingeniously availed themselves of this fact, to take credit for the workhouse system as the cause ; but they stopped short of the remainder of the letter, in which the writer attributed the improvements to the provisions of the Police Act, which had recently been introduced into the place, and to its being lighted. Here we have a notable example of the *suggestio falsi* as well as the *suppressio veri.* The same device was practised by the Factory Commissioners in the suppression of Mr Stuart's Report.

Doubts have been thrown, and a meaning attempted to be wrested from the first and declaratory clause of the 43 Elizabeth, for the relief of the poor without the shadow of right or reason. The parish was bound to take order *for setting the poor to work,* " having no means to maintain them," and for the necessary relief of the aged, &c. The providing with work was compulsory ; the object was the maintenance of the poor ; if there be no work to be had, that might be a misfortune, but it could not discharge the parish from the resulting obligation of the maintenance of those willing and able for any work that might be found. Work and maintenance are clearly in the act synonymous or convertible terms, which the weak or the wicked alone can misapprehend the relative import of. By the same act of Elizabeth, it is ordered that "convenient houses of dwelling for the impotent poor" shall be erected on the "waste or common" lands of the parish, upon consent of and agreement with the Lord of the Manor, or by order of the Justices of the Peace, such "cottages" not to be used or employed at any time after for any other purposes. By the Whig system observe the difference: the "cottage" is superseded by the workhouse, from which the desolate inmates are allowed no egress, and by windows above reach, are debarred even the sight of the earth beneath. The intent of the "cottages" was the decent and affectionate provision for family ties and family affections, which are mercilessly sundered and inhumanly disregarded under the Whig law, by which the father or the husband immured in one workhouse, is rigorously isolated and denied all communication with the desolate partner of his life and the hapless child who are relegated to a separate dungeon in some other portion of the Union ; and in both cases, with a refinement of cruelty scarcely credible, the places of confinement are so calculated, under the instruction expressed or implied of the central despotism, as to withdraw them, by interposing the greatest practicable distance, from the communion and consolation of the more special friends and relatives of each. Is it to be wondered at that the poor, the aged and impotent poor, prefer to die of starvation, as they are daily dying by hundreds, in their own dear though miserable cottages at home, rather than be consigned to lingering misery in tombs, which, like the graves when dead, cut them off living from the most wretched solaces of earth ? Shall we be surprised that weeping friends and relatives take leave and bewail the fate of victims thus sentenced to excommunication, as if the workhouse, like the churchyard, were part and parcel of those gloomy regions from whose "bourne no traveller ere returns?" Ulloa records the same thing in Peru of the factories : " The order to go and work," says he, " in the *obrajes* or factories, causes more terror in the Indians than all the rigorous cruelties impiously invented against them. The married women, the mothers, begin to bewail the death of their husbands and children the moment of their condemnation to this penal la-

bour. With respect to their parents the children do the same, and there is no means left untried by parents to procure the liberation of their children from the labour of these *obrajes*." Once incarcerated, we may add, it was a sentence for life. When all efforts have proved unavailing, their despair is inconsolable ; they (the Indians) "direct to Heaven their clamorous complaints, seeing that all on earth conspire against them." Hear what the great and good Pitt said, as quoted by Mr Walter—" The law which prohibited relief, where any visible property remained, should be abolished. That degrading condition should be withdrawn. No temporary occasion should force a British subject to part with the last shilling of his capital, and descend to a state of wretchedness from which he could never recover, merely that he might be entitled to a casual relief." And yet under the workhouse system, so long as a stick of furniture can be found in the poor man's cottage, or a shilling in his possession, he is not entitled even to the luxuries of the Union gaol. Nay, distress warrants have been issued, and execution levied, to recover by public sale of his goods the defalcation of contribution assessed upon the son of a pauper earning twelve shillings a-week, and on the point of being married, for the parish outlay upon his mother.

Whatever amendments the original Workhouse Bill received in the House of Lords, one of which we have gratefully particularized, we are far from being content, after every allowance for the popular excitement of the time and the peculiarity of their position, with the conduct of the Conservative party upon the Poor Law trial. In all times care for the material interests of the poor had been a distinguishing feature of the aristocracy, gentry, and great manufacturers of the country ; they should have left the Whigs and Radicals-utilitarian with the monopoly of odium accruing from their own crusade against the non-voting working classes. We are not of the opinion of those who think a " red herring" good enough for the unfortunate beings who cannot work, or who are unable to procure work, or that food to the amount of two pence per day can keep soul and body together, or that paupers should not after death be buried in the same churchyard endeared to them as the repository of the bones of their fathers, or that families should be divided and the affections of kindred alienated by a line of demarcation in workhouses as broad and as impassable comparatively as the intervention of an ocean. A passage of the humane protest against the Workhouse law, recorded in the Peers' journals, by a right rev. Prelate, and several members of that House, in which it is denounced as " unjust and cruel to the poor," is well worthy of a place here, to the lasting honour of those who signed it. " We think that the system suggested in the bill, of consolidating immensely extensive unions of parishes, and establishing workhouses necessarily at great distances from many parishes, and thereby dividing families, and removing children from their parents merely because they are poor, will be found justly abhorrent to the best feelings of the general population of the country." This is language which affectingly contrasts with the doings of a right rev. Prelate who headed the first commission, and lost sight of Christianity in the delusions of utilitarianism, who himself subsequently, and in more reflecting moments, thus stigmatized the bill for workhouse imprisonment when advocating one benevolent clause. " It is about the only one in the bill that bears a kindly feeling towards the poor on the face of it." Better had he done to have deposed his mitre rather than have countenanced it.

The commissioners have declared that, for the due administration of this exterminatory enactment, stern, unflinching, and unfeeling executors (executioners, they should have said) are the best and the only qualified tools. There is a point at which resistance, we are told, becomes lawful, and Mr Fielden has intimated his opinion that the limit of endurance is reached. If the workhouse system be persevered in, a social revolution, in companionship with the one political, seems inevitable. The masses— the strong—who have foregone the privilege of strength to " take who can," on a condition and a right, not enacted only by Elizabeth, but coeval with Nature herself, will redress their own wrongs. The poor cannot, will not, ought not, to starve whilst any " visible property remains," as the great Pitt said. To this truism

and compact founded on it, the weak, the property classes, acceded. If the seal be " railed off the bond" wo to the rash innovators. If the law remain unchanged, unmodified, the Corn Laws cannot stand—to uphold them would be a paltering with principles which can meet no sympathy with us. If they are abolished, as abolished they must be, what becomes of the farmers? We shall be among the last to consent to their being victimized— we shall be among the first to insist upon an " equitable adjustment" of leases and rents. Prices will fall, and so must wages. We shall be found in the front of the battle for the operatives also, that wages may not be depressed beyond the fall point of corn values. But, great God! what a convulsion—what ruin—misery universal must be the consequence of heartless experiments for determining the extreme minimum of food upon which soul and body can be just kept from final separation! We have been told indeed—we are assured every day—that the abolition of the corn laws would raise wages. That frothy person Dr Bowring, in the debate on the factory bill, slashingly bids us " abrogate our corn laws —liberalize our commercial system ; thus shall we raise wages." And Colonel Thompson, a gentleman who should be much better informed, and who is infinitely superior in talent, has himself given and preached from the same text. But Prussia has no corn laws, and yet wages do not rise ; according to the evidence of Mr Grey before the committee on commerce and manufactures, a political economist of much higher repute than the touring Doctor, manufacturing wages at Bonn in Prussia were only two shillings and sixpence per week, and the operatives were condemned to live on black bread and sour wine. Neither are there any corn laws in Switzerland, where the workmen live on chickory for coffee three times a-day, with potatoes, although, as the Doctor acknowledges, " they naturally prefer better living when they can obtain it." Are the working classes of England to be brought to this—will they submit to it ? In passing, we may notice the opinion of a writer upon the Doctor's boasted morality of Switzerland manufacturing, whose literary reputation as far transcends his, as does the integrity and trustworthiness of his facts. M. Chevalier is quoting from the letter of a friend who was sojourning at Aran, in the canton of Argovia, which, as the Doctor prides himself on his French, we give in the original. " Je vois l'industrie qui envahit les montagnes, et arrache des bras aux terres les plus fertiles. Je puis voir aussi combien elle emancipe et combien elle démoralise. En passant à côté de l'étranger le paysan ou l'ouvrier ne le saluent plus ; la jeune fille ne murmure plus son *Dieu vous salue!* mais elle le regarde fixement et sourit." This is language the Doctor will fully comprehend, and we should not be astonished if his employer of the Trade Board were tempted by the picture to a tour in Switzerland himself.

Thus to the Government and to the Utilitarian Radicals the working classes are indebted for the Reform Bill, which deprives them of a share in the representation—for the proposition of the Ballot which would fleece them of the fraction of political influence in remainder—for the abuses of the Factory system—for the Workhouse system with all its horrors. In exchange they are amused with unmeaning balderdash about Church rates, which they do not pay—about an Irish Municipal Bill, of which Irish hodmen understand little, and for which they care less—about " despotism and Don Carlos," which they value as moonshine. The middle classes are, on the contrary, the special pets of Whig and Utilitarian solicitude. These they have made the depositaries of political and municipal powers—these they seek to conciliate with freedom from poors rates—these they would bribe with the surrender of church rates. The middle classes ought to know how to appreciate their selfishness and hypocrisy—the working classes their ingratitude, their tergiversations, the turpitude of their changeling policy. They court the middle classes now—when not in office, and before the Reform, they excited the lower classes against them. The lessons of experience should not be lost upon either. Mr Roebuck, on the Utilitarian side, has defended the Centralization system of the workhouse, because the poor are a national concern. If so, as this shallow legislator asserts, why is not poor law pro-

vision administered equably, rateably, uniformly in allowance throughout the kingdom ? Why is the administration split into parishes with the rates of some differing 50 per cent with those of others ? Paving, lighting, watching and warding, are to the same extent national concerns. Upon what principle are these left to the absolute direction of parish boards or town councils ? Why should they be better qualified to adjudge upon outlays of hundreds and thousands upon town halls and gas works, than upon the shillings and pence to helpless paupers? Why should the self-government about which he dilates, without grasping the principle, be more operose, or impracticable of application to the offices of local charity than to those of local police ? Why should those who are assessed to the rates be disqualified for dispensing and controlling their expenditure? No central board of despots sits enthroned, or would be tolerated at Washington, for coercing or disposing at its pleasure of the poor of the American Union ; not even a State Assembly interposes to limit or influence the action of legal and local authority. The select men apply the law, and superintend its execution in the township, against whose decisions appeal is allowed to the justices of the peace in session—as here under the old law. The system is found to work satisfactorily both to the poor and the rate payers ; for there are poor even in America ; a recent report states the existence of 2000 in the city of Boston alone. The local Board of Guardians, which by the workhouse system has been created, is the mere slave, and not the delegation of the central despotism. It is a body without vitality —a corporation without power—official without functions—having option or volition none, save to register the decrees which emanate from the triune tyranny of Somerset House. Men who servilely consent to accept the style and title of guardians, without one single right or privilege to the care and superintendence of the poor, must stand degraded in self-esteem, as they are in public opinion. The Government has invested them with no trust, the people repose in them no confidence. They are the ostensible agents of oppression, which they have not sanctioned, but are powerless to qualify—they are the helpless utensil

for the reception of that popular execration, which unshared, might suddenly overwhelm the Workhouse system with all its authors and abomina-
tions.

Let the middle classes take heed in
time ; for upon them, as the foundation of power, as the order, more tangible, more hated and envied, the reaction of popular vengeance, for the
ills of the Factory system, and the
atrocities of the Workhouse system,
will surely be discharged the first.
Savings in wages, by the slow immo-
lation of factory children, and of rates,
by the decimating consequences of
workhouse incarceration and workhouse starvation diet, will be found
cheerless and unfructifying economy,
when corn ricks are blazing, cotton
mills are fired, and the masses, manufacturing and agricultural, with their
Jack Cades and Wat Tylers at their
head, are in open insurrection. At
the best, and if successful in the struggle, the county rate of one year may
chance to absorb all the wretched and
recklessly purchased parsimonies of
the poor's rate outlay for twenty. The
sound and thinking portion have foreseen this, but in the presence of a factious majority in the Legislature, and
agitators in the Government, they remain inert and passive. The clergy
of the national church have distinguished themselves as becomes their
holy calling, by active endeavours to
mitigate the evil, and by remonstrance
against the barbarity of the system.
But not one of the dissenting ministry
has ventured forth to plead the cause
of the people, nor dare they. The
wealthy and well-doing, and such only
do they covet for their flocks, are there
with the Voluntary principle in hand,
and *in terrorem* over them. Their salaries, the supplies of the recusant
preacher would be stopped, who also
has a sordid interest in diminished
rates.

With these dangers impending on
the one hand over them, no inconsiderable portion of the middle classes,
of the sectarians chiefly, are rushing
blindly on towards—are infected with
insane longings for—the establishment
of a pure democracy on the ruins of
the mixed Constitution, under which
they, as all, have grown in wealth and
happiness. M. Chevalier notes it as
a distinctive characteristic of the English and Anglo-American race, that

whilst they trample on, or disdain all
below them in the social scale, they
are jealous, and would pull down to
their own level all above them. The
bourgeoisie, or middle orders of America, have already passed under the
absolute yoke of the masses. They
are shorn of all power, deprived of all
dignity, degraded and confounded
among the common herd of matter
without mind—robed in all the arbitrary absolutism of universal suffrage.
Not alone does the majority, in the
plenitude of its tyranny, exclude them
from political dominion or participation in it, but its scrutinizing jealousy penetrates and persecutes them
in the details of private life. Woe
to the citizen, rich though he be,
who indulges too ostentatiously in the
luxuries of private life. The sight of
a carriage would scarcely be tolerated
in Broadway — in Wall Street the
gaudy nuisance would breed a riot ;
the tenant would be hooted for lordly
affectation of superiority—the pride
of " equality" would be shocked, the
majesty of the workie insulted. " In
Europe," says M. Chevalier, " where
great cities abound, every bourgeoisie
which should fail in supporting the
throne or the aristocracy, would be
exposed to a worse fate than that of
the American bourgeoisie." Let it not
be imagined that the prosperity and
advancement of America is referable
in whole, or to any extent, to her republican institutions. De Tocqueville,
a writer equally favourable to the democratic principle, and calculating upon its inevitable triumph with the one
before quoted, acquaints us, that " the
population of America (in which is
included her progress economically
and socially), increased as rapidly
under the colonial system as it does
at the present day ; that is to say, it
doubled in about twenty-two years.
But this proportion, which is now applied to millions, was then applied to
thousands of inhabitants ; and the
same fact which was scarcely notice-
able a century ago, is now evident to
every observer." He continues to
show that the " British subjects in
Canada, who are dependent on a King,
augment and spread almost as rapidly
as the British settlers of the United
States, who live under a Republican
Government."

Here we must draw to a conclusion.
Interests well understood, should lead

the middle classes rather to strengthen their connexion with the aristocracy and monarchy, than jealously to weaken powers and forms essential to the preservation of their own supremacy, and which never can seriously endanger it. But the social and political superiorities of both bourgeoisie and aristocracy, will be jeopardised if the crusade of the first, and the acquiescent march of the last, against the rights of the poor be madly persisted in. The industrial world is every where in the throes of a convulsion—in the United States, in France, in Germany, as well as here. Overstrained production is succeeded by a violent reaction of falling values. Widely spread ruin and bankruptcy are inevitable results of a decline in prices, of 30, 40, or 50 per cent. Consumption is arrested without a medium of barter or exchange, and can only be re-established when the par is re-adjusted, and the downward race between nations decided at the common goal of diminished rates, as well as diminished production. Long before that period, nay, before the expiration of another year perchance, thousands, and tens of thousands, in the manufacturing districts, may be cast out of work. They will cry out for bread, and a stone, a workhouse will be offered. The next encampment of one hundred thousand raging spirits, will not be in Warwickshire, but in Lancashire. No Olivers, or Parkeses, backed with Treasury franks, will be wanting to excite them—for betrayed they will be powerless. A populace incomparably more intelligent, and leaders infinitely more desperate than those of Birmingham, may be banded in mortal strife against the " monarchy" of the middle classes," whilst these are rashly as besottedly occupied in sapping the foundations of the monarchy aristocratical. Where, in so solemn a conjuncture, is the empire to look for safety and protection? In presence of the coming tempest there is a Government only less imbecile than unprincipled—a majority in the Commons' House compounded of traitors more than suspected, of Radicals utilitarian and destructive, of Whigs venal and time-serving—the authors, abettors, and supporters of the workhouse system—the implacable foes of the poor. Come the crash will, meet it who may. A rural police will be nerveless to prop up workhouses tumbling to their ruin. The firmament of Whiggery is, however, calm and unclouded as on a summer's day. The cries of the poor or the oppressed cloud not the atmosphere respired in Downing-street—yet rebellion is silently and sombrely hatching in Ireland—Lower Canada is in open revolt—even the little rock of Malta is in quasi insurrection. Russia captures our ships, and wars against our commerce—Portugal bars us out with prohibitory tariffs—General Evans, the hero of Lord Palmerston, with his legion and an army half as strong as that which, at Vittoria, under Wellington, triumphed over, and chased before it, 50,000 of the *élite* of the troops of Napoleon, is so disgracefully defeated at Hernani by a band of raw mountaineers, that the wreck owed its safety and escape, though within the walls of St Sebastian, only to the cool intrepidity of the Royal Marines, who protected the flight. Brookes's is all agog with peerages expectant, and commoners coronetted but not ennobled. Nay, four hundred baronets have formed an union to enforce their rights to—the Ulster badge!!! Such was the feasting, such the idle revelries in Belshazzar's palace at the ominous moment of the " handwriting on the wall." So Nero sang, danced, and fiddled, whilst Rome was blazing!

THE MINISTRY AND THE PEOPLE, THE WORKHOUSE SYSTEM, THE FACTORY
SYSTEM, AND THE TEN HOURS' BILL.

So far back as January, 1836, in an article on the *Zoll Verein*, or Prusso-Germanic customs league,* we took occasion to call the serious attention of the Ministry, the legislature, and the country, to the commercial storm which, amidst the lurid glare of a deceitful sunshine, was darkly gathering on the horizon. On six several occasions, subsequently, our warnings were repeated, and the signs and tokens abroad pointed out. The second-sighted seer of the north stood alone in his denunciations of the wrath to come; the false prophets, daily, monthly, and quarterly, were paid and arrayed against him. Their salaams were still as ever to their patrons—oh! Whigs and Radicals Utilitarian live for ever; the sun of your glory is but in its earliest dawn—the land fructifies a hundredfold, under its cheering beams—the nations of the earth are bewildered with the effulgence of its splendour. In the Commons' House, and out of the Peers' House ministerial minstrels tuned their harps to the same grateful theme. Parker touched the chord of Whig-Radical prosperity in strains so glowing, from notes furnished by Treasury and Trade-board

repositories, and withal so gratefully laudatory of his Whig-inspirers as the givers of all good things to the nation, as to be recompensed instanter for the magnificent apotheosis of Whiggery with a seat at the Admiralty Board, and the profits and appurtenances thereunto appertaining. There sits the briefless barrister, who has brought Sheffield to market, blundering between Admiral Blackwood and Judge Blackstone, and in his dealings with the gallant sailor tribe, confounding cannon with the canon law. The pious Lord Glenelg, too, on occasion of the dinner at Inverness, previous to the opening of the Session, claimed, with due and solemn deference to an Almighty power as the first great cause, the secondary agency in boundless national prosperity for the Whigs, senile and juvenile. "It is proved (said he) that the resources of this country have been developed; that commercial enterprise has been called forth to new enterprise and exertions; that science, and intelligence, and reason, and all the efforts of the mind have been called forth to their utmost expansion, in order to meet the growing demands of a mighty people call-

---

* The iniquity of the principles, the malignity of purpose, and the falsehood of pretext on which this league was founded, had been ably exposed before, more especially by our respected contemporaries of the *Foreign Quarterly* and the *Times*; but the facts, figures, and comparisons were wanting by which the subject could be simplified and rendered intelligible; for the logic of words alone must ever be unsatisfactory when not illusive in the absence of practical data, where such are attainable and ought to be applied. We furnished those facts and figures, to this hour uncontradicted; translated as they have been in France and Germany, and largely circulated. The Prussian Government can deal with works astutely enough, and against them can be free of its arithmetic; it *would have replied* to our *exposure* of pretence and practice had the task been possible, but on reference to *commercial authorities* the undertaking was abandoned. It has lately attempted to do it by a side wind through Dr M'Culloch, whose utter ignorance and unfairness, not deliberate we hope, we shall perhaps have occasion to expose. It may be well to notice, that the Right Hon. Mr Herries, formerly Chancellor of the Exchequer,,,was, it is reported, so impressed with the force of the practical evidence adduced, that he intended to have moved for a Committee of Enquiry on the subject, but on announcing his views with the courtesy usual in other times to Mr P. Thompson, that gentleman, we have heard, begged his forbearance, on the ground that negotiations were then on foot with the Cabinet of Berlin, the successful issue of which might by such a motion be prejudiced. With a patriotic statesman such an appeal was of course irresistible—the motion was not made. Eighteen months have since elapsed, but of the negotiations, if any there really were, which may be doubted, not one word has transpired or one effect been visible. As a man of business statesman, there is not a more able and far-seeing man than Mr Herries, and it may be hoped that he will not lose sight of the subject during the present Session.

ing forth every vigorous energy of the mind in the career of power and substantial greatness.—(Immense cheering of his auditors). This cannot be denied * * * *. But is it true that human agency has had no part in these transactions and in these blessings, and which, eminent as they are, we no doubt must ascribe to that great Providence which dictates the fate of nations? But then we know that there are *secondary agents*, and instruments to carry into effect those designs, and to *these is to be ascribed the existing state of things.*" This was the language of that saintly and softly reposing personage, upon which in our February number the challenge so openly given was fairly accepted. Our words were, " the *secondary agents* then have inflated the great balloon of national prosperity—be it so. * * * The *secondary agents* who boast of national prosperity as their exclusive creation— —false and hollow as that prosperity appears—are bound, now and hereafter, to accept all the responsibility of national reverses and national degradation." To the same purport, but in commonplace not worth the repetition, were previous preachings of Lord John Russell at Stroud and Bristol; of that same Lord John who, in the very last month of May, when questioned about the disastrous aspect of public *prosperity*, pertly rejoined, that "the Government had nothing to do with it"—or words to that effect, for we quote from memory, as the precise sayings or doings of such a person are scarcely worth the trouble of more special reference.

The Whigs and Radicals Utilitarian are fixed therefore out of their own mouths with the balance of the prosperity and adversity accounts, whatever that may be, which we shall perhaps have occasion to advert to. In Maga of April we opened to their astonished eyes, for the first time, for the only time the revolting truth has been exhibited, the full measure of their unpopularity then, and since on the increase to almost universal execration. The triumphant re-election of Sir Francis Burdett since and so lately by the most popularly constituted electoral body of the empire is even but a faint glossary of the text—is but a shadowy illustration of more signal disgraces to come. We warned them that the next great meeting of 100,000

men would not be the gathering of a political union in Warwickshire, but a more northern and fearful muster to anathemize the horrors of the anti-Poor Law bill. Twice 100,000 have already on Harthead Moor verified our prediction. We opened to their gaze the abyss threatening to engulf them from the abuses of the factory system, the exterminatory operations of the workhouse system, and from the ballot proposed, by which the people were to be cheated of the only privilege left them by the Reform bill. To judge of the consternation of their patrons by the outcries and recriminations of the Ministerial press, of the *Morning Chronicle*, more especially, their leading champion, the discovery must have been equally surprising, although not quite so grateful as that of *terra firma* to the rebellious crew of Columbus. Conservative testimonies in behalf of the workhouse system were ostentatiously invoked; the authority of the great Duke, and the more guarded acquiescence of Sir Robert Peel, were triumphantly appealed to against us, though on all other subjects vociferously repudiated by the same appellants. We knew it all, and with the reverence due to such names we had duly weighed all in the balance and found it wanting. The Lords and the Commons were led by their natural leaders, and to them surrendered their judgment. But we were without the pale of that influence; of the people ourselves, we judged for the people, as we have ever done, with independence, perfect, unshackled, and disinterested. However our affections may incline, no man who has read us aright can accuse us of fawning with our ready homage upon the Conservative body in the legislature; few will deny how little tender we have been of the errors or wanderings of those to whom with fidelity unshaken we have adhered in times of evil and ill-merited report, and around whom we have rallied and concentrated the elements of public opinion, which had been led astray and chained to the car of mercenary ministers and unscrupulous factions. But we have and can have no community of feeling with the " red herring" philosophy of the workhouse system. Sir Robert, whose assent to the new Poor Law bill was in the first instance qualified, has already seen cause to think that it has been executed " too harshly," and that some of its enactments want revision and " amendment." The only wholesome " amendment that we know of would be to repeal it altogether, to send the trio of Commissioners adrift to seek a more honest means of livelihood, and despatch the secretary penny-a-liner to superintend the felonry of New South Wales, where, among faces familiar to him of old in Bow Street or the Old Bailey, he may more worthily apply the Bastile system, to which, through a confusion of ideas and associations incident perhaps to habits and practice, he has subjected guiltless paupers at home. Of the atrocious spirit which presides in the administration of the new law, volumes of evidence have already been published, whilst, as if evidence were wanting, a Committee of the House of Commons is still sitting day by day accumulating more, and piling Pelion upon Ossa. Sickening as is that evidence, and irrefragably conclusive upon all matters of detail, we will not stake, we have never staked the merits of the case even on that issue. We have protested *in limine* against that abominable provision of the workhouse system, by which a bargain is driven with destitution, and a jail made the inexorable alternative for scanty rations of gruel pottage. And we protest against it with greater solemnity and more entire conviction, as being the inevitable precursor, the stepping-stone, to the fell and final abolition of all poor relief laws whatever—to a formal declaration by legislative enactment against the right, whether in or outside a prison—to the abrogation, by Act of Parliament, of the first clause in the great bond of social union, of the most sacred obligation of nature, consecrated from the beginning by the word of God, and centuries ago inaugurated as the law of the land. That such is the ulterior object, the *arrière pensée*, will not be questioned by those who have been in the habit of perusing the writings of the economists, the one-sided reports of the Commissioners, or the insidious anti-poor law sophisms of Senior. But in truth the trouble of reference to them has been spared us, as their organ, as the mouthpiece of the Whig Ministry and the Poor Law Commission, Lord Brougham, then Lord High Chancellor of England, and the fountain-head of law if not of justice, did,

with all the imposing gravity of the highest office, and from the highest judgment-seat in the realm, pronounce first the non expediency of poor laws and the advantages to be derived by sweeping away every vestige of them hereafter from the statute-book ; and next the keeper of his Majesty's conscience, did not only doubt, but resolutely deny the existence of any rights of the able-bodied poor to relief. Whatever may be thought of the discretion of those judicial decisions, their honesty and boldness unhesitating leave nothing to be desired.

The mischievous errors and the ill-considered declarations into which Conservative Lords and Commoners have been betrayed, are deeply to be deplored, for they forcibly tend to the severance of social relations, and of the kindly dependences which bind man to man. Moreover, they widen the already invidious line of demarcation between classes, and lay the foundation of a storm of odium against castes. Lord Ellenborough vindicates the workhouse system, upon the plea that private benevolence is stimulated in the inverse ratio that poor law charity becomes less compulsory, and decreases in amount. This is the O'Connell doctrine imported into the House of Lords ; it is some consolation to find it patronised by no more weighty authority. In the individual case of his lordship, it is pleasing to believe that such an effect can have flowed from a cause so contradictory. The reverse, it is notorious, occurs in Ireland, and it will require something more substantial than his eloquence and example to inoculate Irish paupers with his own convictions. In Lyons and its suburbs 50,000 operatives out of work are now encumbering the streets by day, or perishing of cold and hunger on the *pavés* by night. There is no compulsory provision for the poor, and therefore " ample scope and verge enough" for the display of private charity the most unbounded. It is not the less true, however, that they die like dogs for want of food and shelter—by scores daily—surrounded with 20,000 bayonets, and all the " pride and pomp" of military array, to repress the sudden mutiny, and drown the groans of the dying. If, indeed, the voluntary principle through private charity is likely to work such wonders, in the relaxation or the ab-

sence of poor laws, the sooner they
are nullified at once and for ever, the
better for the poor.    There must be
more philosophy, after all, in Joe Miller than we dreamt of, who thus im-
mortalizes a paradoxical extravaganza
of two wags, one of whom gave commencing vent to his amorous furor in
the following line :—

My wound is great because it is so small,

which the other appropriately concluded thus :—

Then 'twould be greater were it none at
all !

Just so would private benevolence,
doubtless, expand as compulsory des-
cended to zero.

The Conservative press, for the
most part, has, with zeal and talent
unrivalled, taken more large, and liberal, and philanthropic views of the
Poor Law Question.    Let them not
be discouraged by discrepancies of
opinion between themselves and those
to whom they have been accustomed,
perhaps sometimes too implicitly, to
defer.    Theirs is the noble mission of
upholding the good old principles of
law, order, and the Constitution.    The
rights of the poor constitute the very
outpost and rampart of all property ;
when the one is forced the other will
quickly be undermined.    The ability
consummate with which that press is
now conducted,* and the commanding
influence in public opinion to which it
has attained over contemporary representatives of opposing factions, fully
entitle it to take the lead, and must
ultimately compel those to follow who
now do not disdain to owe to it, although not to own, their happiest inspirations.    The pauper *mittimus* act
of general incarceration is even now
almost a dead letter.    Lord Brougham
warned the Lords, when moving it,
that if not passed, their estates, in the
course of years, would be swallowed
up in poors' rates.    As a rider to his
lordship's startling discovery, we will
add a forewarning more startling still.
Let the workhouse system be attempted
now in the manufacturing districts,
and then neither their lordships' estates
nor Lord Brougham's pension will
be found bargains too marketable at

twelve months' purchase.    We need
say nothing upon the other false assurances of the same learned person
upon matters of fact, under the impression of which the Bastile bill was
passed ; assurances as false as those of
Lord John Russell about the number
of assistant commissioners, and the extent of trial operation to which the new
bill was to be limited—as false as his
pledge that all Irish police appointments
should be at the disposal of Col. Shaw
Kennedy, as absolutely as in reality
they are at that of Mr Dan. O'Connell.    Although tolerant of Lord
Brougham's senseless exaggerations,
for they were chastised by no rebuke,
let us not be unmindful that every essential mitigation in the interest of humanity in the original of the new poor
law bill, and several such there were,
was effected by the Peers.    They
might, and they would have done more
assuredly, but there was the people's
house robed in all the despotism of
popularity, and the people out of doors,
reform drunk, to whom change of
any sort, even for the worse, was
alone welcome, and they willed it
otherwise.

Against the workhouse system our
stand is determined, and not the less
so against the abuses of the factory
system, and in behalf of the infant labourers.    Our zealous, however humble exertions in that sacred cause, will
testify for us how sincere our convictions, how entirely enlisted our feelings.
But upon the proposed " ten hours'
bill" we are compelled to pause.    Deep
and painful reflection has led us to
doubt its practicability, and to question
its expediency.    For it is not sufficient
to enact a law in order to its execution, if that law, as in the case of the
pauper prison discipline, alias the jail
and gruel system, be opposed to the
moral fitness of things on the material
concerns of the common weal.    Whether considered in the sense of the interests of the operative exclusively
(if such a thing were possible as the
losing sight of mutual dependencies),
or in the more rational light of the
combined and inseparable interests of
employers and men ; whether, in fine,
viewed nationally, or sectionally with
reference to a class, we must regard

---

* The provincial press, perhaps, more especially, in which, during the last few years,
a developement of talent is apparent truly extraordinary.

it as an experiment which ought not to be hazarded, because failing, as fail it must, it will have jeopardized without remedy or recal, every substantial element of the industry and prosperity of the land. We who have been the unflinching friends of the working orders, in all times and circumstances, in many an uphill fight, as still we truly are, and whether politically they were favourable or hostile to our opinions—we tell them this in most sober and anxious earnestness—let them weigh well the gravity of the reasons we shall adduce in the course of that general review of the question we propose to undertake. First, however, we have to deal with certain calumnious imputations against the friends of infant factory children, and the supporters of the Ten Hours' Bill, widely circulated in Whig and Utilitarian publications, but for our purpose more conveniently condensed, although with more commendable moderation stated, in a bulky pamphlet, recently from the pen of Mr Robert Hyde Greg, a wealthy, and no less intelligent, manufacturer, of Bury (we believe), near Manchester, and purporting to be a reply to an article on the " Factory Question," in the *Quarterly Review* of last December. We have not seen the article alluded to, nor if we had, should we have volunteered a defence which, if needed, cannot be in more able hands. It is not unlikely, however, that we may be found to differ in opinion with the writer, as from the tenor of Mr Greg's remarks we are induced to suspect ; our strictures, however, will be construed as bearing upon the general case and the general accusations of Mr Greg alone.

This gentleman commences by attempting to fasten a charge upon those whom he calls Tories, of having taken up the factory question and the Ten Hours' Bill as a " party" and " political " question, in order to " strengthen themselves and weaken Ministers, by adopting what they consider the popular side." No more irrefragable testimony need be adduced to show the groundlessness of the charge than what may be found in his own subsequent statements. The first man who, in 1802, brought forward and carried through a measure for the protection of cotton factory children was the late Sir Robert Peel. Did he, a Tory, propose it " from party " motives,

and with a view to " weaken " the Tory administration of that day ? In 1816 another bill was passed, extending the shield of law to the protection of *all* children, factory workers in cotton mills, which, by the former bill, was confined to children apprentices only. The most indefatigable agent in this transaction, no less wise than humane, was the late Mr Nathaniel Gould of Manchester, also a Tory, a name honourably renowned in the annals of benevolence ; he was ably assisted by several conscientious individuals, as well as by the late Sir Robert Peel. Did Mr Gould make the question a stalking horse of factious opposition against the Tory Ministers of that day ? We well remember, as Mr Greg may also, the bitter revilings, the insolent reproaches, the storm of slander with which that good man and his supporters were assailed by the merciless and intolerant among the mill-owners, more notably those of the Unitarian clique, of which Mr George Phillips (now Sir George) was then the worthy representative in the Commons House. And lastly, was Sir John Hobhouse animated by the spirit of " party " and factious dislike against his Whig-Radical friends, the then, as now, Ministers, when, in 1831, he brought forward and got passed another bill, by which the principle of infant protection was still further carried out, and which placed under the same legal safeguard as in cotton mills all children, workers in woollen, worsted, flax, and silk mills ? The Tories of that day were not so intolerant as to brand the praiseworthy exertions of Sir John with the stigma of partisanship or an undue craving after popularity. Why, with less provocation, should Mr Greg hazard accusations so utterly falsified by antecedent as well as contemporary evidence? None better than he himself knows, or should know, or not knowing be more chary of abuse, that the Conservatives as a party were divided in sentiment upon the infant factory question, not certainly as to the principle, but the measure of its application. Upon the Ten Hours' Bill he must be aware they are still more divided, and that individuals among them of unquestionable philanthropy, whose character and station would lend authority to any cause, entertain opinions the most opposite respecting it.

In the same tone of misrepresentation Mr Greg asserts that the mill-owners were denied a Parliamentary Committee for the reception of testimony on their side, replicatory to that given before Mr Sadler's Committee. The fact is, however, that had the mill-owners pressed the claim in earnest, the Ministry, which had early declared for them, would not have refused ; but a *modus operandi* was proposed, much more to their satisfaction. The " Parliamentary Commission," as he fancifully styles it, being in truth no other than a Whig commission under the Great Seal, was so far from being " with difficulty obtained," as he asserts, that it is sufficiently well known the expedient was joyfully hailed by the mill-owners as a desirable means of avoiding the Parliamentary inquisition, by the Government as a plausible source of jobbery and patronage. After, however, stating that the Commission was conceded on the *demand* of the masters, our consistent author, with a querulousness amusing enough, complains that by the " advocates " of the Ten Hours' Bill, it was pretended the Commission was the *master's commission*. Whose then was it ? Not that of the Ten Hours' Bill people, for they protested against it *ab origine* as an ex parte tribunal, constituted not to enquire into the merits of the case impartially, but to get rid by a side wind of a case established in open court. To the report of the Commission thus suspiciously inaugurated, Mr Greg appeals as to the court of *dernier resort,* and insists that the " facts collected by it * * * *form an official and authenticated mass of evidence to which all must bow;*" and this *dictum*, to render it more absolute, is posted in italics. In this self-satisfied conclusion he fortifies himself by calling in aid certain extracts from an article on the factory question, in the *London and Westminster Review !* Of course the Bury manufacturer is innocently unconscious of the current rumour that the article in question, so laudably encomiastic of the Report and the Commission, was the fruit of the learned leisure of one of the members of the identical commission ! ! We doubt whether advocacy from such a quarter, and in such taste, will pass for authority any where out of the narrow circle in which the work is ever heard of; we more than doubt whe-

ther nine-tenths of the masters themselves may not be visited with conscientious qualms about the righteousness of their cause, when they shall learn that its leading champions are to be sought in the clique of Unitarians, Infidels, and Destructives, who are understood to be the presiding genii over the publication, cited as Sir Oracle. We entirely demur to the competency of the tribunal—we repudiate the summary jurisdiction of Mr Greg and the golden calf he has set up for worship. We assert, and could fill this whole number with damning proof of the fact, that the report of the Commission is not an " authenticated mass of evidence to which all must bow," but that, on the reverse, it too often betrays the latent leaning in favour of one of the parties to a suit, not unaccountable in fee'd agents. Some of the fee'd agents, the Commissioners, as at Leeds, refused binding themselves to record all the evidence tendered or given in favour of the factory children, thus reserving to themselves a discretion to omit and to garble it at pleasure. These " petty tyrants," moreover, decided to sit with closed doors, and that publicity and daylight might not, by any possibility, dawn upon their acts, no party was permitted to attend for the purpose of taking notes of the proceedings. As if this exposure of the real purport of their errand was not patent enough, these disinterested officials are next heard of feasting at the sumptuous board of the richest mill-owner of the district, having at the very moment depositions on oath in their pockets undenied, undeniable, of the common practice in the mill of which he was the proprietor of the most flagrant barbarities upon the helpless children in his employ—we feel bound, however, to express our conviction without his cognizance. And yet the report of these persons is to pass for an *authenticated mass of evidence!* When we are told that the " names and characters of the Commissioners place them beyond suspicion," we are justified in pleading " non-content," and in appealing from the sack to the sample. But did Mr Greg, or any body else, ever hear, or read, before the Gazette told the tale, aught of the " names and characters " of the majority of the tribe, migratory or stationary ? They were notoriously selected, as nearly as possible of one political complexion, and as saturated with the dye of the same anti-social tendencies. The milk of human nature was fortunately not dried up or soured in all of them; several honourable exceptions there were to whom thrilling contact with infant woes and human suffering left no longing for the gastronomic dainties of the rich master's table. In them the generous sympathies of kind were aroused, and they did the duty least expected and most unwelcome—they boldly bore testimony to the truth. It may be as well to enlighten Mr Greg, however, as to some of the "names and characters" he refers to so confidently as the *del credere* of the report. We can spare little room, and will therefore take in the order in which they stand the Central or Stationary Board, consisting of three members. The first is Mr Thomas Tooke, a gentleman deeply imbued with the economical heresies of the day, well-read in the doctrine of redundant population, but, withal, a man of some science and ability. We next arrive at Mr Edwin Chadwick, *Barrister*, late penny-a-liner! The life of this gentleman, a brief space excepted, was passed, and his education accomplished, in the London police courts—in the Old Bailey, and other places of trial for criminals, and occasionally in assisting at hanging exhibitions, or the gallows, in the humble but useful capacity of a police reporter for the daily press of the metropolis. Paid for his services by the line, his utmost ingenuity was laudably taxed to the extent of his powers in spinning out a story, accumulating expletives, and amassing verbiage. The organ of destructiveness, in such a vocation, became somewhat largely distended, and naturally inclined him, so far as he could understand it, to the Benthamite philosophy, which teaches, that as for the reduction of surplus population, hanging and burking upon a large scale is impracticable, and therefore a means inadequate to the end, so the object can only be safely, silently, and more *mercifully* attained by the more slow but wholesale process of workhouse incarceration, and starvation diet for adults; for those of tender years the strap, the billy-roller, and factory labour—for mercy, as the play-actors say, is a point to be made. Our Factory Commissioner

was thus seasoned with a spice of the "killing no murder" philosophy, and enriched his vocabulary with a few of its slang phrases, such as " fund for subsistence to be reproduced "—that is, masses must die before their time to fatten the soil and " reproduce " for the survivors; " moral effects which *I am deploring*," which is greatly like Jack Ketch " deploring " the exit of a wretch by whose dying he is living; " increased fund for the payment of wages by the diminution of rates;" that is, surplus labour pressing upon the market and upon the parish, wages can only be enhanced and rates diminished by putting to rest with the spade the superabundant mouths; " the combination of workhouses, and substituting a rigid administration," signifies merely a Central Board and well paid secretaryship. Thus finished, he started as an economist, and became qualified for a Factory and Poor Law Commissioner. With submission to Mr Greg, we must doubt whether the school in which this man was bred was favourable to the developement of sound moral feeling and humanity. Of human nature, he had been conversant only with the blackest and most disgusting side. His calling had placed him in contact only, as it were, with murderers, felons, prostitutes, pickpockets, and pauper impostors—with executioners, turnkeys, thief-catchers, and police-officers —with crime, vice, depravity, misery, in their most hideous and demoralizing phases. He who touches pitch, we are told, shall not escape defilement. Can such pursuits fit best for the office of humanity, of charity, of equity? Must they not inevitably tend to encourage and produce callosity of heart, and deaden the nobler impulses of nature? Do they not lead to a base and degrading estimate of the human species—to confound virtue with vice—innocence with guilt— to range all mankind under one category of condemnation—to place them under one ban of social excommunication? Such would be inferences, not overstrained or too far-fetched, from the premises specified. The central Commissioner may, we will not deny, have escaped intact from contagion; he may be, and doubtless is, an exception from the rule; but, we ask Mr Greg, is he of the class, or of the antecedents, or of the repute from which a paternal government would have chosen a guardian for helpless infancy, or for poverty, honest and not less helpless ? Of Dr Southwood Smith, the last of the trio of the Central Board, little is known, beyond the fact, that he also is a thorough-going Benthamite, ready and reckless in carrying out theories whose substratum is pure and naked destructiveness. Such were the trio who mixed up the ingredients of the Factory Report, and seasoned the contents of the cauldron to Whig palates. In the description of the central worthy of the three we have been the more special, in order to display those peculiar qualifications for the performance of all sorts of work, which, in the Poor-Law Commission, so fitly earned for him all the eulogistic notoriety which the flash and froth of Lord Brougham's eloquence could bestow, and because also Mr Greg has challenged to the invidious task, and left no option, by his ostentatious parade of the "names and characters" constituting the unimpeachable "guarrantee" of his great authority. We shall here quit the subject, and throw the Report on which the last factory law was founded overboard for ever, as no better than an imposture, disgraceful to the parties by whom it was perpetrated ; and this on their own showing. " The Report of the Factory (Central) Commissioners" (writes Mr Stuart to them, one of the district Commissioners himself, whose report was entirely suppressed), " is no more the Report of the twelve persons appointed to see things with their own eyes, and to report their observations on them, than of any twelve gentlemen whom one may by chance meet in St Paul's Churchyard. It is the Report of three gentlemen residing in London, who, for aught that appears in the Report, never visited a cotton factory nor a flax factory in their lives." With the value of that body of evidence collected by the district Commissioners, and quoted by Mr Greg as " *unimpeachable,* and, we believe, *unimpeached,*" the three judges were so awfully impressed, that they cast it to the winds, or, to use their own more emphatic language, they state, that our " opinions and recommendations are *not* founded on that evidence ;" having, as a climax of shuffling chicanery, previously published in the *Spectator* newspaper, which, with other journals, they were in the habit of priming, *anonymously,* but not unavowedly, that their " Report contained a clear and faithful analysis of the evidence, and a perfectly intelligible statement of the opinions and recommendations of the Central Board, *founded on that evidence.*" The central penny-a-liner has not rubbed against and among thieves and thieves' attorneys at the Old Bailey for nothing ; but surely a respectable man like Mr Greg should be sure of his man before he volunteers a certificate of " character." *

We need offer no excuse for declining to rip up the question of the comparative health and mortality of the factory and non-factory population. The common sense of the public has long passed sentence, and it is equally bad taste and wrong judgment in Mr Greg to disturb the verdict, in which, after all, the utmost industry can only encounter failure. Statistical tables, constructed upon partial or limited data, collected and applied to confined districts, influenced by local and other circumstances, such as the greater or less influx or change of adults, can be no safe criterion for decision. According to the animus of the calculator, they may almost be made to assume any shape by agents appointed and paid for the object. The late good and highly-gifted Sadler blew the bubble creations of the paid commissioners into airy nothing, and overwhelmed the puny whipsters of arithmeticians with well-merited ridicule, as Messrs Drinkwater, Baker, and Baines can testify. Mr Greg, like all one-sided observers, omits any reference to antagonist authorities, such as the tabular demonstrations of Mr Sadler, indisputably the most profound political economist, as well as the most ready and practically scientific mathematician of his day, nor does he once allude to the late most able and complete pub-

---

* The same petty larceny spirit of falsification, as if indeed in the same handwriting, is seen in the Reports of the Poor-Law Commissioners ; witness the Petworth and the Cholesbury cases.

lication and researches upon the question which has yet appeared, of Mr Charles Wing, surgeon to the Royal Metropolitan Hospital for Children, &c. a gentleman certainly of higher public repute than one-half of the Factory Commissioners, and as deservedly esteemed as the first in standing amongst them. The balance of credit, conceding the quality of evidence to be equal, would doubtless incline with all unbiassed people in favour of the unpaid, *unbought* advocates of the factory children and the factory operatives, over the paid, and with respect to certain of them, *suborned* opponents. We cheerfully admit, however, to their honour, that several of the Factory Commissioners rose superior to the odious nature of the service upon which they were sent, and arbitrated well and wisely between the Ministry and the poor.

The proofs most incontestible of the effects of the factory system upon health and longevity must be sought in the population tables of Mr Rickman, whose results present the comparison of totals instead of fractional parts, of counties instead of towns and sections of districts. It is not denied, however the question of comparative healthiness be disputed, that the term of life is shortened by it, and that the spinner dies of premature decay. Nor is this unhappy consequence peculiar to the factory system of this country alone. Mulhausen reciprocates the fatality of Manchester. The researches of M. A. Penot, in 1828, establish the fact that the mean duration of life at Mulhausen was one-fourth less than in the rest of France. Nor can this enormous difference be attributed to the unhealthiness of the climate, for the air of that town, as that of Alsace in general, is represented as clear, bracing, and generous, and it contains little more than 20,000 inhabitants. The mean term of life notwithstanding is stated at twenty-five years only, whilst for the rest of France it is about thirty-three. Mulhausen, like Manchester, is a city of cotton factories and power-looms. This precocious mortality is more particularly observable in children below ten years of age. M. L. Levrault ascribes it to the Factory System still. He says, " *C'est encore au regime des fabriques qu'il faut l'attribuer. Les femmes enceintes continuent*

*à se rendre aux ateliers jusqu'au dernier ou à l'avant-dernier jour des couches ; elles y retournent le plutôt possible, car ce n'est pas tout de donner la vie à l'enfant, il faut vivre, et à Mulhouse l'on ne peut vivre un jour qu'en travaillant tout le jour. Les malades ont tort aux yeux de l'industrie, elle ne donne ou plutôt ne vend à vivre qu'aux bienportans. . . . Puis, à peine dressés sur leurs débiles jambes, ces malheureux enfans ne sont que trop souvent entraînés par leurs parens à respirer près d'eux l'air malsain des ateliers.*" The same writer observes, that one " need not be astonished at the great number of *ghastly* faces, pitiful, stunted, deformed beings (*êtres chétifs, rabougris, défaits*), which are met wandering like spectres," &c. in the town. How strikingly does the picture correspond with that drawn by Dr Hawkins, one of the Factory Commissioners ! " I believe that most travellers are struck by the lowness of stature, the leanness, and the paleness, which present themselves so commonly to the eye at Manchester, and, above all, among the factory classes. I have never been in any town in Great Britain, nor in Europe, in which degeneracy of form and colour from the national standard has been so obvious." The morality of manufactures is not worth the pains of discussion. We could easily show Mr Greg that it is pretty nearly on a par in most countries, in France, Switzerland, Germany, and Belgium, as in England. The case of the rising manufacturing town of Lowell, in Massachusetts, United States, is one apart. It is an exception arising out of a state of things of transitory duration not difficult to account for, which serves only to confirm the rule. Comparative returns of illegitimacy is the mode least conclusive of the superiority of manufacturing over agricultural habits, for physical causes may be adduced to reconcile the smallest proportion of births with the greatest possible existence of female depravity. The population (say 25,000) of Merthyr Tidvil, the capital of the great mining districts of South Wales, is equal to about one-eighth that of Manchester and Salford. It is probable (we have not the data at hand) that the bastardy ratio may be higher in the former than the latter place ; but, from information and observation in both towns, we are satisfied that the *pro rata* of prostitution, almost indiscriminate in Manchester, is perhaps not less than fifty to one over Merthyr. On such points statistics, even if vice were officially recognised and registered, as in Paris, can teach us little, compared with the every-day exercise of the organs of sight and hearing. Nor ought much stress to be laid on the less weighty pressure upon poor's rates and the workhouse. In concentrated communities, such as the manufacturing, benefit societies can be arranged, and do exist upon a large scale ; add the allowances and expenditure of these to the poors' tax of Manchester, or any other considerable town, and the balance of saving and pauperism will diminish, or nearly disappear. Such mutual guarantee societies can rarely be established in thinly peopled agricultural districts, where therefore every man must stand by his own resources, or appeal to the common stock of the parish. With every advantage of concentration, even nothing but the higher rate of manufacturing wages could support benefit clubs ; the hand-loom weavers have long been struck with the same paralysis of incapacity to that end as their rustic brethren.

We have, however, been led astray from our main intent much farther than, it will have been seen, was contemplated, by the unjust aspersions and unfounded assumptions of Mr Greg, the champion of his order, and of the mill-owners ; aspersions upon the supporters of the Ten Hours' bill, and of the factory children, unjust because undeserved, and betraying a lamentable lack of good feeling and forbearance ; assumptions unfounded, because reposing on no more solid

substratum than culled portions from so much of the reports of the *Master's* Factory Commission, as would suffice to eke out a case. We are willing to admit, as on former occasions we have admitted, that although cotton factory labour is, from the nature of the raw material, somewhat more injurious to health than woollen or flax spinning, yet there is no question that the infant cotton operatives have been subjected to no such appaling barbarities as were proved before the committee of Mr Sadler, and not less irrefutably before the master's commission afterwards, to be of very common occurrence in the woollen and flax mills. These, in justice be it said, were not chargeable upon the masters, but the overlookers or adult operatives. The superiority of cotton factory regulations, however, in every respect was solely attributable to acts of Parliament, humanely, not less than judiciously framed for their government, in the benefits of which, until the act of 1831, the infant operatives in wool and flax were not admitted to participate. Having thus discharged our conscience, let us proceed to a brief review of the state and prospects of trade, with reference to the practicability of a Ten Hours' bill for labour ; we shall take the cotton trade only as being by far the most extensive of our manufactures, as well as the most sensitive, because most dependent upon the accidents of foreign demand and foreign competition, and also because we have no more than a fragment of space to dispose of.

The importance of the subject with which we have to deal, in a national point of view, will be duly estimated by the following returns :—

Total Exports of the Produce and Manufactures of the United Kingdom.

|  |  |  |  |  |  |  |
|---|---|---|---|---|---|---|
| 1835, | Declared value, | . | . | . | . | £47,372,270 |
| 1836, | Do. | . | . | . | . | 46,796,937 |

Of which the export in cotton manufacture was

|  |  |  |  |  |  |  |
|---|---|---|---|---|---|---|
| 1835, | . | . | . | . | . | £22,128,304 |
| 1836, | . | . | . | . | . | 25,019,619 |

So that something more than one-half the foreign traffic in our indigenous productions is made up of cottons alone. Furthermore, it appears that

more than one-half* of the raw cotton imported and worked up in this country is consumed, not at home, but abroad. Thus :—

---

* Mr Greg says, " three-fourths, or probably four-fifths in quantity ; perhaps two thirds to three-fourths in value, would be near the truth." These calculations appear to be overcharged, if the official accounts and " Burn's Commercial Glance " are to be

Total weight of Cotton imported for consumption, that is working up.

Lbs.

1836, . . . . . . 367,713,963
Of which exported in the shape of
Manufactured or piece goods, . 111,644,210 ⎫
Yarn, . . . . 85,195,702 ⎬ 198,860,910
Thread, . . . . 2,020,998 ⎭

Left for home consumption only, . 168,853,053 lbs.
It is not necessary to encumber the account with the fractional items of waste, which would not affect the result either way.

Assuming, which would not, perhaps, be much wide of the truth, that the cottons consumed in Great Britain were of equal value with the real or declared value of those exported, it would seem that the annual movement of the trade reached to the enormous money quantity of *fifty millions sterling !* The last, and the one preceding, having been years of extraordinary excitement, and an extravagant rise in prices, must be regarded as furnishing rather an exaggerated view. Allowing, however, an abatement of one-fifth, or 20 per cent, on the amount, which will reduce the appreciation more nearly to that of ordinary times, the prodigious sum total must still excite astonishment.

Cottons exported, . . . . £20,000,000
Consumed at home, . . . . 20,000,000

Forming an extraordinary circulation of values annually
in this magnificent manufacture of . . £40,000,000
The manufacture gives bread to operatives and families
consisting of not fewer persons than . . 1,500,000
Amongst whom are distributed in wages yearly not less
than . . . . . £20,000,000 *

Now, it must be admitted that this is an interest of importance so vast, that, compared with it, all others, save agriculture, seem to fade into insignificance. It is one, therefore, which should awaken all our solicitudes rather to surround it with every guarantee for its future progress, than to run the slightest risk of impairing its permanence by undue interference with those conditions of existence under which it has advanced to its pinnacle of present greatness. For it is not an industry of which, like iron, or coal, or hardware, or earthenware, or woollens, we hold the keys in our own possession, but one artificially created, dependent, and therefore at the mercy of other continents for the very first necessary of its being. Nor, prodigious as in its dimensions it appears, and resembling more the gigantic product of the energies of a world than of an islet, is it a monopoly which we can claim and control as our own. Its very grandeur will be the primary cause of its fall, whenever the hour of its fall arrives. It provoked the wrath and the unprofitable covetousness of Napoleon, and gave birth to the continental system ; followed by the prohibitory tariffs of the Bourbons, by which alone the mighty rivalship of France was called into action. It awakened the cupidity, at the same time that it opened

trusted. The quantities speak for themselves. Taking into account the more expensive quality of the goods fabricated and retained for home consumption, and coupling it with the fact of the vast proportion which yarn bears to the whole export, which may be considered an article in the first stage of manufacture only, and therefore of low comparative value, we are satisfied that the value of the home consumption of cotton equals, if it do not transcend that of the export trade.

* See Blackwood for March, 1836, article " Cotton Manufacture," since which the quantities consumed and values circulated have increased probably as above noted.

to the people of Massachusetts and America a way by which they might mortally harm Great Britain, with which they were then at war, and profit themselves. The people of New England, says Mr Cheozlier, after deep reflection, said to themselves, " the best war against the English is that which will attack their prosperity ; what is the principal source of the riches of Great Britain ? Her manufactures. — Among these which which are the most productive ? The manufacture of cottons.

Then we also will build factories and establish manufactures ; this shall be our war against England." So also judged Frussia, when we refused to take her corn and timber, to abandon our own colonies, and ruin our agriculturists, in order to enrich a land which made us no return ; and hence the German custom's league. It may be well cursorily to glance at the degree of progression of our competitors in the race. The raw cotton wrought in the manufactures of France amounted only in

|  |  |
|---|---|
| 1812 to . . . . | 6,343,230 Kilogrammes, |
| or less than . . . . . | 14,000,000 lbs. |
| In 1833, it had risen to . . | 35,609,819 Kils. |
| 1835, . . . . | 38,759,819 |

These are the quantities, as stated in the *Tableau General* of commerce, the official record, and are the latest official returns published. From Mr Greg's pamphlet, however, we learn that the consumption of

|  |  |
|---|---|
| 1836 was . . . . . | 353,005 bags. |
| Against in 1835, . . . . . | 308,736 |

The two corresponding years for Great Britain give,

|  |  |
|---|---|
| 1836, . . . . . | 1,031,904 bags. |
| 1835, . . . . . | 937,616 |

The increase therefore in France was more than one-seventh, whilst that of Britain was less than one-ninth. The total export of manufactured piece-goods from France was,

|  |  |
|---|---|
| 1833, to the amount of . . . | 56,663,351 francs. |
| It had risen in 1835 to . . . | 61,608,731 |

Not having the French official reports before us for 1834, we shall pursue the comparison of the same two years for this country. Declared value of British cottons exported,

|  |  |
|---|---|
| 1833, . . . . . | £18,486,401 |
| 1835, . . . . . | 22,128,304 |

France, therefore, exported more, relatively, that is, nearly five millions additional against an advance here of less than three and three quarter millions. The French exports meet ours in the same markets, more especially Spain, Belgium, the United States, Sardinia, &c., about one-seventh of the whole of her exports only being to her own colonies. Upon the whole, there-

fore, it will be seen that the career of this industry in France is more accelerated than here, which can be satisfactorily accounted for, only, we think, by the daily greater equality of skill, combined with superior economy of production.

The manufactures of America absorbed no more than 10,000 bales in 1810. In

|  |  |
|---|---|
| 1830 they converted into cloth . . | 126,512 bags. |
| 1832 . . . . . | 173,800 |
| 1834 . . . . . | 197,000 |
| 1836 . . . . . | 237,000 |

So that in seven years the consumption was not far away from being doubled. Within the same period the British speed was,

|  |  |
|---|---|
| 1830, . . . . . | 805,250 bags. |
| 1836, . . . . . | 1,031,904 |

Increase at the rate of about 28 per cent only. The export of piece-goods reached,

|  |  |
|---|---|
| 1831, to the value of  .  .  . | 1,126,313 dollars. |
| 1835,  .  .  .  .  . | 2,856,681 |

That is, it had much more than doubled in five years. Two of the chief articles were,

|  |  |
|---|---|
| 1831, Printed and coloured piece-goods, | 96,931 dollars. |
| White and grey ditto,  .  . | 947,932 |
| 1835, Printed, &c.,  .  .  . | 397,412 |
| White, &c.,  .  .  . | 2,355,202 |

Our own movement was,

|  |  |
|---|---|
| 1831, declared value of cotton exports, | £17,257,204 |
| 1835,  .  .  .  . | 22,128,304 |

Immense as this advance must be justly deemed, it is only one-fourth part of the speed at which our Transatlantic brethren have raced. They little comprehend the indomitable and untiring energies of the Yankee character, who shall opine that once embarked in the contest they will ever be found lagging behind. Men who grudge the indispensable half-hour of meal time as a deduction of so much per cent from the day's profits, and who glory in calling and in thinking themselves the " first nation in the world" —the " State Empire"—will cease not, shrink not, from toil and trial until they have achieved, are first at, the goal. They have skill, ingenuity, the raw products, capital — English capital—all in their favour. Speculation is a necessity of their nature ; the reverses of to-day disturb not their imperturbable phlegm ; their cry tomorrow is still—Go a-head !* And go a-head they will if the spirit of the mother-land be caught slumbering in fancied security. During all the late fury of land-jobbing schemes in the west, of building extravagances in the east, of bancomania every where, which have involved all other, the commerce, agriculture, and industry of the Union in bankruptcy, the cotton manufacture alone remains unscathed, luxuriating in profits, and tempting the cupidity of fresh adventurers. The late ruinous results of all other descriptions of enterprise will serve to draw the attention and whet the appetite of the industrial community and of capitalists. The assurance of better wages will tempt labour from less beneficial employment in agricultural and other pursuits, in a country where families emigrate a thousand miles any way with less scruple than here a change of ten would be resolved on. Iron and coal are abundant, and the progress of mining has kept pace with that of the cotton manufacture. The latest return at hand of the iron production comes down unfortunately only to 1830.† There were in that year in action in the States say

|  |  |
|---|---|
| 1830. Furnaces,  .  .  .  .  . | 202 |
|  | Tons of 28 cwts. |
| Producing, converted into the shape of bar-iron, | 96,621 |
| And of castings from the blast furnaces,  . | 28,273 |
| Importation of foreign iron,  .  .  . | 33,986 |

---

* In the late session of the legislature of Massachusetts several bills were passed incorporating more companies, with large subscribed capitals, for establishing cotton-spinning and manufacturing concerns on the largest scale.

† This article was suggested to us, whilst on a tour in the manufacturing districts of Lancashire, in the middle of last month, by the perusal of Mr Greg's pamphlet, which about that time made its appearance, and by the great meeting on Hartshead Moor of the operatives, against the Workhouse system. We intended to have taken up the subject at a more distant day, and with that view had not been neglectful of observation and notes. The circumstances stated, decided us to execute our resolve off hand, and rather to risk being incomplete than out of season. Of course our means of reference were often beyond reach.

Thus, the importation entered into the consumption for rather more than one-fifth only. Besides the coal mines of Virginia, the discovery in 1814 of the mines of Anthracite, in Pennsylvania, has opened new and inexhaustible sources of supply of a mineral now made available for all purposes. The quantities extracted and brought to market stand thus :—

|         |   |   |   |   |   | Tons.   |
|---------|---|---|---|---|---|---------|
| 1820,   | . | . | . | . | . | 365     |
| 1825,   | . | . | . | . | . | 33,699  |
| 1830,   | . | . | . | . | . | 173,734 |
| 1835,   | . | . | . | . | . | 557,000 |

The whole product of France in 1834 was but 2,500,000 tons ; and that of Belgium, the richest mineral country in Europe after Great Britain, no more than 3,200,000.

There are no precise data for estimating the progress of the cotton manufacture in Prussia and Germany, but we are already enabled to judge of the effect of the German custom's league upon our own industry. We intimated on a former occasion that the operation of that confederacy against us would not probably be felt materially during a season of high prices, or until the continental spinneries could supply the increased and increasing demands of the weaver. For the tax being laid upon weight and invariable, as prices rose or continued high its per centage pressure was less, as they diminished it gradually advanced to a prohibition. Even upon high prices its influence has exceeded our anticipations. The following table, extracted from Burns's Commercial Glance for this year, exhibits the march of the Prussian system.

EXPORTS TO GERMANY AND THROUGH THE HANS TOWNS AND HOLLAND, INCLUSIVE.

|                                    | 1833.      | 1834.      | 1835.      | 1836.      |
|------------------------------------|------------|------------|------------|------------|
| Dimities   .   .   .               | 107,484    | 42,343     | 45,963     | 26,419     |
| Calicos, printed   .   .           | 38,926,442 | 31,194,439 | 34,766,587 | 32,690,029 |
| Ditto, plain   .   .               | 20,954,809 | 17,449,192 | 20,618,448 | 21,685,113 |
| Cambrics and Muslins   .           | 5,598,143  | 5,129,242  | 3,223,106  | 2,347,774  |
| Ginghams and Checks   .            | 354,830    | 119,771    | 20,639     | 152,944    |
| Nankeens   .   .   .               | 17,448,609 | 243,116    | 2,022,951  | 1,592,139  |
| Velveteens, Velvets, Cords, and Jeans   .   . | 6,022,286  | 5,510,640  | 4,724,442  | 3,553,744  |
| Yards,                             | 79,412,603 | 59,688,743 | 65,422,136 | 62,048,062 |

Showing a decrease in four years of more than seventeen millions of yards, or above one-fifth. The decrease would doubtless be in reality much more marked if it were possible to deduct from the total amount the separate imports of Hanover, Brunswick, Mecklenburgh, Holstein, and Oldenburgh, which have not, we believe, joined the league, and whose united population amounts to about three millions. As it is, the trade is in course of rapid annihilation ; whilst judging from the multiplying demand for yarns from hence, over and above what is furnished by the numerous factories latterly constructed (and others more numerous in course of construction) in Rhenane Prussia, Saxony, Baden, and elsewhere, the condition of the manufacturers of fabrics must be highly flourishing. The despatch of cotton yarns to Prussia and Germany through the Hans Towns and Holland had ascended as follows :—

1833,   .   .   .   .   .   34,871,589 lbs.
1834 (adding more than 5,000,000 lbs. sent through
    Belgium that year, from some temporary cause),   38,000,000
1835,   .   .   .   .   .   43,912,058
1836,   .   .   .   .   .   45,928,153

Thus, the excess of supply taken off within four years by looms in Germany amounts to nearly one-third. The Prussian Tariff is based upon the fraudulent pretext of a ten per cent *ad valorem* tax, which, by some hocus pocus more fraudulent still, is juggled to mean a poundage duty of 1s. 6d. per pound upon all foreign cotton cloths. The difference may be thus explained:—The average price of cotton prints exported for the last year is stated at 14s. per piece; add agency charges and freight, and say:—

| | | | |
|---|---|---|---|
| 1 piece of print, length 28 yards, weight 4 lb., value | . | L.0 15 | 0 |
| 10 per cent, *ad valorem*, would be | . . . | 0 1 | 6 |
| Poundage at 1s. 6d., on 4 lb., is | . . . | 0 6 | 0 |

or 40 per cent. Plain white calicoes are a case still stronger in point:—

| | | | |
|---|---|---|---|
| 1 piece calico, length 24 yards, weight 5 lb. 8 oz., value | . | L.0 1 | 0 |
| 10 per cent, *ad valorem* | . . . . . | 0 1 | 0 |
| Poundage at 1s. 6d. | . . . . | 0 8 | 2 |

or 82½ per cent. Dr M'Culloch, who appears to have been entrusted by the Prussian Government to make out a vindication for it, has imagined a case of fine cotton prints at 2s. 6d. per yard, upon which he operates accordingly, and brings out the poundage at no more than 8¾ per cent. The answer is easy—there are not perhaps twenty thousand pounds worth of that costly article exported to Prussia and Germany in any one year. The right way, after all, is to decide upon the point by the gross quantity, and not by isolated instances. Take the whole exports, calculate the weight, and the value, according to ascertained rates—those of Mr Burn, for example—and the real result may be arrived at. This we have done heretofore* in ample detail, and need not repeat it here. The result is, that the actual duty levied, or with which the commodities are struck, by the poundage system, amounted, on the whole actual export, to about 45 per cent. Prices have already considerably receded below those of last year. Printing cloth which then sold currently at 10s. 6d. per piece, ranges now about 6s. 6d. or 7s. only, so that the poundage duty will equal, if not exceed, the cost price.

It will be perceived, therefore, that some of our former most extensive customers are not only rapidly supplying their own consumption, but partially meeting us in other markets. Assuming the first cost of manufacture to be equal in Germany, France,† the United States, and Great Britain, it is clear that all the difference of the tariffed amount, say thirty, forty, or fifty per cent of protecting duties, goes into the pockets of our manufacturing rivals, creates the capital wanted, and is and will be laid out in mills and machinery. But the first cost is not generally equal. The following shows at one view the mean rate of wages in one of the largest establishments of Mulhausen or the neighbourhood. M. Ed. Collomb, by whom it has lately been published, does not name the firm, but he answers for the exactitude of the figures.

### STATISTICS OF A LARGE MANUFACTORY ON THE HAUT RHIN.

| | Men and Boys. | Women and Girls. | Total Workpeople. | Mean Wages per day and per head. |
|---|---|---|---|---|
| Spinning, | 93 | 327 | 420 | 1 franc 11 cents. |
| Weaving, | 836 | 930 | 1766 | 0        94 |
| Printing, | 564 | 99 | 663 | 1        69 |
| Mechanics, Machine-Men, &c. | 262 | — | 262 | 1        67 |
| | 1755 | 1356 | 3111 | 1 franc 35 cents. |

The mean average per head of 1832 was 1 franc 16 cents only, so that wages had advanced.

---

* See Blackwood, January, 1836.

† The Tariff of France, honest towards us, if not neighbourly, is—prohibition.

The mean wages, 1 franc 35 cents, are equal to 13½d. per day per head, or per week, 6s. 9d.  The wages of spinners at Lille, where the finer yarns are spun, are 3 francs per day, or 15s. per week.  At Mulhausen, 2 francs 34 cents, or nearly 12s. per week.  The scale of wages for the following places we take from Mr Greg and the Report of the Commissioners.

|                         |        |            |
| ----------------------- | ------ | ---------- |
| In the Tyrol (Germany), the spinner earns | | 9s. weekly. |
| Vienna,                 | . . . . | 12s.     |
| Baden, adults,          | . . . | 8s. 4d.   |
| Bonn (Prussia),         | . . . | 5s. 6d.   |
| Switzerland,            | . . . . | 10s.    |

The last is, we think, understated.  M. A. Kœchlin, the very intelligent French manufacturer, and member of the Chamber of Deputies, rated them rather higher, if our memory do not deceive us, for we have not the authority at hand.  But to understand these rates, quantities produced and qualities are necessary.

The operatives at Lowell, in the State of Massachusetts, are paid probably higher than in any part of the United States.  The following, according to an authentic source, are the mean rates:—

OPERATIVES.

|                         |                   |
| ----------------------- | ----------------- |
| Preparations, carding, &c. | . 12s. 11d. per week. |
| Spinning,               | . . . 13s. 4d.   |
| Weaving,                | . . . 13s. 11d.  |
| Dressing, &c.           | . . 15s. 7d.     |

These were the rates paid in May, 1834, as furnished by the Merrimack Corporation Manufacturing Company to M. Chevalier, who is certainly an unexceptionable authority.  We have always been inclined to distrust the evidence of Mr James Kempson, the American cotton manufacturer, as taken before the Commons' Committee on Manufactures.  He proved too much.*  The average rate of Factory earnings in England for all classes of operatives are estimated at 10s. 6d. per

week, so that in America the difference so far is in our favour.  But other advantages, even taking the disadvantages of a higher rate of interest and greater cost of machinery into account, help to kick the beam against us.  For instance, the superior cheapness of water-power, which is an immense saving, and the economy of the raw material, nearly at their door, untaxed.  The average wages of two principal classes in Manchester and the neighbourhood are stated in the Factory Report thus:—

|                         |                   |
| ----------------------- | ----------------- |
| Spinners,               | . . . . . 25s. per week. |
| Power-loom weavers, male and female adults, male and female non-adults, but chiefly females, | 10s. 10d. |

The fine spinners of course earn considerably more in proportion to the higher numbers and the quality.  The average wages in calico printing, men and boys included, have been calculated at 10s. per week.

The daily duration of labour appears to be—

|                         |          |
| ----------------------- | -------- |
| In France,              | . . 13 hours. |
| In the Tyrol, rather more than | 12 |
| In Vienna, more than    | . 14¼   |
| In Switzerland,         | . . 13  |
| In the United States,   | . 12     |
| In England,             | . . 12  |
| For Children,           | . . 8   |

We shall frankly own that the rapidly comparative view of the state of the cotton manufacture at home and abroad, as here sketched, does not salute us as over cheering.  If to the lower rate of wages, and many other

---

* Witness his statement about rates of living.  " I have paid (in America) 8s. per week for board, lodgings, and washing, and lived as well as I could live in equal lodgings in a village in England for L.2 a-week."  The assertion is a gross absurdity.

essentials of superiority now existing against us abroad, we add an additional bonus in a ten-hours' bill, by which the manufacturer will be expected to pay the same amount of wages as now for the labour of twelve hours, our case will not be improved. Supposing that the demand remain steady it must add one-sixth to wages already double those of some, and one-third more than those of other neighbouring states. Moreover, to produce the same quantities the number of mills, print-works, &c. as well as of hands, must be increased by one-sixth. But mills cannot be created in one day, nor could such an augmentation be possible for years. On the Continent they can build nearly as fast, and in America equally so perhaps, as we can here. In the mean time higher prices would check consumption at home and abroad. But the additional number of mills would not be built here, because capital would seek the places which promised the most profitable returns. The rates of profit are low here—they are exorbitant elsewhere, through protecting tariffs and low wages. Let us not deceive ourselves. Capital is not so locomotive as in America; but when once the stream sets, and set it has, the tributary streamlets are inevitably attracted to the same course. We fear not Switzerland, nor Belgium, a mightier rival still, backed by the ponderous capitals of its manufacturers, merchants, and the *societé générale*. The incipient tornado does not take its rise in those quarters, but in France, Austria, the Germanic Customs Confederation, and the United States. In these there are all the elements of manufacturing prosperity; large populations, cheap living, low wages, immense internal consumption alone. We leave Russia out of the question at present, because, largely as she imports of our yarns, sixty millions of people are not so soon supplied with fabrics at home.

If there be progress here, the progress elsewhere is still of a more formidable character. It betokens the possession of capital, the certainty of its increase, the security of employing it, the immense returns for investing it. For the Continent of Europe this is a new feature, where, so long ravaged by wars, the people hoarded, and dared not lay out their gains for accu-

mulation. Every post now brings intelligence of new and gigantic enterprises. From Baden we are informed that "many manufactories, spinneries, &c., have been established in the vicinity of Carlsruhe, and the Brisgau * * * which may be attributed to the abundance of capital, the low rate of labour, and perhaps to the favourable climate." Of manufacturing companies, and enterprises established and projected, we have information that would fill more space than we have to spare. Not only is commercial attention directed to cotton manufactures, but to other speculations. Independent of the great railroad undertakings from Aix-la-Chapelle to Cologne, and in divers parts of Austria, to facilitate, accelerate, and cheapen the means of transport and outlet (without particularizing the steam navigation from the Danube to the Black Sea), it will not be amiss to give our readers an outline of some of the vast enterprises in train of execution, and projected by Saxony alone—comparatively a small state—to say nothing of Prussia Rhenane:—

A Railroad from Dresden to Leipsic. All the shares taken and paid up.

The Railroad of the Erzebirge. From the Elbe, traversing the Moldau, through Chemnitz to Zwickau, with a tunnel of several hundred yards. Thirty thousand shares, of 100 rixdollars each, subscribed in a few days.

Steam Navigation Company, from Dresden to Hamburg. Capital, One hundred and fifty million rixdollars.

Coal Mining Company of Pottschappel. It is calculated that these mines cannot be exhausted for three centuries. Capital three hundred thousand rixdollars.

Brewing Company at Dresden, to relieve Saxony from the importation of foreign beer. Capital, four hundred thousand rixdollars.

Iron-Works and Machine-making Company of Uebingen, near Dresden. Capital, five hundred thousand rixdollars.

Machine-making Company. Capital, one million rixdollars; for the manufacture of cotton and wool-spinning, and weaving machinery.

No more need be cited, we apprehend, to show the extraordinary accumulation of capitals, and the boundless spirit of enterprise now pervading Germany, so lately and so long impoverished and needy. These capitals have been accumulated chiefly by the golden profits accruing out of the cotton manufacture, through the combined operation of high protecting tariffs, against competition from abroad, and low wages with cheap rates of living at home.

With all respect to Mr Greg, for of all respect as a worthy master and friend of his operative labourers, he is worthy, and with all deference to his superiority in practical knowledge, and well-known intelligence besides, we have made use, in these pages, of no more of the information he has published, than what has been acknowledged—valuable as we confess that information appears to us. Unknown to him as we are, he will, we trust, consider it no mark of disrespect that we have preferred to rely upon our own resources rather than be influenced by his authority, weighty as that doubtless is. It has served to incline our minds very seriously to the consideration of the subject in hand. Last year only we gave a guarded adhesion to the Ten Hours' Bill, influenced by the sanguine expectations of various practical men of well-known humanity, and tenderness for the operative classes, that the state of trade and of profits could well support the sacrifice, as then doubtless they could. We are entirely satisfied now of the reverse. The evil that hereafter we have to pray against is, *the reduction of wages,* without any reduction of time-working. We entertain little doubt that before the end of this year 100,000 operatives will be out of employ within a radius of 20 miles round Manchester inclusive. The question is not, therefore, cannot be, working shorter time for the same wages, but retaining the same wages for the same quantity of work and of hours. In a manufacture depending so largely, one-half, upon export, and one-half the annual value of which is paid in wages alone among the workers, those wages hereafter may chance to become the sole barometer for determining its high or low condition. Our skill and ingenuity may discover new and improve old processes for economizing labour, but we no longer enjoy a monopoly of skill and ingenuity. Step by step other nations accompany us in our progress. At the last year's public exhibition of products and manufactures at Mulhausen, not to speak of splendid machines, embracing all the most recent improvements for spinning yarns, making paper, grinding corn, &c. &c. which were shown, the display of samples of fine yarns, and embroidered and printed muslins, is said to have been extraordinary for execution and splendid for taste. Samples of the highest range of numbers of fine yarns, up to No. 300 French count (340 or 350 British, we believe), were to be seen from the spinneries of Mulhausen, Thann, Guebwiller, Cernay, and Kaizerberg. The No. 300 of M. A. Herzog, of Logelbach, was said to be a specimen of most perfect fabrication. It is asserted, and believed among our neighbours of those parts, that although they cannot yet produce sufficient of these fine yarns for the wants of the manufacturer, still that the qualities are superior to the corresponding counts produced here. The Austrian printed cottons, sent to the same exposition by M. Spærlin, of Vienna, are reported to rival those of Manchester, and to be executed in the same sort of styles.

The present Factory Act we believe to be impracticable, and to have been designedly so contrived by the Ministry, in order to render abortive the zeal of the friends of the factory children, and disgust the operatives themselves. The plan of eight hours' labour, with relays, will end, can end, only in the adults being eventually condemned to sixteen hours daily toil, instead of twelve. Two alternatives alone seem to present themselves—either to prohibit the employment of children under twelve years of age altogether, and repeal the eight hours clause for all above it—that is, under thirteen—or to render the system of relays practicable and reconcilable with the twelve hours daily labour of the adult, enact a six hours bill for children.* If practicable, the last plan would, we think, be most advantageous, as well as satisfactory for all parties. But

---

* We first heard this plan suggested by Mr Robert Stuart, a respectable and intelligent master spinner of Manchester.

the obstacles appear to be almost insuperable. In towns there would perhaps be little difficulty in procuring a supply of the requisite number of infant hands for the system of relays ; but in country districts, and about isolated spinneries, it would scarcely be possible. One or the other proposition, however, must, we think, be entertained, for, maugre the opinion of Mr Greg, the present absurd piece of Whig legislation cannot work without eventual detriment to the adult operative.*

To conclude, for we have already trespassed beyond our limits, we take leave to add our strenuous recommendation of Mr Greg's advice to the master spinners, of the *"propriety of cultivating a better understanding with their people."* There has been too much of distance, of neglect, shall we add of disdain almost, exhibited towards them. These are not times for the manifestation, for the perpetuation, of unfriendly dispositions, even in the worldly sense ; the Christian obligation is imperative in all times and under all circumstances. Let the bonds of good understanding, of amity, of confidence, be drawn closer, and cultivated more and more. The welfare of the operatives may be promoted by a kindly interest and superintendence, as much as by the payment of weekly wages. Let the masters, imitating the meritorious examples of Messrs Ashton, Greg, and many other meritorious manufacturers, attend to the comforts and the education of the infant labourers, so that they may early be trained in the path of religion and morality as well as of industry.

In the mean time, we counsel the Legislature to lose no time in repealing and consigning to the tomb of eternal ignominy the execrable workhouse system,† forged for the oppression of the working classes of England, and as if to chastise them for their protest against the crying abuses of the Factory System,‡ and their invocation in behalf of the helpless progeny which seemed born only to inherit and perpetuate bondage, disease, and misery. Until the advent of that day, which sooner or later will arrive, we trust that Mr Oastler, the devoted friend of the operative orders, will not relax in his determined but peaceful agitation, and that the Member for Berks, honourably—how can a man be more honourably—distinguished in his own county as " the poor's man magistrate," will not be discouraged in the same noble cause, by the host of foes by whom he is now thwarted at every step, and maligned on every occasion. We exhort the property classes, more especially the middle orders, to advance boldly to the rescue. Now is the time to promote union, and cement harmony among and between all denominations of society ; strike down the monster Poor Law Abolition Act—it will be accepted as a peace offering—the security of home and property will be fortified—the " flood of mutiny " will be dammed up and dried at its source—contentment and concord will revisit the land. If not, worse may betide—we are yet only in the beginning of the end.

---

* Mr Greg unjustly charges the friends of the operatives with agitating for the purpose of undoing their own work. In the first place, the Factory Bill was not their work, but passed under protest from them. In the second, the masters, or Mr P. Thomson, their representative, commenced the agitation by moving the repeal of the clause relating to the 13th year of age, before even it had been tried.

† The old law was sufficiently stringent. The mere substitution of *paid* for gratuitous and interested overseers, to be appointed by the Magistrates in Quarter Sessions, or by any other local independent authority, would have been efficient for the correction of all abuses. But there would have been no Whig jobs !

‡ Before concluding, let us not omit the confession of our obligations for much ready information and easy reference to " Wheeler's History of Manchester "—a work as full of facts almost as of words, and a complete compendium of every thing relating to that important town and its various branches of industry unparalleled.

B2